# PageMaker 7:
# The Complete Reference

# PageMaker 7:
# The Complete Reference

Carolyn M. Connally

**McGraw-Hill**/Osborne

New York   Chicago   San Francisco
Lisbon   London   Madrid   Mexico City
Milan   New Delhi   San Juan
Seoul   Singapore   Sydney   Toronto

**McGraw-Hill**/Osborne
2600 Tenth Street
Berkeley, California 94710
U.S.A.

To arrange bulk purchase discounts for sales promotions, premiums, or fund-raisers, please contact McGraw-Hill/Osborne at the above address. For information on translations or book distributors outside the U.S.A., please see the International Contact Information page immediately following the index of this book.

**PageMaker 7: The Complete Reference**

1234567890 CUS CUS 01987654321

ISBN 0-07-219358-1

**Publisher**
    Brandon A. Nordin

**Vice President & Associate Publisher**
    Scott Rogers

**Acquisitions Editor**
    Megg Bonar

**Senior Project Editor**
    Betsy Manini

**Acquisitions Coordinator**
    Tana Diminyatz

**Technical Editor**
    Jena Ball

**Full Service Compositor**
    MacAllister Publishing Services, LLC

**Illustration Supervisor**
    Lyssa Wald

**Series Design**
    Peter F. Hancik

I dedicate this book to my three children: Judy Irish, Jim Stroud, and Nancy Beck, whose patience has been unbounded; and to Ben, Amanda, and Jackson Irish and Katie Beck, my wonderful grandchildren who bring so much joy into my life.

I also want to include in this dedication my mother, Esther Connally, who has supported me through the writing of this book, has tolerated the pressures of deadlines and late night hours, and has not allowed me to skip any meals.

## About the Author

**Carolyn M. Connally** studied advertising design at the University of Texas at Austin. She put the skills she learned there to use as the advertising specialist for a national manufacturing company where she designed advertising, catalogs, and other marketing materials using one of the earliest versions of PageMaker. She also spent many years doing freelance design for a number of industries.

As a professional trainer since the early 1990s, she trained for Fred Pryor Seminars and SkillPath seminars, teaching computer courses among other topics. In addition to *PageMaker 7: The Complete Reference*, she is the author of *Effective Executive's Guide to Office XP*.

She is the mother of three and the grandmother of four wonderful children. Carolyn lives in Temple, Texas.

# Contents at a Glance

# Contents

**Part I**

**Getting Started with PageMaker**

Part II

PageMaker Essentials

## Part III

### Managing PageMaker Documents

## Part IV

### Using PageMaker's Advanced Features

## Part V

### Using PageMaker with Other Programs

# Acknowledgments

First and foremost, of course, I want to acknowledge the team at McGraw-Hill/ Osborne. Megg Bonar, Acquisitions Editor, was incredibly supportive and always had a kind word. Jena Ball, Technical Editor, who did such a great job of ensuring that I included all the steps and called items by the correct names, has also become a friend and ego-booster when I need encouragement. Tana Diminyatz, Acquisitions Coordinator, and Betsy Manini, Senior Project Editor, kept me on my toes and on deadline. Beth Brown, with MacAllister Publishing Services, nudged me from time to time, but always gently. And there were many others with whom I was not in direct contact, but whose dedicated work made this book possible. Thanks, guys.

I also want to thank Paul Kim, Product Manager at Adobe. Paul provided invaluable and rapid assistance when I encountered a technical problem with which I needed help. Thanks also to Adobe's Jennifer Brieger and Ed Meadows who helped in many ways throughout the process.

Jody Donaldson and Gloria Wilcox of American Printing in Temple, Texas, generously spent time with me discussing the practical and innovative aspects of working with commercial printers to produce PageMaker documents. I appreciate your professionalism and your willingness to help.

And to all the friends and family members whose support and unwavering belief in me kept me going during some stressful life crises that occurred in the midst of writing this book, I send my love and eternal gratitude.

# Introduction

You do not have to read far into this book to know that I really enjoy PageMaker. I've used it since before Windows had icons and have thrilled with every update and innovation across all the years. I've written this book as a means of sharing that enjoyment with others.

PageMaker is sometimes perceived as being a bit daunting and complicated. Although it is a very powerful program, PageMaker is *not* that hard to use. I hope that this book will enable previously intimidated individuals to give this great program a try.

I've written this book with a dual purpose in mind. I hope that *PageMaker 7: The Complete Reference* can be used as a tutorial, instructing the reader in the use of PageMaker one chapter at a time. But I also want the book to serve as a reference, a book where the PageMaker user can find the answers to the problems confronting them as they design a publication.

## This Book's Target Readership

They say that a book cannot be all things to all people, but I've tried to do so here. Although I've assumed that the reader has a fundamental knowledge of Windows, parts of this book, particularly the first six chapters, are basics, targeted to the PageMaker beginner. There are plenty of chapters for the intermediate and advanced PageMaker user as well. However, it is my intention to provide a book with which a beginner can start out with the basics and progress to an advanced level of use.

# Conventions Used in This Book

I've tried to write this book so that the instructions are easily understood by the novice as well as by the more experienced reader. Only a few conventions may need explanations.

When a combination of keystrokes is required to accomplish a function, I state the first key, a plus sign (+), and then the second key; for example: CTRL+A. In that instance, you would press and hold the CTRL (control) key, then press the A key, and finally release both.

Instead of using some cryptic format to describe menu and submenu selections, I use the following conventions.

- I refer to a selection on a menu as a command, and occasionally as an item.
- I state the menu first, then the command, and if necessary the item on a submenu. For example: *Select the File menu's Preferences Command. Then select General from the submenu.*

When I refer to text that appears on a dialog box, I write that text in title case (the first letter of each word capitalized), even though many of the words on the dialog box may not be capitalized. This is to help you discern the referenced wording from other text.

# The Structure of This Book

If you wish to use this book as a reference, the comprehensive index will guide you to the information you need.

For use as a tutorial, I've divided *PageMaker 7: The Complete Reference* into six parts, containing a total of 26 chapters, loosely arranged from PageMaker basics to the program's more advanced functions. I have, however, placed the Printing section last because that seems the most logical place for it.

## Part I: Getting Started with PageMaker

If you are a beginner looking to learn PageMaker, or if you just want to know enough to create a quick design, this is the place to begin. The six chapters in Part I describe the very basics of creating a PageMaker publication, using basic text and graphic functions, and applying color. The only thing you need to know about creating a simple document that is not included here is printing, which is discussed in Part VI.

## Part II: PageMaker Essentials

This part, containing five chapters, moves the reader into a greater understanding of how PageMaker works. Discussions include how to save a document and how to work with its elements, such as graphics, text, and color.

## Part III: Managing PageMaker Documents

The eight chapters of Part III cover ways of working with publications from setting preferences to utilizing some of the exciting PageMaker features, such as data merge, creating books, and building booklets. Also included here are instructions on how to create Adobe PDF documents.

## Part IV: Using PageMaker's Advanced Features

Three chapters are included in Part IV. The topics discussed are object linking and embedding, color management, and color separation.

## Part V: Using PageMaker with Other Programs

Part V includes two chapters, which discuss aspects of interfacing with other programs. Chapter 23 covers the processes of converting documents, which have been created in other programs, into PageMaker publications, while Chapter 24 is about importing graphics and text from the World Wide Web and exporting PageMaker publications to HTML so that they can be posted on the Web.

## Part VI: PageMaker Printing

Whether you are printing a PageMaker document on your desktop printer or sending it to a commercial printing house for publication, Part VI has the information you need. It includes information on how to package your document and associated files into a format that is easily used by commercial printers. The printing process and print options are discussed in detail.

Carolyn M. Connally

# The
# Complete
# Reference

PageMaker
7

# Part I

## Getting Started with PageMaker

The Complete Reference

PageMaker 7

# Chapter 1

## What's New in PageMaker 7

A dobe PageMaker 7 is the latest in a long line of PageMaker products that have proven for years to be a premier page layout program for use in both Windows and Macintosh operating systems.

I have used PageMaker since very early in its existence. I remember fondly the anticipation of anxiously awaiting each new version and the exhilaration of discovering all the new bells and whistles of the latest program. Every version was filled with new and exciting tools (and toys) that made the design of print materials faster, easier, and more sophisticated. I greeted this latest PageMaker with the same delight.

PageMaker 7 is no disappointment. The new innovations are every bit as exciting as those that have come before, and just as much fun to work with. This chapter looks at the additions and innovations that have been added to PageMaker since version 6.5.

## The New PageMaker Toolbar

The one big change to the PageMaker environment since PageMaker 6.5 is the addition of a *PageMaker Toolbar* (shown below). This handy collection of all the most common commands and tasks is a welcome addition to the PageMaker screen. Now familiar commands such as New, Save, and Print, as well as new features such as Indent, Bullets and Numbers, and Export to PDF, are just a mouse click away. The commands and tasks available through the PageMaker Toolbar are discussed throughout this book.

**Note**    *Although PageMaker 6.5 Plus included a Toolbar; I'm listing it here as new. PageMaker 6.5 Plus was a nice addition to the 6.5 version, but since many people did not have the Plus addendum, I'm not using it for reference.*

## New Text Management Functions

Earlier versions of PageMaker presumed that any text in a document would be imported from an outside source already edited and spell checked, and therefore few text management functions were available. With each new version, however, the text management capabilities of PageMaker have increased. The changes in PageMaker 7 bring the management of text closer to the ease found in word processing programs.

# A Streamlined Spell Check

At last, checking spelling in PageMaker is as easy as it is in word processing programs. Instead of the two-step process that spell checking required in the last several versions, one click on the Spell Check button on the PageMaker Toolbar places the document into Edit-story mode and activates the Spelling dialog box (see the following illustration). (For more details on using text in your PageMaker documents, see Chapters 4 and 9.)

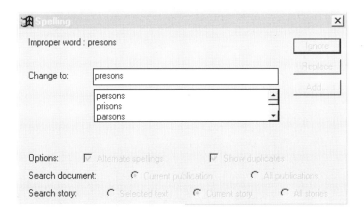

# The New Bullets and Numbering Feature

Now, bulleted or numbered lists can easily be achieved in PageMaker by using the Bullets and Numbering dialog box (see Figure 1-1). Various bullets and numerous numbering styles are available. Just select the text to be affected, click the Bullets and Numbering button on the PageMaker Toolbar, and make your selections. The use of this feature is discussed in detail in Chapter 9.

# Outdent and Indent Toolbar Buttons
# Move Text with One Click

The Outdent and Indent buttons on the PageMaker Toolbar move selected text to the left (Outdent) or to the right (Indent) as desired. Each click on the appropriate Toolbar button moves selected text in half-inch increments; however, text cannot move beyond established margins. For more information on the use of indents and outdents, see Chapter 9.

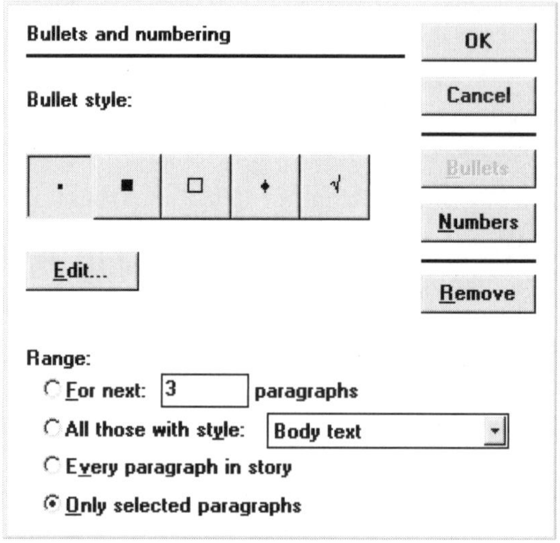

**Figure 1-1.** *The Bullets and Numbering dialog box*

# New PageMaker Functions

Several new functions have been added to PageMaker 7 that increase its capability to produce professional-quality print and Web-based documents. These new functions are indicative of PageMaker 7's tight integration with other Adobe programs as well as its smooth interface with Microsoft Office applications.

## New Data Merge Capabilities

The most exciting of PageMaker 7's innovations is its capability to merge text and graphics stored in other programs, such as database and word processing applications, into PageMaker documents. Now you can create form letters, mailing labels, catalogs, and much more right in PageMaker. For example, if you design a sales piece, you can merge a list of targeted customers into the document and create original pieces with the name of the individual or company, as well as other specific details, in the document. Then you can use the same data list to create mailing labels for the envelope in which you mail the finished piece. This function is discussed in detail in Chapter 14.

# Create Adobe Acrobat Portable Document Format (PDF) Files

For some time, PageMaker has been closely integrated with Adobe Acrobat. But now the alignment is even closer. It is no longer necessary to finalize your PageMaker document before printing it in Portable Document Format (PDF). With PageMaker 7, you can create PDF files, continue to edit them, and modify security and compatibility options without leaving PageMaker. Chapter 19 outlines these functions in detail.

## Placing PDF Files in a PageMaker Document

Although it has long been possible to distill PageMaker publications into PDF files, PDF files previously could not be placed in a PageMaker document. With PageMaker 7, all things are possible. Well, maybe not all things, but you can now take PDF documents, import them into PageMaker, and make them a part of the publication.

## Import Photoshop and Illustrator Files

Documents created in Adobe Photoshop or Adobe Illustrator, two programs frequently used in concert with PageMaker, may now be placed in PageMaker documents in their native form. This means that valuable time does not have to be spent converting those files to other formats. The native version of an Illustrator or Photoshop file is now compatible with PageMaker 7.

## PageMaker 7's Converter Utility

New in PageMaker 7, the Converter utility (see Figure 1-2) converts files from QuarkXPress and Microsoft Publisher directly into a PageMaker-acceptable format. Also, importing and exporting text and graphics to and from Microsoft Office applications, such as Word and PowerPoint, are simplified.

# New Palettes

A helpful innovation that presents needed tools or choices in one convenient package is PageMaker's palettes, which are provided as part of the PageMaker software. For example, the Toolbox Palette contains the general tools for designing documents in PageMaker, the Color Palette provides colors and access to the Color Libraries, and the Master Pages Palette permits the selection and utilization of document masters.

Some palettes, such as the Toolbox Palette, always remain the same. The Control Palette, on the other hand, is contextual; it changes according to the tool you have chosen from the Toolbox. Others, such as the Picture Palette discussed later, can be customized.

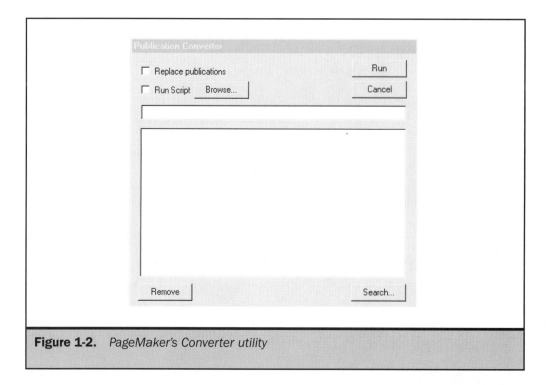

**Figure 1-2.** *PageMaker's Converter utility*

> **Note**
>
> *Although the Template Palette and the Picture Palette, discussed here, are new since PageMaker 6.5, they were included in an intermediate release named PageMaker 6.5 Plus. However, we are including them here for those who are coming to PageMaker 7 from Version 6.5.*

New palettes have been added in PageMaker 7 that have effectively changed the face of PageMaker for new users.

## The Template Palette

Particularly for the new PageMaker user, the Template Palette (see Figure 1-3) is a convenient way to set up the type of document you want to produce with just a simple selection. In the Template Palette, templates are grouped into 20 categories that range from Ads to TriPak. When selected, they provide all of the layout parameters for that type of document.

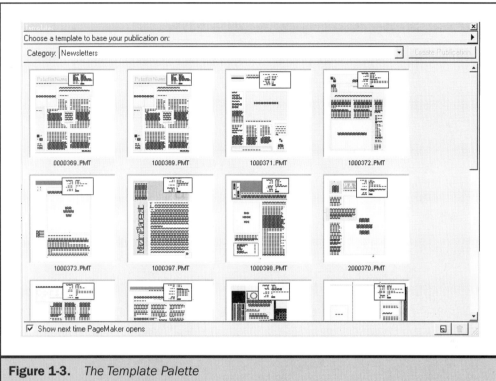

**Figure 1-3.**  *The Template Palette*

## The Picture Palette

This palette is a clip art gallery that provides storage and easy accessibility to graphics and photographs. The Picture Palette (see Figure 1-4) comes with some graphics, but you may add more as you wish.

## The Data Merge Palette

The Data Merge Palette (see Figure 1-5) presents the choices that you may need in the process of merging data from outside applications into a PageMaker document (see Chapter 14).

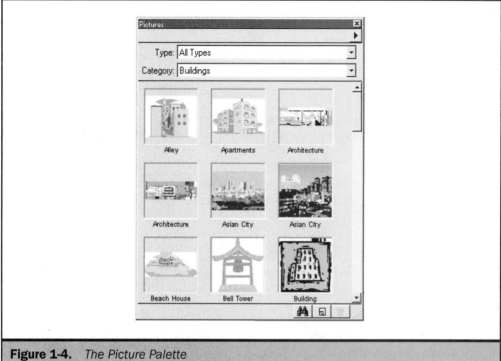

**Figure 1-4.**   *The Picture Palette*

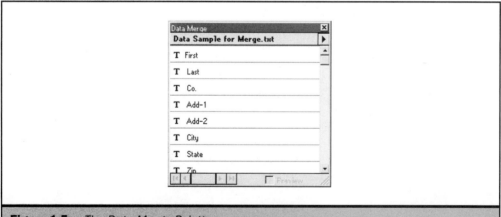

**Figure 1-5.**   *The Data Merge Palette*

# Summary

PageMaker 7 presents a number of new features that enable you to easily layout quality documents for print or the Web.

Among the new features found in PageMaker 7 is the new PageMaker Toolbar that provides instant access to the essential commands for page layout. PageMaker 7 also comes with new Text Management functions, such as a streamlined, easy-to-use spell checker, bulleted and numbered list creation, and text indent capabilities.

With the release of PageMaker 7, you can now merge data from other applications into PageMaker documents, and PageMaker's tight integration with Adobe applications and Microsoft Office programs makes document interfacing a snap.

Particularly for the new PageMaker user, the Template Palette takes the guesswork out of document setup. Another new palette, the Picture Palette, provides storage and organization of graphics and photos.

# Chapter 2

## The PageMaker Environment

Just as you need a map to find your way around a new community, or directions to the washroom to feel comfortable in a new office situation, the first thing you need to know about PageMaker is how to find your way around its environment. Those of us who use computers as a primary tool in our work and in our lives know that you can learn a lot about a new application by just "playing" with it, experimenting with the menus and toolbars and just taking it out for a spin. However, those of us who have worked in training also know that a good, solid foundation of information always takes us a lot further, faster.

I encourage you to take PageMaker out for a spin, play with its tools, and seek out and identify its bells and whistles. But if your goal is to use PageMaker to its fullest capacity, as soon as possible, a solid foundation of information is essential.

In this chapter, I discuss the basic elements of a PageMaker screen and the tools that you need to know as you get started.

## The PageMaker Window

Because I am writing about PageMaker as it runs in the Windows operating system, it is necessary to discuss the PageMaker window. The PageMaker window appears much as the program window in most other Windows-supported applications (see Figure 2-1).

**Note**    *Although this book addresses PageMaker for Windows, using PageMaker on the Macintosh is very similar. The PageMaker for the Mac environment differs slightly and some of the keyboard shortcuts require different key combinations; however, the essential functions of PageMaker 7 are the same.*

When you launch the program, an empty PageMaker window appears; that is, the PageMaker window opens without an active document. If you are accustomed to working in the Windows operating system, many elements of the window are familiar to you. You see the Title Bar at the top, the Control Buttons to the right of the Title Bar, and the Menu Bar and Toolbar below. Although the use of these items is identical to that in other applications, for the sake of clarity, I briefly discuss them here.

In addition to the typical Windows elements, several palettes appear when you launch PageMaker. The Toolbox Palette and the Control Palette are important parts of the PageMaker window that I leave open in my window all of the time. The Template Palette appears at launch to help you select the type of new document you wish to work with, and the Picture Palette and Colors Palette are made available for your convenience in choosing clip art or in coloring graphics or text. Additionally, the Styles Palette appears as a tab behind the Colors Palette. You can use the Styles Palette to select styles to apply to text (see Chapter 9 for more information on styles).

### The Title Bar

The Title Bar is the colored heading at the top of the PageMaker window. The words Adobe PageMaker 7.0 at the left edge of the Title Bar indicate that you are working in

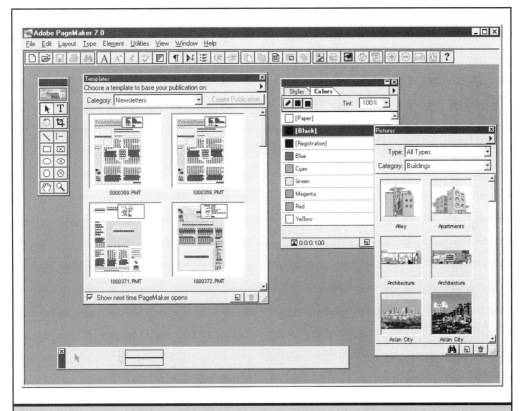

**Figure 2-1.** *The PageMaker window*

PageMaker. Once a document has been opened (see Chapter 3), the Title Bar displays the name of the active document as well. If the document is saved, the name of the document appears in the Title Bar. If the document is unsaved, it is identified as Untitled 1 (or 2, 3, and so on).

# The Control Buttons

The Control Buttons: Minimize, Maximize/Restore, and Exit, located to the right of the Title Bar (shown below), are exactly what their name implies; they control the status of the PageMaker window.

## The Minimize Button

Clicking the Minimize Button causes the PageMaker window to become inactive and to be reduced to a button on the Windows Task Bar. This is handy if you wish to return to the Windows Desktop for some reason, and it is also one way to activate another application that may be running at the same time as PageMaker. Once the PageMaker window is minimized, it can be restored to the screen by clicking its button on the Task Bar.

## The Maximize/Restore Button

This dual-purpose button toggles between Maximize and Restore:

- When the button shows a representation of one large window, clicking it causes the window to become as large as it can be on the computer monitor screen.

- When the window is maximized, the button is in its restore configuration showing two smaller windows. Clicking it then returns the window to the condition it was in at the time it was maximized.

## The Exit Button

The Exit Button does exactly that. It closes the PageMaker window, which closes PageMaker. Once the PageMaker window has been closed, the program must be launched again.

# The Menu Bar

The topics across the gray area below the Title Bar represent the PageMaker menus, as shown below. Most of the PageMaker functions can be located and activated using the Menu Bar; however, frequently there are other, sometimes quicker, ways to accomplish the same thing. Although I do not discuss every use of the menus and their commands in this chapter, most are discussed in the course of this book. Nonetheless, in order to get started with PageMaker, you need to understand how to use them and their general functions.

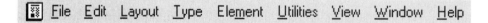

## Accessing a Menu

The most common way to access a PageMaker menu is to click it with the mouse. The menu opens, as shown in the following illustration, to reveal the menu items or menu commands that are available to you. You then make your selection by clicking the item of your choice. If an item is grayed, it is not available to you at that time.

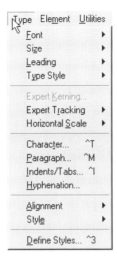

## Using the Keyboard

PageMaker is greatly mouse-driven; therefore, by its very nature, PageMaker is not easily operated solely by keyboard commands. However, there are some keyboard techniques that you will wish to use from time to time. Activating menus by using the keyboard may be one of them.

Take these steps to activate PageMaker menus without using the mouse:

1. On the computer keyboard, press the ALT key and the underlined letter of the menu name.

   The menu appears just as if you had clicked it with the mouse.

2. Select the menu item or command.

   Use the keyboard arrow keys to move the highlight down the menu until the item or command of your choice is highlighted.

3. Activate the menu item.

   Press the ENTER key on the keyboard to activate the menu item. The menu closes and the appropriate item opens or the command is executed.

## Closing a Menu Without Selecting an Item or Command

If you activate a menu, but want to close it without selecting a menu item or command, press the ESC key on the keyboard. The menu closes.

Table 2-1 identifies each of the PageMaker menus and gives a general description of their functions.

When you first launch PageMaker, the PageMaker window appears without an active document. Many of the menu items are unavailable to you when there is no document active, but those that are available enable you to establish defaults. Learn more about this in Chapter 12.

| Menu | Description of Function |
|------|--------------------------|
| File | The items and commands in the File menu pertain to document management. Use these commands to open and close files, save and save as documents, change document parameters, and print, among other functions. |
| Edit | The Edit menu contains those items or commands that concern making changes to a document. Use these commands to undo an action, cut, copy, or paste, and select all objects on a page, among other functions. |
| Layout | The Layout menu concerns the make-up of the document itself, such as the addition and removal of pages, the use of columns, and autoflow of imported text. |
| Type | As you would expect, the Type menu pertains to all of the characteristics of the text elements of your document. Choosing and sizing type falls under this menu, as well as leading, kerning, indents, tabs, and much, much more. |
| Element | Each part of a document is an element. With these menu items, you can specify the parameters of specific elements and how they work together. For example, the Element menu contains commands for stroke settings, object fills, grouping and ungrouping, and wrapping text around objects. |
| Utilities | The Utilities menu contains such useful commands as Find, Change, Spelling Check, and Index and Table of Contents creation. Also on this menu are additional PageMaker functions, called Plug-ins, which you may choose to install. |

**Table 2-1.** *The PageMaker Menus and Their Functions*

| Menu | Description of Function |
|---|---|
| View | The items and commands in the View menu control what you see on the PageMaker screen and how you see it. For example, such items as rulers and guides are hidden or displayed through the View menu. View menu commands also control the magnification of the page. |
| Window | The Window menu enables you to display or hide PageMaker palettes such as colors, styles, and master pages. If you have multiple PageMaker documents open, you may switch from one to the other using the Window menu. |
| Help | Access to PageMaker help is found in this menu, as well as a list of PageMaker keyboard shortcuts. |

**Table 2-1.**  *The PageMaker Menus and Their Functions* (Continued)

## The PageMaker Toolbar

Immediately below the Menu Bar is the PageMaker Toolbar (shown below), a feature new in PageMaker 7. The Toolbar is composed of buttons that provide shortcuts to the most frequently used commands. Clicking a toolbar button activates a specific command or provides a dialog box from which you make choices or establish parameters. These shortcuts are especially convenient as they cut down on the number of mouse-clicks necessary to achieve the results you want. If you are uncertain as to the shortcut associated with a certain button, rest your mouse pointer over the button. After a short delay, a tag appears identifying the button.

Table 2-2 displays the buttons on the toolbar and their functions.

| Button | Name | Function |
|--------|------|----------|
| | New | The New Button displays the Document Setup dialog box. From this, you can choose the way you want a new document to be configured. |
| | Open | Use of the Open Button activates the Open Publication dialog box, which enables you to locate and open an existing PageMaker document. |
| | Save | If you have not saved your PageMaker document, clicking the Save Button will display the Save Publication dialog box where you name and save the document for the first time. However, if the document has already been named, the Save Button will save any changes made since the last save without opening a dialog box. |
| | Print | Clicking the Print Button will automatically send all pages of your document to the default printer. One copy will be generated. |
| | Find | Use the Find Button to display the Find dialog box, which will enable you to search a text box, the entire document, or several documents for a particular word or phrase. |
| | Character Specifications | Clicking the Character Specifications Button brings up the dialog box of the same name. In this dialog box, you set text parameters such as Font, Size, Color, Text Effects, and much more. (See Chapters 4 and 9 for more information.) |
| | Increase Font Size | Clicking this toolbar button increases the size of selected text by one-tenth of a point. Leading is automatically adjusted as well. |

**Table 2-2.**    *The PageMaker Toolbar Buttons and Their Functions*

| Button | Name | Function |
|---|---|---|
| | Decrease Font Size | Clicking this toolbar button decreases the size of selected text by one-tenth of a point. Leading is automatically adjusted as well. |
| | Spelling | The Spelling Button, sometimes called the Spell Check Button, opens an edit story screen and launches the Spelling dialog box. Each word in the active story (text box) is compared to the dictionary. Words not found in the dictionary are highlighted and suggested spellings are listed, if any are available. |
| | Fill and Stroke | A stroke is another term for a line. When lines form simple graphic shapes, they may be filled with solid colors or patterns. The Fill and Stroke Button opens a dialog box from which you may select the specifications of the stroke and the color, tint, or pattern of the fill. |
| | Paragraph Specifications | This button opens the Paragraph Specifications dialog box. From it, you can establish specifications such as indents, space before and after paragraphs, paragraph alignment, and other paragraph options. |
| | Indents/Tabs | In PageMaker, paragraph indents and tabs are set on a special ruler that can be accessed through the Indents/Tabs Button on the toolbar. |
| | Bullets and Numbering | The Bullets and Numbering dialog box appears when you click this toolbar button. The specifications that you choose from the dialog box will affect selected text. |
| | Outdent | Each click on the Outdent Toolbar Button moves selected text to the left in half-inch increments; however, text cannot move beyond the established margins. |

**Table 2-2.**   *The PageMaker Toolbar Buttons and Their Functions* (Continued)

| Button | Name | Function |
|--------|------|----------|
|  | Indent | Each click on the Indent Toolbar Button moves selected text to the right in half-inch increments; however, text cannot move beyond the established margins. |
|  | Insert Pages | Clicking the Insert Pages Button displays a dialog box from which you may choose the number of pages you wish to insert and where you wish them to be inserted. |
|  | Remove Pages | The Remove Pages Button presents a dialog box from which you can indicate a range of pages to be deleted. |
|  | Frame Options | Click this button when you wish to establish parameters for a frame and control the way it relates to its contents. Frames are discussed in Chapter 9. |
|  | Text Wrap | The Text Wrap Button opens a dialog box that controls text's relationship with a graphic. Text can wrap around one or both sides of a graphic, it may fit closely to odd-shaped graphics, or it may flow through the graphic. |
|  | Update Links | Clicking the Update Links Button checks all links and updates any changes in the original objects. |
|  | Picture Palette | The Picture Palette is displayed when you click on its button on the toolbar. This palette contains and organizes a collection of clip art and other graphic material. |
|  | Place | The Place Button opens the Place dialog box, from which you locate and open text or other objects you wish to place in your PageMaker document. |
|  | Photoshop | This button opens Adobe Photoshop if it is present on your computer. |

**Table 2-2.**  *The PageMaker Toolbar Buttons and Their Functions* (Continued)

| Button | Name | Function |
|---|---|---|
| | HTML Export | The HTML Export Button does just that. It converts selected data into HTML and exports it to another document or the Web. |
| | Export PDF | Use the Export PDF Button when you wish to convert PageMaker data to Adobe Acrobat PDF format. |
| | Zoom In | The Zoom In Button magnifies your PageMaker document along a preset magnification sequence of 25 percent, 50 percent, 75 percent, 100 percent, 200 percent, and 400 percent. |
| | Zoom Out | The Zoom Out Button provides the opposite effect as Zoom In. The preset reduction sequences are the same as those in Zoom In: 400 percent, 200 percent, 100 percent, 75 percent, 50 percent, and 25 percent. |
| | Actual Size | When you click the Actual Size Button, the page you are viewing is displayed at an approximation of the size it would be if printed. In reality, however, the effect of Actual Size depends upon the size of your computer monitor screen. |
| | Fit in Window | The Fit in Window Button causes the current PageMaker page to be visible in its entirety in the PageMaker window. |
| | Help | Clicking the Help Button activates the PageMaker Help feature. |

**Table 2-2.** *The PageMaker Toolbar Buttons and Their Functions* (Continued)

# The Toolbox Palette

The most essential of all PageMaker's palettes is the Toolbox (see the illustration below). This palette appears on your PageMaker window by default whenever you launch the program. From it, you select the Text or Pointer tools, activate the basic graphic tools, or choose to rotate, crop, and zoom. I keep this palette open on my PageMaker window at all times. If it gets in the way, you can easily move it by grabbing its title bar with the mouse and dragging it to a new location.

Table 2-3 shows the tools found in the Toolbox Palette and their function.

If the Toolbox Palette is not visible, select the Window menu's Show Tools command. The Toolbox appears toward the left side of your PageMaker window.

| Tool | Name | Function |
|------|------|----------|
| ▶ | The Pointer tool | The Pointer tool selects, moves, and resizes graphics and text blocks. |
| | | If you wish to resize a graphic, for example, you would use the Pointer tool to first click on the graphic to select it and then, still using the pointer tool, grab one corner of the object and drag it to the desired size. (For more information on using the Pointer tool, see Chapter 5.) |

**Table 2-3.**   *The Toolbox Palette Tools and Their Functions*

| Tool | Name | Function |
|------|------|----------|
| T | The Text tool | The Text tool creates text boxes, and selects and edits text. |
| | | You would click and drag the Text tool to create a text box into which you could type text. The Text tool would also be used to highlight text that you wish to format. Essentially, anything that directly affects the text of your document requires the Text tool. (Chapter 4 discusses the use of this tool in more detail.) |
| (rotate icon) | The Rotate tool | The Rotate tool selects and rotates objects such as graphics and text boxes. |
| | | An example of using the Rotate tool would be if you wished to have text rotated 90°. You would select the Rotate tool and click on the text box you wish to transform. Then, still using the Rotate tool, click on any corner of the text box and move it to the desired position. (See more about using this tool in Chapters 4 and 5.) |
| (crop icon) | The Crop tool | The Crop tool trims imported objects. |
| | | Occasionally, you may import an image that needs to be trimmed down to show only a portion of its original view. By selecting the Crop tool and using it to click on the image, you may then move the edges of the image in until only the portion of the picture on which you wish to focus remains. (Learn more about this technique in Chapter 10.) |
| (line icon) | The Line tool | Use the Line tool to draw lines from one point to another in any direction. |
| | | Whether you wish to place a line (also called a stroke) as part of a graphic or as an element of your page layout, the Line tool enables you to draw the line from any point to any other point with no restriction as to direction. (See more about strokes in Chapters 5 and 10.) |

**Table 2-3.** *The Toolbox Palette Tools and Their Functions* (Continued)

| Tool | Name | Function |
|---|---|---|
| \|– | The Constrained Line tool | The Constrained Line tool draws lines that are horizontal, vertical, or at a 45° angle. |
| | | If you wish to be certain that a line is exactly horizontal or vertical, the Constrained Line tool is the one to use. When you click the Constrained Line tool and drag across your page, the line only draws vertically, horizontally, or at a 45° angle. (See Chapter 5.) |
| ▭ | The Rectangle tool | The Rectangle tool draws rectangles or squares. |
| | | Use the Rectangle tool to draw rectangular-shaped graphics on your page. These graphics may be filled with color, rotated, and sized. (See Chapter 5.) |
| ⊠ | The Rectangle Frame tool | The Rectangle Frame tool creates a rectangular placeholder for graphics or text. |
| | | As you design your PageMaker page, use this tool to create a rectangular space into which you later place either graphics or text. This enables you to layout the page without having to enter the text or place the graphic at the same time. (See Chapters 9 and 10.) |
| ◯ | The Ellipse tool | The Ellipse tool draws ellipses and circles. |
| | | Use the Ellipse tool to draw oval- or round-shaped graphics on your page. These graphics may be filled with color, rotated, and sized. (See Chapter 5.) |
| ⊗ | The Ellipse Frame tool | The Ellipse Frame tool draws an elliptical placeholder for graphics or text. |
| | | As you design your PageMaker page, use this tool to create an elliptical space into which you later place either graphics or text. This enables you to layout the page without having to enter the text or place the graphic at the same time. (See Chapters 9 and 10.) |

**Table 2-3.**    *The Toolbox Palette Tools and Their Functions* (Continued)

GETTING STARTED
WITH PAGEMAKER

| Tool | Name | Function |
|------|------|----------|
| ⬡ | The Polygon tool | The Polygon tool draws basic polygons such as hexagons, pentagons, and even stars. |
| | | Use the Ellipse tool to draw polygonal shapes on your page. These graphics may be filled with color, rotated, and sized. (See Chapter 5.) |
| ⊗ | The Polygon Frame tool | The Polygon Frame tool draws polygonal placeholders for graphics or text. |
| | | As you design your PageMaker page, use this tool to create a polygonal space into which you later place either graphics or text. This enables you to layout the page without having to enter the text or place the graphic at the same time. (See Chapters 9 and 10.) |
| ✋ | The Hand tool | The Hand tool repositions the page on the screen. |
| | | Use the Hand tool to move the page to a position that shows the portion of the page you wish to see. (See "Using the Hand Tool" later in this chapter.) |
| 🔍 | The Zoom tool | The Zoom tool magnifies or reduces an area of the page. |
| | | Use the Zoom tool to magnify or reduce the PageMaker page so that you may view the area of the page you wish to see. (See the section on the Zoom tool under "Page Views" later in this chapter.) |

**Table 2-3.**  *The Toolbox Palette Tools and Their Functions* (Continued)

# The Control Palette

Another essential PageMaker component is the Control Palette. This contextually sensitive panel places most of the common settings and commands within convenient reach of the user, saving multiple steps involved in activating menu commands and working within dialog boxes.

The Control Palette automatically changes to reflect the context of the tool that is being used. For example, if you are working with text using the Text tool, the Control Palette reflects the current text settings (font, font size, leading, text effects, and so on) and enables convenient adjustment of those settings. However, if you have a graphic selected using the Pointer tool, object settings are displayed. Figure 2-2 shows the Control Palette in text mode, that is, when the Text tool is being used. Figure 2-3 displays the control panel in the object mode that occurs when the Pointer tool is selected.

If the Control Palette is not visible, select the Window menu's Show Control Palette command. The Control Palette appears toward the bottom of your PageMaker window.

Like the Toolbox Palette, I leave the Control Palette open in my PageMaker window at all times. If it gets in the way of my work, I use the mouse to drag it by its Title Bar to another position on my screen. (Unlike most windows and palettes, the Title Bar of the Toolbox Palette is vertical across the left side of the palette.) I find it to be a most useful tool and I like having it right there to make the changes that I need to make, quickly and conveniently. However, if you find that it is not helpful to you (some people just prefer to use the menus), close it by choosing the Window menu's Hide Control Palette command or by clicking the Exit Button at the top of the Title Bar.

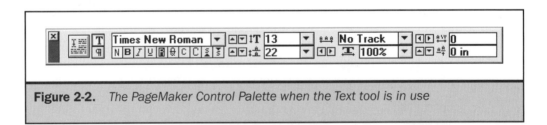

**Figure 2-2.** *The PageMaker Control Palette when the Text tool is in use*

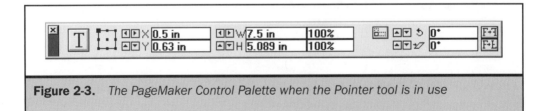

**Figure 2-3.** *The PageMaker Control Palette when the Pointer tool is in use*

I explain the many uses of the Control Palette throughout this book as I discuss applying various settings to your PageMaker document.

## The Template Palette

By default, the Template Palette appears when you launch PageMaker (see Figure 2-4). This feature, new to PageMaker 7, is particularly useful to new PageMaker users or to those who want the layout parameters of their document to be automatically configured for them. The Template Palette provides 20 categories ranging from Ads to TriPak. Each category contains numerous individual templates from which you may choose.

If the Template Palette does not appear in the PageMaker window when you launch the program, you can take these steps to display it:

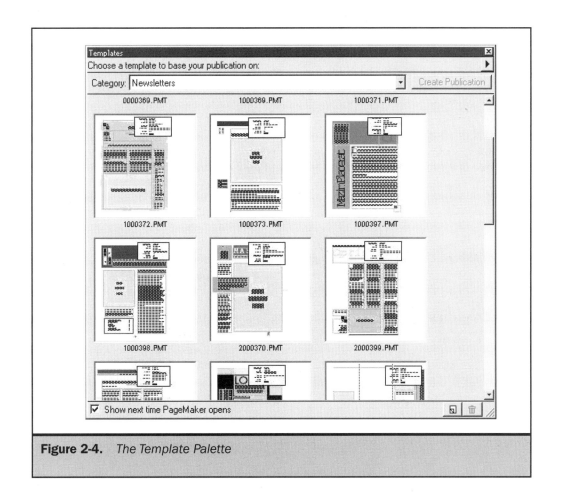

**Figure 2-4.** *The Template Palette*

1. Open the Window menu.

   Click on the Window menu on the Menu Bar and the Window menu drops down.

2. Open the Plug-in Palettes sub-menu.

   Select the Plug-in Palettes menu item and the sub-menu appears.

3. Open the Template Palette.

   Click the Show Template Palette command. The Template Palette appears in the PageMaker window.

If the Template Palette does not automatically appear whenever you launch PageMaker, and you wish it to do so, click in the selection box beside Show Next Time PageMaker Opens. As long as the check mark is in the selection box, the Template Palette will open every time you launch PageMaker.

If you do not want the template to appear every time you open the PageMaker program, deselect the box. You may still open the palette when you wish to by following the steps outlined previously. More information about using the Template Palette will be given in Chapter 3.

## The Picture Palette

PageMaker 7's Picture Palette (see Figure 2-5) is a graphics gallery in which you can access the clip art and images that come with PageMaker, and to which you can add your own, frequently used art. The Picture Palette offers two styles of art: clipart, which is drawn graphics, and images, which are photographs. Within the collection of graphics there are 24 categories of each style with multiple graphics from which to choose.

The first time you launch PageMaker, the Picture Palette is shown in the PageMaker window. Subsequently, when you open PageMaker, the Picture Palette will only be shown if it was open at the time PageMaker was shut down. However, the Picture Palette is easily accessed. Just take these steps:

1. Open the Window menu.

   Click the Window menu on the Menu Bar and the Window menu drops down.

2. Open the Plug-in Palettes sub-menu.

   Select the Plug-in Palettes menu item and the sub-menu appears.

3. Open the Picture Palette.

   Click the Show Picture Palette command. The Picture Palette appears in the PageMaker window.

More information on using the Picture Palette is given in Chapter 5.

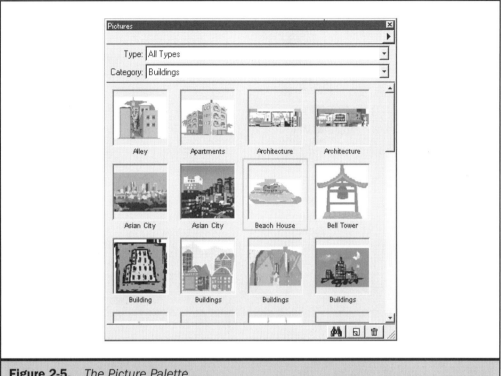

**Figure 2-5.**  *The Picture Palette*

## The Colors Palette

The Colors Palette, as shown in Figure 2-6, is not new to version 7; however, it is an important part of the PageMaker window. From this palette you choose the stroke colors and the fill colors that you wish to apply to graphics that you create within PageMaker.

**Note**  *The Colors Palette is one tab of a two-tab palette, Style being the other tab. When you first launch PageMaker, however, it is the Colors Palette tab that is selected.*

On the title bar of the Colors Palette are two control buttons. One, the Exit Button, closes the palette. The other, the Minimize Button, hides all but the palette's heading. When you wish to display the entire palette, clicking the button again will restore it to its full configuration. This is convenient because it ensures that the Colors Palette is not in the way of your layout while you work on your document, but the palette is handy and easy to restore when you need it.

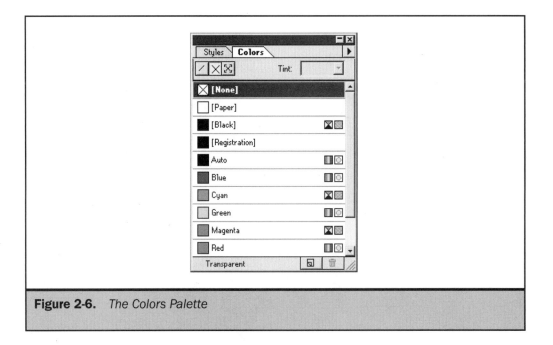

**Figure 2-6.**   *The Colors Palette*

The Colors Palette comes with ten colors or fill states. However, you may easily add more colors from PageMaker's color libraries. The palette enables you to determine whether you wish the selected color to affect the stroke or the fill of the graphic, or both.

The first time you launch PageMaker, the Colors Palette is shown in the PageMaker window. Subsequently, when you open PageMaker, the Colors Palette will only be shown if it was open at the time PageMaker was shut down. However, the Colors Palette is easily accessed. Just take these steps:

1. Open the Window menu.

   Click the Window menu on the Menu Bar and the Window menu drops down.

2. Open the Colors Palette.

   Click Show Colors. The Colors Palette appears.

I will discuss the Colors Palette in more detail in Chapter 6.

# Viewing the PageMaker Page and Pasteboard

In PageMaker, the active page of your document is situated in the center of an area called the pasteboard. The amount of pasteboard that is visible depends upon the view settings. This pasteboard enables you to place objects beyond the boundaries of your page to hold them for later use. Each page that you create is in the center of the same pasteboard so that items placed on the pasteboard may be retrieved at any time onto any page (see Figure 2-7).

## Using Scrollbars

As you probably know, the scrollbars at the right and bottom of the PageMaker window move the document up, down, right, or left when you click the appropriate scrollbar arrow, enabling you to better see the elements on the page. Scrollbars in PageMaker operate much the same as in any other windows-supported application with a notable exception: Moving the vertical scrollbar button to the very top of the scrollbar moves you farther than the top of the current page; it moves you to the top of the pasteboard.

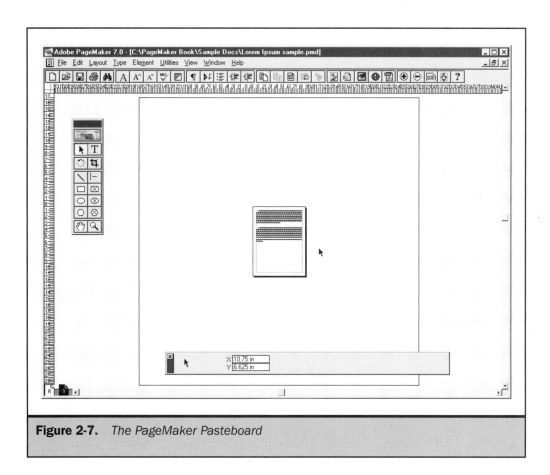

**Figure 2-7.** *The PageMaker Pasteboard*

The PageMaker scrollbars are used not only to see what is on your current page, but everything that is on the pasteboard as well. Centering the scrollbar buttons in the horizontal and vertical scrollbars centers the page on your screen.

## Using the Hand Tool

In addition to using the scrollbars, the Hand tool may be used to adjust the portion of the page or pasteboard visible on your monitor. The Hand tool is best used for smaller adjustments.

Follow these steps to adjust your page using the Hand tool:

1.  Select the Hand tool.

    Click the Hand tool in the Toolbox. The mouse pointer turns into a representation of a hand.

2.  Click on the page.

    Once the Hand tool has been selected, click and hold the mouse at a location convenient to the direction in which you wish to move the page.

3.  Move the page.

    Continuing to hold down the mouse button, drag the mouse so that you see the part of the page you want to see.

4.  Continue to move the page until you reach the area you wish to view.

    If you move the Hand tool as far as it will go on the screen and you still have not located the part of the page or pasteboard you are looking for, release the mouse button and grab the page at another location that enables you to move farther in the direction you want to go. Continue to reposition the Hand tool and drag until you have located the portion of the page or pasteboard you desire.

In moving the page with the Hand tool, think of the process as if you actually grabbed a piece of paper with your hand. Moving your hand down (or towards you) brings the top of the paper closer. Moving your hand away makes the bottom of the page visible.

## Page Views

PageMaker offers you an almost unlimited range of page magnification: from viewing the entire pasteboard to a 400-percent magnification of a specified area of a page. You can choose to view your entire document page in the PageMaker window, or you may wish to zoom in so that one area is greatly enlarged. There are several ways of accessing the view that is right for you.

## The View Menu

The View menu, as shown below, provides several predetermined choices.
The View menu choices are defined in Table 2-4.

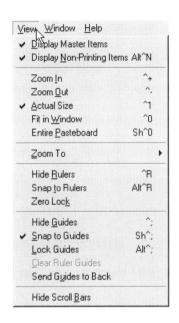

## The Shortcut Menu

Another and somewhat faster way to change the magnification of your PageMaker page
is to use the Shortcut menu (see Figure 2-8), which is obtained by clicking the right
mouse button. Among other convenient commands, the Shortcut menu contains Actual
Size, Fit in Window, and Entire Pasteboard, which operate just as they do when selected
from the View menu. If you right-click on a graphic or in text, the Shortcut menu also
contains the Other View command, which enables you to enter any percentage of
magnification, in 1-percent increments, from 8 to 731 percent (see Figure 2-9). If you
right-click anywhere else on the page or the pasteboard, the percentages are shown on
the menu.

| View | Description |
|------|-------------|
| Zoom In | Choosing this command causes the page to enlarge. The preset magnification sequence is 25 percent, 50 percent, 75 percent, 100 percent, 200 percent, and 400 percent. If you were viewing the page at 63 percent, for example, clicking the Zoom In command would move the page to the next increment of magnification, 75 percent. Zoom In focuses on the center of the page. |
| Zoom Out | This command is the opposite of Zoom In. Selecting Zoom Out from the View menu causes the page to reduce in size. The preset reduction sequences are the same as those in Zoom In: 400 percent, 200 percent, 100 percent, 75 percent, 50 percent, and 25 percent. |
| Actual Size | This command supposedly presents the page in the actual size it will be when printed. In reality, however, the size of the objects on the page depends upon the size of your monitor. For working purposes, however, Actual Size provides a good, moderately close-up view that enables you to easily read text and see the intersections of graphics. |
| Fit in Window | The Fit in Window command does just that; it causes the entire page to be viewable in the PageMaker window. In this view, you see very little of the pasteboard above or below the page and only some to the right and left. |
| Entire Pasteboard | This command reduces the entire pasteboard so that it is entirely visible in the window. Although you see the entire pasteboard and, of course, the page, few details will be visible because of their reduced size. |
| Zoom To | This command enables you to zoom to any of six preset magnifications: 25 percent, 50 percent, 75 percent, 100 percent, 200 percent, and 400 percent. |

**Table 2-4.**   *Zoom Commands from the View Menu*

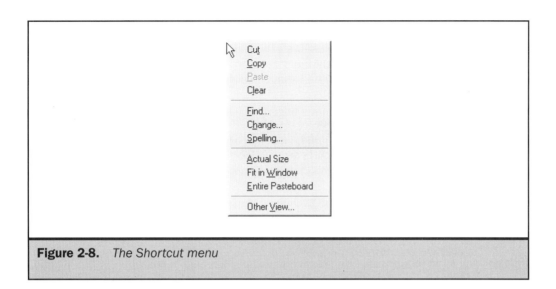

**Figure 2-8.** *The Shortcut menu*

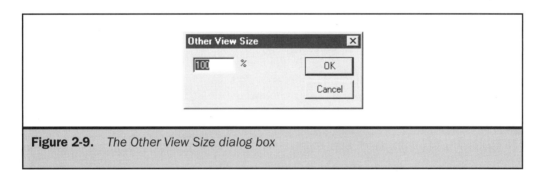

**Figure 2-9.** *The Other View Size dialog box*

## The Zoom Tool

You will remember the Zoom tool from the discussion on the Toolbox Palette. This is a handy tool for incrementally magnifying or reducing the size of the page.

Here's how to use the Zoom tool to zoom in (magnify):

1. Select the Zoom tool.

   To make use of the Zoom tool, click the Zoom Tool Button on the Toolbox Palette. Your mouse pointer changes from an arrow to a picture of a magnifying glass with a plus symbol (+) in its center (shown below).

2. Select the focus of the zoom.

   Place the mouse pointer over the portion of the page that you wish to view at magnification. Repositioning the mouse pointer with each increment of magnification keeps that area in the center of the screen.

3. Click to magnify.

   Each mouse click increases magnification along a preset sequence of 25 percent, 50 percent, 75 percent, 100 percent, 200 percent, and 400 percent. In other words, if you start at a magnification of 37 percent, the next increment takes you to 50 percent, the next to 75 percent, and so on.

The Zoom tool may also be used to zoom out (reduce the size of the page). Just follow these easy steps:

1. Select the Zoom tool.

   To make use of the Zoom tool, click the Zoom Tool Button on the Toolbox Palette. Your mouse pointer changes from an arrow to a picture of a magnifying glass with a plus symbol (+) in its center.

2. Change the plus symbol (+) to a minus sign (-).

   When the Zoom tool is selected, pressing and holding the CTRL key on the keyboard causes the plus sign in the center of the Zoom tool to change to a minus sign (-) (see illustration below). This also changes the function of the tool from zooming in (magnifying) to zooming out (reducing). Be sure to continue holding down the CTRL key until you have reached the reduction that you want.

3. Click to zoom out.

   Each mouse click reduces the size of the page along a preset sequence of 400 percent, 200 percent, 100 percent, 75 percent, 50 percent, and 25 percent.

## The Toolbar Buttons

You may also use the Zoom In and Zoom Out Buttons on the PageMaker Toolbar. Clicking the Zoom In Button (the one with the plus sign) enlarges the view of the page along a preset sequence of 25 percent, 50 percent, 75 percent, 100 percent, 200 percent, and 400 percent. The Zoom Out Button reduces the view along a sequence of 400 percent, 200 percent, 100 percent, 75 percent, 50 percent, and 25 percent.

## Using Keyboard Commands

As you work in your document, you may want to frequently switch between
Actual Size and Fit in Window. Use the following keyboard command to quickly
toggle between the two views:

Press CTRL and right-click the mouse

# Switching Between Documents

Multitasking, working in more than one document at a time, is one of the hallmarks of
any windows-supported application, and PageMaker is no exception. Why would you
want to work on more than one PageMaker document at a time? It all depends upon
what project or projects you are working on, of course, but consider the following:

- Copying objects from one document to another. The copying and pasting
  process is much simpler with both documents open.

- Creating two similar, but not identical documents for different purposes. For
  example, you may create a flyer for sales promotion to be mailed to regular
  customers with a special discount. You also want a flyer to distribute within
  your retail environment that looks similar, but does not contain the special
  offer. Creating these two documents simultaneously is easy and it is most
  convenient if both of them are open at the same time.

- While working on one project, you are called on to make changes on another.
  No need to shut the first one down while you edit the second.

- Creating multiple documents that comprise a set, such as letterhead, envelopes,
  invoice forms, and business cards.

There certainly are more reasons for working on two or more PageMaker
documents at a time, and switching between them is simple. Here's how:

1. Open the Windows menu.

   Click Windows on the Menu Bar to reveal the Window menu.

2. Select the document you wish to make active.

   Each of the PageMaker documents that are currently open is listed at the
   bottom of the Window menu, as shown in Figure 2-10. The document shown
   with the check mark beside it is the active document. Click on the document of
   your choice and the document becomes active in the PageMaker Window.

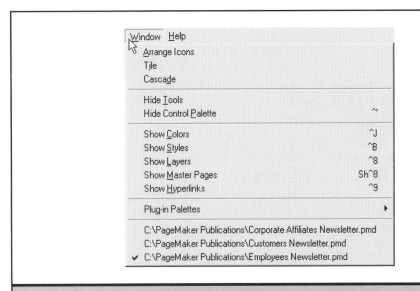

**Figure 2-10.**   *Multiple open documents shown in the Window menu*

# Summary

This chapter provides you with a roadmap of the PageMaker environment through discussions of the PageMaker window, viewing the PageMaker page, and switching between documents.

**The PageMaker Window**   The PageMaker window contains some elements that are consistent with most Windows-supported applications, such as the Title Bar, the Control Buttons, and the Menu Bar. However, the PageMaker window also contains two application-specific palettes, the Toolbox Palette and the Control Palette.

**Viewing the PageMaker Page and Pasteboard**   Not only can the PageMaker page be seen on the screen in a number of views, but the PageMaker pasteboard (an area surrounding the page where objects may be temporarily placed) is visible as well. Portions of the page and pasteboard can be magnified or reduced as required to see items in larger or smaller form. The View menu, the Shortcut menu, and the Zoom tool from the Toolbox Palette may each be used to access the view that you desire.

**Switching Between Documents**   You may need to have more than one PageMaker document open at the same time. You can easily switch between documents by selecting the document you want to make active from the Window menu.

The
Complete
Reference

PageMaker
7

# Chapter 3

## The Basics of Creating
## a New Document

T he product of your work in PageMaker may be a newsletter, a Web page, a brochure, or any of myriad other print or online items. Whatever you intend the end result to be, the piece-in-progress in PageMaker is referred to as a document and, sometimes, a publication. This document is the frame into which all of the PageMaker elements are placed in order to produce the design you desire.

Since Part I of this book concentrates on the basic skills you need to get you off to a quick start, in this chapter I'm focusing on generating documents through the use of the Template Palette as well as the basics of creating a new document through the Document Setup dialog box. Chapter 7 gives you more information on fine-tuning documents. Before you actually create your document, however, it is important that you know what you want your end result to be.

# Thinking Ahead

A document may have multiple pages and can be formatted to seemingly endless variations of size and specifications. Although it is not important that you know exactly how your document will look when it is completed, it is important to have a general idea. For example, if you are designing an advertisement, you should know the approximate size of the ad space in order to create a document that will fit that space. Pages can be adjusted as you go along, but some adjustments affect multiple elements and take some time. Having the parameters in mind and, better yet, writing them down before you start are always the most efficient ways to begin.

Keeping these items in mind, conceptualize your project before you create a document:

- What do you want your piece to achieve?

   What is the job of the piece you are developing? Is it a sales piece? Is it intended to provide information? Maybe its job is to persuade others to your point of view. Perhaps its sole purpose is to entertain. It is important to be very clear about a document's purpose before you begin not only concerning the type of document you need, but from a design quality perspective as well. Documents that do not have a clearly defined purpose usually are ineffective.

   Sometimes a document will have multiple purposes, but one should be predominant. For example, you may wish to create an information piece that holds interest because it is also entertaining. Even though it is entertaining, its primary purpose is to inform. Although a sales piece may be formatted as an information piece, its intent is still to sell a product or service. Just make certain that the primary purpose is clear.

- What kind of document are you creating?

   Now that you know the purpose of your document, you need to determine what kind of document will achieve that purpose. You can use PageMaker to design most any type of print document and many types of Web pages.

Working from the intent of your piece, determine what type of document you wish to use to achieve that result. A sales piece could be an ad layout, a brochure, or even a newsletter. An information piece could take the form of a newsletter, a booklet, a flyer, or other document types. Consider the audience you are reaching with your document and what type of document would do the best job in reaching them.

■ What size do you want the document to be?

Documents from ads to tri-fold brochures can be created in any size you wish. Although newsletters frequently are 8$^1$/$_2$-by-11 inches, folded down from 11 by 17 inches, they can be any size, from small to very large. Brochures are frequently 8$^1$/$_2$-by-11-inch pages folded, but they too can be just about any size you want them to be. This same thing is true of most types of documents.

In considering the size of a print document, there are some things you need to keep in mind. If you are producing the document on your own printer, obviously you are limited to the size of paper your printer uses. If you are having the document produced by a commercial printer, keep in mind that printing on standard sizes of paper costs less than using large parent sheets of paper stock or cutting sheets to conform to a smaller size. Check with your printer about costs before you decide.

The size of your printed document also impacts how you can deliver it to your target market. For example, a tri-fold brochure printed on 8$^1$/$_2$-by-11-inch paper fits nicely in a standard business envelope. Larger brochures must be designed as self-mailers, or large envelopes must be found or created. Outsized printed pieces cost more postage to mail as well.

Think beyond your piece's creation to its use as you decide on a size. For example, an advertisement must be sized to conform to the requirements of the publication in which it will be published.

■ How will you deliver your document to your target market?

Obviously, a Web page will be delivered via the Internet, but there are a lot of ways in which a print piece can be delivered: as a self-mailer, mailed in an envelope, as a newspaper insert, in a display rack, and so on. Thinking through the delivery method will help you to understand elements that must be included in your document, such as a bulk mail insignia or an attention-getting design that can be seen when the piece is displayed in a brochure rack.

■ How many pages will your document have?

Brochures usually have only two pages (the front and back of the same piece of paper). But newsletters can have two pages (front and back), four pages (two sheets printed front and back or one large sheet of paper printed front and back, and folded), or any number in multiples of four (multiple sheets of paper printed front and back, and folded). Knowing the number of pages you expect to have before you create a document allows you to set those pages up at the same time, saving adjustments later.

■ Will your document be in color or black and white?

Deciding color usage is an important factor in the development of your print piece. Many PageMaker templates have specifications for color that can be customized to your requirements. Conceptualizing color requirements is a major step in selecting the best template, particularly if you are creating your document using a PageMaker template.

Once you have answered these questions, think about any other document parameters that need to be taken into consideration. Don't hesitate to sketch your document out. It doesn't have to be great art, just a readable representation.

The result is what I call the *concept document*. The concept document may be held in your mind, but I strongly urge you to put all of your answers to the previous questions, as well as any other ideas and concepts you have, down on paper. The written concept will serve as a guide to keep you on track as you design the document you want to create.

# Creating a New Document with the Template Palette

The Template Palette (see Figure 3-1) is new to PageMaker since PageMaker 6.5. It is a collection of preformatted documents in a variety of types and styles that you can use as the basis of your document. The Template Palette contains 20 categories and 310 templates that are typical of the documents frequently created using PageMaker. Opening a document template creates a new document (I'm calling this a template document) in which all of the essential elements are in place.

If the document you have conceptualized in the previous exercise fits one of the templates available on PageMaker's Template Palette, using that template is the easiest way to create your document. If the layout of the new document is exactly as you wish your piece to be, all you have to do is replace the sample text with your text and the graphic holders with your graphics. Of course, you may make additional adjustments as well; you are not limited to the parameters of the template.

Becoming familiar with the templates provided in the Template Palette is a good idea. If you spend a little time exploring all of the templates, it will save you time selecting templates with this and subsequent documents.

## Exploring the Template Palette's Templates

Obviously, the Template Palette must be open before you can explore it. As discussed in Chapter 2, the Template Palette is open by default the first time you launch PageMaker.

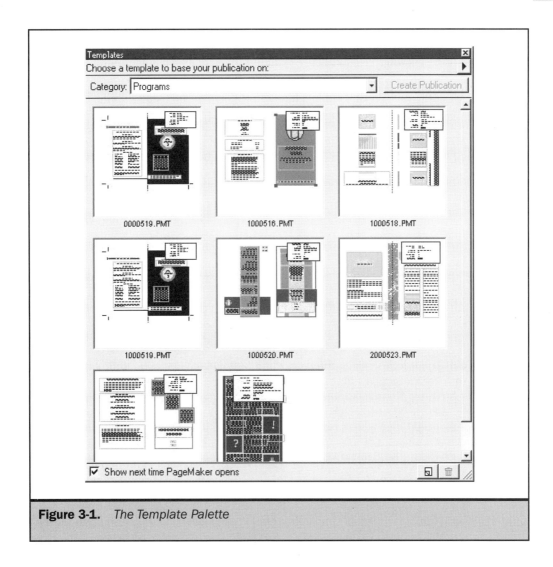

**Figure 3-1.**  *The Template Palette*

If you wish it to be open every time you launch PageMaker, select the Show Next Time
PageMaker Opens box. If the Template Palette is not open in the PageMaker window,
you can quickly and easily open it. Just follow these simple steps:

1.  Open the Window menu.

    Click the Window menu on the Menu Bar and the Window menu drops down.

2. Open the Plug-in Palettes sub-menu.

   Select the Plug-in Palettes menu item and the sub-menu appears.

3. Open the Template Palette.

   Click on the Show Template Palette command. The Template Palette appears in the PageMaker window.

With the Template Palette open, templates are displayed from the category that is shown in the Category menu box at the top of the Template Palette. Click the drop-down arrow to the right of the Category menu box to reveal additional categories (see Figure 3-2). Clicking the category of your choice displays the templates in that category.

A concern I have with PageMaker 7's Template Palette is that unless you have a very large computer monitor, the templates that are shown in the Template Palette are so small that discerning a template's features and layout is impossible without opening the template as a template document. This means that in order to explore the templates in the palette, and to find the template that matches or comes close to your concept document, you must open and close a lot of documents.

To open a template as a new document, double-click the template you wish to open or select the template with one click, and then click the Create Publication Button located to the right of the Category drop-down arrow. The template opens as an unnamed template document. Untitled-1 (or 2, 3, and so on) appears in the Title Bar.

If the template contains fonts that you do not have on your system, before opening the template as a template document PageMaker prompts you to select a substitute font (see Figure 3-3) or to accept the default font, Courier. I dislike Courier—a lot!—and I never allow it to remain in any of my documents. Just select the font that needs a substitute and locate another from the drop-down font menu at the bottom of the Panose Font Matching Results dialog box. Indicate whether you want the substitution to be temporary or permanent. Once all the substitute fonts have been selected, click OK. PageMaker then asks if you want to save these substitutions. Click Yes or No.

**Note** *As with all templates, a template document is based on the template and is not the template itself. So, if you close the document unsaved, you are not affecting the template.*

To close a template document, select the File menu's Close command, just as you would with any PageMaker document. PageMaker will ask if you want to choose the Save the Changes You Have Made option to Untitled-1. Selecting No closes the document completely. (If you would like to save the document, of course, select Yes; then name and save it in the Save As screen that appears. This process is described in more detail in Chapter 8.)

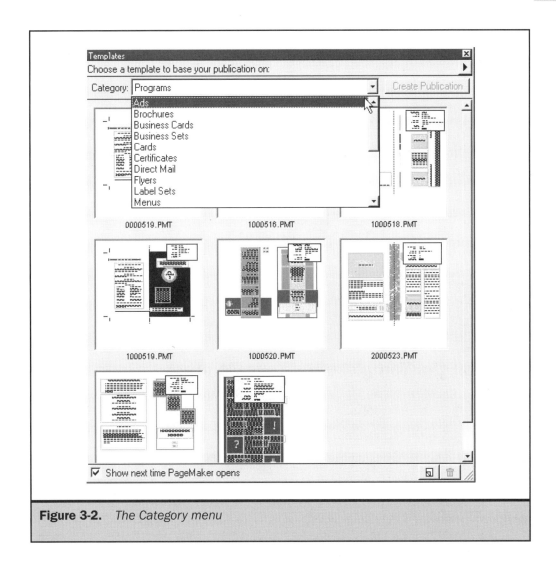

**Figure 3-2.**    *The Category menu*

Once you have selected a template and opened a template document, the Template Palette closes. If you want to open it again to select another template, you can follow the previous steps. The Template Palette reappears on your screen.

Explore the templates provided in PageMaker by opening and closing documents as much as you need to in order to get a good look at what is available in the category or categories of your choice. If you wish, documents may be printed before closing or even saved in a file on your computer's hard drive to have a more convenient record of the selection.

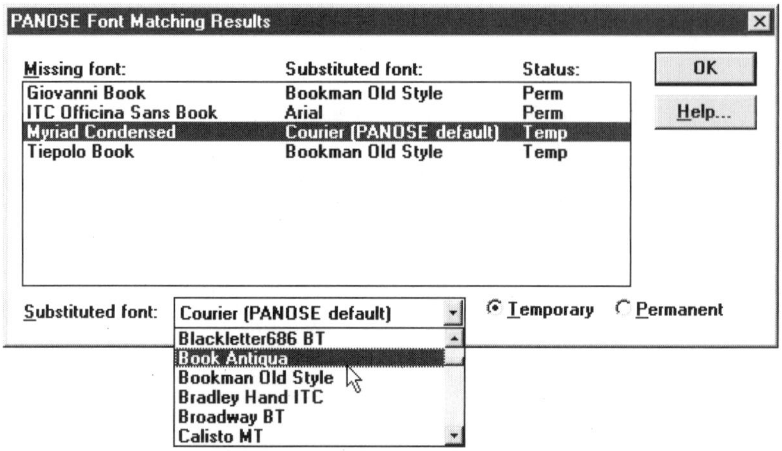

**PANOSE Font Matching Results**   [x]

| Missing font: | Substituted font: | Status: |
|---|---|---|
| Giovanni Book | Bookman Old Style | Perm |
| ITC Officina Sans Book | Arial | Perm |
| Myriad Condensed | Courier (PANOSE default) | Temp |
| Tiepolo Book | Bookman Old Style | Temp |

OK

Help...

Substituted font:   Courier (PANOSE default)   ⊙ Temporary   ○ Permanent

Blackletter686 BT
Book Antiqua
Bookman Old Style
Bradley Hand ITC
Broadway BT
Calisto MT

**Figure 3-3.**   *The Panose Font Matching Results dialog box*

# Deciding on the Template for Your Concept Document

In exploring the templates available to you in PageMaker, look for the one or two that are as close as possible to your concept document. It is very possible that an exact match can be found. It is also quite likely that the templates you examine will give you additional ideas that you can add to yours.

Each PageMaker template document has a specifications label (see Figure 3-4) within the document area. This non-printing rectangular box provides information such as the template type, code, description, fonts used, production notes, and technical level of the project. Many of the concepts that you wish to match will be listed there. If the specifications label is in the way of part of the document, drag it aside.

If you do not find a template that is a good match for your concept, you can choose to create a document using the Document Setup dialog box. For more information on this way to create a document, see the section, "Creating a New Document Using Document Setup," later in this chapter. However, if your document concept and a PageMaker template are pretty close, the template may be the best technique to use. It accomplishes several steps automatically, and most document parameters created by a template can be adjusted quickly and easily. I discuss the fine-tuning of a document in Chapter 7.

Once you select a template on which to base your document and open it in the PageMaker window, name and save it (see Chapter 8). You have created the document from which your piece will be built.

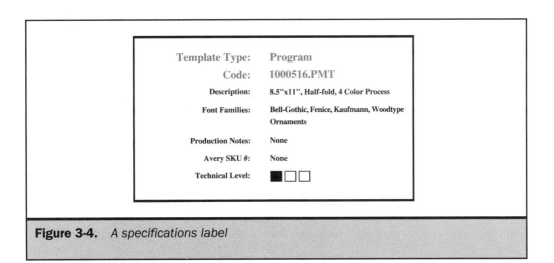

| Template Type: | Program |
| Code: | 1000516.PMT |
| Description: | 8.5"x11", Half-fold, 4 Color Process |
| Font Families: | Bell-Gothic, Fenice, Kaufmann, Woodtype Ornaments |
| Production Notes: | None |
| Avery SKU #: | None |
| Technical Level: | ■ □ □ |

**Figure 3-4.** *A specifications label*

# Replacing a Template Document's Text with Your Own

The template document is a shell into which you place the appropriate information to make it your own unique design. The first step is to put your copy in place of the existing text in the template document.

Do not be surprised if you cannot read most of the text in the template document. The body text that is shown in the template document may have a few words of instruction or identification, but most of it will be nonsense text called *greeking*. Greeking can take many forms, and the most common form looks remarkably like Latin, but actually contains no real words at all.

Take a look at the different uses of text in the template document. Depending upon the template you have selected, there may be any number of different uses of text (see Figure 3-5 for examples).

Table 3-1 defines some of the types of text you may find.

Of course, you may rearrange the template document's layout however you wish. But if the template is a close match to your concept document, it is a good idea to keep the text types the same. For example, replace headlines with headline copy, body text with body copy, and so on.

Replacing text, whatever the type, is a simple process. Here is how to do it:

1.  Place the insertion point.

    Using the Text tool, click in the text that you want to replace. This indicates to PageMaker which text box is to be affected.

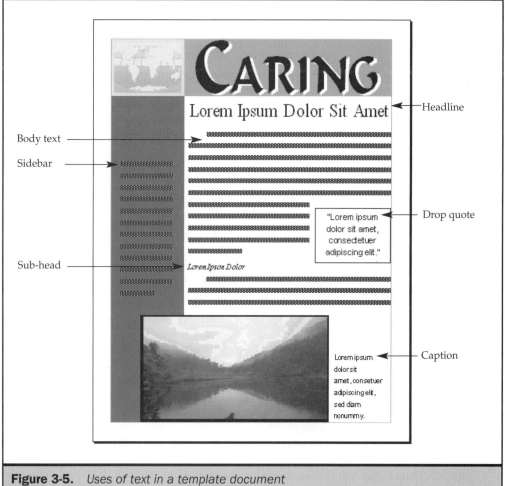

**Figure 3-5.**    *Uses of text in a template document*

2. Press CTRL-A.

   Simultaneously pressing the CTRL key and the A key causes the entire text block to be highlighted.

3. Begin typing your text.

   Any highlighted text will be replaced by the next keystroke. So, as soon as you begin typing your own text, the text from the template document disappears and only your typing remains.

| | |
|---|---|
| Headline | A headline is a short statement that identifies the contents of a text block. Headlines are also used to draw the user into the copy. |
| Sub-head | A sub-head is a very short statement that breaks up longer text blocks. Sub-heads are frequently used to identify topics contained in the text. |
| Body text | The main blocks of text in a document are called body text. In some types of documents, body text composes the major element of the piece. |
| Caption | A caption identifies and sometimes explains graphics and tables. Although a caption usually is placed below the element it is defining, it also may be placed above or on either side. |
| Sidebar | A short story that accompanies a larger one is called a sidebar. Sidebars contain information that's different from the major story, but related. |
| Drop quote | A drop quote is a quotation taken from the text of a document, placed prominently and in large type for emphasis. |

**Table 3-1.**   *Types of Text and Their Definitions*

If you already have your text typed in a word processing document, it is possible to import the text into PageMaker without having to retype it. Importing text is discussed in Chapter 9.

# Replacing a Graphic Placeholder with Your Own Graphic

Just as a template document has text in place so that you can see its effect, graphics may be in place as well. Almost every template uses a graphic of some sort, even if it is just a line of color or a box that indicates where you should place your logo. Some template documents have bold graphic statements as part of their design; many are much more subtle in the use of graphics. Several template documents have a small box, called a graphics placeholder, that says Place Artwork Here, as shown in Figure 3-6.

Although the location of artwork can be changed, the placement of a graphic in the template document is indicative of good design technique and should be considered for your customized piece. To move a graphic or a graphic placeholder, merely click on it

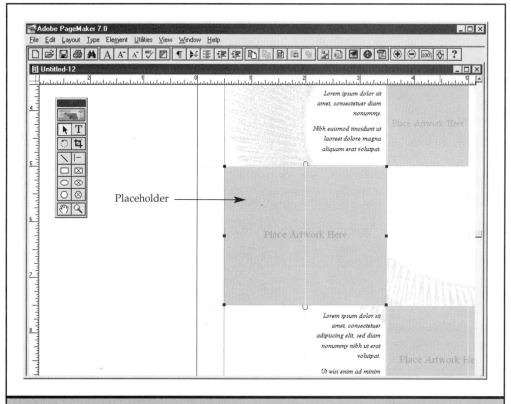

**Figure 3-6.** *A template document with a graphics placeholder*

with the Pointer tool and drag it to a new location. To replace a placeholder with your own artwork, follow these steps:

1. Select the graphic.

   Click the Pointer tool, and then click on the graphic or graphic placeholder. A selected graphic has small boxes called *sizing handles* at each corner and in the middle of each side (see Figure 3-7).

2. Open the Place dialog box.

   Select the File menu's Place command. The Place dialog box opens as shown in Figure 3-8.

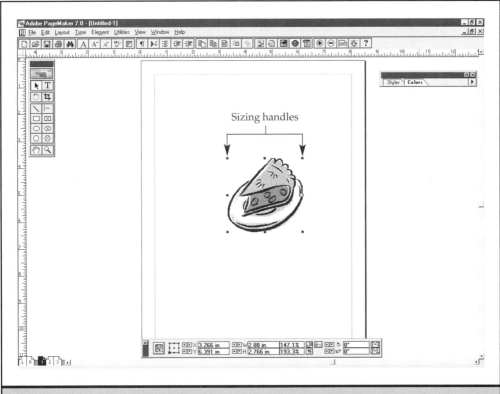

**Figure 3-7.** *A selected graphic*

## Using the Keyboard

The Place dialog box is quickly and easily opened by using the keystrokes CTRL-D.

3. Locate your graphic.

   Click the drop-down arrow to the right of the Look In menu box. From the resulting menu (see Figure 3-9), select the drive and open the folder where your graphic is located.

4. Open your graphic.

   From the appropriate folder, open your graphic by double-clicking its icon, or by selecting it with a single-click, and then clicking the Open Button. Your graphic appears in place of the template's placeholder.

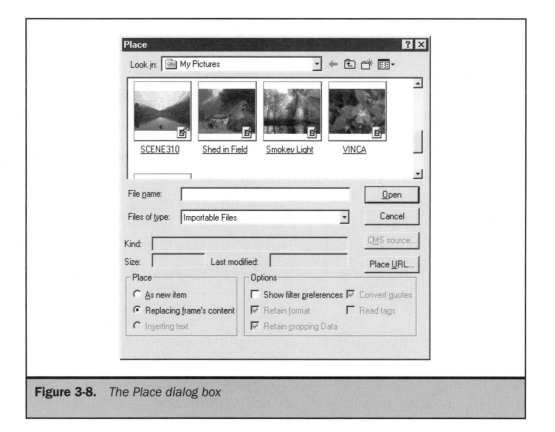

**Figure 3-8.** *The Place dialog box*

*The directions given in this book are based on a classic setting in Windows' Folder options. If you have your folders set for a single-click style, single-click to open the graphic or rest the mouse pointer on the graphic to select it, and then click the Open Button.*

## Creating and Saving a New Template in the Template Palette

If you have customized a template document or have created a new document that you want to use as a template, you can save the document as a template and store it in the Template Palette. There, it will always be easily available to create new template documents.

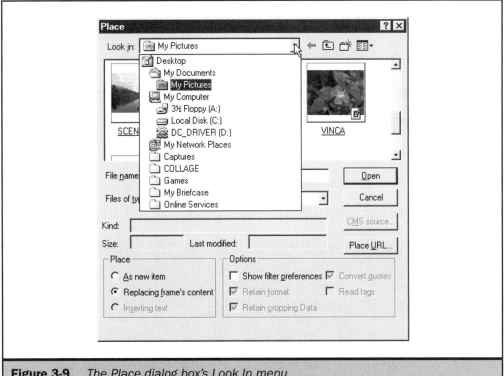

**Figure 3-9.**   *The Place dialog box's Look In menu*

## Save the Document as a Template

Your document may be saved as a regular document, but to store it on the Template Palette it must be saved as a template as well. Saving the document as a template is much the same process as a regular save. The following instructions tell you how:

1.  Open the Save As dialog box.

    Click on the File menu's Save As command. The Save As dialog box opens. This is different from a regular save in that it enables you to make certain selections that are not available with the Save command.

2.  Locate the folder in which you wish to save the file.

    Click the drop-down arrow to the right of the Save In menu box. From the resulting directory tree (see the following illustration), select the drive and open the folder where you want to place the template.

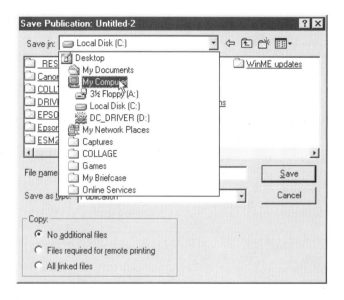

3. Name the document.

   In the File Name box, replace the existing text with the name you wish to give the document.

4. Select the document type.

   Click the drop-down arrow to the right of the Save As Type menu box. With the menu displayed, select Template.

5. Save the Document

   Click the Save Button. The document is saved as a template and the Save As dialog box closes.

## Add the New Template to the Template Palette

Once a document has been saved as a template, it can be added to the Template Palette. Here's how:

1. Show the Template Palette.

   If it is not already open, display the Template Palette by clicking the New Button on the PageMaker Toolbar.

2. Display the Template Palette's shortcut menu.

   Click the right-pointing arrow to the right of the bar immediately below the Template Palette's Title Bar. The Template Palette's shortcut menu appears as shown in Figure 3-10.

Shortcut menu

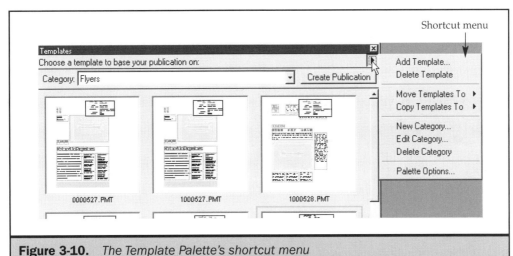

**Figure 3-10.**   *The Template Palette's shortcut menu*

3. Open the Add a Template dialog box.

   Select the shortcut menu's Add Template command. The Add a Template dialog box appears.

4. Name the template.

   In the Name text box, enter the name you want to give to the new template. This may well be the same name you gave the document when you saved it as a template, but you can call it something else if you wish. The templates that are already in the Template Palette have numbers for names. Set up your own system for keeping track of your templates.

5. Locate the template.

   There are two possible steps you may use to indicate the template that you want to add to the palette:

   ■ If the active document is the template (as it will be if you have just saved it as a template and have not yet closed it), click the Create From The Currently Active Document Radio Button.

   ■ However, if the active document is *not* the document you are adding to the palette, select the Add An Existing PageMaker Template File Radio Button. Then click the Browse Button and locate the file using the resulting directory tree.

Once you have located the file, double-click to open or select it and click the Open Button. Your template will appear on the Template Palette to the right of the template that is selected, as indicated by the surrounding yellow box.

# Creating a New Document Using Document Setup

The primary difference between using the Template Palette and the Document Setup dialog box to create a new document is that a template comes with the document parameters already selected; in Document Setup, you have to select them yourself. In this section I discuss some of the basic document parameters, how they affect your document, and when you should use them. Additional document parameters are covered in Chapter 7.

## The Document Setup Dialog Box

All of the basic document parameters are found in Document Setup (see the following illustration). Document Setup is a dialog box that is used to set the specifications of a document you are about to create, or it is used to change the specs of an existing document. There are two ways to access the Document Setup dialog box: through the File menu's New command or the File menu's Document Setup command. To open the Document Setup dialog box to create a new document, select the File menu's New command.

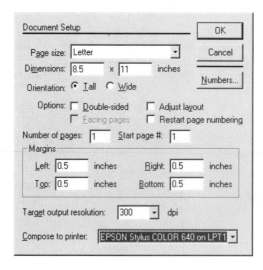

When the Document Setup dialog box is opened using the File menu's Document Setup command, it displays the current specifications of the active document. Using this to make changes to a document is discussed in Chapter 7. However, if no document is open and the Document Setup command is selected, changes made to the dialog box will establish the default settings for future documents. See Chapter 12 for details.

# Selecting Parameters for a New Document

Once the Document Setup dialog box is opened, you are faced with a number of choices. These settings determine the size and scope of your document when it is created, as well as many of the factors of how it looks. This section discusses page size, orientation, margins, Target Output Resolution settings, and Compose to Printer settings.

## Page Size and Dimensions

PageMaker 7 offers you a choice of 21 preset page sizes as well as a custom setting through which you can set dimensions that are not included in the menu. Page sizes include common print document dimensions as well as browser pages, magazine layouts, video settings, and compact disc case labels. Click the drop-down arrow to the right of the Page Size menu box and, using the scroll bar, scroll through the selections. Make your choice of page size by clicking on the selection. Once a page size is selected, the page dimensions are shown in the Dimensions area immediately below.

Actually, you can establish your document size in the Dimensions boxes as any size, from as small as $1/2$ inch to as large as 42 inches. Changing Dimensions to a range not consistent with one of the predetermined sizes causes the Page Size box to read Custom.

## Orientation

Orientation is the arrangement of a page in respect to the direction of the long and short edges. In PageMaker, the terminology used to indicate orientation is *Tall* and *Wide*. Tall, of course, means that the short edge of the page runs horizontally and the long edges run vertically. Wide is the opposite, with short edges appearing vertically and long edges, horizontally. In other computer programs, the terminology is sometimes Portrait (for Tall) and Landscape (for Wide), reflecting the corresponding orientation in art. To choose the orientation for your new document, click the appropriate Radio Button for either Tall or Wide.

## Margins

Your document's margins are set in the four margin boxes identified as Left, Right, Top, and Bottom. An easy way to set the margins is to double-click in the Left box to highlight the existing data, and then enter the desired margin in the decimal equivalent of inches. Next, press the TAB key. The cursor moves to the next box and the existing setting is highlighted, simply requiring that you type the new margin in the box. Tab again and type. Then tab one more time and enter the final margin setting.

## Target Output Resolution

The Target Output Resolution dots per square inch (dpi) setting is the resolution with which the document will be created. This setting assures that the document that you are creating conforms with the resolution in which the document will ultimately be produced. In other words, if your goal for the document is to print on a desktop printer and your printer is a 600-dpi printer, select the 600-dpi Target Output Resolution setting. If you are creating for high-resolution 3300-dpi output, make that selection. Likewise, if you are creating a document to publish electronically, select the resolution best suited for your document on the Internet.

## Compose to Printer

Like the Target Output Resolution, this setting's purpose is to coordinate the document with the printer from which it will eventually be produced, even if, in the case of Web pages and other non-print media, the printing is just for proofing. In actuality, before a document is printed, PageMaker will recompose the document to conform with the printer; therefore, the setting is more to establish an accurate representation on the computer monitor.

Make this setting by clicking the drop-down arrow to the right of the Compose to Printer menu box and selecting the printer to which you wish to compose the document.

# Create the Document

Once these settings have been made, click the OK Button. The Document Setup dialog box disappears and is replaced by your document.

In creating a document using the Document Setup dialog box, you have an empty canvas on which to build the elements of your concept document. The next several chapters discuss basic techniques on creating text blocks and placing graphics.

# Summary

PageMaker is capable of creating an almost unlimited variety of documents. This chapter discusses the two ways in which you can create a PageMaker document to achieve your desired end result.

**Thinking Ahead**    An important step in creating a PageMaker document is conceptualizing that document first. Think through what you want your piece to achieve, which type of document you want to do the job for you, the page size you will use, and the delivery techniques for the final result. Once these things have been conceptualized and written down, you are ready to create your document.

**Creating a New Document with the Template Palette**    New to PageMaker since version 6.5, the Template Palette presents a collection of preformatted documents in a variety of types and styles on which you can base your document. From these templates, choose one that matches or nearly matches your concept document. Then substitute your text for the text in the template document and place your graphics in the graphic placeholders. Documents that you have customized or designed can be saved as templates and stored in the Template Palette.

**Creating a New Document Using Document Setup**    When your concept document does not match any of the templates in the Template Palette or when you just like a more hands-on approach, you can create a new document by using the Document Setup dialog box. In Document Setup, document settings such as page size, orientation, and margins are entered. When the settings are okayed, the new document is created. The new document is an empty canvas on which you build the elements of your concept document.

The
Complete
Reference

PageMaker
7

# Chapter 4

## The Basics of Using PageMaker Text

In some ways, PageMaker uses text just as a word processing program. In other ways, it is quite different. Chapter 4 provides the basic skills needed to work with text in PageMaker. I discuss how to create a text box, how to move and size it, and how to edit and format text that is in place.

PageMaker text is contained in a text box, which establishes the configuration of the block of text. In word processing programs, the entire document is usually one big block of text, even if it is hundreds of pages long. But, because PageMaker is concerned with the placement of both text and graphics, each graphic or text box is a separate element. One text box (also called a story) may run to subsequent pages, and there may be several text boxes on a page. This enables the management of articles individually.

Working with text in PageMaker requires the Text tool, found on the Toolbox Palette. Use this tool whenever you want to create a text box, enter text, or edit text. Click on the tool to select it (shown below) and the mouse pointer turns into an I-beam.

## Creating a Text Box

In order to place text into a PageMaker document, you must first create a text box. In doing so, you establish the width of the block of text (the length is determined by the amount of text that you enter). For many types of documents, this is very important as text is a design element in the document and text block size contributes to the overall design.

There are two ways to create a text box. The first enables PageMaker to create the text box from existing document parameters. The second way is to drag to create the box to your own specifications.

## Allowing PageMaker to Create a Text Box

To allow PageMaker to create a text box for you, select the Text tool and click on the page at the vertical location where you want the box to begin. PageMaker establishes the box between two existing margins. For example, if the page has only one column (as in a letter), the text box extends from one margin to another. The top edge of the new text box aligns with the point where you clicked.

If your page is divided into columns, the text box extends between the margins of the column in which you clicked. And again, the top edge of the text box aligns with the point where you clicked.

## Dragging to Create a Text Box

When you want a text box width that extends across column margins or is smaller than the distance between margins, you can create the text box to the size you wish. First, select the Text tool; then click in the location where you want the text box to begin and drag to the width you desire.

Once a text box is created, enter text immediately. You can always go back and edit what you have typed and you may also add to it, but PageMaker automatically removes a text box that contains no text. You do not see the borders of a text box unless you click on it using the Pointer tool.

## Deleting a Text Box

When you wish to delete an entire text box, you must use the Pointer tool. Select the Pointer tool by clicking on it in the Toolbox Palette, as shown below. The mouse pointer becomes an arrow. Click anywhere in the text box to select it and then press the DELETE key. The text box is removed.

# Moving and Sizing a Text Box

Once created, a text box can be manipulated in a number of ways. For example, you can stretch the text box to increase or decrease its width; you can also move the text box to another location. In order to do this, you must be able to view the borders of the text box.

To view the text box, first select the Pointer tool as described previously, and the mouse pointer becomes an arrow. Click on the text. The borders and other components of the text box appear (see Figure 4-1).

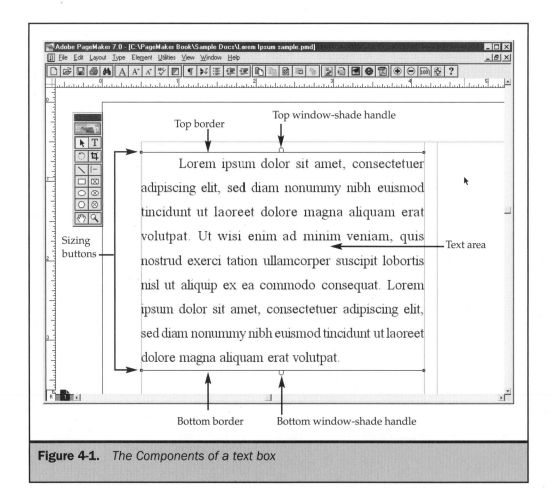

**Figure 4-1.** *The Components of a text box*

## Moving a Text Box

You can move a text box to a new location on the page by simply clicking with the Pointer tool anywhere within the text box and dragging it to the new location. You can also move the text box upward vertically by dragging the top window-shade handle up.

*Dragging the lower window-shade handle down does not correspondingly move the text box down, however. The bottom window-shade handle is used to manage text flow and is discussed in detail in Chapter 9.*

## Sizing a Text Box

To increase or decrease the width of a text box, grab one of the sizing buttons on either side of the top or bottom border using the Pointer tool and drag to the width you wish.

# Editing Text

Editing text in PageMaker is remarkably similar to working in a word processing program. If you are familiar with Word, Word Perfect, or similar programs, the editing techniques in PageMaker will hold few surprises. As mentioned in Chapter 1, even the Spell Check function in PageMaker 7 is now streamlined and launches with one-click convenience.

In this section, I discuss selecting text, making corrections, and spell checking.

## Selecting Text

Selecting text, sometimes called highlighting, is an important text skill. Some text correction techniques require highlighted text, and text must be selected before any text effects or formatting can be applied. Highlighted text is shown reversed; that is, where the text is usually black on a white background, selected text is white on a black background, as shown in Figure 4-2.

The primary technique for selecting text is simple: Using the text tool, just click at the beginning and drag the text tool's I-beam through to the end of the text you want to select. There are shortcuts, however, that make the selection of text much quicker and easier (see Table 4-1).

Before performing the Select All or the CTRL-A technique, make sure that you are using the Text tool. If you use these methods while the Pointer tool is selected, PageMaker selects all objects on the visible pages and pasteboard.

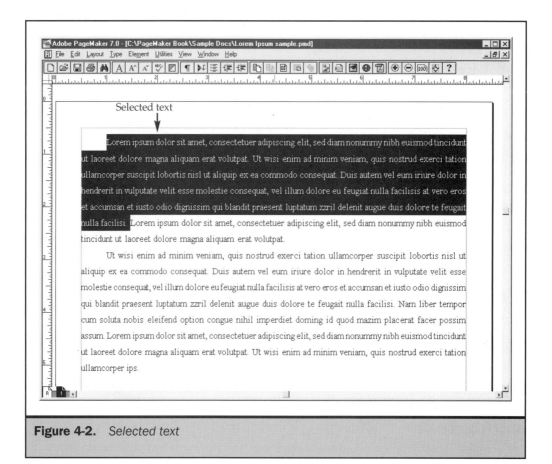

Selected text

**Figure 4-2.**  *Selected text*

# Making Corrections

Whether we mistype or merely change our minds, all of us must correct what we have written from time to time. Just as in word processing, there are several ways to do so.

## Delete Characters

If you want to take out just a few letters, you can use either the BACKSPACE key or the DELETE key on your computer's keyboard:

- Place the insertion point to the right of the text you wish to eliminate and press the BACKSPACE key until the unwanted text is no long there. Remember the BACKSPACE key removes text to the left of the insertion point.

- Place the insertion point to the left of the text you want to get rid of and press the DELETE key until the text is gone. Remember, the DELETE key removes text to the right.

| Technique | Results |
|---|---|
| Double-click a word. | The word is selected. |
| Triple-click anywhere in a paragraph. | The entire paragraph is selected. |
| Place the insertion point at the beginning of the text you are selecting; then hold down the SHIFT key and use the right arrow key to extend the highlight. | Text characters are selected one character at a time until you have highlighted the desired block of text. |
| Place the insertion point at the beginning of the text you are selecting; then hold down the SHIFT key and use the up and down arrow keys to extend the highlight. | Text is selected one line at a time until you have highlighted the desired block of text. |
| Place an insertion point at the beginning of the text you want to select; then holding down the SHIFT key, click at the end of the text. | The entire block of text between the two points is highlighted. |
| Click the Edit menu's Select All command. | The entire text box is selected. |
| Hold down the CTRL key and press the A key. | The entire text box is selected. |

**Table 4-1.**  *Selection Techniques*

## Replace Text

If you wish to replace existing text with new characters, here are two techniques that will get the job done for you:

- Delete the unwanted text using either technique discussed previously. Then, with the insertion point in place where the unwanted text was eliminated, type the new text. The new text is inserted in the old text's place.

- Highlight the unwanted text. Begin typing the new text. The old text disappears with the first keystroke and the new text is inserted in its place.

# Checking Spelling

Although spell checking has been around in computer programs for quite a while now, I'm still in awe of a computer's capability to keep watch on our work this way. I'm particularly delighted with the advancements made by PageMaker 7's Spell Checking feature. Checking spelling in PageMaker is now as simple as in any word processing program and has even more features. You can spell check one story (text box), every story in a document, or a selection of text within a story. You can even direct PageMaker to check all PageMaker documents that are open.

Spell checking works by checking each word in your document against the PageMaker dictionary. If a word you have written is not located in the dictionary, the Spell Checker brings that word up for your attention. If you have asked it to do so in the Spelling dialog box (see the following step 4), the Spell Checker will suggest words that might be the correct spelling of the word that you intended to use. Although the PageMaker dictionary is very large, occasionally you may use words that are not in the dictionary, but are legitimate words. The Spell Checker enables you to ignore those words and continue the spell check.

Here are the steps to use the PageMaker 7 Spell Checking feature:

1. Click in a text box.

   If you are checking one story, it is a good idea to have your insertion point in that story. If you are checking all stories in a document or checking more than one document, it is not necessary to have the insertion point in a text box; you instruct PageMaker to make those checks in a subsequent step.

2. Open the Spelling dialog box.

   Click the Spelling button on the PageMaker toolbar. PageMaker opens the story in a separate window. The Spelling dialog box (see below) also opens; however, it remains inactive.

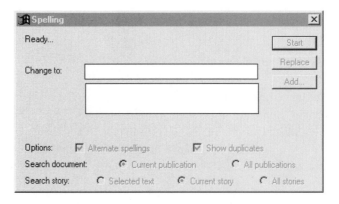

3. Activate the Spelling dialog box.

   Click anywhere on the Spelling dialog box to activate it. Once active, numerous choices are made available at the bottom of the dialog box (show below).

4. Select the Options you wish to use.

   Selecting the Alternate Spellings box means that PageMaker will suggest replacement words for the words that are not in its dictionary. As this is an important part of the spell-checking process, make this selection if it is not already checked. The Show Duplicates box causes the Spell Checker to indicate words that are repeated. This also is an important check to make.

5. Select the publications (documents) you wish to check.

   There are round selection buttons (called Radio Buttons) on the line that reads Search Document. You may choose to spell check the Current Publication or check All Publications that are currently running. Just click the appropriate radio button. Only one may be chosen at a time.

6. Click to select the story or stories you want to check.

   The line that reads Search Story affords three choices. The first item, Selected text, is discussed later in this chapter. If you selected Current Publication in step 5, both Current Story and All Stories are available to you. By choosing the Current Story radio button, you ask PageMaker to check only the text box in which you have placed the insertion point. Selecting All Stories means that PageMaker's Spell Checker searches every text box in your document.

   If, however, you chose All Publications in step 5, the Current Story selection is not available. The All Stories item is selected by default. That means that every text box in every open PageMaker document will be checked.

7. Start the spell check.

   Click the Start button on the Spelling dialog box. PageMaker's Spell Checker begins comparing the words in your document to the PageMaker dictionary. Words that are unmatched with words in the dictionary appear in the Change To text box (see the following illustration).

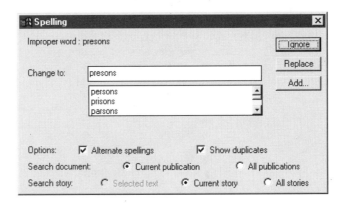

8. Ignore, replace, or add the unmatched word.

   Almost all of the spell check process is automatic, but at this point you must make a decision. Consider the following questions:

   ■ Is the word in the Change To box misspelled?

   ■ Is the correct spelling shown in the box beneath the Change To box?

   ■ Is the word in the Change To box a word that is correctly spelled? Is it one you use frequently?

   The following list outlines your three choices and explains what each entails.

   Ignore:  As you would expect, this button ignores the word and proceeds to the next word not found in the dictionary.

   Replace:  When you click on a word from the list in the box below the Change To box, it appears in the Change To box. Clicking the Replace Button then substitutes the selected word for the unmatched one.

   If the correct spelling of your word does not appear in the list, click in the Change To box and correct the spelling manually. Clicking the Replace Button then substitutes the edited word for the unmatched word.

Once the change has been made, the Spell Checker moves to the next unmatched word.

Add: This choice adds the unmatched word to the dictionary and then moves to the next unmatched word.

Be very careful using the Add feature. If you add a misspelled word to the dictionary, it will no longer be identified as unmatched by the Spell Checker.

9. Close the Spelling dialog box and the spell-checked stories.

Once every unmatched word has been presented for your consideration, the Spelling dialog box displays a message that says Spelling Check Complete. To complete the process, close the dialog box by clicking the Exit button in the upper right corner of the box. Each story that was opened for checking must also be closed in the same manner. This will return you to the PageMaker page where you began.

If you want to check a block of text rather than a full story or stories, highlight the text you wish to search before you begin the spelling check. When the Spelling dialog box is activated, selected text in the Search Story line is automatically selected (see Figure 4-3).

# Formatting Text

When text is an essential part of a document's design, as it is particularly in advertisements, newsletters, letterhead, and even sometimes in Web pages, its formatting or appearance is crucial. There are myriad ways to format text in PageMaker 7. The basics such as alignment, font face, font size, and text effects (also called text style) are discussed here. More advanced text manipulations are addressed in Chapter 9.

## Aligning Text

Text alignment has to do with how the text is situated between the margins. In PageMaker, alignment affects whole paragraphs; you cannot apply alignment styles to individual words or characters. In PageMaker, you have five alignment styles from which to choose:

- **Align Left**, also called left justification, aligns the text flush against the left margin, leaving text next to the right margin uneven or ragged (see Figure 4-4). If you have created an indent in the text, the Flush Left command honors it by left-aligning all but the indented line or lines. By default, text created in

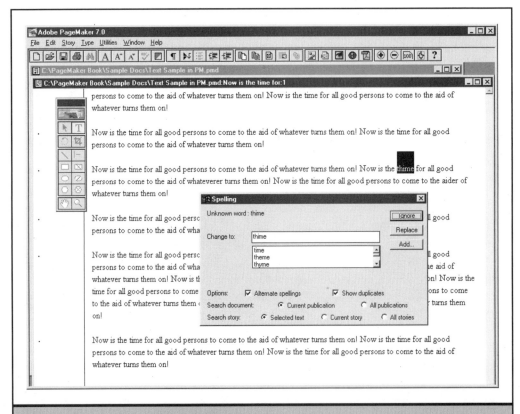

**Figure 4-3.** *Spell checking selected text*

PageMaker is left-justified. Left justification is the most commonly used of all alignment styles. It is an informal style and therefore is frequently the choice of graphic designers who wish to project a reader-friendly image.

- **Align Center** aligns the text between the two margins, leaving both left and right text edges ragged, as shown in Figure 4-5. Center alignment is usually reserved for headlines and other short lines of text. Larger blocks of centered text are difficult to read.

- **Align Right**, called right justification, aligns the text flush against the right margin, leaving the text near the left margin ragged (see Figure 4-6). This is the least used of all alignment styles. Right alignment is appropriate only when its use is crucial to the design of a page.

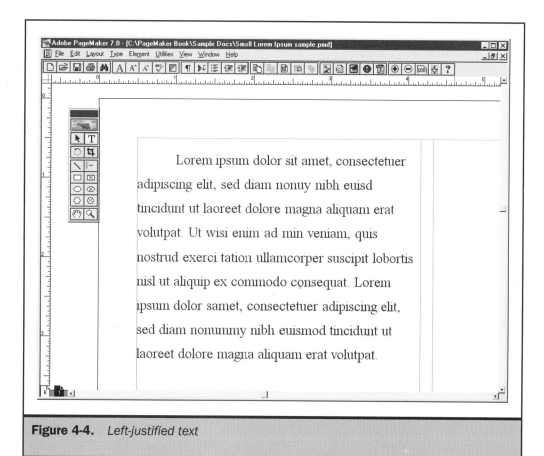

**Figure 4-4.**   *Left-justified text*

- **Justify,** also known as full justification, aligns the text flush against both the right and left margins except for a partial last line in a paragraph (see Figure 4-7). This alignment style is more formal. Its use is common when the target market of any document is conservative and conventional. Although justification provides neat, crisp margins to text, it also produces a phenomenon referred to as rivers of white space. The irregular spacing caused by forcing each line of type to the right margin causes white space (the blank spaces between words) to seem to flow through the text, as shown in Figure 4-8.

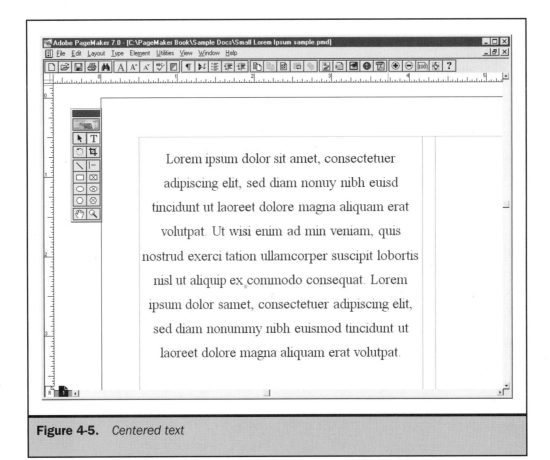

**Figure 4-5.** *Centered text*

- **Force Justify** produces the same result as Justify, except that all lines are justified, even an incomplete line at the end of a paragraph. Be aware that if the last line in a paragraph is short, force justification creates some unattractive spacing (see Figure 4-9).

Take the following steps to apply an alignment style to your text:

1. Indicate the text you want to align.

   Using the Text tool, click the text to place the insertion point in the paragraph to which you want to apply an alignment style. If you want to apply an alignment style to more than one paragraph, highlight those paragraphs.

GETTING STARTED
WITH PAGEMAKER

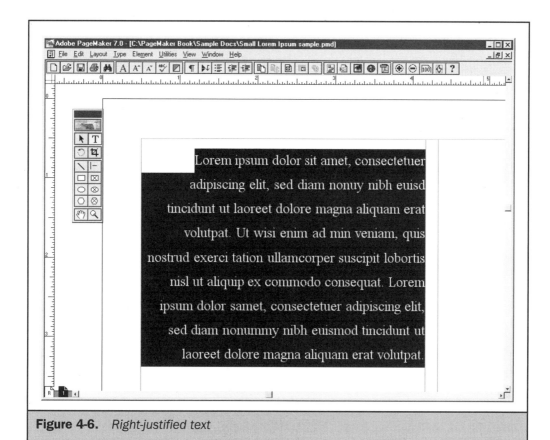

**Figure 4-6.**   *Right-justified text*

## Using the Keyboard

I usually use the keyboard to apply alignment to paragraphs. Just make sure that the insertion point is in the paragraph to which you want to apply the alignment style, or, if you want to affect multiple paragraphs, see that those paragraphs are highlighted. Then choose the keystroke commands from the following list.

| | |
|---|---|
| Align Left | CTRL-SHIFT-L |
| Align Center | CTRL-SHIFT-C |
| Align Right | CTRL-SHIFT-R |
| Justify | CTRL-SHIFT-J |
| Full Justify | CTRL-SHIFT-F |

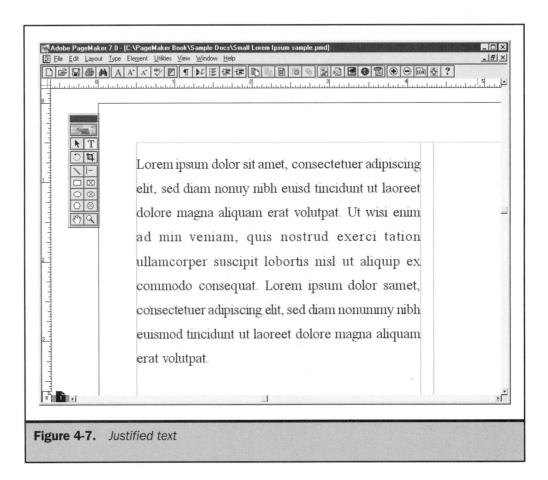

**Figure 4-7.** *Justified text*

2. Select the Alignment command.

   From the Type menu, click the Alignment command; a sub-menu opens, displaying the alignment styles, as shown in Figure 4-10.

3. Choose an alignment style.

   Click on the style you wish to apply to the paragraph or paragraphs you have indicated. The text is formatted to the selected style.

# Changing Font

One of the biggest advantages of the computer (over the typewriter, which I used for years) is the ease with which the text font can be changed. And it is easy, if sometimes inadvisable, to have many different font faces in one document.

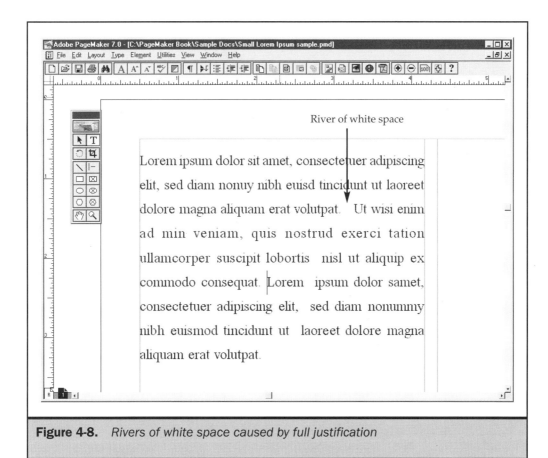

River of white space

Lorem ipsum dolor sit amet, consectetuer adipiscing elit, sed diam nonuy nibh euisd tincidunt ut laoreet dolore magna aliquam erat volutpat. Ut wisi enim ad min veniam, quis nostrud exerci tation ullamcorper suscipit lobortis nisl ut aliquip ex commodo consequat. Lorem ipsum dolor samet, consectetuer adipiscing elit, sed diam nonummy nibh euismod tincidunt ut laoreet dolore magna aliquam erat volutpat.

**Figure 4-8.** *Rivers of white space caused by full justification*

Highlight the text you want to format. In addition to selecting large amounts of text like paragraphs and whole stories, you can select one word or even one letter if you wish. If you want to change an entire document, each text box must be highlighted and formatted separately.

In PageMaker, there are three techniques that can be used to change the font in which your text appears; one uses the Character Specifications dialog box, another uses the Font menu, and the third utilizes the Control Palette. I, personally, prefer the Control Palette. I always have it open and handy in my PageMaker window, so making a change takes just a couple of mouse movements. But, of course, the choice is yours. All three techniques are discussed here.

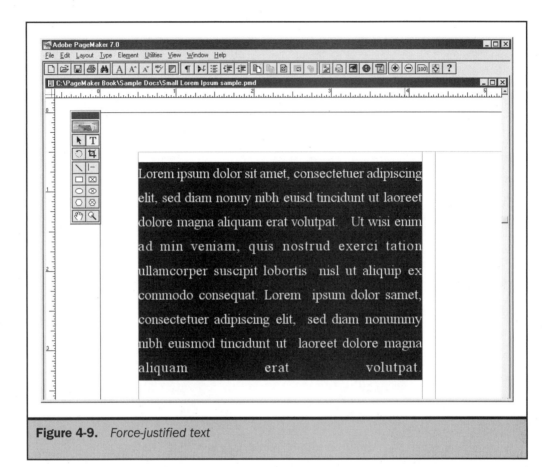

**Figure 4-9.** *Force-justified text*

## Using the Font Menu

If you know the font you want to change to, this is really easy. Follow these steps:

1. Select the text.

   As mentioned previously, you must highlight all of the text you want to format. (Refer to the section "Selecting Text" earlier in this chapter.)

2. Open the font list.

   Click the Type menu's Font command. A list of fonts available from your computer system is displayed. If you have more fonts installed on your system than can be displayed in one list, open additional lists by clicking the More command at the top of the list (see Figure 4-11). As long as the More command appears at the top of the last list, there are more fonts available to list.

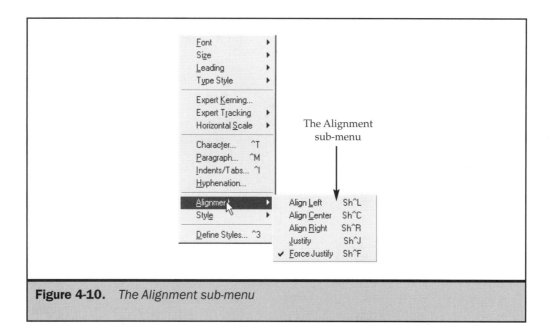

**Figure 4-10.**  *The Alignment sub-menu*

3. Make your selection.

   Click on the name of the font that you wish to use. The list (or lists) close and
   the highlighted text changes to the new font.

## Using the Character Specifications Dialog Box

The advantage of using the Character dialog box (see Figure 4-12) is that you can make
a number of text changes in one operation. Changes that involve font, size, effects
(style), color, leading, scale, and much more can be changed in this one spot. In this
section, using the Character dialog box to change font is discussed; changing size and
applying text styles are presented later in this chapter. Please see Chapter 9 for
information about the other selections available on the Character dialog box.

   A new font face is applied using these steps:

1. Select the text.

   Highlight all of the text you want to format. (Refer to the section "Selecting
   Text" earlier in this chapter.)

2. Open the Character Specifications dialog box by clicking on the Type menu's
   Character command.

   Click on the Type menu's Character command. The Character Specifications
   dialog box opens.

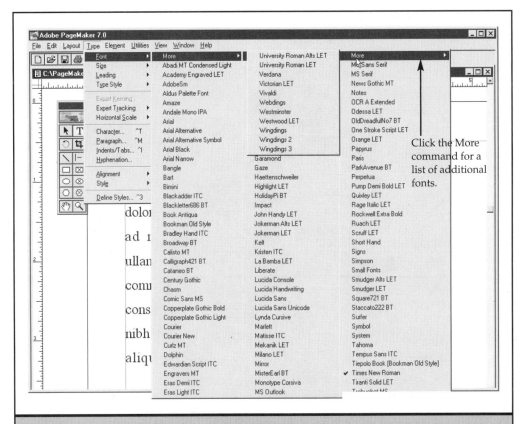

**Figure 4-11.** *Multiple font lists displayed*

3. Display the Font menu.

   Click the drop-down arrow to the right of the Font menu box. A menu appears showing all of the fonts installed in your system (see Figure 4-13). The font currently in use is selected.

4. Select a font.

   Scroll through the menu using the vertical scroll bar. Click on the font you want to use. The name of the new font appears in the Font menu box.

5. Click OK.

   When you click the OK button, the Character Specifications dialog box closes and the new font is applied to the highlighted text.

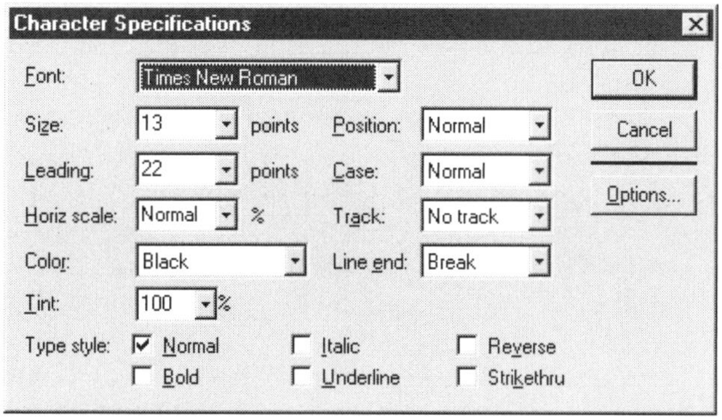

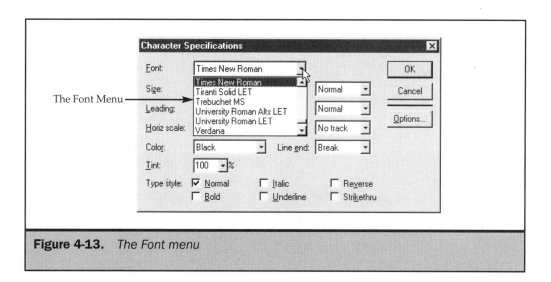

**Figure 4-12.**   *The Character Specifications dialog box*

The Font Menu

**Figure 4-13.**   *The Font menu*

## Using the Control Palette

The Control Palette plays an important role in using PageMaker with precision. With it, you can achieve font formatting and adjustments, manipulate the size and position of PageMaker elements, and other tasks. The Control Palette is contextual; that is, it changes according to the tool you are using and the task you want to accomplish.

Although any task that can be performed with the Control Palette can also be achieved using menus and dialog boxes, the Control Palette provides ease and convenience. I have known PageMaker users who never open the Control Palette and work well without it. But, as I have stated before, I rely on it and leave it open in my PageMaker window all the time. I encourage you to give yourself the opportunity to become comfortable with the Control Palette.

In this section and the ones following, I discuss using the Control Palette for basic text formatting.

Here is how to change the font by using the Control Palette:

1. Highlight the text.

   Just as in the other font-changing techniques, you must select the text you want to change before you begin the process. Click the Text tool and then click and drag through the block of text you wish to highlight or use any of the text selection techniques discussed earlier in this chapter. You may select several paragraphs, an entire story, or one word.

2. Display the Control Palette.

   If the Control Palette is not open, display it by clicking on the Window menu's Show Control Palette command. If the text tool is still the active tool, the Control Palette will display the text-formatting controls, as shown in the following illustration.

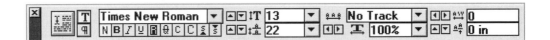

3. Display the Font menu.

   Click on the drop-down arrow to the right of the Font menu box to display the Font menu, as shown below. The current font is selected.

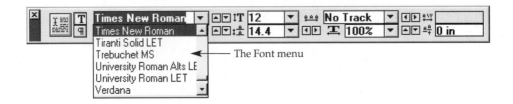

4. Choose a new font.

   Use the scroll bar to move through the menu. Locate the font you want and click on it. The menu closes and the new font is applied to the highlighted text.

# Changing Font Size

PageMaker text can be any size from 4 points to 650 points, and changing font size is every bit as easy as changing the font face. There are three techniques to choose from for this procedure, and they copy almost exactly the processes used in changing the font.

*Font sizes are in points, the sizing system traditionally used by printers for hundreds of years. There are 72 points to an inch; therefore, 18-point type is ¹/₄ of an inch tall. Type is measured, not by the height of the upper-case letters, but from the highest ascender (for example, the highest level of the letter h) to the lowest descender (such as the lowest level of the letter p) of the lower-case letters.*

## Using the Character Specifications Dialog Box

Apply a new font size using these steps:

1.  Select the text.

    Highlight all of the text you want to format. (Refer to the section "Selecting Text" earlier in this chapter.)

2.  Open the Character Specifications dialog box by clicking on the Type menu's Character command.

    Click on the Type menu's Character command. The Character Specifications dialog box opens.

3.  Display the size menu.

    Click on the drop-down arrow to the right of the Size menu box. A menu appears showing preset font sizes (see below). The size of the highlighted text is selected. If the highlighted text contains more than one size type, the size box will be blank.

The Size
menu box ⟶

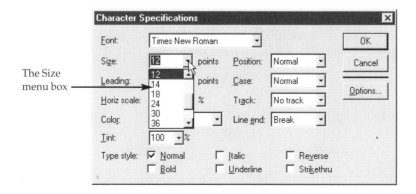

4. Select a font size.

Scroll through the menu using the vertical scroll bar. Click on the size you want to use. You may choose one of the preset sizes by clicking it. Or you may designate a different font size by typing it in the size box, and then pressing the ENTER key. The new font size appears in the Font Size menu box.

5. Click OK.

When you click the OK button, the Character Specifications dialog box closes and the new font size is applied to the highlighted text.

## Using the Size Menu

This works just like the menu option in changing the font face. Follow these steps:

1. Select the text.

You must highlight all of the text you want to format. (Refer to the section "Selecting Text" earlier in this chapter.)

2. Open the Size menu.

Click the Type menu's Size command. A menu appears showing preset font sizes.

3. Make your selection.

Click on the font size that you wish to use. (In this technique, you can only select from the preset sizes.) The menu closes and the highlighted text is resized.

## Using the Control Palette

Here is how to change the font size by using the Control Palette:

1. Highlight the text.

Select the text you want to change before you begin the process. Click the Text tool and then click and drag through the block of text you wish to highlight or use any of the text selection techniques discussed earlier in this chapter. You may select several paragraphs, an entire story, or one word.

2. Display the Control Palette.

If the Control Palette is not open, display it by clicking on the Window menu's Show Control Palette command.

3. Display the Size menu.

Click on the drop-down arrow to the right of the Size menu box to display the menu, as shown in the following illustration. The current font size is highlighted.

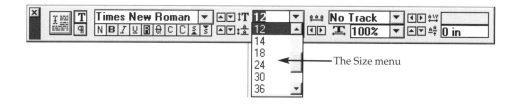

The Size menu

4. Choose a new size.

Scroll through the menu using the vertical scroll bar. Click on the size you want to use. You may choose one of the preset sizes. You may also designate a different font size by highlighting the existing data and typing the new size in the size box. Then press the ENTER key. The new font size appears in the Font Size menu box.

# Adding Text Effects

Text effect is the term I use when talking about bolding, italicizing, underlining, striking, and reversing text. The term type style is also used to refer to the same thing. As I will later discuss PageMaker Styles, using the term *effect* here will create less confusion later on.

Table 4-2 explains the PageMaker text effects and shows examples.

Text effects, except for Strikethru, are used to add extra emphasis to your copy. Overuse can quickly diminish their effectiveness, so use them cautiously. Also keep in mind that text to which the Reverse effect has been applied cannot be seen unless it is placed on a dark background.

There are three techniques that can be used to apply an effect to text: the Type menu's Type Style sub-menu, the Character Specifications box, and the Control Palette. These techniques are discussed below.

## Using the Type Style Menu

This works just like the menu option for changing the font face or the type size. Here are the steps:

1. Select the text.

Highlight the text you want to format. (Refer to the section "Selecting Text" earlier in this chapter.)

2. Open the Type Style menu.

Click the Type menu's Type Style command. A menu appears listing Normal and five text effects: Bold, Italic, Underline, Strikethru, and Reverse.

| Text Effect | Definition | Example |
|---|---|---|
| Bold | Because bolded text is created with a broader line than regular text, it appears darker and stands out among regular text. | An example of **Bolded** text. |
| Italic | Italicized text is created on a slight slant and some of the letter forms are different from regular text. | An example of *Italicized* text. |
| Underline | As you would expect, the underline effect causes a line to be placed under the text. | An example of <u>Underlined</u> text. |
| Reverse | Reversed text appears white. This is used so that text shows against a dark background | An example of Reversed text. |
| Strikethru | Strikethru is an effect that enables text to be deleted while still remaining in place and readable. | An example of text with the ~~Strikethru~~ effect applied. |

**Table 4-2.**   *PageMaker Text Effects*

3. Make your selection.

   Click on the text effect that you wish to use. The menu closes and the text effect is applied to the highlighted text.

If you want to apply more than one effect, you must follow the steps again. Using the Specifications dialog box (see the following steps) enables you to select more than one effect at a time.

## Using the Character Specifications Dialog Box

Apply a text effect or several effects using these steps:

1. Select the text.

   Highlight the text you want to format. (Refer to the section "Selecting Text" earlier in this chapter.)

2. Open the Character Specifications dialog box by clicking on the Type menu's Character command.

   Click the Type menu's Character command. The Character Specifications dialog box opens.

3. Select the text effect.

   Select the text effect of your choice from the list at the bottom of the Character Specifications dialog box. Except for the normal selection, multiple selections can be made at one time, if you wish.

4. Click OK.

   When you click the OK button, the Character Specifications dialog box closes and the text effects are applied to the highlighted text.

## Using the Control Palette

Here is how to apply text effects by using the Control Palette:

1. Highlight the text.

2. Select the text you want to change before you begin the process. (Refer to the section "Selecting Text" earlier in this chapter.) Display the Control Palette.

   If the Control Palette is not open, display it by clicking on the Window menu's Show Control Palette command.

3. Select a text effect.

   Buttons for the text effects of Normal, Bold, Italic, Underline, Reverse, and Strikethru appear on the Control Palette below the Font menu (see Figure 4-23). Click on the effect or effects you want; the effects are applied to the highlighted text.

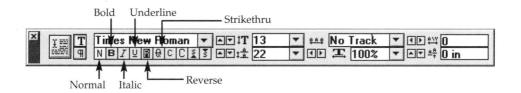

# Summary

PageMaker uses text as a design element. PageMaker text is contained in a text box and each text box in a document is treated as a separate element. Therefore, unlike word processing, there may be multiple text boxes in a document or even on a page. Creating a text block and editing text requires the use of the Text tool. Working with text blocks may also entail the Pointer tool.

**Creating a Text Box**   PageMaker will automatically insert a text box when you click with the Text tool between existing margins. Or you can use the Text tool to click and drag a text box to the size you wish. Although it takes a Text tool to create a text box, to delete one you must click it with the Pointer tool and then press the DELETE key.

**Moving and Sizing a Text Box**   PageMaker text boxes can be moved or sized by using the Pointer tool. Click in the text and drag to move the box. Click and drag one of the sizing buttons on either side of the top or bottom border to increase or decrease the box's width.

**Editing Text**   Editing text in PageMaker is remarkably similar to working in a word processing program. Some text correction techniques require that the text be highlighted before beginning the process. There are several selecting techniques that can be used.

PageMaker's Spell Checker program is streamlined in PageMaker 7 compared to previous versions. You can check selected text, a story, several stories, or all open documents. The Spell Checker works by comparing each word in the selected text or story to the PageMaker dictionary. When PageMaker finds an unmatched word, the word is identified in the Spelling dialog box. You can ignore the unmatched word, change it, or add it to the dictionary.

**Formatting Text**   Formatting text is important to its role as an element in the design of a page or document. Text alignment has to do with how the text is situated between the margins of a document. Changing font and font size, as well as applying text effects, is easily performed through the Character Specifications dialog box, menus, or the Control palette.

# The
# Complete
# Reference

PageMaker
7

# Chapter 5

# The Basics of Using
# PageMaker Graphics

As important as text is to a PageMaker document, graphics are just as important and, in certain types of documents, even more so. Graphics make up a large part of the design elements of any printed piece and are pivotal to a successful Web page.

In PageMaker there are essentially two types of graphics, simple graphics created within PageMaker using the graphic tools in the Toolbox Palette and those that are imported using either the Picture Palette or PageMaker's Place command. This chapter provides the basics of creating simple graphics and placing graphics from the Picture Palette. For more detailed information about fine-tuning graphics, especially those that you have imported, please see Chapter 10.

## Using Simple Graphics

The graphics that you create using the graphics tools in the Toolbox Palette are what I am calling simple graphics. The tools you use are the Line tool, the Constrained Line tool, the Rectangle tool, the Ellipse tool, and the Polygon tool. Table 5-1 identifies and briefly describes each of these tools. Also, refer to Chapter 2 for a list of all of the Toolbox Palette tools.

The use of one graphic tool is much the same as another, yet there are special considerations that you need to understand when working with each simple graphic. In this chapter, I am providing directions for the use of each tool individually. Although

| Button | Tool Name | Description |
|---|---|---|
| ◻ | The Line tool | Draws a line from one point to another in any direction. |
| ◻ | The Constrained Line tool | Draws lines that are horizontal, vertical, or at a 45° angle. |
| ◻ | The Rectangle tool | Draws rectangles or squares. |
| ◻ | The Ellipse tool | Draws ovals and circles. |
| ◻ | The Polygon tool | Draws basic polygons such as hexagons and pentagons. With adjustments, these graphics can be converted into stars. |

**Table 5-1.** *Simple Graphics Buttons*

this provides a bit of redundancy if you are reading straight through the book, it enables each tool to stand on its own when the book is used as a reference.

# Create and Modify Lines

There are two tools used to create simple lines: the Line tool and the Constrained Line tool. The Line tool draws a line at any angle on the page, while the Constrained Line tool draws only horizontal, vertical, or diagonal lines.

Keep in mind that a line is, indeed, a graphic in PageMaker terms as well as in general graphic design principles, and that a line is an important element in creating many designs. Although it seems simpler than, say, a rectangle, it is extremely flexible in its parameters of length and weight (the width of the line).

Length is created at the time you draw the line and can be adjusted later. The original weight of the line depends upon the default line weight setting. But any line weight can be adjusted after it is created.

In addition to length and weight, a line also may have a style. The most used line style is solid, but dashed, dotted, double, or triple lines are available as well.

## Creating a Line

1.  Select the Line tool you want to use.

    If you want your line to draw across the page at any angle, click the Line tool to select it. However, if you want only a horizontal, vertical, or diagonal line, the Constrained Line tool is the best choice. (See examples of each of these lines in Figure 5-1.) Each works the same. Once either Line tool has been selected, your mouse pointer changes to a small cross.

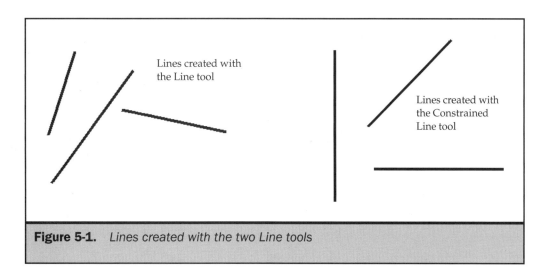

**Figure 5-1.**  *Lines created with the two Line tools*

2. Drag to create the line.

   Place the cross where you want the line to begin. Click and drag the mouse pointer until the line is the length you desire (see Figure 5-2). You may drag in any direction you wish; however, if you use the Constrained Line tool, the mouse pointer will snap to a horizontal, vertical, or diagonal position. When you release the mouse, the line is complete.

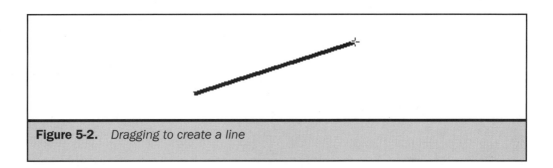

**Figure 5-2.**   *Dragging to create a line*

## Adjusting Line Length

It is very common when working with a layout in PageMaker to want to adjust a graphic after you have created it, and a line is no exception. Making a line longer or shorter after it is created is an easy task that uses the Pointer tool. Here's how:

1. Select the Pointer tool.

   Click the Pointer tool to select it. The mouse pointer then becomes an arrow.

2. Select the line.

   The line must be selected before it can be adjusted. Using the Pointer tool, just click the line to select it. Once selected, sizing handles, small black boxes, will appear at each end of the line.

3. Click and drag.

   Click the sizing handle and drag to stretch the line, that is, to make the line longer or shorter. Take care to not change the angle of the line if its placement is important. Even if the line was created using the Constrained Line tool, it is easy to move the line to a new angle while stretching it. And holding down the SHIFT key keeps a line at a horizontal, vertical, or diagonal angle.

## Adjusting Line Weight

Line weight is measured in points, just like text (refer to Chapter 4). A very fine line may be 1 point or even 1/2 point in width. Bolder lines are usually 8 points or less, but line weight can be adjusted to as much as 800 points. (I can't conceive of a use for an 800-point line, but it is possible in PageMaker.)

Adjusting the weight of the line takes a few more steps than changing its length, but it is still a simple process. Here are the steps to take:

1.  Select the Pointer tool.

    Click the Pointer tool to select it. The mouse pointer then becomes an arrow.

2.  Select the line.

    The line must be selected before it can be adjusted. Using the Pointer tool, just click the line to select it. Once selected, sizing handles will appear at each end of the line.

3.  Open the Stroke menu.

    Click the Element menu's Stroke command. The Stroke menu appears, as shown in Figure 5-3.

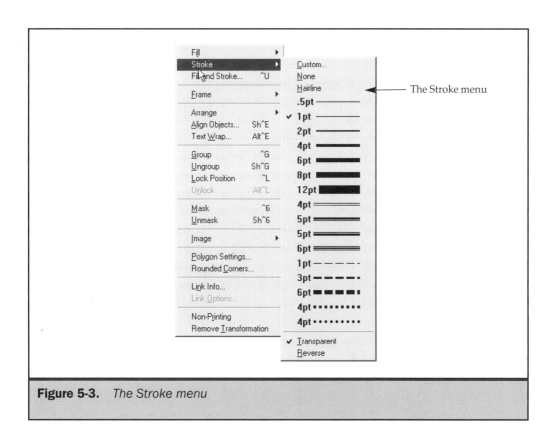

**Figure 5-3.** *The Stroke menu*

4.  Select a line weight.

    Click the line weight you want. Once you have selected a weight, the menu closes and the weight of your selected line is adjusted.

    If the line weight you want is not shown on the Stroke menu, click the menu's Custom command and, in the resulting dialog box (see below), enter the point value of the weight you desire. Then click the OK button. The dialog box closes, as well as the menu, and the weight of the selected line is changed.

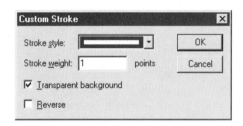

## Adjusting Line Style

There are several line styles available in PageMaker (see Figure 5-4). The style of a line can make a strong graphic statement in your finished product. For example, the two line styles that have a narrow line coupled with a bolder one can be used to draw your eye into or away from another page element much like a portion of a picture frame. A bold solid line can be a major splash of color across your piece.

Each of the PageMaker line styles may be set in any weight up to 800 points.
Here is how to change the line style:

1.  Select the Pointer tool.

    If it is not already selected, click the Pointer tool. The mouse pointer then becomes an arrow.

2.  Select the line.

    The line must be selected before its style can be changed. Using the Pointer tool, just click anywhere on the line to select it. Once selected, sizing handles will appear at each end of the line.

3.  Open the Stroke menu.

    From the Element menu, click the Stroke command. The Stroke menu appears, as shown in Figure 5-3.

4.  Select a line style.

    Click the line style you want. Once you have made a selection, the menu closes and the new style is applied to your selected line.

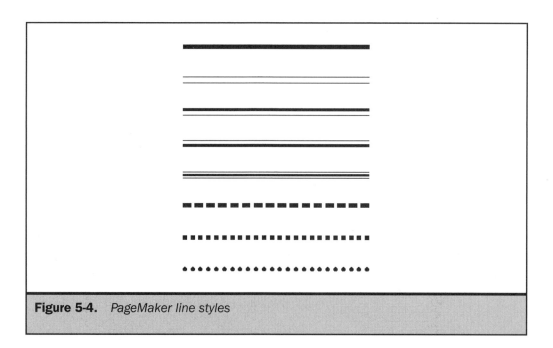

**Figure 5-4.** *PageMaker line styles*

**Note** *You may also change the line weight or style in the Fill and Stroke dialog box. One way to access this box is by clicking on the Fill and Stroke button on the PageMaker toolbar.*

## Moving a Line

The steps for moving a line are so simple that they almost don't require steps at all. But for the sake of clarity, here are two steps to follow if you want to relocate your line:

1.  Select the line.

    In order to move a line, you must first select it using the Pointer tool. Just click the Pointer tool and then click on the graphic. Once selected, the sizing handles appear at each end of the line.

2.  Click and drag.

    Grab the line with the mouse anywhere except for the sizing handles and drag it to a new location. Be sure not to click one of the sizing handles, however. Instead of moving the line, dragging a sizing handle will change its length and maybe its orientation.

# Create and Modify Rectangles

Depending upon how you use PageMaker, you may find that you use rectangles a lot. Some common uses of the rectangle shape are to identify areas of a page, to add color and interest to a document, to highlight another graphic, or to create a focal point. In a complicated layout, you can use a rectangle to balance other elements of the page.

In addition to adjusting its parameters of length and width, a rectangle can be modified in other ways. For example, the line that creates the rectangle can be modified, its corners can be rounded, and it also can be filled with color.

## Creating a Rectangle

You will find that the steps used in creating a rectangle are very similar to the steps used in creating a line. This is not surprising, because the rectangle is created by a line.

Here are the steps:

1. Select the Rectangle tool.

   Click the Rectangle tool to select it. Once the Rectangle Tool has been selected, the mouse pointer changes to a small cross.

2. Drag to create the rectangle.

   Place the cross where you want the rectangle to begin. Click and drag the mouse pointer until the rectangle is the length and width you desire (see below). You may drag in any direction you wish. Once you release the mouse, the rectangle is complete.

If you wish the rectangle to be a perfect square, constrain the graphic while dragging by holding down the SHIFT key. Be sure to release the mouse before you release the SHIFT key.

## Adjusting the Size of the Rectangle

Once created, a rectangle is anything but static. Using the Pointer tool, it can be stretched to enlarge or reduce it, or to change its orientation.

Here are the simple steps to adjust the size of a rectangle:

1.  Select the Pointer tool.

    Click the Pointer tool to select it. The mouse pointer then becomes an arrow.

2.  Select the rectangle.

    The rectangle must be selected before it can be adjusted. Using the Pointer tool, just click the line surrounding the rectangle to select it. Once selected, sizing handles will appear at each corner of the rectangle and midway along each side.

3.  Click and drag.

    Click any sizing handle and drag to change the proportion of the graphic. Dragging a corner sizing handle enables you to move both horizontally and vertically at one time. If you drag the top or bottom handles, you will size the graphic vertically. Dragging the left or right side handles will change the rectangle's horizontal size.

## Adjusting the Line Style of a Rectangle

Changing the style of its outline effectively changes a rectangle's impact on the document layout. It is an especially important consideration in creating the end effect you desire. For example, one line style makes the rectangle appear as a picture frame, another as a coupon to be cut away from a printed page.

As discussed, there are several line styles available in PageMaker. Figure 5-5 shows rectangles with different line styles.

Here is how to change a rectangle's line style:

1.  Select the Pointer tool.

    If it is not already selected, click the Pointer tool. The mouse pointer then becomes an arrow.

2.  Select the rectangle.

    The rectangle must be selected before its style can be changed. Using the Pointer tool, just click the rectangle's outline to select it. Once selected, sizing handles will appear in a box shape around the graphic.

3.  Open the Stroke menu.

    Click the Element menu's Stroke command. The Stroke menu appears, as shown earlier in this chapter in Figure 5-3.

4.  Select a line style.

    Click the line style you want. Once you have made a selection, the menu closes and the new style is applied to the rectangle.

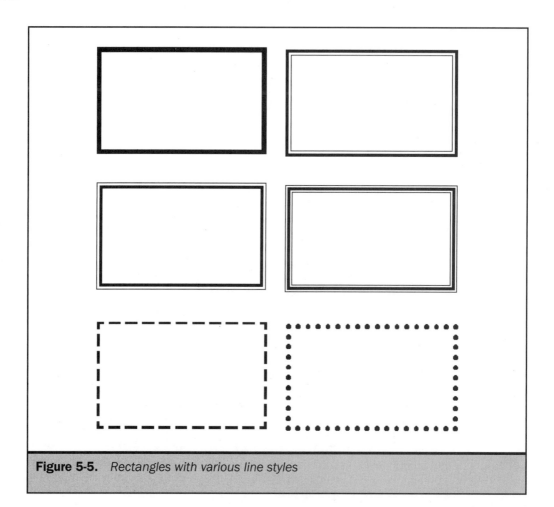

**Figure 5-5.** *Rectangles with various line styles*

## Adjusting the Rectangle's Line Weight

The weight of a rectangle's outline affects the rectangle's impact on the design of a document. With a lightweight line, a rectangle carries less importance than one with a bolder line and the rectangle attracts less attention. You may want to emphasize or de-emphasize a rectangle, depending upon its place in your design. Figure 5-6 shows rectangles with various line weights.

Adjusting the weight of a rectangle's line only takes these few steps:

1.  Select the Pointer tool.

    Click the Pointer tool to select it. The mouse pointer then becomes an arrow.

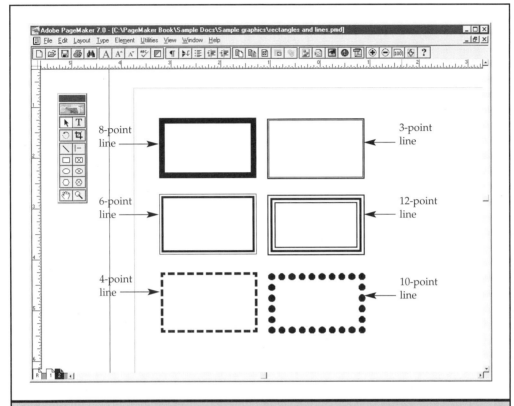

**Figure 5-6.**   *Rectangles with various line weights*

2.  Select the line.

    The rectangle must be selected before its outline can be adjusted. Using the Pointer tool, just click anywhere on the outline to select it. Once selected, sizing handles will appear at each corner of the rectangle and midway along each side.

3.  Open the Stroke menu.

    Click the Element menu's Stroke command. The Stroke menu appears, as shown in Figure 5-3.

4.  Select a line weight.

    Click the line weight you want. Once you have selected a weight, the menu closes and the weight of your rectangle's outline is adjusted.

If the line weight you want is not shown on the Stroke menu, click the menu's Custom command and, in the resulting dialog box, enter the point value of the weight you desire. Then click the OK button. The dialog box closes, as well as the menu, and the weight of the selected rectangle's outline is changed.

*You may also change the line weight or style in the Fill and Stroke dialog box. One way to access this box is by clicking on the Fill and Stroke button on the PageMaker toolbar.*

## Rounding the Corners of Your Rectangle

Rectangles are automatically created with square corners, but you can soften the effect, if you wish, by applying rounded corners to the rectangle. Rounded corners can serve as an attention-getter: If most of the graphics in your layout are squared off, a rectangle with rounded corners will stand out and draw the eye. Another effect of the use of softer corners is to make a layout more contemporary or casual. Conservative pieces will have sharper angles and harder edges.

These steps will round the corners of your rectangle:

1.  Select the Pointer tool.

    Click the Pointer tool to change the mouse pointer to an arrow.

2.  Select the rectangle.

    Click the line that creates the rectangle to select it. Sizing handles indicate that the rectangle is selected.

3.  Open the Rounded Corners dialog box.

    Click the Element menu's Rounded Corners command. The Rounded Corners dialog box appears, as shown in the following illustration, with the square corners choice selected.

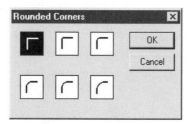

4.  Select a Rounded Corners style.

    The Rounded Corners dialog box shows a total of six rounded corners styles, ranging from square corners to very rounded. I advise that you experiment with the styles until you are comfortable with the various effects that the styles provide. For example, if the selected rectangle is very small, the most rounded style will create an oval or a circle.

5. Click OK.

   Once you have made your selection, click the OK button to apply the rounded corners style to your rectangle.

## Moving a Rectangle

The steps for moving a rectangle are identical to moving any simple graphic. Here are the two simple steps:

1. Select the graphic.

   Before you can move a rectangle, you must first select it using the ointer tool. Just click the Pointer tool and then click the outline of the rectangle. Once the rectangle is selected, the eight sizing handles appear.

2. Click and drag.

   You may grab the rectangle anywhere on its outline and drag it to a new location. Be sure not to click one of the sizing handles, however. Instead of moving the rectangle, dragging a sizing handle will change its proportion.

# Create and Modify Ellipses

An ellipse is an oval. It can also be a perfect circle. Whatever form they take, ellipses are used often in the design of a document to provide graphic interest, add spots of color, or establish focal points.

   Just like a rectangle, an ellipse has length and width, which are easily adjusted. As a matter of fact, once it has been created, an ellipse can be modified in several ways.

## Creating an Ellipse

These steps are similar to the steps used in the creation of other simple graphics.

1. Select the Ellipse tool.

   Click the Ellipse tool to select it. Once it has been selected, the mouse pointer changes to a small cross.

2. Drag to create an oval or a circle.

   Place the cross where you want the ellipse to begin. Click and drag the mouse pointer until the graphic is the length and width you desire (see the following illustration). You may drag in any direction you wish. Once you release the mouse, the oval is complete.

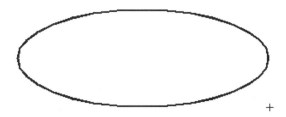

If you wish the ellipse to be a perfect circle, constrain the graphic while dragging by holding down the SHIFT key. Be sure to release the mouse before you release the SHIFT key.

## Adjusting the Size of the Ellipse

Once created, the ellipse, like the line and the rectangle, can be adjusted. Using the Pointer tool, it can be stretched to enlarge or reduce it, or to change its orientation. Here are the simple steps to adjust the size of an ellipse:

1.  Select the Pointer tool.

    Click the Pointer tool to select it. The mouse pointer then becomes an arrow.

2.  Select the ellipse.

    The graphic must be selected before it can be adjusted. Using the Pointer tool, just click the outline of the ellipse to select it.

    Once selected, eight sizing handles will appear in a box formation around the ellipse, as shown in Figure 5-11. The top and bottom sizing handles will be at the upper and lower points of the ellipse, and the right and left sizing handles will likewise be at the left and right points. However, the corner sizing handles are positioned away from the ellipse, forming the corners of the sizing box.

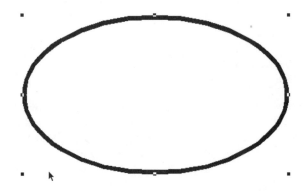

3. Click and drag.

Click any sizing handle and drag to change the proportion of the graphic. Dragging a corner sizing handle enables you to move both horizontally and vertically at one time. If you drag the top or bottom handles, you will size the ellipse vertically. Dragging the left or right side handles will change the graphic's horizontal dimension.

## Adjusting the Line Style of the Ellipse

Changing the line style of its outline changes the entire look of an ellipse and the way it works with the other design elements on a page. As discussed above, there are several line styles available in PageMaker.

Here is how to change an ellipse's line style:

1. Select the Pointer tool.

If it is not already selected, click the Pointer tool. The mouse pointer then becomes an arrow.

2. Select the ellipse.

Any graphic must be selected before its line style can be changed. Using the Pointer tool, just click the ellipse's outline to select it. Once selected, eight sizing handles will appear in a box formation around the ellipse.

3. Open the Stroke menu.

Click the Element menu's Stroke command. The Stroke menu appears, as shown earlier in this chapter in Figure 5-3.

4. Select a line style.

Click the line style you want to apply to the selected ellipse. Once you have made a selection, the menu closes and the new style is applied to the ellipse.

## Adjusting the Line Weight of an Ellipse

Just as with a rectangle, the weight of an ellipse's outline also affects the graphic's impact on the design of a document. Bolder outlines make the ellipse more noticeable. A double line calls attention to the ellipse, especially if all of the other lines on the page are unremarkable.

Adjusting the weight of the line only takes a few steps:

1. Select the Pointer tool.

Click the Pointer tool to select it. The mouse pointer then becomes an arrow.

2. Select the line.

The ellipse must be selected before its outline can be adjusted. Using the Pointer tool, just click the outline to select it. Once selected, sizing handles will appear at each corner of the ellipse and midway along each side.

3. Open the Stroke menu.

   Click the Element menu's Stroke command. The Stroke menu appears, as shown in Figure 5-3.

4. Select a line weight.

   Click the line weight you want. Once you have selected a weight, the menu closes and the weight of your rectangle's outline is adjusted.

   If the line weight you want is not shown on the Stroke menu, click the menu's Custom command and, in the resulting dialog box (refer to Figure 5-4), enter the point value of the weight you desire. Then click OK. The dialog box closes, as well as the menu, and the weight of the selected ellipse's outline is changed.

**Note**    *You may also change the line weight or style in the Fill and Stroke dialog box. One way to access this box is by clicking on the Fill and Stroke button on the PageMaker toolbar.*

## Moving an Ellipse

It is easy to relocate an ellipse to elsewhere on your PageMaker page:

1. Select the graphic.

   In order to move an ellipse, you must first select it using the Pointer tool. Just click the Pointer tool and then click the outline of the ellipse. Once selected, the eight sizing handles appear.

2. Click and drag.

   Click the ellipse's outline and drag it to a new location. Be sure not to click one of the sizing handles, however. Instead of moving the graphic, dragging a sizing handle will distort it.

# Create and Modify Polygons

A *polygon* is a graphic figure with multiple sides. In the early versions of PageMaker, users were unable to create any multiple-sided graphics except the rectangle. Although PageMaker 7 is not the first PageMaker version that enables us to create triangles, pentagons, and other polygons, I still find myself delighted with the ability to do so.

The PageMaker polygon is a remarkably versatile graphic. PageMaker provides the capability to establish the number of sides you want a polygon to have, as well as the capacity to inset the sides of the figure, creating a star. I find that a triangle and the star settings are frequently valuable in creating a detailed layout.

The default polygon (the figure you initially draw using the Polygon tool) is a hexagon, a figure with six sides (see below). From there, you can adjust the figure to the formation that you prefer. It is possible to change the default to produce an initial figure with a different number of sides (see Chapter 12).

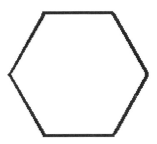

This section takes you through the process of creating a polygon and manipulating it to create the graphic that you desire.

## Create a Polygon

Creating a basic polygon takes essentially the same steps as you use in creating other graphics:

1.  Select the Polygon tool.

    Click the Polygon tool to select it. Once the Polygon tool has been selected, the mouse pointer changes to a small cross.

2.  Drag to create a six-sided polygon.

    Place the cross where you want the polygon to begin. Click and drag the mouse pointer until the graphic is the length and width you desire (see below). You may drag in any direction you wish. Once you release the mouse, the polygon is complete.

If you wish all of the sides of the polygon to be equal in length, constrain the graphic while dragging by holding down the SHIFT key. Be sure to release the mouse before you release the SHIFT key.

## Changing the Number of Sides of a Polygon

Once the polygon has been created, it is a fairly simple process to make the changes to create exactly the figure that you want. Follow these steps:

1. Select the polygon.

   If you have just created the polygon and have not clicked elsewhere on the paper, the polygon remains selected. However, if the figure is no longer selected, it must be reselected before you can make changes to its number of sides.

   To select the polygon, click the Pointer tool and then click the outline of the polygon to reveal the sizing handles.

2. Open the Polygon Settings dialog box.

   Select the Element menu's Polygon Settings command. The Polygon Settings dialog box opens (see the illustration).

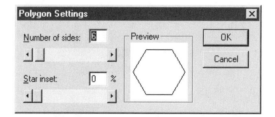

3. Adjust the number of sides.

   You may select the data already in the Number of Sides box and type in a new number to replace it, or you may change the number by using the scroll box below the Number of Sides. Select the number of sides you wish your polygon to have. Clicking the arrow to the left of the scroll bar decreases the number; the arrow to the right increases the number. As you scroll through the numbers, the preview graphic in the dialog box will adjust to show the configuration of the new graphic.

   The number of sides available ranges from 3 to 100. However, once the polygon has more than ten sides or so, it loses much of its character and looks like a circle. It is unlikely that a polygon with more than ten sides will be an effective element in your design.

4.  Click OK.

Click the OK button on the Polygon Settings dialog box. The box closes and the new parameters are applied to the selected polygon.

## Adjusting the Size of the Polygon

In addition to adjusting the number of sides a polygon has, you may change the size of the figure, just as you changed the size of the rectangle and the ellipse. Using the Pointer tool, it can be stretched to enlarge or reduce it, or to change its orientation. Here are the simple steps to adjust the size of a rectangle:

1.  Select the Pointer tool.

Click the Pointer tool to select it. The mouse pointer then becomes an arrow.

2.  Select the polygon.

The graphic must be selected by the Pointer tool before it can be adjusted. Just click the outline of the polygon to select it. If you have just created the polygon, it may appear to be selected with the sizing handles showing. However, in order to size it, you must have the use of the Pointer tool. Selecting the Pointer tool deselects the graphic, making it necessary to click it again, this time using the Pointer tool.

Once selected, eight sizing handles will appear around the polygon, as shown below. The sizing handles appear in a box around the polygon and align with the most extreme points of the graphic. Depending upon the sides selected for the polygon, the sizing handles may or may not actually touch the graphic's sides.

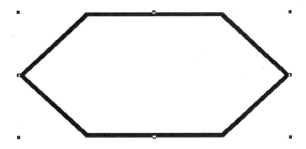

3. Click and drag.

Click any sizing handle and drag to change the proportion of the graphic. Dragging a corner sizing handle enables you to move both horizontally and vertically at one time. If you drag the top or bottom handles, you will size the polygon vertically. Dragging the left or right side handles will change the graphic's horizontal dimension.

If you wish to maintain equal sides on the polygon, hold down SHIFT as you drag. Make sure to release the mouse before you release the SHIFT key.

## Adjusting the Line Style of a Polygon

Changing the line style of its outline changes the entire look of a polygon. There are several line styles available in PageMaker.

Here is how to change a polygon's line style:

1. Select the Pointer tool.

If it is not already selected, click the Pointer tool. The mouse pointer then becomes an arrow.

2. Select the polygon.

Any graphic must be selected before its line style can be changed. Using the Pointer tool, just click the polygon's outline to select it. Once selected, eight sizing handles will appear in a box formation around the polygon.

3. Open the Stroke menu.

Click the Element menu's Stroke command. The Stroke menu appears, as shown earlier in this chapter in Figure 5-3.

4. Select a line style.

Click the line style you want to apply to the selected polygon. Once you have made a selection, the menu closes and the new style is applied to the polygon.

## Adjusting the Line Weight of a Polygon

Just as with other graphics, the weight of a polygon's outline also affects its impact on the overall layout of a page or document. The best line weight for your polygon depends upon how you want to use it in the layout. If you want it to make a strong statement, a heavier line should be used. Conversely, use a lighter weight line for an understatement.

Adjusting the weight of the line only takes a few steps:

1. Select the Pointer tool.

Click the Pointer tool to select it. The mouse pointer then becomes an arrow.

2. Select the graphic.

The polygon must be selected before its outline can be adjusted. Using the Pointer tool, just click the outline to select it. Once selected, sizing handles will appear in a box formation around the polygon.

3.  Open the Stroke menu.

    Click the Element menu's Stroke command. The Stroke menu appears, as shown in Figure 5-3.

4.  Select a line weight.

    Click the line weight you want. Once you have selected a weight, the menu closes and the weight of your polygon's outline is adjusted.

    If the line weight you want is not shown on the Stroke menu, click the menu's Custom command and in the resulting dialog box (refer to Figure 5-4) enter the point value of the weight you desire. Then click the OK button. The dialog box closes, as well as the menu, and the weight of the selected polygon's outline is changed.

**Note**   *You may also change the line weight or style in the Fill and Stroke dialog box. One way to access this box is by clicking on the Fill and Stroke button on the PageMaker toolbar.*

## Adjusting the Inset Value of a Polygon

By default, the sides of a newly created polygon have an inset value of 0 percent. That means that the sides are straight. It is easy, however, to change the appearance of the polygon to add interest or to create a star formation. The higher the percentage of the inset value of a polygon's sides, the more the sides angle toward the center of the graphic (see the following illustration).

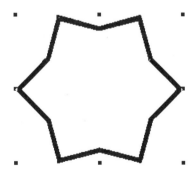

Here are the steps to take to increase the inset value of a polygon:

1.  Select the polygon.

    To select the polygon, click the Pointer tool and then click the outline of the polygon to reveal the sizing handles.

2.  Open the Polygon Settings dialog box.

    Select the Element menu's Polygon Settings command. The Polygon Settings dialog box opens.

3.  Adjust the inset value.

    You may select the data already in the Star Inset box and type in a new number to replace it, or you may change the number by using the scroll box below Star Inset. Select the inset value you wish your polygon to have. Clicking the arrow to the left of the scroll bar decreases the value; the arrow to the right increases it. As you scroll, the preview graphic in the dialog box will adjust to show the polygon's new configuration.

    The percentage of insets possible ranges from 0 to 100. A percentage of 0 establishes straight sides. A value of 100 percent eliminates the sides altogether and presents a star seemingly composed of straight, crossed lines.

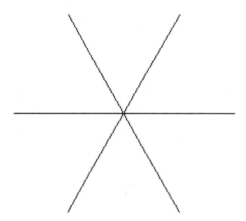

4.  Click OK.

    Click the OK button on the Polygon Settings dialog box. The box closes and the new parameters are applied to the selected polygon.

## Moving a Polygon

The steps for moving a polygon are just like the steps for moving any simple graphic:

1. Select the graphic.

   In order to move a polygon, you must first select it using the Pointer tool. Just click the Pointer tool and then click the polygon's outline. Once selected, the eight sizing handles appear.

2. Click and drag.

   Click anywhere on the polygon's outline and drag it to a new location. Be sure not to click one of the sizing handles, however. Instead of moving the polygon, dragging a sizing handle will distort it.

## Creating a Free-Form Polygon

In addition to the standard polygon form discussed previously, you can create irregularly shaped, closed, or unclosed forms using the Polygon tool.

Instead of clicking and dragging, using the Polygon tool click (then release the mouse), move to a new location, and click again. A line segment forms between the two locations. Continue to move the mouse and click where you want a line segment to end.

The Polygon tool continues to create line segments until one of three things happens:

- You close the polygon at the beginning of the first line segment. A closed form is created.

- You double-click with the Polygon tool or press the ESC key. The line is released and the form remains open.

- You press any key on your keyboard *except* for BACKSPACE, DELETE, or ESC. The form will then close with a line segment between the last click and the beginning point.

# Organize and Place Graphics Using the Picture Palette

In addition to the simple graphics described earlier, another basic graphic source is the Picture Palette, an organizational matrix or gallery for clip art and other images (see Figure 5-7). The Picture Palette provides convenient categorizing of the images as well as ease of placement into a document when you want to use one of the pictures.

Rather than storing actual images, the Picture Palette holds links to graphics that are stored elsewhere on your system or on a removable disk. No matter where a graphic is located, an image link can be duplicated and categorized in the Picture Palette, making it possible to access one graphic from multiple categories. PageMaker 7 comes with a

**Figure 5-7.** *The Picture Palette*

library of graphics on a CD and image links to those graphics are already placed in the Picture Palette. You can add graphics from your files, if you wish.

In this section, we discuss the techniques of placing and organizing graphics with the Picture Palette.

# Opening the Picture Palette

Obviously, the first step to using the Picture Palette is to have it open in your PageMaker window. As discussed in Chapter 2, the first time you launch PageMaker, the Picture Palette is displayed. Subsequently, when you open PageMaker, the Picture Palette is shown only if it was open at the time PageMaker was shut down. However, it is easily accessed. Just take these steps:

1. Open the Window menu.

   Click the Window menu on the menu bar and the Window menu drops down.

2. Open the Plug-in Palettes sub-menu.

   Select the Plug-in Palettes menu item and the sub-menu appears.

3. Open the Picture Palette.

   Click the Show Picture Palette command. The Picture Palette appears in the PageMaker window.

*Even faster, click the Picture Palette button on the PageMaker toolbar. The Picture Palette opens.*

## Selecting the Graphic

Before you can place a graphic that is cataloged in the Picture Palette, of course, you must select the picture you want to place. Follow these steps to locate your image:

1. Select the type of graphic you wish to place.

   Click the drop-down arrow to the right of the Type box to display the Type menu (see Figure 5-8).

*Don't let the term type confuse you here. In this case the word refers to the type of graphic rather than to a font.*

   By default, there are three choices on the Type menu: All Types, Clipart, and Images. Clipart is generally line drawings and other hand-created art, while images are usually photographs. Obviously the All Types selection combines the Clipart and Images graphics into one selection.

   Select the type of graphics you want from the Type menu by clicking on it. Once selected, the Type menu closes.

2. Choose the category.

   Click the drop-down arrow to the right of the Category box to display the Category menu (see Figure 5-9). Use the scroll bar to the right of the Picture Palette to scroll through the 24 categories to find the one that best meets your needs.

   Click the category of your choice to select it. Once selected, the Category menu closes. Thumbnail images representing the graphic links stored in the selected category are displayed in the Picture Palette.

3. Insert the disk that contains the graphic you want.

   If the graphic you want is on your system, you can just skip this step. However, if the graphic is on a removable disk, place the disk in the appropriate drive so that the link to the graphic is in place.

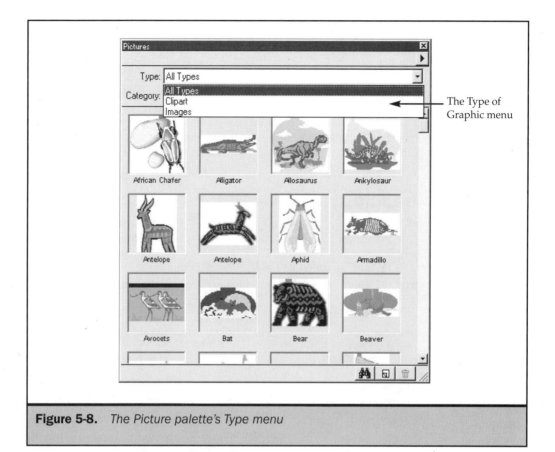

The Type of
Graphic menu

**Figure 5-8.** *The Picture palette's Type menu*

4. Select the graphic.

   Use the scroll bar to the right of the Picture Palette to scroll through the thumbnail images shown in the category you selected. Once you have located the picture that you need, click it to select it.

# Placing Graphics Using the Picture Palette

There are two techniques that you may use to place a picture into a PageMaker document. Each accomplishes essentially the same thing with one method providing slightly more control over the size of the placed graphic. I discuss the method with less control first.

GETTING STARTED
WITH PAGEMAKER

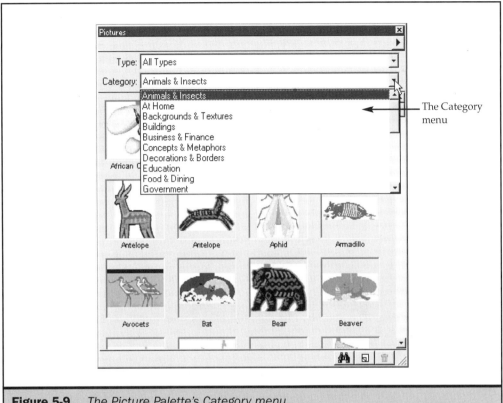

**Figure 5-9.**   *The Picture Palette's Category menu*

## Clicking and Dragging the Picture

This method of picture placement is exactly that: clicking and dragging the thumbnail image from the Picture Palette to your document. You do not need to select the Pointer tool. Whichever tool is selected, when you place the mouse pointer over the Picture Palette, it becomes an arrow. Just click the picture of your choice, and drag it off of the Picture Palette onto the PageMaker document open in the PageMaker window. The location of the pointer at the time you release the mouse determines where the picture will be placed. (Don't worry; you can move it to a new location if you want.)

If you forget to load the disk on which the graphic is stored, PageMaker reminds you with a message box that asks you to locate the graphic. Merely place the appropriate floppy disk or CD in the drive and click OK. Click and drag the picture again. With the graphic's link re-established, the graphic appears on the page.

Depending upon the size of the graphic, you may see a dialog box that states the size of the picture and asks if you want to include it as a part of the document (see the following illustration). The choice offered here enables you to decide whether or not you want the added data of the picture saved as a part of your document. If storage space on your system is a problem, select the No option. As long as the document resides on your computer, the graphic will be linked to the original graphic in the file and will display correctly. However, if you are going to have the document printed or otherwise removed from your system, it is important to select the Yes option. This creates a much larger file (some graphics take up a lot of storage space), but assures you of a quality reproduction of the document outside of your system.

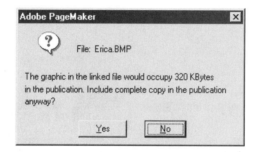

When the graphic has been dragged to the document and the dialog box, if any, has been dealt with, the graphic appears in your document in the same size as it is in the original (that is, the original in the file, not the thumbnail in the Picture Palette). Please see subsequent sections for information on sizing and moving the placed graphic.

## Double-Clicking the Thumbnail Image

The technique in which you double-click the picture provides more control in that it enables you to establish the size of the graphic in your document as well as the location at the time you place it. Take a look at these steps:

1. Double-click the graphic.

   You do not need to select the Pointer tool for this technique. Whichever tool is selected, when you place the pointer over the Picture Palette, the mouse pointer becomes an arrow.

   Double-click the thumbnail of the graphic you want to place. At first, it may appear that nothing happened; however, move the mouse pointer over the document and see that the mouse pointer has changed.

**Note** *The shape that the mouse pointer changes to depends upon the type of graphic selected. The mouse pointer could resemble a brush, a square with an X drawn through it, the letters P or S, or other shapes.*

**Note** *Remember, PageMaker's graphics, which have links that are already included on the Picture Palette, are stored on a separate disk that came with your PageMaker software. If you forget to load the disk on which a graphic you want is stored, when you double-click PageMaker reminds you with a message box that asks you to locate the graphic. Merely place the appropriate floppy disk or CD in the drive and click OK. Double-click the picture again. With the graphic's link re-established, the graphic appears on the page.*

2. Click and drag to size.

   Place the mouse pointer at the location in the document where you want the upper-left corner of the picture to be located. Then click and drag the mouse pointer to the desired location of the lower-right corner of the picture to determine the space that you want the picture to fill. In other words, you can cause the picture to be as big or as small as you want in the placement step.

   Be careful, however, to create the same proportion (the ratio between width and height) in the placed graphic as exists in the original. It is very easy to distort the picture by placing it disproportionately. If you distort the picture when you place it, you can eliminate the distortion by using the Pointer tool to drag the sizing handles to realign the proportion (see the following section for more information).

## Adjusting the Graphics Once They Are Placed

Whichever method you use to place the graphic in your document, you can change its location, its size, and even its proportion if you wish.

### Moving a Placed Graphic

The steps for moving a placed graphic are identical to moving a simple graphic that you have created with PageMaker's tools:

1. Select the graphic.

   In order to move a placed graphic, you must first select it using the Pointer tool. Just click the Pointer tool and then click the graphic. Once selected, the eight sizing handles appear.

2. Click and drag.

   You may click anywhere within the placed picture and drag it to a new location. Be sure not to click one of the sizing handles, however. Instead of moving the picture, dragging a sizing handle will distort it.

## Sizing a Placed Graphic

In the section on double-clicking to place a graphic earlier in this chapter, I discussed dragging the mouse pointer while placing a graphic to create the size you want. If you have your spot picked out and know just the size you want, that is well and good. However, if you change your mind or need to make an adjustment to a previously placed picture, the technique for sizing a placed graphic is simple. And it is very similar to the technique for sizing simple graphics. Here are the steps:

1. Select the Pointer tool.

   Click the Pointer tool to select it. The mouse pointer then becomes an arrow.

2. Select the placed graphic.

   Just click anywhere in the picture to select it. Once selected, the sizing handles appear around the graphic.

3. Click and drag.

   Clicking and dragging on any sizing handle will increase (or decrease) the size of the graphic in the direction of the drag; however, that also causes the picture to stretch, creating a distortion (shown below).

There may be times when, for effect, you really do want to stretch a picture, but most of the time you will want to keep the graphic proportional. To prevent the distortion of the picture due to stretching, just hold the SHIFT key as you drag. Be sure to release the mouse before you release the SHIFT key.

For other transformations that may be applied to placed graphics, see Chapter 10.

# Customizing the Picture Palette

The Picture Palette is quite versatile. Although it comes with a number of graphics already in place, the links to any or all of them may be deleted, and a link to any graphic that you have on your system can be added to the collection. Also, you can easily create new categories of graphics.

## Adding Graphics to the Picture Palette

Adding a graphic to the Picture Palette is somewhat similar to adding a template to the Template Palette. Here's how:

1.  Show the Picture Palette.

    If it is not already open, display the Picture Palette by selecting the Window menu's Plug-in Palettes command and then clicking on the Show Picture Palette command from the sub-menu. You may also open the Picture Palette by clicking on the Picture Palette button on the PageMaker toolbar.

2.  Select the type.

    Open the Type menu by clicking on the drop-down arrow to its right. Select the type of graphic (either Clipart or Image) you want to add.

3.  Select the category.

    The graphic you are adding will be placed in the category that is currently selected. If the current category is not appropriate for the new graphic, open the Category menu by clicking on the drop-down arrow to its right and select the best category from the menu.

4.  Display the Picture Palette's Shortcut menu.

    Click the right-pointing arrow to the right of the bar immediately below the Picture Palette's title bar. The Picture Palette's Shortcut menu appears, as shown in Figure 5-10.

5.  Locate the picture on your system.

    Select the Shortcut menu's Add Pictures command. The Open dialog box appears. Using the Open dialog box's Look In menu and thumbnail pictures, locate the graphic you want to add to the Picture Palette.

6.  Open the picture.

    Click the picture you want to select and then click the Open button on the Open dialog box. The Open dialog box closes and the picture is shown in the Picture Palette as the type and in the category you have chosen.

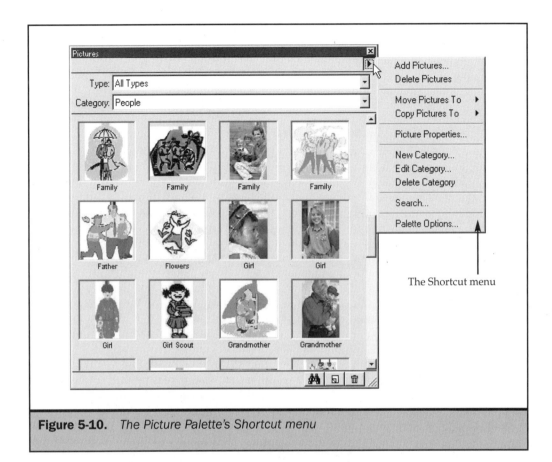

**Figure 5-10.** *The Picture Palette's Shortcut menu*

## Deleting Graphics from the Picture Palette

Deleting graphics is a much simpler operation than adding them:

1. Select the picture or pictures you want to delete.

   Just select the graphic you want to delete from the Picture Palette by clicking on it. You can select several pictures by clicking the first graphic and then holding the CTRL key while you select others.

2. Open the Picture Palette's Shortcut menu.

   Open the Picture Palette's Shortcut menu by clicking on the right-pointing arrow to the right of the bar immediately below the Picture Palette's title bar. The Picture Palette's Shortcut menu appears, as shown in Figure 5-10.

3.  Delete the picture or pictures.

    Select Delete Pictures from the Shortcut menu. The selected pictures are deleted from the Picture Palette.

*An even faster way of removing pictures from the Picture Palette is to select the picture or pictures you want to delete and then right-click the mouse. Choose Delete from the menu and the pictures disappear.*

## Creating a New Category in the Picture Palette

Although the categories that come with the Picture Palette by default are generally pretty good, you may want to create some new ones that apply specifically to you. I created a category for family pictures under the Image type. I also have some clip art from a purchased package that I like a lot and I have created a category just for them in my Picture Palette. Creating custom categories improves the organization of your graphic collection and makes location and placing a snap. Follow these steps:

1.  Open the Picture Palette's Shortcut menu.

    Open the Picture Palette's Shortcut menu by clicking on the right-pointing arrow to the right of the bar immediately below the Picture Palette's title bar. The Picture Palette's Shortcut menu appears, as shown in Figure 5-22.

2.  Display the New Category dialog box.

    Select the Shortcut menu's Add Category command. The New Category dialog box appears, as shown below.

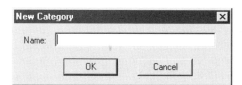

3.  Name the new category.

    In the New Category dialog box's Name box, enter the name you have chosen for the new category. Click the OK button. The dialog box disappears and the Picture Palette shows the new category ready for you to add the graphic links, which can be done by following the previous directions for adding pictures.

## Deleting a Category

Just as you can add new categories, you can also delete unwanted categories. Here's how:

1. Select the category you wish to delete.

   Open the category you want to delete. Keep in mind that any links contained in that category will be deleted with the category. (Just the links will be removed, however, not the graphics themselves.)

2. Open the Picture Palette's Shortcut menu.

   Open the Picture Palette's Shortcut menu by clicking on the right-pointing arrow to the right of the bar immediately below the Picture Palette's title bar. The Picture Palette's Shortcut menu appears, as shown in Figure 5-10.

3. Delete the category.

   Select the Shortcut menu's Delete Category command and a warning message appears, asking you to confirm the deletion of the category. Once you have clicked on Yes, the category and all of its associated thumbnails are removed.

## Moving and Copying Images to Another Category

In using the Picture Palette to organize your graphics, you may want to move pictures from one category to another or copy them so that they appear in multiple categories. Whichever you choose, moving or copying, the process is essentially the same:

1. Select the picture.

   Select the picture or pictures you wish to move or copy. Multiple pictures may be selected by holding down CTRL while clicking.

2. Open the Picture Palette's Shortcut menu.

   Open the Picture Palette's Shortcut menu by clicking on the arrow to the right of the bar immediately below the Picture Palette's title bar. The Picture Palette's Shortcut menu appears, as shown in Figure 5-10.

3. Choose to move or copy.

   Choose *Move Pictures To* to take them out of one category and move them to another. Select *Copy Pictures To* to leave them where they are and place a copy in another category.

4. Select the new category.

   Once you have selected either the Move or the Copy command, a menu appears listing the available categories. Click the category to which you are moving or copying the graphic. The graphic appears in the selected category.

# Summary

Graphics are an important part of layout design. In PageMaker there are many ways of working with graphics. This chapter discussed the creation and customization of simple graphics and the placing and adjusting of graphics using the Picture Palette.

**Using Simple Graphics**   To create simple graphics such as lines, rectangles, ellipses, and polygons, use the graphic tools on the Toolbox Palette. Clicking on its respective tool and then clicking and dragging the tool on the PageMaker page produces each of the simple graphics.

Simple graphics can be modified in various ways. They can be resized by dragging on sizing handles that appear when the graphics are selected. Line style and weight can be adjusted by selecting the Element menu's Stroke command. Using other Element commands, a rectangle's corners can be rounded, and a polygon's sides can be inset, forming a star. All simple graphics can be relocated on the page by selecting them with the Pointer tool and dragging them to the new location.

**Organize and Place Graphics Using the Picture Palette**   The Picture Palette, new since PageMaker 6.5, is a convenient matrix in which you can organize and store links to any graphics stored on your system. Graphics, shown on the Picture Palette as thumbnail images, can be dragged onto a PageMaker document or can be placed by double-clicking, allowing sizing at the time of placement.

Although the PageMaker Picture Palette comes with many graphic links already in the matrix, new pictures can be added or any pictures removed. Additionally, new categories can be added to the Picture Palette, providing customization. Like simple graphics, placed graphics can be moved, sized, or even stretched out of shape.

The Complete Reference

PageMaker 7

# Chapter 6

## Applying Color to Simple Graphics

Color is one of the most effective elements that you can place in your documents to attract attention, direct focus, and establish status. Not only that, color is an effective communicator. Closely tied into cultural connotations, color sometimes carries significance even beyond the printed (or electronically produced) word.

This chapter discusses the application of color to the simple graphics discussed in the previous chapter. In Chapter 5, I discussed the process of creating simple graphics to use in PageMaker layouts. These graphics put interesting shapes in your document and, through the application of color, they have an even greater impact on your document.

PageMaker has powerful color management capabilities that I discuss elsewhere in this book; however, this chapter focuses on the basics of color usage: applying color to simple graphics. In addition, I add a few words to point you in the right direction for using color if you are publishing your document electronically.

A key player in the use of color in a PageMaker document is the Color Palette, a somewhat unassuming tool in appearance. But the Color Palette packs a powerful wallop when put to its full use. I discuss the Color Palette as I describe the process of applying color to simple graphics. However, the Color Palette can do a lot more than the basics described here. Make sure to see more information on this useful tool in Chapter 11.

Simple graphics (except for simple lines, obviously) have two components that are subject to color: the outline, also known as the stroke, and the interior space created by the outline, generally referred to as the fill. Even though there is much similarity in the techniques for adding color to these components, I address them individually.

# Coloring Lines

In discussing the application of color to lines, it is important that I make it clear that I am not just talking about a line as a simple graphic, but the lines that outline and create other simple graphics as well. It is fully possible to have a graphic with a line of one color and a fill of another; and it is not uncommon that graphics are set with no line (the None selection) in order to create a "clean" graphic with a fill that stands on its own. Couple these techniques with the line weight and style choices discussed in Chapter 5 and you see that you have a lot of flexibility in the creation of graphics.

The application of color to a line can be accomplished in two ways. The first uses the Color Palette, the second, the Fill and Stroke dialog box.

## Using the Color Palette

In order to apply color to a line using the Color Palette, the line must be selected (of course) and the Color Palette must be open, as shown in the illustration.

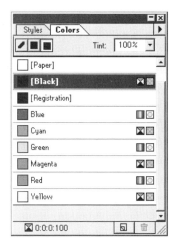

As you know from the discussion on lines in the previous chapter, all you have to do to select a line is to click on it using the Pointer tool. You know the line is selected when you see sizing handles at each end of the line. If you are applying color to the outline of a simple graphic, click on the outline and eight sizing handles appear around the graphic.

The Colors Palette appears in your PageMaker window as soon as PageMaker is launched the first time. However, subsequently it will only appear when PageMaker is launched if it was open when PageMaker was closed down. Some PageMaker users find the Colors Palette to be in the way and like to keep it closed. The Colors Palette is one of those PageMaker window elements that I prefer to keep open or at least handy. Like all of PageMaker's palettes, it is easy to show the Colors Palette. Just select the Window menu's Show Colors command and the Colors Palette appears. If it appears in an inconvenient place, move it to a new location by clicking and dragging it by the Title Bar.

With your line selected and the Colors Palette displayed, you are ready to apply color. Here's how:

1. Select the Line Color Application box.

   Just below the tab at the top of the Colors Palette are three small boxes I call the Color Application boxes. These boxes tell the Colors Palette whether you want to apply color to a line, to a fill, or to both (shown below).

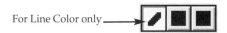

For Line Color only

Click the first box to indicate that the color should be applied to the line only. If you are coloring the outline of a simple graphic, all three boxes are available. However, if you are coloring a line as a simple graphic, the second and third boxes will not be available and the first will be selected by default.

2. Click on the color.

Click on the color of your choice to apply that color to your line. None, Paper, Black, Blue, Cyan, Green, Magenta, Red, and Yellow are provided in the color list. Additional colors can be added to the list. Information on adding colors to the Colors Palette and creating a color library is given in Chapter 11.

Once you click on a color in the list, the color is applied to the selected line.

*Registration, also in the list, is used in color separations. Please see Chapter 22 for more information on using this selection.*

## Applying a Tint to a Line

Lines may also be colored with a tint. A tint is just an application of color in a percentage of the solid color. In other words, a 50-percent tint of red will produce a color that is half-red and half-white: a medium pink.

If you wish your line to be colored with a tint, take these steps:

1. Select the line.

All you have to do to select a line is to click on it using the Pointer tool. You know the line is selected when you see sizing handles at each end of the line. If you are applying color to the outline of a simple graphic, click on the outline and eight sizing handles appear around the graphic.

2. Open the Colors Palette.

If the Colors Palette is not open, select the Window menu's Show Colors command. The Colors Palette appears in your PageMaker window.

3. Select the color you want.

Choose the color you want from the color list in the Colors Palette. PageMaker applies the color to the line.

4. Open the Colors Palette's Tint menu.

Click the drop-down arrow to the right of the Tint box at the top-right of the palette. The Colors Palette's Tint menu appears, as shown in the illustration.

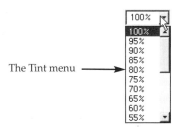

The Tint menu

5.  Select the tint percentage.

Use the scroll bar on the right of the Tint menu to scroll through the
percentages. Select the tint that you want by clicking on the percentage. The
Tint menu closes and the tint is applied to your selected line. If the line's tint is
not what you want, just open the Tint menu again and select another
percentage. Continue until you are satisfied.

Unlike some dialog boxes and palettes, the Colors Palette does not close
automatically once a color is selected. If the Colors Palette is in the way, you
may want to minimize it until you need it. Clicking the Minimize Control
Button (see Figure 6-4) rolls the palette up and leaves the header on your
screen, taking up much less room. To redisplay the colors list, select the
minimize Control Button again. The palette rolls down, displaying the
color list.

The Minimize button

# Using the Fill and Stroke Dialog Box

Another technique for applying color to a line is to use the Fill and Stroke dialog box.
You can use this box to select line weight and style at the same time if you wish. Here
are the simple steps:

1.  Select the line.

Before it can be adjusted in any way, the line must be selected. Using the
Pointer tool, click anywhere on the line. When you see the sizing handles, you
know the line is selected.

2. Open the Fill and Stroke dialog box.

   Click the Element menu's Fill and Stroke command or click the Fill and Stroke button on the PageMaker toolbar. The Fill and Stroke dialog box appears on the screen (shown in the illustration).

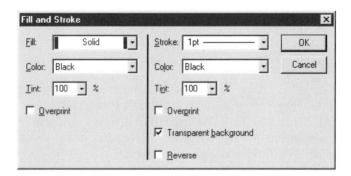

   Note that the dialog box is divided into two parts. The left half of the dialog box pertains to the fill of a graphic and is covered in another section in this chapter. The right half provides settings for the selected line.

3. Select a color.

   Click on the drop-down arrow to the right of the Color box to display the Colors Palette menu. Use the scrollbar to scroll through the menu. The colors listed there are identical to the colors on the Colors Palette. If you have added any colors to the Colors Palette's color list, they will appear on this list as well. For more information on adding colors to the color list, please see Chapter 11.

4. Select a tint if you wish.

   While the Fill and Stroke dialog box is open, the color you have chosen may be adjusted to a tint. A tint is just a percentage of a color. In other words, a 50-percent tint of red will produce a color that is half-red and half-white: a medium pink.

   Click on the drop-down arrow to the right of the Tint box and select a percentage of the color you want to apply (see the following illustration). If the Tint box is set to 100 percent, the color will be full strength.

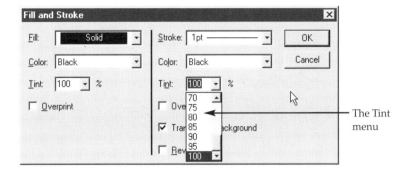

The Tint menu

Once a percentage is clicked, the menu closes.

5.  Click OK.

When you click the OK button, the Fill and Stroke dialog box closes and the selected color or tint is applied to your line.

# Applying Fills

A *fill*, as I mentioned previously, is the space inside a graphic that is surrounded by an outline. There are four kinds of fills from which you may choose to fill a simple graphic: None, Paper, Solid, and Pattern. Table 6-1 explains their use.

All of the fills can be applied from the Fill and Stroke dialog box. And all fills except Pattern can be applied using the Colors Palette. The Element menu's Fill command provides a selection of patterns that you may select. Color can then be applied to the lines of the pattern through the use of the Colors Palette.

## Applying a Fill Using the Colors Palette

1.  Select the graphic.

Your graphic, of course, must be selected in order to apply a fill. Click the Pointer tool, and then click on the outline of the graphic. Once the graphic is selected, sizing handles appear in a box formation around it.

2.  Select the Line Color Application box.

Just below the tab at the top of the Colors Palette are three small boxes I call the Color Application boxes. These boxes tell the Colors Palette whether you want to apply color to a line, to a fill, or to both.

If you wish to color only the fill, click the second box. If you want to color the fill and the outline with the same color at the same time, select the third box (see Figure 6-1).

| Fill | Use |
|------|-----|
| None | This is exactly what it says: no fill. A simple graphic with no fill is only the shell created by the outline. This is particularly useful when you want an element of your design to show through the graphic. |
| Paper | A Paper fill on first glance may look like it has no fill. However, a Paper fill provides a solid white fill that is opaque. This is particularly useful when you want to block the view of another element. |
| Solid | A Solid fill applies a solid block of color to your graphic. This too is opaque, but can be set to display fills from a seemingly endless library of colors.<br><br>A Solid fill can be tinted. A tint is achieved by mixing a color with a percentage of white to produce a lighter version of the original color. |
| Pattern | You can fill your graphic from a wide selection of patterns. Each pattern is made up of lines in various configurations and only the lines carry color. |

**Table 6-1.** *Types of Color Fills*

3. Click on the color.

   Click on the color of your choice to apply that color to your line. None and Paper, as well as the Solid fill colors of Black, Blue, Cyan, Green, Magenta, Red and Yellow, are provided in the color list. (See Chapter 11 for information on adding colors to the list.) The Solid fill colors can also be used to color the pattern lines if a Pattern fill has been applied to the graphic.

   Once you click on a color in the list, the color is applied to the selected graphic.

## Filling a Graphic with a Tint

Not only can you set a solid fill to any color in PageMaker's library of colors, but you can set it to percentages of color, called tints, as well. This provides an exciting range of possibilities. For example, a 50-percent tint applied to a Red fill creates a medium pink; a 25-percent tint creates a light pink.

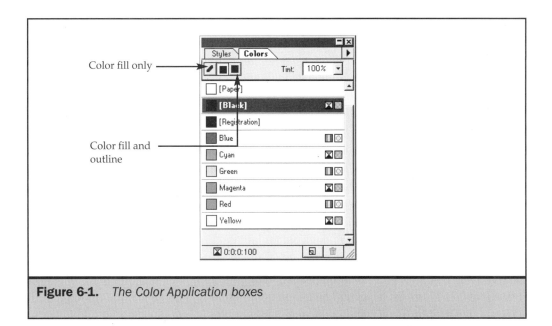

**Figure 6-1.** *The Color Application boxes*

If you wish your simple graphic to be colored with a tint, first select the graphic and the color you want. Then open the Colors Palette's Tint menu by clicking the drop-down arrow to the right of the Tint box at the top right of the palette. Use the scroll bar on the right of the Tint menu to scroll through the percentages. Select the tint that you want by clicking on the percentage. The Tint menu closes and the tint is applied.

# Applying a Fill Using the Fill and Stroke Dialog Box

The Fill andStroke dialog box can also be used to apply a color fill. You can use this box to select line weight, style, and color at the same time if you wish. Here are the simple steps:

1. Select the graphic.

   Before it can be adjusted in any way, a graphic must be selected. Using the Pointer tool, click anywhere on the graphic's outline. When you see the sizing handles, you know the line is selected.

2. Open the Fill and Stroke dialog box.

   Click the Element menu's Fill and Stroke command or click the Fill and Stroke button in the Toolbar menu. The Fill and Stroke dialog box appears on the screen (see the following illustration).

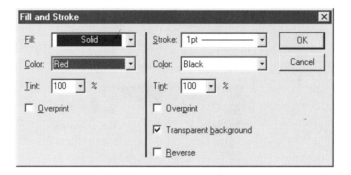

Note that the dialog box is divided into two parts. The left half of the dialog box pertains to the fill of a graphic. The second half provides settings for a line and has been discussed previously in the chapter.

3. Select a color.

   Click on the drop-down arrow to the right of the Color box to display the Color menu. Use the scrollbar to look through the menu. The colors listed there are identical to the colors on the Colors Palette. If you have added any colors to the Colors Palette's color list, they will appear on this list as well. For more information on adding colors to the color list, please see Chapter 11.

4. Select a tint if you wish.

   While the Fill and Stroke dialog box is open, the color you have chosen may be adjusted to a tint. A tint is just a percentage of a color. In other words, a 50-percent tint of red will produce a color that is half-red and half-white, a medium pink.

   Click on the drop-down arrow to the right of the Tint box and select a percentage of the color you want to apply (shown below). If the percentage in the Tint box is set to 100 percent, the color will be full strength.

   Once a percentage is clicked, the menu closes.

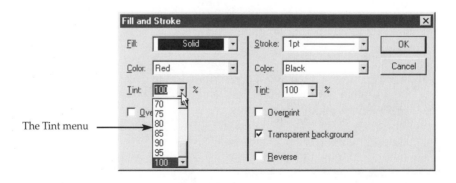

The Tint menu

5. Click OK.

When you click the OK button, the Fill and Stroke dialog box closes and the selected fill color or tint is applied to your graphic.

# Using Colors in Electronic Documents

If you are looking to publish your PageMaker document on the Web or in Adobe's Portable Document Format, only specific colors can be used. Web browsers, the medium that displays documents on the Web, use only a subset of 216 colors. Any color outside of those specific 216 will not display accurately on the Web.

PageMaker provides a library of colors that are appropriate for use in electronically published documents. The Online Library is accessible through a special link on the Colors Palette or through the Utilities menu's Define Colors command. Because this is a more advanced technique than is appropriate to this "basics" chapter, please see Chapter 11 for information on making this color library available.

# Summary

Color is an effective means of adding interest and attention-getting drama to your document. In this chapter, I described how to add color to lines and to the inside space of simple graphics, called fills. More advanced color techniques are discussed later in the book.

**Coloring Lines**   Adding color to a line dramatically impacts its effect on your document. You can add color to a line, whether a simple graphic or the outline of a simple graphic, by using the Colors Palette or by using the Element menu's Fill and Stroke dialog box. A color list found in either of these sources provides basic colors and the capability to create percentages of those colors, called tints.

**Applying Fills**   There are four kinds of fills that can be applied to a simple graphic: None, Paper, Solid, and Pattern. Just as in coloring lines, either the Colors Palette or the Fill and Stroke dialog box can be used to add color to a solid fill. These sources can also be used to add a tint (a percentage of a color) to a fill.

A Pattern fill must be created in the Fill and Stroke dialog box or in the Element menu's Fill menu. Then you can add color to the pattern's line by using the Fill and Stroke dialog box or the Colors Palette.

**Using Colors in Electronic Documents**   Only certain colors reproduce accurately in electronically published documents. A library of online colors is available. More information on accessing this library is given in Chapter 11.

# The Complete Reference

PageMaker 7

# Part II

## PageMaker Essentials

# Chapter 7

## Managing
## Document Layout

Layout, the parameters of your page and the way you arrange it, is the heart of a quality document, whether you create a print piece, a Web page, or some other type of document. The layout of a document can be even more important than the words or the graphics of your page in attracting and retaining readers or viewers. PageMaker provides numerous ways of managing your layout. Although subsequent chapters deal with managing text or graphic objects, this chapter is about the tools PageMaker presents to help you place text and graphics for the most effective layout.

In Chapter 3, I discussed two ways of creating a new PageMaker document. In the discussion of one of those techniques, the document's basic layout design settings were selected in the Document Setup dialog box as part of the creation process. Only the basic document design parameters are discussed in Chapter 3 in order to keep your first exposure to PageMaker documents simple, as the chapter's title requires; however, there are other settings in the Document Setup dialog box that you may want to apply to your documents, as you grow more comfortable in the PageMaker environment. As part of the focus on layout, in this chapter I'm discussing the settings from the Document Setup dialog box that are not discussed in Chapter 3. These features may be elected at the time you create a new document or may be set after it has already been established.

Crucial to the development of quality design is the layout grid. This grid provides the skeleton of the layout. The last part of this chapter discusses the layout grid, what it is composed of, and how to create and manage grids.

# The Document Setup Dialog Box

The most common use for the Document Setup dialog box (see Figure 7-1) is the creation of a new document. Selections are made in the dialog box and when the OK button is clicked, the new document appears with the selected parameters in place. However, the Document Setup dialog box can also be used to adjust the parameters of your document after it has been established.

Selecting the File menu's Document Setup command reveals the Document Setup dialog box. Document settings are grouped loosely by category.

Selecting the page size, dimensions, and orientation of a new document, the first three items on the Document Setup dialog box (discussed at length in Chapter 3), is simple.

Here are the steps to select a page size:

1. Open the Page Size menu.

   To reveal the Page Size menu, click the drop-down button to the right of the Page Size box.

2. Select the Page Size of your choice.

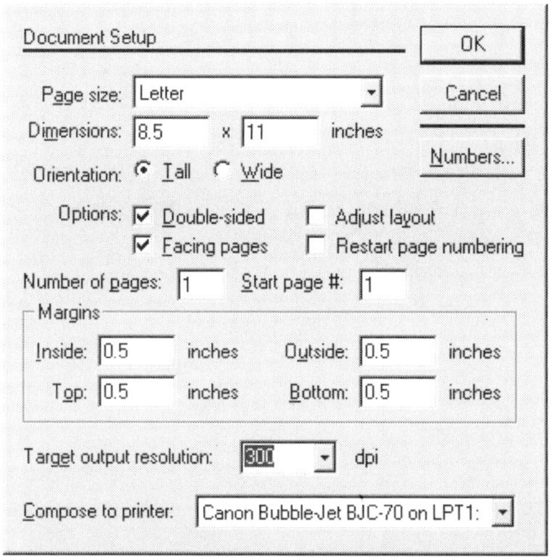

**Figure 7-1.** *The Document Setup dialog box*

Use the scroll bar to locate the page configuration that you want. Keep in mind that although the term *page* is used, this menu contains far more options than just standard pieces of paper.

Once you click on a selection, the menu closes and the page size you chose is displayed in the Page Size box.

The measurements of a page size selection appear in the Dimensions boxes. If you change the measurements that are in the Dimensions boxes, the page size box reflects the Custom setting.

Orientation is selected by clicking on the appropriate radio button in the Orientation section. Tall is also called Portrait; Wide is also called Landscape.

If you wish to change any of these settings once the document has been established, just open the Document Setup dialog box and, using the techniques described above and in Chapter 3, change the previous settings to the new one. Once you click the OK button, the document adjusts to the new parameters.

## Options

The Options section of the Document Setup dialog box consists of four selection boxes: Double-Sided Pages, Facing Pages, Adjust Layout, and Restart Page Numbering.

## Double-Sided Pages

This setting configures separate settings for the right and left pages of a document. This is particularly important in a printed document such as a book. Pages that will be on the right side of a document will be bound on the pages' left side; conversely, pages on the left side of the document will be bound on their right. Therefore, additional margin space may be required in the inside areas to accommodate binding. When the Double-Sided check box is selected, the Margin section displays boxes for Inside and Outside settings instead of the usual Left and Right.

## Facing Pages

The Facing Pages box is only available if Double-Sided is selected. This setting determines how double-sided pages are displayed on your screen. When selected, two pages (a left and a right) are shown side by side in the PageMaker window at the same time, as shown in Figure 7-2. If you start the document with an odd page number, such as Page 1 (see the section "Start Page Number"), the first page will appear alone.

## Adjust Layout

Adjust Layout automatically revises your layout to fit the new parameters when you make changes in the Document Setup dialog box. For example, if you change the margins of your document, the elements on the page may no longer fit appropriately. However, with Adjust Layout selected, PageMaker automatically adjusts the text and graphics on each page to fit the new settings. This is a handy tool to have around.

If you don't like the results of a layout adjustment, individual objects may be rearranged as you wish. Also, you may control the way PageMaker adjusts a document's elements by establishing criteria in the Layout Adjustment Preferences dialog box (see Chapter 12).

## Restart Page Numbering

Page numbers are an important part of some documents. Chapter 13 discusses placing page number codes on master pages. However, some important page numbering parameters are set in the Document Setup dialog box.

If you are creating a multiple publication document, such as a book, you may want a new series of page numbers to begin at certain places in the document, such as following the introduction or at the start of an appendix, for example. Follow these steps to set up the page numbers appropriately:

1. Select the check box for Restart Page Numbering.

   Clicking on the Restart Page Numbering selection instructs PageMaker to use special instructions in establishing the page numbers for that publication in the book. If this selection is not made, all pages in a multiple publication document will be numbered consecutively.

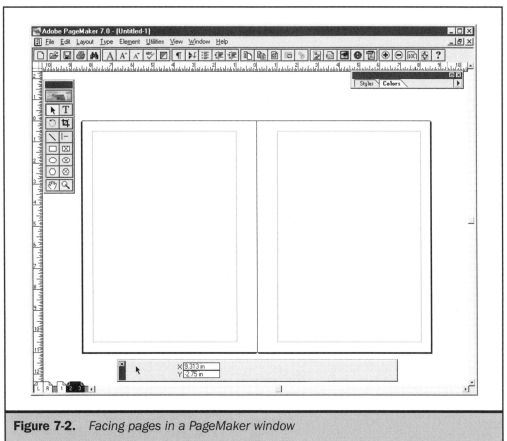

**Figure 7-2.**   *Facing pages in a PageMaker window*

2.  Open the Page Numbering dialog box.

Click the Numbers button in the Document Setup dialog box. The Page Numbering dialog box opens, as shown below.

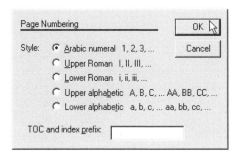

3.  Select the numbering scheme you want.

    You may choose from Arabic numerals, upper-case roman numerals, lower-case roman numerals, upper-case alphabetic, or lower-case alphabetic. Click the Radio Button for the style of your choice. If you want a special prefix to appear before a page number, enter it in the TOC and Index Prefix box.

4.  Click OK.

    Clicking the OK button closes the Page Numbering dialog box and sets the style of numbers for your document.

5.  Enter the starting number.

    Enter the number or letter with which you want your document to begin in the Start Page # box.

If you do not want to restart numbering in one publication of a multiple publication document, deselect the Restart Page Numbering check box. PageMaker then automatically calculates page numbers based upon the publication's location in the book.

## Number of Pages

If you have a good idea how many pages your document will be, you can create those pages at the same time you create the PageMaker document. Just enter the number of pages you want in the Number of Pages box. Once you have clicked OK to close the Document Setup dialog box, the document appears with the selected number of pages.

If you want to add pages to an existing document, you can do it here as well. Any pages added here appear at the end of the document. I always add pages through the Layout menu's Insert Pages command. However, I have recently discovered that some use the Document Setup dialog box to do so. Just adjust the number in the Number of Pages to reflect the additional pages you want. When you click the OK button, the additional pages appear in your document.

## Start Page Number

As described previously, this setting is to establish the starting number for documents that are part of a multiple publication document. Just enter the number with which you want the publication to start.

## Margins

As described in Chapter 3, margins are established by entering the desired margin in decimal equivalents of an inch in the appropriate boxes. You can easily go from one box to another by using the TAB key. When you tab to a Margin box, the previous setting is selected. All you have to do is type the new margin setting and tab again to go to the next one.

Keep in mind, however, that if the Double-Sided Pages selection in the Document Setup dialog box is selected, the Margin items will be Inside, Outside, Top, and Bottom, rather than Left, Right, Top, and Bottom.

# Target Output Resolution

The Target Output Resolution dots per square inch (dpi) setting is the resolution with which the document will be created. This setting ensures that the document that you are creating conforms with the resolution in which the document will ultimately be produced. In other words, if your goal for a document is to print on a desktop printer, and your printer is a 600-dpi printer, select the 600-dpi Target Output Resolution setting; if you are creating for high-resolution 3300-dpi output, make that selection. Likewise, if you are creating a document to publish electronically, select the resolution best suited for your document on the Internet.

## Compose to Printer

Like the Target Output Resolution, this setting's purpose is to coordinate the document with the printer from which it will eventually be produced, even if, in the case of Web pages and other nonprint media, the printing is just for proofing. In actuality, before a document is printed, PageMaker will recompose the document to conform with the printer; therefore, the setting is more to establish an accurate representation on the computer monitor.

Select this setting by clicking the drop-down arrow to the right of the Compose to Printer menu box and selecting the printer to which you wish to compose the document.

Once you have made all of the selections you want in the Document Setup dialog box, click OK to close the box and apply the settings.

# The Layout View

There are two views you may use for text in PageMaker. The PageMaker window, as described in Chapter 2 and throughout this book, uses the default view in PageMaker: the Layout view. Unless I am performing a spell check, I never vary from the Layout view because it shows the document as it appears when published. All of the elements are shown in place and any editing of text or graphics can be accomplished there.

The alternative view is the Story Editor and is effective only in text editing. The Story Editor focuses on text and operates as a word processing environment. There is minimal formatting and the screen redraw is faster than in the Layout view. If you are editing text that contains a lot of graphics, using the Story Editor is faster because PageMaker does not have to be redraw graphics. To see text in Story view, select the Edit menu's Edit Story command. To return to the Layout view, click the Edit menu's Edit Layout command.

# Creating Text Columns

We are accustomed to seeing large amounts of text set into multiple columns. This is common in newspapers, magazines, newsletters, and many other print publications. Readers usually will not read very much text when the lines are long. It is awkward and easy for a reader to lose his or her place. Therefore, single columns of text with long lines should be reserved for very short paragraphs, say, three lines or less. Columns divide text into manageable line lengths for ease of reading and reader retention.

In PageMaker, column guides are a part of the layout grid (see "Creating and Using a Layout Grid" later in this chapter), into which all elements of your page design are placed. Graphics may be fitted into the column grid or placed across column guides for added interest. Text is placed into a column structure as described in Chapter 9.

When you place columns guides on a PageMaker page, the guides appear only on that one page. However, you can cause guides to appear throughout your document by placing the guides on a master page. See Chapter 13 for more information.

Here are the simple steps for creating a column grid on a PageMaker page:

1. Open the page where you want the columns to appear.

   If the page where you want the column guides to appear is not already active on your screen, open the document and click on the appropriate page number icon in the lower-left area of your PageMaker window. If you want to place the guides in a master page, click the Left or Right master page icons in the far left corner of the screen (see the following illustration).

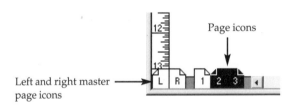

2. Open the Columns dialog box.

   Select the Layout menu's Column Guides command. The Column Guides dialog box appears.

3. Enter the number of columns.

   In the Number of Columns box, enter the number of columns you want. The maximum number of columns you may create is 20. However, there is not much text that can be placed in very narrow columns. Very narrow lines of text run readers away even faster than very wide ones. So, select the number of columns that will work best with your design and keep the reader/viewer happy.

4. Enter the space between columns.

   The space between columns, also called a gutter or columnar gutter, can be set in the Column Guides dialog box as well. The default is 0.167 inches. For documents such as a newsletter, I recommend leaving the default in place. However, for three-fold brochures and certain other types of documents, I widen the gutter to a half-inch or so.

   Whitespace, the unused space around elements in a layout such as columnar gutters, is important. It keeps the document from being over heavy and intimidating to the reader or viewer. However, too much white space between columns looks amateurish.

   Enter your selection in decimal equivalents of inches based on the best look for your document. Select the Adjust Layout box if you wish the text on the page to be adjusted to the column configuration.

5. Click OK.

   When you click the OK button, the Column Guides dialog box closes and the column guides appear in your document. See the following illustration for an example of a three-column grid.

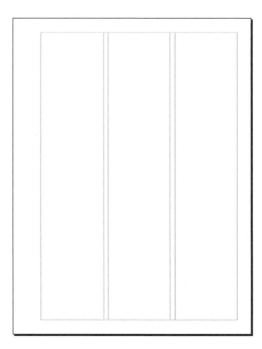

Column guides may also be created using the Grid Manager. See the section "Using the Grid Manager" later in this chapter.

# Creating and Using a Layout Grid

In graphic design, a layout grid is the pattern with which a document is designed. For example, your newsletter may have a narrow left column, with wider middle and right columns, and all of your newsletters and all of their pages may be based on this grid. (See Figure 7-3 for an example of a layout grid for the first page of a newsletter.) Or perhaps each of the brochures you publish has a broad stripe of color running vertically down the fold of the front panel. Web pages have layout grids as well. You will frequently see a Web page with links on the left and copy in the remaining portion of

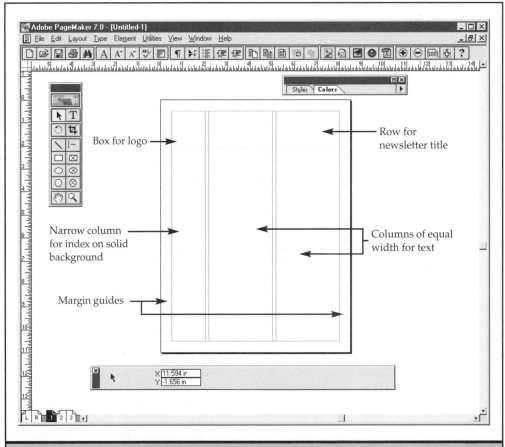

**Figure 7-3.** *A layout grid for the first page of a newsletter*

the page to the right. Or maybe links are on both the right and left with copy in the center.

Layout grids provide consistency and when you use a grid on a regular basis, it becomes a recognizable design element to your piece, like a logo or a typeface. A layout grid does not have to be something you use consistently, however. You may set up a grid for a one-time flyer just as a way of providing the structure for your design.

In PageMaker, a grid consists of nonprinting guides that provide a skeleton for the placement of text and graphics. Guides such as column guides and margin guides are placed on a page when you establish certain settings such as the margin selections in the Document Setup dialog box or create them using the Column Guides dialog box (see the previous section on Column Guides).

Another type of nonprinting guide, referred to as Ruler Guides or simply Guides, may be placed manually by eye, manually using the ruler as a guide, manually using the data on the Control palette, or by using the Grid Manager. This section discusses all of these, but first let's discuss rulers, which are an important element in a grid.

# Rulers

Horizontal and vertical rulers appear on the left and upper edges of the PageMaker window by default. The rulers can be hidden, but I keep mine visible all of the time. I'm very dependent upon the PageMaker rulers. I like to have an understanding, all of the time, of where on the page I'm placing a graphic or otherwise working, and the rulers provide a quick visual reference.

However, if you want to hide your rulers, you can. Just select the View menu's Hide Rulers command. The rulers disappear. To show the rulers again, select the View menu's Show Rulers command and they appear around your window.

## Repositioning The Zero Point

By default, the rulers are aligned with the zero point, the beginning measurement of the rulers (shown below) at the upper-left corner of a single page. On facing pages, the zero

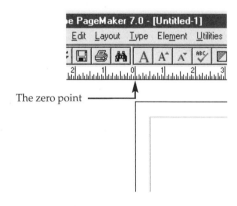

The zero point

point rests between the two pages, and the ruler runs right to left on the left page and left to right on the right page, as shown in Figure 7-8.

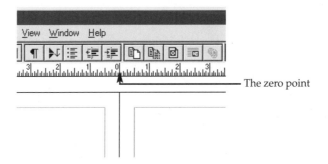

The zero point

But the zero point can be moved. You may want to move the zero point to coincide with the left edge of a graphic in order to accurately measure that graphic or perhaps as a guide in sizing it. If you are designing a very large graphic and have to print it in letter size tiles in order to produce a copy of the document for proofing, you may want to move the zero point to establish where specific tiles begin. See Chapter 27 for more information on printing in tiles.

To reposition the zero, just click anywhere in the area where the horizontal and vertical rulers meet, which I call the zero box and drag to the location you desire (see Figure 7-9). Keep in mind, however, that when you drag the zero you are moving it both vertically and horizontally. Make sure that the point is properly aligned where you want it—on both rulers.

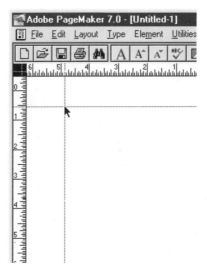

Does it hurt anything to move the zero point? Absolutely not! Just understand that your ruler is not giving an accurate measurement of the width or depth of your page if the zero has been repositioned. And repositioning the zero on one page moves it on all pages in the document as well. It is usually a good idea to put the zero back when you no longer need it to be in another position.

To reposition the zero to its default position, double-click in the zero box. The zero returns to its original position.

## Locking the Zero Point

If you want to make sure that you do not inadvertently move the zero, you may lock it by selecting the View menu's Zero Lock command. To unlock the zero, reverse the process by deselecting the View menu's Zero Lock command.

# Ruler Guides

Ruler guides, also called nonprinting guides or guides, are pale blue lines that you can position anywhere on the page. You can use them to align objects horizontally or vertically, to create a guide box to place a graphic in, or in any way in which a structured but nonprinting line would be helpful. Usually, guides appear only on the page they are positioned on, but they can be duplicated by placing them on master pages or by copying them as described later in this section.

## Placing Guides Manually

To position a guide on your page, place your mouse pointer in either ruler, and then click and drag the guide onto the page. You can judge placement by eye or align your guide with the marks on the rulers. If aligning a guide with the ruler seems a bit tedious, you may also use the data shown on the Control Palette to place your guide precisely where you want it.

The Control Palette is an exceptionally versatile tool that changes according to the items you are working with. No matter which Toolbox tool you have selected, when you drag a guide from a ruler onto your page, the X and Y boxes on the Control Palette change to show the exact position of the guide in relationship to the zero point on the ruler (see Figure 7-4). Guides pulled from the vertical ruler move horizontally and therefore show X-axis data; guides from the horizontal ruler move vertically and are shown as the Y-axis.

As you drag the guide, look at the placement information on the Control Palette and position the guide exactly where you want.

A guide can be repositioned by dragging it to a new location on the page using the Pointer tool. If you place one guide directly over the position of another guide, the two guides merge and become one.

I cannot determine any limit to the number of guides that you can place on a page in PageMaker. I placed over 100 guides (50 from each ruler) in a document to see if there was a limit. Of course, my document was filled with so many light blue lines that it

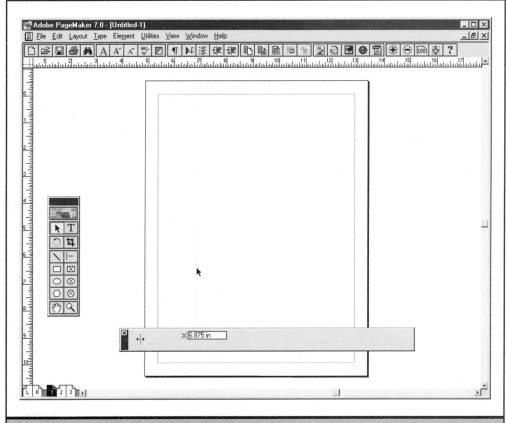

**Figure 7-4.**    *The Control Palette showing the placement of an X-axis guide*

would have given me a headache to work in it, but the guides just kept coming. Suffice it to say, you can create as many guides as you need to establish a workable layout grid.

If you get too many guides on your page, like I did with those 100 or so, you can clear them all at once by selecting the View menu's Clear Ruler Guides command.

On complicated layouts, I sometimes find that I have so many guides that I cannot clearly see my design. I don't want to clear them; I just want to get them out of the way for a moment so I can see my layout. So, I hide them. To do this, just click the View menu's Hide Guides command. To show them again, select the View menu's Show Guides command and the guides reappear on the page.

## Placing Guides With the Grid Manager

If you need to create a number of guides to create a layout grid, and if you know where you want to place them, using the Grid Manager is the quickest and easiest way to do so. See the following "Using the Grid Manager" section.

## Copying Guide Configuration

If you have created a grid of ruler guides that you particularly like, you may want to save it to use it again. This is a great idea for recurring publications such as newsletters, catalogs, and reports. Information on how to save a guide configuration is given in the following section on using the Grid Manager.

# Using the Grid Manager

The Grid Manager is a PageMaker plug-in that is a recent innovation in PageMaker and is one of those tools that fills me with delight. With this dialog box, you can create guides and rearrange them. You can save guide configurations (grids) and copy them into any document you wish. You can even create column guides with the Grid Manager, then modify the number of columns, and adjust the width of the gutter. All in all, the Grid Manager is a handy tool to have. I don't know what I ever did without it.

To open the Grid Manager, click the Utilities menu's Plug-in command, and then select Grid Manager from the sub-menu list. The Grid Manager appears (see Figure 7-5).

## Setting up a New Grid

1.  Select the type of guide.

    In the Define Grid area, click the drop-down arrow to the right of the Guide Type box. Select the type of guide from the list. These guide types are defined here:

    - *Columns* divides the page or pages vertically with column guides. This is just another way to establish columns in your document.

    - *Rulers* divides your page or pages vertically (called columns but still ruler guides) or horizontally (called rows) using ruler guides. If you are viewing facing pages, a horizontal ruler guide spans both pages. Vertical guides are set for left and right pages separately.

    - *Baseline* inserts horizontal ruler guides based on the leading (line spacing) you have chosen for your document. For more information on leading, see Chapter 9.

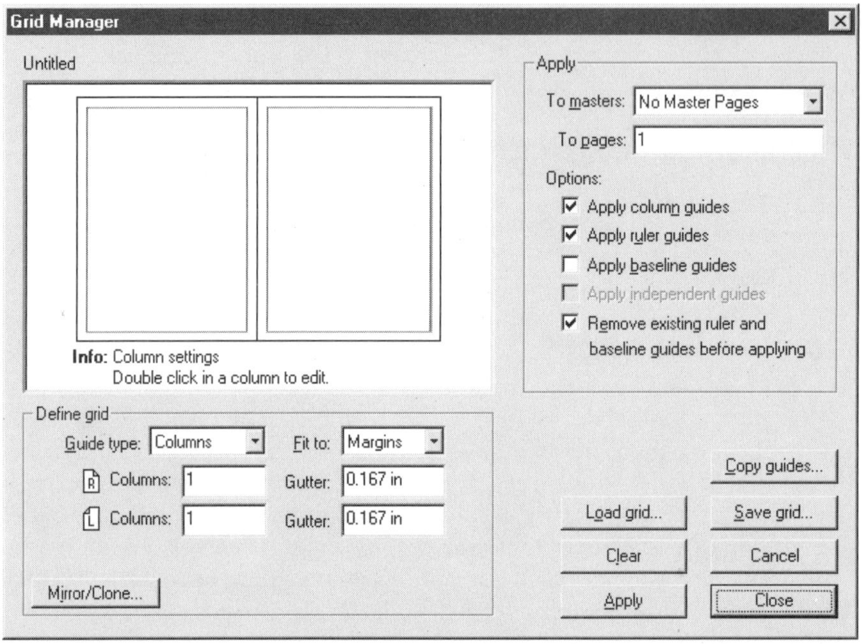

**Figure 7-5.** *The Grid Manager*

2. Enter the number of rows and columns you want.

If you have selected Rulers as the type of guide, you can set the number of columns and rows you want. If you selected Columns, the Rows setting is not available.

Enter the number of columns you want in the Columns boxes beside the Right and Left page icons. PageMaker sets the column width according to the amount of space that you have available. The default setting for the column gutters is 0.167 inches. You may change that if you wish by entering a new value in the Gutter box.

Enter the number of rows you want if that choice is available to you.

As soon as you enter a figure into a Column or Row box, the corresponding guides appear in the preview at the top of the Grid Manager.

3.  Specify the Fit-to parameters.

    Click the drop-down arrow to the right of the Fit-to box. Select Margins or Page from the menu. This setting determines whether the columns and rows you have created will be based between the margins or within the dimensions of the whole page.

4.  Apply the grid.

    If you want these guides to be applied to multiple pages in the active document, enter the page numbers of the pages that the grid will be applied to in the To Pages box. Place commas between the page numbers of discontiguous pages (3, 7, 12) and a hyphen between the lowest and highest page numbers of a contiguous group (15-36).

    If you want to apply the grid to a master page, use the drop-down button to the right of the To Masters box to select the master page to which you wish to apply the grid.

    In the Options section of the Grid Manager, select the types of guides you want to apply to the selected pages. If the pages already have guides in place, be sure to select the Remove Existing Ruler and Baseline Guides Before Applying checkbox so that the old guides will be removed before the new ones are put in place.

    Then click the Apply button to apply the grid you have created to the page or pages. When you are through with the Grid Manager, click the close button to close the dialog box.

> **Note**
>
> *You can create a grid using one type of guide, and then add additional guides to the same grid using another type.*

## Customizing a Grid

I prefer to use asymmetry in my document design most of the time. For example, I think that a column of white space, smaller than two adjoining equally spaced text columns, is more interesting and more inviting than three equally spaced columns. But if PageMaker creates columns of equal width based upon the distance between margins (or page edges), how can I add the asymmetrical punch that I am looking for?

Well, of course, the designers of PageMaker have thought of that, too. Take these steps to customize the width of existing columns:

1.  Select the column or row you want to modify.

    Place your mouse pointer over one of the columns in the preview at the top of the dialog box. A note at the bottom of the preview window tells you the width of the column or the height of the row. There is also a message that says

Double-click in a Column to Edit. When you place the mouse pointer over a column, the message changes to Double-click to Set the Column's Width.

Double-click the column or row you wish to change. The Set Width or Height dialog box appears (shown below).

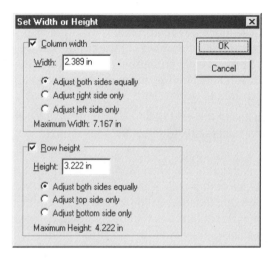

2. Set the adjusted width or height.

   In the Set Width or Height dialog box, change the existing data to the measurement you want. Note that there are two sections to the dialog box. The top reflects the column; the bottom shows the row. If you have only one (either columns or rows) in your grid, the other will not be available.

3. Select the change options.

   With the check boxes in the Options section, you can elect to change the width of a column in one of three ways: equally from both sides, from the right side only, or from the left side only. Your choices when customizing a row are to change from both sides equally or from the top or bottom.

4. Click OK.

   Click the OK button. The Set Width or Height dialog box closes and your changes are shown on the preview. You may then apply the changes as you wish.

   If you change an inside column from both sides equally, the columns on either side of it will adjust to the column's new measurements absorbing the change. If you change an outside column in the same way, however, the column loses its relationship to the margin and either pulls away from the margin or floats over it, depending upon whether you increased or decreased the size. Only the column next to the changed one adjusts; the other column or columns, if any, do not, leaving them imbalanced. The same thing applies to changing a row.

**Note**

*To change an evenly distributed three-column grid to an asymmetric one consisting of a narrow column to one side of two columns of equal width, I have to first change the center column to the measurement I want for the narrow, outside column using the Adjust Both Sides Equally selection. The columns on each side of the narrow one adjust to equal dimensions. Then I change the outside column to the same narrow dimensions using the Adjust Right or Adjust Left setting, depending upon the location of the neighboring column. The column next to the outside column adjusts, leaving one narrow column and two wider columns the same size.*

## Saving a Grid Created in Grid Manger

When you have used Grid Manager to create a grid that you want to use over and over, you can save it and apply it whenever you wish. Here's how:

1. Open the Save As dialog box.

   Click the Save Grid button. The Save As dialog box opens (see the following illustration). Although this looks very much like the Save As dialog box you use to save a file, it is set up to save the grid settings as a Guides file into the Guides folder.

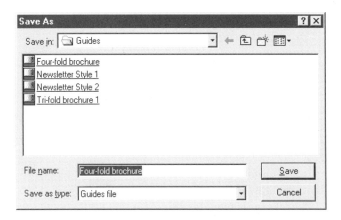

2. Name the grid.

   In the File Name box, enter the name you want to give to the guide configuration.

3. Save the grid.

Click the Save button. The guides configuration is saved and is available to be applied to other documents using the Grid Manager.

## Saving a Grid Created Manually

If you like a grid you have created by manually placing ruler guides, you can save it in the Grid Manager as well. Follow these steps:

1. Display the grid.

You must have the page open that contains the grid you want to save.

2. Open Grid Manager.

Select the Utilities menu's Plug-in command. Then select Grid Manager from the sub-menu. The Grid Manager opens.

3. Copy the grid.

Click the Copy Guides button. The Copy Guides dialog box appears (shown below).

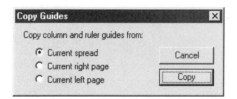

4. Select the grid to save.

If you have facing pages, you are asked if you want to save the guide configuration across the two-page spread or if you merely want to save one page or another. Click the appropriate radio button.

If you do not have facing pages selected, only one choice will be available to you.

5. Copy the grid.

Click the Copy button. The Copy Guides dialog box closes and the grid is displayed in the preview window of the Grid Manager.

6. Save the grid.

Save the copied guides by clicking the Save Grid button and naming the guide configuration as discussed previously.

## Applying a Saved Grid

Once a guide configuration has been named and saved, it is an easy matter to apply it to any document. Just follow these simple steps:

1. Open the document.

   Open the PageMaker document on which you wish to apply the grid.

2. Open Grid Manager.

   Select the Utilities menu's Plug-in command. Then click Grid Manager in the sub-menu.

3. Load the grid.

   Click the Load Grid button. The Open dialog box appears. From the list, select the name of the grid you want to apply. Click the Open button. The grid appears in the Grid Manager's preview window.

4. Apply the grid.

   If you want the grid to be applied to multiple pages in the active document, enter the page numbers of the pages that the grid will be applied to in the To Pages box. Place commas between the page numbers of discontiguous pages (3, 7, 12) and a hyphen between the lowest and highest page numbers of a contiguous group (15-36).

   If you want to apply the grid to a master page, use the drop-down button to the right of the To Masters box to select the master page to which you wish to apply the grid.

   If the pages already have guides in place, be sure to select the Remove Existing Ruler and Baseline Guides Before Applying checkbox.

   Then click the Apply button to apply the grid you have created to the page or pages.

5. Close the Grid Manager.

   The Grid Manager does not close automatically. Click the Close button to close it.

## Mirroring or Cloning a Grid

If you have created a grid for one side of a two-page spread, you can use that grid as the basis for the other page. Mirroring a grid means that you flip the grid so that it is the reverse of the original. Cloning means that you copy the grid exactly as it is to the other page.

To apply the guides from one page to a facing page, follow these steps:

1. Display the pages.

   Open both pages so that they are facing each other in the PageMaker window by clicking on the appropriate page icon to the left of the horizontal scroll bar.

2. Open the Grid Manager.

   Click the Utilities menu's Plug-in command. Then select the Grid Manager from the sub-menu. The Grid Manager opens.

3. Copy the guides.

   Click the Copy Guides button to load the grid into the Grid Manager.

4. Open the Clone/Mirror dialog box.

   Click the Mirror/Clone button. The Mirror and Clone dialog box appears (see the following illustration).

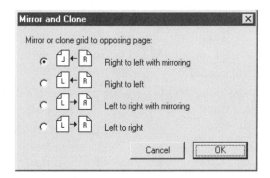

5. Select the operation you wish.

   From the several choices in the Mirror and Clone dialog box, select the operation that is appropriate for what you want to do.

6. Apply your selection.

   Click the OK button. The Mirror and Clone dialog box closes. The grid is applied to the page in the Grid Manager preview.

7. Apply the grid to your document.

   Using the Apply instructions listed previously, apply the grid to your document.

# Summary

The term *layout* means the parameters of your documents, the way you place its elements, and their relationship to one another. PageMaker provides many ways of managing your layout from the settings in the Document Setup dialog box where you establish the parameters of your document, such as paper size, the appearance of pages on your screen, margins, and the creation and management of guides and layout grids.

**The Document Setup Dialog Box** The Document Setup dialog box is most commonly used for the creation of a new document. As described in Chapter 3, you can set the parameters you want in Document Setup, click OK, and a new document appears. However, if you want to make changes to your document, such as change from one size of paper to another, you can do so in the Document Setup dialog box at any time, even after a document is established. You can even elect for PageMaker to automatically adjust your layout to fit the new parameters, if you wish. Page numbering, double-sided pages, and margin controls are also available in the Document Setup dialog box.

**The Layout View** There are two views in PageMaker. The view used most and generally discussed in this book is the Layout view. In it, you see things in the PageMaker window as they will appear when printed or published. The other view, Story Editor, operates much like a word processing program. There is limited formatting and page layout is not revealed.

**Creating Text Columns** Text columns are frequently used in text-heavy documents such as newsletters. It is good to divide text into columns; it makes the copy easier to read. Text columns are guides into which you may place or enter text. They are easily placed on a page through the Layout menu's Column Guides command.

**Creating and Using a Layout Grid** Whether using the computer or creating a design manually, graphic designers almost always use a layout grid, a guide to the placement of graphics and text that assures balance and effective composition. In PageMaker, this layout grid is composed of guides, nonprinting lines that identify margins and columns and indicate the structure of your piece.

The rulers that appear, by default, above and to the left of the PageMaker window are an important part of creating a layout grid. I keep rulers visible all the time, but they can be hidden if you wish. The zero point of the rulers appears at the upper left of a single page and at the midpoint of facing pages, but it can be adjusted.

Ruler guides are nonprinting guides that you can place manually on your page or create using the Grid Manager.

The Grid Manager is a tool that makes the creation and management of layout grids a piece of cake. Using the Grid Manager, you can create a grid, save it for future use, copy and save manually created grids, and create mirror images for facing pages.

# Chapter 8

## Managing Documents

If you have worked with computers for any time at all, you know how important it is to properly manage your files—if you want to see them or use them again. As a trainer, I am sometimes slightly embarrassed to keep harping on the same old truisms: "Save, save, save" and "Keep your files organized." It seems to me that computer users surely must already know this and furthermore are tired of hearing it again and again. But, unfortunately, I've found that even the most experienced computer users need to be reminded from time to time. So, here we are at the chapter in this book where I get to remind you about saving and organizing files.

If you are familiar with the way most Windows-based programs manage files, you will not find PageMaker much different. The Save, Save as, and file organization features work the same way, mainly because they are not solely a PageMaker utility, but part of Windows' function as the operating system. However, PageMaker offers some special features, such as PageMaker's MiniSaves and the Revert option, that depart from other Windows-based programs.

If you feel that you know all there is to know about the Saving process in Windows-based programs, I urge you to not abandon this chapter altogether. The special features that PageMaker offers really are *special* and you wouldn't want to miss them.

## Naming and Saving a PageMaker Document

Once you have created a PageMaker document, it is a good idea to name and save it right away. Doing so performs two very important functions: It establishes the file on your hard drive where it can be accessed later (until your file is saved the first time, it is just running in your computer's memory) and it provides a location for the file so that you can find it when you want to access it again. In addition, when you save, you select the type of file you want to save it as and whether you want to include additional files as a part of the saved document.

When saving a file for the first time, the Save As dialog box (see Figure 8-1) is always used for the process. Subsequent saves do not require a Save As unless you want to create an identical second document with a new name or location.

Before discussing the steps for performing a save, exploring the parts of the Save As dialog box is a good idea. Table 8-1 identifies each section and explains their functions.

Here are the steps you take to name and save your document:

1. Open the Save As dialog box.

   You can open the Save As dialog box in one of three ways:

   ■ Clicking the File menu's Save As command
   ■ Selecting the File menu's Save command

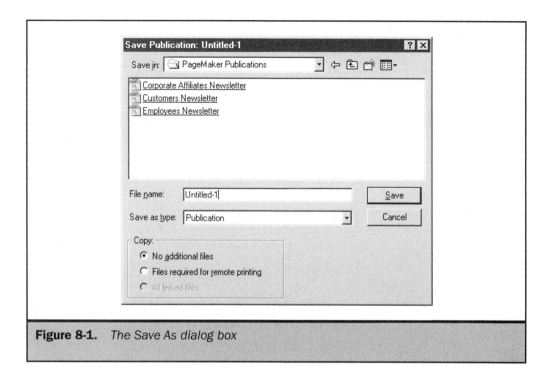

**Figure 8-1.**   *The Save As dialog box*

■ Clicking the Save toolbar button

Once the document has been named and saved, subsequent use of the Save command or the Save button do not bring up the Save As dialog box, but perform a behind-the-scenes save of changes to the document.

2. Open the folder where you want to store the document.

Unless the folder that appears automatically in the Save In box is the folder where you want to store your document, you must use the directory tree to locate that folder. If your target folder is already in the Save In box, go on to Step 3.

The directory tree is a list of all the folders in your computer where files are stored. Double-clicking a folder in the directory tree opens it to reveal the folders stored in it. The files stored in the folder are shown in the file list.

| Section | Function |
|---------|----------|
| Save In | This part of the Save As dialog box enables you to store the file so that you can find it again. The folder that is currently open is shown in the Save In box. However, clicking the drop-down arrow to the right of the Save In box reveals the directory tree where you can open the folder in which you wish to store your document. |
| File List Area | The File List Area displays the files currently stored in the folder shown in the Save In box. |
| File Name | This area is where the name of the file is entered. If a file in the File list area is selected, its name will be displayed in the File Name box. |
| Save As Type | In PageMaker 7, you can save a document as a publication, a template, or as a PageMaker 6.5 file. Clicking the drop-down arrow to the right of the Save As Type box reveals the choices. |
| Copy | The Copy section enables you to save files, such as placed graphics or other placed documents, as part of the document file. If you are moving the file, publishing it on the Web or are taking the file to a printer for publication, you must include these files. If you are producing the document from your computer, it is not necessary to do so. |

**Table 8-1.**   *The Sections of the Save As Dialog Box and their functions*

Click the drop-down arrow to the right of the Save In box. The directory tree is displayed (see Figure 8-2). Double-click the drive (usually the C drive) where the target folder is stored. If the target folder is displayed in the C drive, double-click to open it. Then go on to Step 3.

If the target folder is stored inside another one, double-click the outside folder to show the folders inside it. Continue to open folders until you locate the target folder. Then double-click to open the folder where you want to store your file.

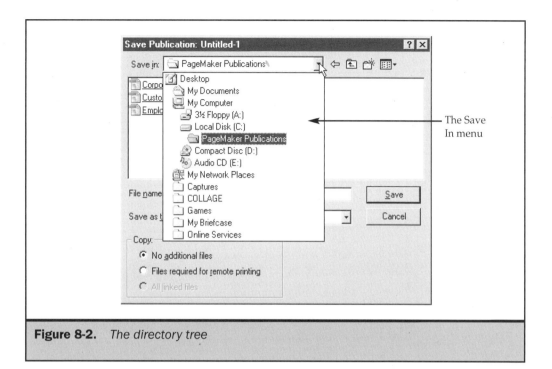

The Save
In menu

**Figure 8-2.**   *The directory tree*

3.   Name the file.

In the File Name box, enter the name you want to give to the file you are saving. The File Name box will have an entry already in the box such as Untitled-1. If the entry is highlighted, you don't have to click in the box or delete the entry, just type the new name.

4.   Select the document type.

Most of the time, I expect, you will save your document as a publication. However, you have two other choices: as a template or a copy in 6.5 format.

If you want to save your document as a type other than publication, click the drop-down arrow to the right of the Save As Type box and make your selection, as shown in Figure 8-3.

Selecting Template will save the document in the Template Palette and it can be used as the foundation for future documents (see Chapter 3 for more information). Choosing a Copy in 6.5 Format will save the document so that it can be opened in the previous version of PageMaker. (See the section on this a little later in this chapter.)

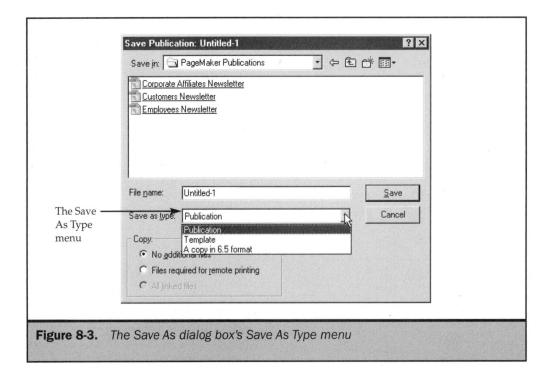

**Figure 8-3.**   *The Save As dialog box's Save As Type menu*

5.  Select the files to save with the document.

Click the appropriate radio button, as shown below, to select the option of your choice.

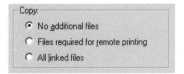

If you have imported files in your document, such as placed graphics or text that you imported into PageMaker, you may wish to save those original files along with the document for better quality printing or publishing. And any links that you have placed in the document may also be saved along with the file.

However, if you are going to continually view or print the document from the originating computer, saving the files along with the document is not necessary.

So long as the document is not moved (changing the path to the placed files), the supporting documents do not need to be saved as part of the file.

Keep in mind that saving supporting files as a part of your document adds considerably to the size of the document.

6. Save the document.

Click the Save button. The Save As dialog box closes and the document is saved.

# Saving Changes to a Named Document

Once a document has been named and saved, save again frequently as you work on the document to save changes to your work. This is the part where I tell you what you already know—but need to be reminded. Changes in your document are being held in your computer's memory until saved. Although today's computer applications frequently have built-in safeguards against losing data because of power failure, unsaved data is fragile and is still at risk.

Save, save, save!

Saving the changes to a named document is a quick and unobtrusive procedure. Just do one of the following:

■ Click the File menu's Save command.

■ Click the Save button on the PageMaker toolbar.

Both operations have the same result. The changes to your document are saved to the named file. You will not see a dialog box or any representation of the operation. You can just keep on working on your document.

A save, as described previously, adds the changes to your document, but does not save the document into its most compact form. If storage space is not a problem, don't worry about it while you are working on the document. However, at the completion of the document, save it once more, accessing the Save As dialog box from the File menu's

## Using the Keyboard

It is so simple to perform a save operation using the keyboard. Use this keyboard combination:

CTRL-S

Once you become accustomed to using it, you can incorporate the keystrokes into your work and save frequently without breaking stride.

Save As command. You don't need to make any changes in the dialog box; just click Save and the Save As dialog box rewrites the documents into a form that uses far less storage space.

# Saving a Document with a New Name or to a New Location

You can use the Save As dialog box to save your document with a new name or in a new location. Keep in mind that this operation creates a second document (the one with the new name or in the new location), leaving the original document in place. This works just about the same as a Name and Save operation; however, there is only one way to get to the Save As dialog box. Here are the steps:

1. Save the document.

   If you want to save the most recent changes in the original document, it is necessary to perform a regular save before you start. If you don't, the changes will be incorporated into the new document, but the original will only be complete up to the previous save.

   Just click the Save button on the PageMaker toolbar or select the File menu's Save command.

2. Open the Save As dialog box.

   Select the File menu's Save As command. The Save As dialog box opens.

3. Locate a folder in which to store the new document.

   If you are placing the new document into a new location, use the directory tree to locate the folder in which you want to store it.

   If you are not changing the document's location, go to Step 4.

4. Rename the document.

   Enter the new document's name in the File Name box.

   If you are not changing the name of the document, you do not need to do this step.

5. Save the new document.

   Click the Save button. The original document is seamlessly replaced by the new document.

   If you changed the name of the document, the new name appears on the title bar of the document window.

   If you changed the location of the new document, but not the name, you may not notice much difference in the appearance of the new document; however, subsequent saves add changes to the new document in the new location.

# Saving a Document So That It Can Be Opened in PageMaker 6.5

If you are taking a document created in PageMaker 7 to another computer on disk, the document can only be opened if the new computer also has PageMaker 7 installed. There is a way, however, to save the document as a PageMaker 6.5 file so that, if the target computer has the previous version of PageMaker, it can be read. These steps tell you how:

1. Open the Save As dialog box.

   Click the File menu's Save As command. The Save As dialog box opens.

2. Select the appropriate drive.

   In the Save In box, use the directory tree to select the drive that contains the disk that you will use to move the document.

   You may use a floppy disk (usually drive A), an external large storage drive (usually designated as D or higher), or a writeable CD drive (also may be designated as D or higher). This depends upon the configuration of your computer and its peripherals.

3. Select the type of file.

   In the Save as Type box, select A Copy in 6.5 Format (shown below).

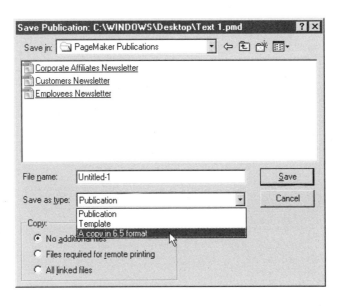

PAGEMAKER ESSENTIALS

4. Save the document.

   Click the Save button. The document is saved so that it can be read by PageMaker 6.5.

   Keep in mind that some features of PageMaker 7 may be lost.

# Closing a Document

Once a document has been named, it may be closed and stored until you need to work with it again. You can close a document in one of two ways:

- Click the File menu's Close command.
- Click the Document Exit control button.

Notice that there are two sets of control buttons. One set, discussed in Chapter 2, controls the application itself. The second set controls the active PageMaker document. Their position depends upon whether or not the PageMaker document is maximized or restored.

If the document is in a maximized state, the document's control buttons appear immediately below the application buttons on the same bar as the PageMaker menus, as shown below.

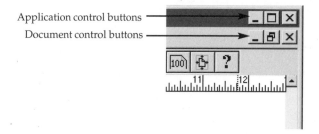

Application control buttons ——————
Document control buttons ——————

If the document is in a restored state, the control buttons appear to the far right of the document's title bar, below the PageMaker toolbar (see the following illustration).
Make sure that you are clicking the correct exit button.

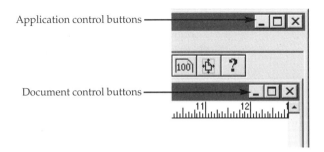

Application control buttons

Document control buttons

# Opening a Document That Has Been Saved

A closed PageMaker document is easily reopened. There are two ways in which you may do so: Use the Open dialog box or the Recent Publications menu.

## Using the Open Dialog Box

Here's how to reopen a document using the Open dialog box:

1. Display the Open dialog box.

   Click the File menu's Open command. The Open dialog box appears, as shown below.

   You may also click the Open button on the PageMaker toolbar to display the Open dialog box.

**Open Publication**

Look in: PageMaker Publications

Corporate Affiliates Newsletter
Customers Newsletter
Employees Newsletter

File name: Corporate Affiliates Newsletter          Open

Files of type: PageMaker Files                       Cancel

Open as:
● Original    ○ Copy

2. Locate the file.

   Click the drop-down arrow to the right of the Look In box to display the directory tree. Locate the file you wish to open. Click it to select it.

3. Select Original or Copy.

   The radio buttons in the lower-left section of the Open dialog box give you the choice of opening the original document or opening a copy of the original. If you select Copy, the document will open but with an Untitled-1 designation.

   The Original button is selected by default. If you want a copy, click the button beside Copy.

4. Open the file.

   Click the Open button on the Open dialog box. The selected file opens.

## Using the Recent Publications Menu

PageMaker provides an easy connection to the last eight files that you have opened. Click the File menu's Recent Publications menu and select the file you want form the sub-menu, as shown next.

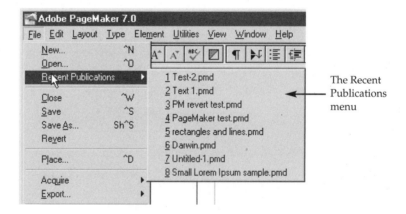

The Recent Publications menu

As soon as you click the document you want to open, the menus close and the file opens in your PageMaker window.

## Using PageMaker's Revert Feature

A nifty feature in PageMaker enables you to abandon the changes you have made in your document since the last full save and return the publication to the way it was at the time of the save.

Why would you ever want to do that? When working on a layout in PageMaker, I've found that some of my design decisions just weren't working out. Rather than having to try to redo all of my actions or start from scratch, I can revert the document to the way it was on my last save. If you are saving frequently, that may not take you very far back, but sometimes it can be a real time-saver.

The process is simple: Just click the File menu's Revert command and click OK when the confirmation message appears (see the illustration below). All actions since the last save are removed from your document.

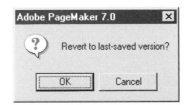

## Using PageMaker's Mini-Save Safety Net

PageMaker automatically performs a mini-save of your document when certain operations are performed. A mini-save is not a true save and will not remain on the computer permanently. It will, however, survive a sudden cessation of PageMaker. The following operations all activate a mini-save:

- Moving to a different page
- Inserting or deleting a page
- Changing the document setup
- Printing
- Switching between layout view and story editor
- Using the Clipboard
- Clicking the active page's icon

There are two uses for a mini-save. You can revert back to a mini-save using the Revert feature instead of reverting all the way back to a Save, and the mini-save version is invaluable in recovering from a crash.

### Reverting to a Mini-Save

Just as you can use the Revert command to abandon all changes since a save, you can also use the Revert command to abandon all changes since a mini-save. Perform the

Revert procedure just as you would in a full revert, but hold down the SHIFT key when selecting the File menu's Revert command. Once you have clicked the OK button on the confirmation box (shown below), the document immediately reflects its state at the time of the last mini-save.

## Recovering from a Crash

It seems that no matter how sophisticated a computer system you may have, an eventual crash is inevitable. Now I'm not talking about a total loss of system (I had one of those recently and it was *ugg-ly*), but the occasional power outage or system lock up that seems inherent with computers. If this happens and your PageMaker document is not closed down correctly, you will be presented with a choice when you reopen the document. A message box appears (shown below), informing you that you can open the last mini-save version or the last full-saved version. Click the button that is the best solution and the document reopens.

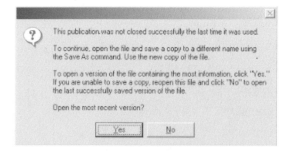

## A Few Words about File Organization

I'm always amazed in a training class when a student says, "Oh, I don't bother with organizing my files; I just dump them all in the same place." I'm not the most compulsive person in the world, so I understand the impulse to not get weird about it, but I can't imagine having to dig through hundreds of files to find the one I want. If you only deal with, say, 20 files a year, we're not talking about a big deal, but I generate hundreds of files in a short period of time, and organization is vital to keeping me sane or nearly so.

Most of the time, failure to keep files organized is the result of not understanding the file management system in the computer. This is particularly true of adults who are new to the computer and have not grown up with it as some people have.

I have learned to use the analogy of the computer's storage system being a filing cabinet, each drive equating to a different file drawer. Each drawer contains folders. Some folders just have pieces of paper in them; some have other folders, which may have even more folders. So, in order to find the piece of paper (document) that you want, you have to go to the right drawer, locate the right folder, and look in it for the document or for other folders that may have the document in it.

I urge you to keep your PageMaker documents well organized in folders named with expressive names that aid you in locating the document you want. Nothing is worse than being under a deadline and having to spend an hour looking for the file you know you saved but just can't find.

## The Importance of Backup

Here is one more topic for the I-already-know-that category and that is *backup*. In this chapter, we have talked extensively about saving files. But managing documents includes backing them up as well. If the files on your computer are at all important, a copy needs to be made of them and stored in a location away from the computer itself. As I said before, computers crash. And, as I recently found out, not all crashes are recoverable. I lost valuable data in the recent crash of my desktop computer because I had not been conscientious about backup. (I know, I know; I should have known better.)

Today, the cost of peripheral hardware is getting lower and lower. Tape backup systems are probably the best, but external, large volume storage drives are useful as well as the new, low-cost writeable CD drives. You can even save some individual files on floppy disks.

Just don't leave your documents to the vagaries of fate.

## Summary

Although we have heard it myriad times before, the importance of saving and organizing documents is significant enough to be repeated. The saving process in PageMaker is very similar to that of other Windows-based applications.

The first time you save a PageMaker document, you name it and place it in a location where you can find it again when you need it. When initially naming and saving a document, you can bring up the Save As screen by using either the File menu's Save or Save As commands. You can also use the Save button on the PageMaker toolbar.

In the saving process, you must stipulate where you want the document to be stored, what name you want it to have, what type of document it will be stored as, and what files you want to store along with it. Once a document has been named and saved initially, subsequent saves are simple and unobtrusive. The Save As dialog box can be used to save a file to its smallest size and also to copy the document with a new name and/or a new location.

Previously saved and closed documents can be opened by using the Open dialog box or by selecting the document's name from the Recent Publications list on the File menu.

PageMaker provides a mini-save feature that automatically saves the publication when certain operations are performed. The mini-save can be used to recover from a computer crash or as a point to revert back to when you want to abandon changes to your document.

File organization and file backup are vital in locating and protecting important documents.

# Chapter 9

## Managing
## PageMaker Text

PageMaker text can be loosely divided into two categories. I think of these as the text-box management category in which text is placed, positioned, sized, and otherwise handled as an object, and the type-setting category in which text is generated, formatted, and edited.

In Chapter 4, I touched on both of these categories in order to give you the skills you needed to get started. But there is a lot more to working with text than the simple ones described there. PageMaker text is highly manipulative. Its placement can be closely controlled or automated to flow from one column to another, from one page to another. It can be created in PageMaker as described in Chapter 4 or it can be imported from another source, such as a word processing program.

Text can be edited in the Layout view so that you can see the effect of the changes on your layout as they are entered, or in the Story Editor where text editing is streamlined for word processing without concern for layout. PageMaker offers professional leading and kerning control, which is the spacing between lines and the spacing between letters, as well as other type-setting techniques that make your document a cutting-edge publication.

In this chapter, I give the rest of the story, as it were, the ins and outs of text management.

## Managing Text As an Object

An object is any element in a PageMaker layout that contributes to the overall design. Objects are specifically graphics, text boxes, and frames. Chapter 10 discusses working with graphics as well as graphics text boxes as they interact with graphics. But here I cover the text box itself: importing text from another source, flowing the text from column to column, and placing text into simple graphic shapes, called frames.

### Importing Text

In earlier versions of PageMaker, I always created my text in a word processing program and imported it into my PageMaker layout. This allowed me to perform all the neat word processing operations such as spell check and certain kinds of formatting before I moved it into PageMaker where, at that time, those techniques were not available. Now PageMaker has all the spiffed-up word processing capabilities that I could want, but I frequently import text anyway. If it is already created in a word processing program, why re-enter all those keystrokes? If you work in a situation where others submit copy to you for inclusion in a PageMaker document such as a newsletter, then you too will want to import those documents into PageMaker. You may edit them before or after placing them.

Before importing text, you must make some preparation. Consider these questions; you will need the answers in the Place dialog box:

- Do you want to retain the formatting of the text you are importing?

- Is the text being imported as a new story, or is it replacing an existing one?

- Do you know where you want the text to be placed in your document?

- Do you want PageMaker's Autoflow feature to automatically flow long text documents from one column to another and then from one page to another, or do you want to manage the text flow manually?

In the following steps, I lead you through the process of placing short text manually without PageMaker's Autoflow feature. Autoflow is discussed later in the section "Using Autoflow."

1. Display the page on which you want to place the text.

   Open the document in which you want to place the text to the appropriate page.

2. Place the insertion point.

   If you are inserting text into the midst of a story, use the Text tool to place the insertion point where you wish the text to appear.

   If you are replacing an entire story, use the Text tool to place the insertion point anywhere in the story you want to replace.

   If you are not inserting or replacing text, it is not necessary to place an insertion point.

3. Open the Place dialog box.

   Select the File menu's Place command or use the Place button on the PageMaker toolbar. The Place dialog box opens, as shown in Figure 9-1.

4. Locate the file to place.

   Click on the drop-down box to the right of the Look In box to display the directory tree.

   Unless the folder that appears automatically in the Look In box is the folder where your document is stored, you must use the directory tree to locate the target folder. If your target folder is already in the Save In box, go on to Step 5.

   As explained in Chapter 8, the directory tree is a list of all the folders in your computer where files are stored. Double-clicking on a folder in the directory tree opens it to reveal the folders stored inside. The files stored in the folder are shown in the file list.

   Start by double-clicking on the drive (usually the C drive) where the target folder is stored. If the target folder is displayed in the C drive, double-click to open it. Then go on to Step 5.

PAGEMAKER ESSENTIALS

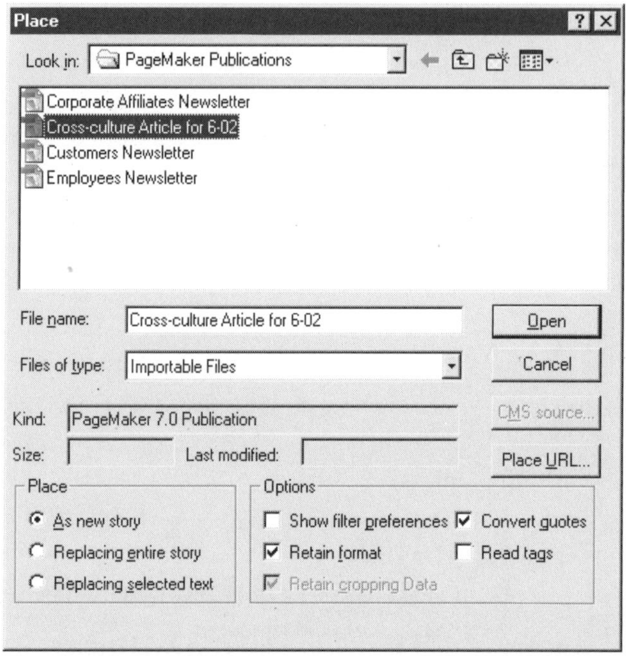

**Figure 9-1.** *The Place dialog box*

If the target folder is stored inside another one, double-click on the outside folder to show the folders inside it. Continue to open folders until you locate the folder that contains your document. Then double-click to open the folder. All of the documents in that folder are shown in the file list area.

5. Select the file you want to place.

In the file list area, click on the file you want to import into your PageMaker document. The document appears in the File Name box along with information on that file, such as the kind of file it is (Microsoft Word Document for example), its size, and the date on which the file was last modified.

6. Select the Place options.

Choose the appropriate radio button in the Place section of the dialog box for your text placement requirements:

- **As New Story** You are placing text where no text currently exists.
- **Replacing Entire Story** This tells PageMaker to remove the existing story and put the new one in its place.
- **Inserting Text** This places the imported text into the existing text at the insertion point.

7. Select the Options boxes.

   Select the appropriate boxes in the Options section of the Place dialog box:

   - **Show Filter Preferences** This makes options associated with certain filters available in a secondary dialog box.
   - **Retain Format** The formatting of the imported text will be retained when it is placed in the PageMaker document.
   - **Retain Cropping Data** This selection is appropriate only for graphics.
   - **Convert Quotes** This will automatically convert old-fashioned straight quotation marks into typeset-quality marks. In other words, "this" becomes "this." Most modern word processing programs convert quotes automatically.
   - **Read Tags** This imports style tags (codes) from the original text.

8. Click Open.

   Click the Open button on the Place dialog box. The box disappears and one of the following occurs:

   - If you selected the Replace Entire Story option, the imported text replaces the previous text.
   - If you selected the Insert Text option, the imported text is placed at the insertion point.
   - If you selected As New Item, the mouse pointer changes to a symbol that looks like a page of text.

9. Place the text.

   If you elected to replace or insert text, your text is already placed in the document. However, if you are placing a new item, you must use the mouse pointer to tell PageMaker where you want the text to appear. Choose one of the following operations to place the text:

   - Click in your document between the margins that you want to contain your text. The text automatically fills the space between the margins.
   - Click and drag with the mouse pointer to create the parameters of the text box that holds your text.

PAGEMAKER
ESSENTIALS

# Managing Text Flow

If you are importing short text boxes, those that are complete on one page or in one column, the information in the previous section is all you need to import and place your story. But if you are working with a long text document, one that continues from one page to another or one column to another (or both), it is important to know how to manage text flow.

## Using Autoflow

PageMaker provides a convenient feature, Autoflow, which can automatically flow long text boxes from column to column and on to additional pages if needed. The text is placed in one long text box divided into column-length sections that are threaded; that is, they are connected in the appropriate order. The following steps take you through the process of placing long text using Autoflow:

1. Make the target document ready.

   Have the page open where you want the text box to begin, and have column guides in place if desired. If your text is going to flow onto the next page or pages, be certain that those pages are prepared as well.

2. Select Autoflow.

   Select the Layout menu's Autoflow command. A checkmark beside the Autoflow command indicates that it is selected.

3. Open the Place dialog box.

   Select the File menu's Place command or use the Place button on the PageMaker toolbar. The Place dialog box opens. The Place dialog box is shown in Figure 9-1.

4. Locate the folder that contains the file you want to place.

   Click on the drop-down box to the right of the Look In box to display the directory tree.

   Unless the folder that appears automatically in the Look In box is the folder where your document is stored, you must use the directory tree to locate the target folder. If your target folder is already in the Save In box, go on to Step 5.

   As explained in Chapter 8, the directory tree is a list of all the folders in your computer where files are stored. Double-clicking on a folder in the directory tree opens it to reveal the folders stored inside. The files stored in the folder are shown in the file list.

   Start by double-clicking on the drive (usually the C drive) where the target folder is stored. If the target folder is displayed in the C drive, double-click to open it. Then go on to Step 5.

If the target folder is stored inside another one, double-click on the outside folder to show the folders inside it. Continue to open folders until you locate the folder that contains your document. Then double-click to open the folder. All of the documents in that folder are shown in the file list area.

5. Select the file you want to place.

   In the file list area, click on the file you want to import into your PageMaker document. The document appears in the File Name box along with information on that file, such as the kind of file it is (Microsoft Word Document, for example), its size, and the date on which the file was last modified.

6. Select the Place options.

   Choose the appropriate radio button in the Place section of the dialog box for your text placement requirements:

   ■ **As New Story**   You are placing text where no text currently exists.

   ■ **Replacing Entire Story**   This tells PageMaker to remove the existing story and put the new one in its place.

   ■ **Inserting Text**   This places the imported text into the existing text at the insertion point.

7. Select the Options boxes.

   Select the appropriate boxes in the Options section of the Place dialog box:

   ■ **Show Filter Preferences**   This makes options associated with certain filters available in a secondary dialog box.

   ■ **Retain Format**   The formatting of the imported text will be retained when it is placed in the PageMaker document.

   ■ **Retain Cropping Data**   This selection is appropriate only for graphics.

   ■ **Convert Quotes**   This will automatically convert old-fashioned straight quotation marks into typeset-quality marks. In other words, "this" becomes "this." Most modern word processing programs convert quotes automatically.

   ■ **Read Tags**   This imports style tags (codes) from the original text.

8. Click Open.

   Click the Open button on the Place dialog box. The box disappears and the mouse pointer changes to a serpentine arrow.

9. Place the text.

   Click the arrow in the column where you want the text to begin. Then sit back and watch PageMaker work its magic. Before you can blink, the text is placed in continuous columns and, when needed, contiguous pages.

## Controlling Flow Manually

The benefit of Autoflow is that it places text automatically, in one rapid process, into columns and pages. But what if you don't want the text to flow through contiguous pages? Maybe you want only one or two columns of text on the first page and the remainder on a later page of your newsletter. Instead of using Autoflow, you can manually place the text.

Follow the previous steps for placing Autoflow text, but skip Step 2; do not select Autoflow. (Check the Layout menu to make sure that there is not a checkmark beside the Autoflow command.) Then, when you place the text with a mouse pointer that looks like a page of text, the text flows only to the end of the column in which it is placed.

The text box indicates that there is more unplaced text by the presence of a red arrow in the bottom window-shade handle. To place a continuation of the text, click on the red arrow on the window-shade handle; the mouse pointer again looks like a page of text (see Figure 9-2). Move the mouse pointer to the location of the text continuation and click. Again, the text will flow only to the end of the column in which it is placed. If even more text remains, click on the red arrow again and repeat until all text is placed.

## Understanding Text Box Sections

Keep in mind that although you may have text spread through numerous columns, and even pages, the text that you have placed using either flow management technique is *one text box*. The text is connected (threaded) so that if you change the height of the first text box section by raising or lowering the top window-shade handle, the text automatically adjusts through all of the sections. If you decrease the height of the section by raising the bottom window-shade handle, the removed text moves to the next section and all sections move throughout the box. If you add or remove text in the middle of the text box, the sections following it adjust. If a large amount of text is added, keep in mind that the last section of the text box will only expand to the bottom of the column in which it is placed. The last section will then show a red arrow in its bottom window-shade handle, indicating that more text remains to be placed.

In addition to the red arrow indicating that more text remains to be placed, other window-shade handle symbols give you information on the section's position in the text box.

- ■ If the top window-shade handle is blank, it is the first section in the box.
- ■ If the window-shade handle at the top of the section contains a plus, you know that the section is a continuation of text elsewhere.
- ■ A blank-bottom window-shade handle indicates that that section is the last section in the text box.
- ■ If the bottom window-shade handle contains a plus, that tells you that there is more text elsewhere that follows.

See Figure 9-3 for examples.

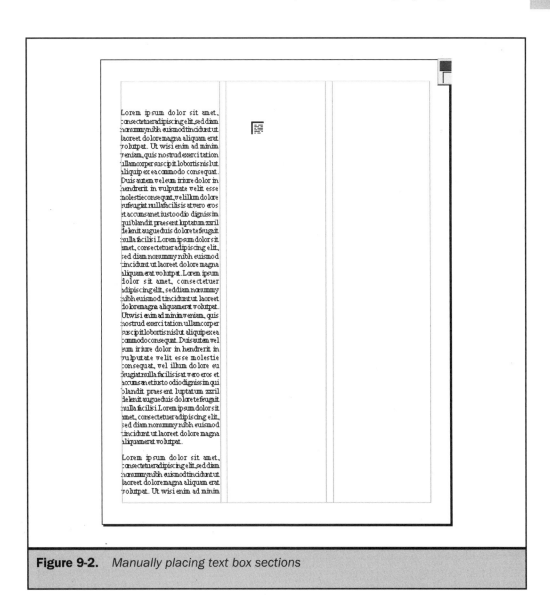

**Figure 9-2.** *Manually placing text box sections*

PAGEMAKER
ESSENTIALS

# Using Text Frames

In addition to text boxes, PageMaker provides an exceptional way to display text: a special object called a frame. Frames come in the same shapes as simple graphics, but have two capabilities not available in the graphics:

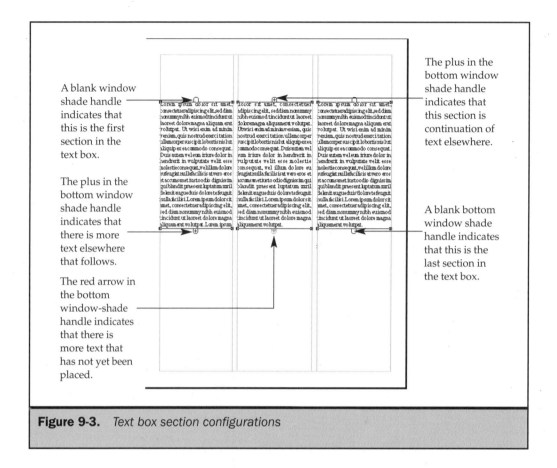

The plus in the bottom window shade handle indicates that this section is continuation of text elsewhere.

A blank window shade handle indicates that this is the first section in the text box.

The plus in the bottom window shade handle indicates that there is more text elsewhere that follows.

The red arrow in the bottom window-shade handle indicates that there is more text that has not yet been placed.

A blank bottom window shade handle indicates that this is the last section in the text box.

**Figure 9-3.** *Text box section configurations*

- Frames hold content, either text or graphics, or can serve as placeholders for content.
- Text frames, even placeholder frames with no text content, can be threaded just like text boxes so that a story can flow from one frame to another.

This chapter discusses text frames. Please see Chapter 10 for information on placing graphics in frames.

Text held in a frame takes on the shape of its frame, which can serve as an interesting element to your page. Just like simple graphics, frames may be displayed without a stroke, which means that the text will appear in the frame shape without the outline. Now, for a rectangular frame that may not be so dramatic, but imagine the effect of text in an elliptical frame or a polygon, maybe even a star.

## Creating Text Frames

In Chapter 5's discussion of simple graphics, you may have noticed that alongside each simple graphic tool in the Toolbox Palette is a similar tool with a non-printing X in its fill space. Those tools are the Frame tools and they are created and placed using the same techniques as the simple graphics. Chapter 5 discusses the creation of each of the simple graphics individually. Those instructions may be applied to the creation of frames as well. The following steps are a general guide to creating all of the frames:

1. Select the Frame tool.

   Click on the Frame tool of your choice in the Toolbox Palette: Rectangle, Ellipse, or Polygon. Once a tool has been selected, the mouse pointer becomes a small cross.

2. Click and drag.

   Click the mouse pointer in the area where you want the upper left of your frame to be and drag diagonally down and to the right to create the size and shape you desire. Remember that if you hold down the SHIFT key while dragging, the frame will be constrained, creating a frame that is a square (rectangular frame), a circle (ellipse frame), or a symmetrical polygon.

3. Customize the frame.

   Once created, frames may be customized just as you customized the simple graphics. Line style and weight may be adjusted, and the frames may be sized or moved.

4. Place text in the frame.

   Using the Text tool, click inside the frame. The insertion point appears. Enter the text that you wish to be held in the frame. The text will wrap to the frame's shape.

## Turning a Simple Graphic into a Frame

Simple graphics can easily be converted into frames. Just select the graphic and select the Element menu's Frame command. From the sub-menu, select Change to Frame. The non-printing X appears. You may enter text into the new frame as described previously or leave the frame empty to serve as a placeholder, as discussed in the following section.

## Using Frames as Placeholders

It is a very common practice in creating quality graphic designs to layout an entire piece using a layout grid and frames as placeholders before adding any text or even graphics. Not only does that allow you to achieve balance on your page before adding any copy, but also you can actually create the text to fit the space available. Figure 9-4 shows the use of frames as placeholders on the first page of a newsletter layout.

**Figure 9-4.**  *A newsletter layout using frames as placeholders*

To use frames as placeholders, just create the frames as described, but do not enter the text. Frames without text show the non-printing X to identify their use as a placeholder.

## Threading Frames

Although text boxes are threaded automatically during the placement process, frames must be connected manually. Frames may be threaded even if they are being used as placeholders. Once text is added to the placeholder frames, it will flow from one frame to another of those you have joined together. All frames do not have to be threaded, just those through which you want the same story to flow.

The following steps lead you through the process of threading frames together:

1.  Select the first frame.

    Using the Pointer tool, select an existing text frame or placeholder frame.

2.  Click the window-shade handle.

    Click the bottom window-shade handle of the selected frame. The mouse pointer changes to the thread icon.

3.  Click the next frame.

    Click anywhere on the frame that you want to thread to. The frames are automatically threaded.

4.  Continue the process.

    Continue to thread frames in this manner until all of the frames are joined.

## Changing the Threading Order

Once frames are threaded, the flow of text can be changed, if you wish. You can completely reorder the frames or add frames into the thread. Here's how:

1.  Select the frame to redirect.

    Using the Pointer tool, select the frame that you want to connect to a different frame.

2.  Break the connection.

    Press CTRL-SHIFT and click on the top or bottom window-shade handle. Clicking the top handle breaks the connection with the previous frame. Clicking the bottom one, of course, breaks the connection to the next frame. Any text in the frame rolls up to the frame preceding the break.

3.  Click the bottom window-shade handle.

    With the frame still selected, click in the bottom window-shade handle. The mouse pointer becomes the thread icon.

4.  Click on the next frame.

    Click anywhere in the frame to which you want to connect. The connection is complete. You can only add frames to the beginning or end of a thread. If the frame you want to connect to is in the middle of a thread, you will receive a message warning you that you can't do that. Either add the frame to the beginning or end of the thread, or disconnect the target frame from its thread.

5.  Repeat.

    Continue the redirection process until the frames are threaded as you wish.

# Professional Techniques for Document Editing and Formatting

Several times in this book, I have celebrated the fact that PageMaker 7 comes closer than ever to providing word processing techniques in the management of text. The addition of spell checking and other conveniences that are traditionally a part of word processing programs makes working with text much easier.

However, in another sense, PageMaker offers, and has always offered, type-manipulation techniques that go far beyond what most word processors provide. These techniques are consistent with professional typesetting practices that have their origins in the days when type was set by hand, one letter at a time. Sometimes it is the use of these techniques that makes the difference in a piece that appears to be professionally designed and typeset and one that looks like it was generated by a less-professional method.

In this half of Chapter 9, I explain editing techniques that go beyond those discussed in Chapter 4, such as Find and Change, Indents and Tabs, Indent and Outdent, Styles, and Bullets and Numbering. I'll also cover more advanced text-manipulation topics, such as kerning, leading, baseline shift, horizontal scale, and tracking.

# Advanced Text-Editing Tips and Techniques

As with all of the chapters in Part I of this book, Chapter 4 discusses only the basic editing skills, just enough to get you started. But there are several other editing techniques that are great time-savers. This section explores these procedures.

## Using Find

The Find utility is useful when you need to search a story for a word or phrase. This feature only operates in the Story Editor view; however, depending upon the selections you make, you may search one story at a time or all stories in a publication. The Find utility continues to find each instance of the target word or phrase until the entire story or stories have been searched or until you cancel the operation.

Here's how it works:

1. Select a story.

   You can launch the Find utility using either the Pointer tool or the Text tool, but one of the following must be in effect:

   ■ A text box must be selected using the Pointer tool.

   ■ Using the Text tool, the insertion point must be placed in the text of a story.

   If you are searching only one story, then the story you are searching must be the selected one or the one with the insertion point. When searching all stories in a document, one of the stories in the document must be selected or have the insertion point in place. If no story is selected, when the Story Editor is opened a blank story is presented.

2. Open the Story Editor view.

   Select the Edit menu's Edit Story command. The Story Editor opens and only text is shown. No layout elements are available (see Figure 9-5).

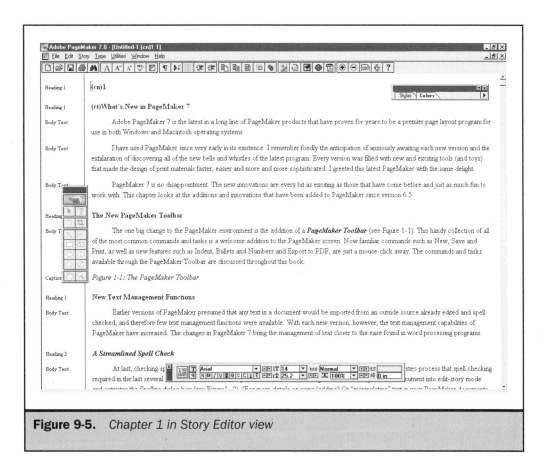

**Figure 9-5.** *Chapter 1 in Story Editor view*

3. Select the Find utility.

   From the Utility menu, select the Find command. The Find dialog box opens, as shown in the following illustration.

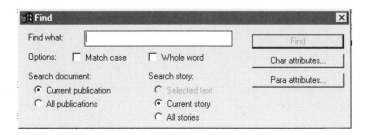

4. Enter the Find What criteria.

   In the Find What box, enter the word or phrase you want to find. Keep in mind that any keystrokes you enter, such as spaces and periods, are also part of the criteria. For example, if you enter key hole, PageMaker will not recognize keyhole as the same word. Once you have entered the word or phrase in the Find What box, the remaining buttons and selection boxes become available to you.

5. Select any options.

   In the Options section of the dialog box, click the appropriate selection boxes for Match Case and Whole Word:

   ■ **Match Case**   Click on this selection box if you want PageMaker to match your criteria exactly, even the use of upper- and lower-case letters. For example, if you entered Book, with this box selected PageMaker would not locate book.

   ■ **Whole Word**   Select this box if you want PageMaker to only locate whole words that match the criteria. For example, if you entered key in the criteria box with this box selected, PageMaker would locate any instances of key, but would not stop on monkey. Without the Whole Word selection, PageMaker would stop on monkey, donkey, and keyhole, and any other words in which the key character configuration appears.

6. Make a Search Document selection.

   You may choose for PageMaker to search the current document for your criteria or any PageMaker document that is currently active. Only one radio button may be selected, of course.

7. Select the Search Story option.

   If you selected Current Publication in the Search Document section of the Find dialog box, the Search Story radio buttons are available to you. (Selected Text is available only if a block of text in the Story Editor is selected.) However, if you selected All Publications, only the All Stories radio button is active. Only one radio button of those active may be selected.

   Here are the Search Story options:

   ■ **Selected Text**   If you selected text before opening the Find dialog box, you may choose only the selected text to be searched. However, even if text is selected, you may still choose either of the following two options instead.

   ■ **Current Story**   This option causes only the story currently in Story Editor to be searched.

   ■ **All Stories**   If you selected Current Publication in the Search Document area, this selection causes all stories in the publication that is currently active to be searched. However, if you selected All Publications, PageMaker will search all stories of all PageMaker publications currently open.

8. Select Character and Paragraph Attribute criteria.

Using the lower two buttons to the right side of the Find dialog box, you can be very specific in your search criteria. Click the Character Attributes button or the Paragraph Attributes button to display the appropriate dialog box:

■ **Character Attributes**  As shown in the following illustration, this dialog box enables you to limit your search to words in which certain character attributes, such as a specific font, font size, or font color, are present. Make your selection of one attribute or several; then click the OK button to close the Find Character Attributes dialog box. The Find utility limits its search to your criteria with those attributes selected.

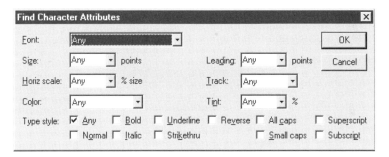

■ **Paragraph Attributes**  The Find Paragraph Attributes dialog box (see the following illustration) works just like Find Character Attributes except with much fewer choices. Select from Paragraph Style, Alignment, and Leading Method and click the OK button to close the dialog box. The Find utility limits its search to the criteria in the Find What box that contains the selected paragraph attributes.

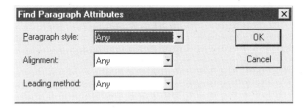

9. Launch the search.

Once you have made all the necessary selections in the Find dialog box, click the Find button. The Find utility searches for the word or phrase you have entered in the Find What box with the attributes you have selected, if any.

The first instance of the word or phrase is located and highlighted, as shown in Figure 9-6. If you were searching for the word to make some adjustment to it or the text around it, you may click in the document and make your changes, leaving the Find dialog box inactive on your screen.

10. Search again.

    If you want to search for other instances of the word or phrase, click on the Find dialog box to reactivate it, if necessary, and click the Find button again. PageMaker immediately goes to the next instance of your Find criteria. You may continue this process until PageMaker has searched the entire story or document.

11. Complete the search.

    When the search is complete, PageMaker displays a Search Complete message (see the following illustration). If the Find utility does not find an instance of the word or phrase, the Search Complete message also appears. Click OK to close the message box.

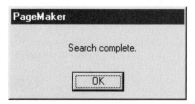

    Close the Find dialog box by clicking on the Exit command button in the upper-right corner of the dialog box.

## Using Find and Change

Closely akin to the Find utility, but even more powerful, is the Find and Change utility. You can use the Find and Change utility to change a word or phrase to another, or to locate that word or phrase and apply attributes to it. Changes to a located word or phrase may be made one at a time, as each instance of the word is located, or you may elect to make the change to all of the instances of the word at one time (a global replacement). Like the Find utility, the Find and Change utility can search one story, all stories in a document, or all stories in all active PageMaker documents.

The Find and Change utility works very similarly to the Find utility:

1. Establish criteria and options.

    Follow Steps 1 through 8 of the Find utility instructions, except, in Step 3, launch the Change dialog box (see the following illustration) by choosing the Utility menu's Change command. As in the Find utility instructions, enter the word or phrase to search for, make selection box and radio button choices, and select character and paragraph attributes for the search criteria.

2. Enter the Change To criteria.

   Enter the word, phrase, or attribute that you want to change to in the Change To box.

   There are many different change configurations possible. See Table 9-1 for examples of some of them.

3. Launch the Search and Change.

   There are two techniques for making changes. In the first, you proceed cautiously, one instance of your target word at a time. In the second technique, you click one button and make all of the changes at once:

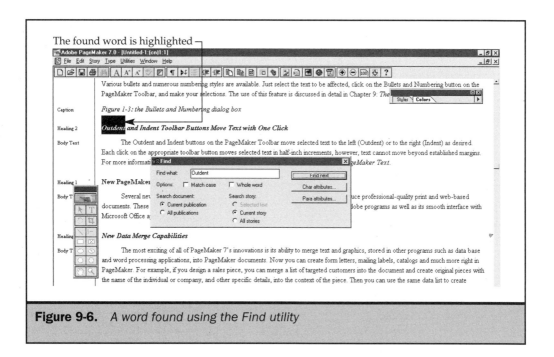

**Figure 9-6.** *A word found using the Find utility*

■ Search for words one at a time by clicking the Find button. When a word is located, click the Change button if you wish to make a change. If you want to make a change and immediately go to the next instance of the word, click the Change & Find button. If you do not want to make a change, click on the Find Next button to go to the next instance of the target word or phrase. Continue until the search is complete. This method is used when not all of the instances of a word require a change or you are unsure.

■ You may also make all of the changes in one action by clicking the Change All button on the right side of the Change dialog box. Called a global change, this is particularly handy when you want to change references of Mr. Brown to Ms. Jones.

Be very cautious when making a global change, however. In this instance, it is a good idea to use the Whole Word option on the Change dialog box. Otherwise, it is easy to make a real mess. For example, if you are making a global change from cat to dog and the Whole Word option is not selected, not only are all cats now dogs, but categories and catalogs are dogegories and dogalogs. That sort of error can be a real nightmare to clean up.

4. Complete the search.

When the search is complete, PageMaker displays a Search Complete message. If the Find utility does not find an instance of the word or phrase, the Search Complete message also appears.

Close the Change dialog box by clicking on the Exit command button in the upper-right corner of the dialog box.

There are any number of change configurations possible using the Find and Change To boxes, along with the Character and Paragraph Attribute dialog boxes. Table 9-1 gives examples of just a few.

## Changing Case

An exceptionally helpful utility is Change Case, which is used when you want to alter the case configuration of selected text. For example, if you typed a heading in all lower case, the Change Case utility can change the entire heading to all upper case or title case in one operation. The Change Case operation can be performed equally well in either Layout view or Story Editor. Here's how:

1. Select the text.

Select the text you want to change.

| From | To | How/Example |
| --- | --- | --- |
| A word or phrase | A different word or phrase | Place the new word or phrase in the Change To box. |
| | | For example, place document in the Find box, and place publication in the Change To box. All instances of document change to publication. |
| A Character attribute | A different character attribute | Click in the Find What box and then select the Character Attributes button. Select the attribute you are searching for. Click in the Change To box. Click on the Character Attributes button and select the attribute you are searching for. |
| | | For example, in the Find box, place the character attribute, such as bold. In Change To, place the character attribute, such as italic. Every instance of bold text changes to italic text. |
| A word with a specific character attribute | A different word with the same character attribute | Place the word to search for in the Find What box and then set the character attribute of that word. Type the replacement word in the Change To box, and set the same attribute for the changed word. |
| | | For example, type Antelope in the Find What box. Set the Find What attribute to bold. Type Deer in the Change To box. Set the attribute to bold. Every instance of **Antelope** changes to **Deer**. |

**Table 9-1.** *Some Change Configurations*

| From | To | How/Example |
|---|---|---|
| A word with a specific character attribute | The same word, but without the attribute | Place the word to search for in the Find What box. Set the character attributes of that word as well. In the Change To box, enter the same word. Open the Character Attributes dialog box and verify that no character attributes are set. |
| | | For example, if you have applied bold to the word Vacation, but wish to change it, enter the word Vacation in the Find What box and set the character attribute to bold. In the Change To box, enter Vacation again, but open the Character Attributes dialog box and deselect the Bold selection, if necessary. Every instance of **Vacation** changes to Vacation. |
| A style | A different style | Click in the Find What box and then click the Paragraph Attributes button. Click the drop-down arrow to the right of the Paragraph Style box. The Style menu appears. Locate the style you want to replace. Click in the Change To box. Click the Paragraph Attributes button and use the drop-down menu to select the style you want to change to. |
| | | For example, in the Find What box, place the paragraph style Heading3. Place the style, bulleted text, in the Change To box. Every instance of the Heading3 style will change to the bulleted text style. |

(For more information on working with PageMaker styles, see the section "Styles" later in this chapter.)

**Table 9-1.** *Some Change Configurations* (Continued)

2. Open the Change Case dialog box.

   Select the Utilities menu's Plug-in command, and then select the Change Case item from the sub-menu. The Change Case dialog box opens, as shown in the following illustration.

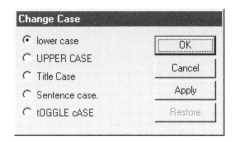

3. Select the case configuration.

   Select the radio button beside one of the following:

   ■ **Lower Case**    All lower-case letters, no capital letters at all.

   ■ **Upper Case**    All capital letters, no lower-case letters at all.

   ■ **Title Case**    The first letter of every word is capitalized. Note that the Change Case utility does not distinguish between articles and other small words that are frequently left in lower case in a title. In the Change Case utility, the first letter of *all* words is capitalized.

   ■ **Sentence Case**    The first letter of the sentence is capitalized. All other letters are lower case.

   ■ **Toggle Case**    If you forget to turn the caps lock off and get a sentence like mR. bROWN AND mS. sMITH WENT TO A PICNIC AT lAKE fRIENDSHIP, the Toggle Case selection can automatically correct the transposition of upper-case and lower-case letters so that you get this: Mr. Brown and Ms. Smith went to a picnic at Lake Friendship.

4. Apply the change.

   Click the Apply button to apply the change to the selected text while leaving the Change Case dialog box open. If the results are not what you want, you may make another selection and apply it.

5. Close the Change Case dialog box.

   When you are satisfied with the change, click the OK button. The dialog box closes.

## Rearranging Text

PageMaker text can be easily arranged using the Clipboard. Although the Clipboard is technically a part of the Windows software, it is still an important tool in working with PageMaker objects. The Clipboard is a memory buffer that captures and holds data for replacement. In other words, text that is placed on the Clipboard may be pasted at a new location.

Here is the Clipboard terminology:

- **Cut**    To cut means to take the text away from its current location and place it on the Clipboard so that it may be put back in a new location.

- **Copy**    To copy is to place the text on the Clipboard while leaving it in its current location. When positioned elsewhere, the text will be in two places.

- **Paste**    The Paste operation copies the text that is on the Clipboard to a new location. The term *copies* is used here because once text is placed on the Clipboard by a cut or copy operation, it remains on the Clipboard and can be pasted as many times as you wish. It will stay on the Clipboard until it is replaced (other text is cut or copied onto the Clipboard) or your computer system is shut down. Because the Clipboard is a part of Windows and not directly a part of PageMaker, you may place text on the Clipboard and paste it in another program; you can even shut PageMaker down and still paste into another location in another program.

The steps to take to rearrange text using the Clipboard are really very simple. Take a look:

1.  Select the text.

    Highlight the text that you want to cut or copy onto the Clipboard.

2.  Place the text on the Clipboard.

    Select the Edit menu's Cut command, if you wish to move the text, or the Copy command, if you want to place a duplicate of it in a new location.

3.  Move to the new location.

    Once the text is on the Clipboard, you may change pages, edit other text, or perform just about any operation except close down your computer. When you are ready to paste the selection, place your insertion point where you want the text to appear.

4.  Paste.

    Select the Edit menu's Paste command. The text is pasted in the new location.

5.  Paste again?

    If you want to paste the text in an additional location, move there and paste again. You may repeat this as often as you wish.

You may notice on the Edit menu that there are two other Paste commands in addition to Paste. Paste Special is a command that provides a connection between original and pasted objects and is discussed in Chapter 20. Paste Multiple is a nifty way of pasting an object several times in one operation and is discussed in Chapter 10.

# Advanced Character Formatting

Text formatting can involve a lot more than just changing font and font size or adding text effects such as bold, italic, and underline. In this section I discuss advanced techniques for formatting characters and for formatting their relationships to one another.

## Horizontal Scale

Although many of today's text management techniques have their origins in the days of hot type, when type was set by hand one character at a time, the ability to adjust horizontal scale became available only with the origination of type-setting computers. Horizontal scale is the width of individual letters. In PageMaker, it is possible, quite easy actually, to change the width of letters. For example, a word like Look! can be changed to appear Look! Long, complicated titles such as Metropolitan Volunteer Council on Community Services and Health and Welfare Actions and Activities can be adjusted to take up less room like this: Metropolitan Volunteer Council on Community Services and Health and Welfare Actions and Activities. Both of those examples were accomplished not by changing the font or font size of the text, but by changing the horizontal scale, the width, of the characters.

Adjusting Horizontal Scale can be done by using the Control Palette or by changing the settings in the Character Specifications dialog box. In both cases, the process is much the same.

To use either technique, follow these steps:

1. Select the text.

   Before horizontal scale can be applied to text, it must be selected. Select only those characters to which you want to apply a horizontal scale adjustment.

2. Show the Control Palette or open the Character Specifications dialog box.

   Open the Character Specifications dialog box by selecting the Type menu's Character command.

   Or if you want to use the Control Palette, display it, if necessary, by clicking the Window menu's Show Control Palette command. The Control Palette appears on your screen.

3. Open the Horizontal Scale menu.

   Click the drop-down arrow to the right of the Horizontal Scale box in either the Character Specifications dialog box or the Control Palette. The following illustration shows the Horizontal Scale menu open in the Control Palette.

PAGEMAKER ESSENTIALS

lla facilisis at vero | et accumsan et

4. Select the scale settings you want.

From the menu, select the Horizontal Scale setting you want to apply to the selected text. Normal, of course, produces text that is normal width, with no horizontal scale applied. Percentages of 90, 80, and 70 reduce the text width, while percentages of 110, 120, and 130 increase the width of your selected text. If you want a percentage that is not shown, just double-click in the box to highlight the existing setting, if necessary, and enter the percentage you want. You may choose any percentage from a range of 5 to 250.

5. Apply the scale adjustment.

If you are making the adjustment using the Character Specifications dialog box, click the OK button. The dialog box closes and the adjustment is applied.

If you are using the Control Palette, pressing the ENTER key applies the adjustment.

Once you are accustomed to using Horizontal Scale, you will find many uses for it. I sometimes adjust scale slightly to fit over-long text into a set space, but I also use it for effect, such as increasing the width of title text on the front page of a booklet. This is one of the most fun and effective techniques in PageMaker.

## Kerning

Kerning, the adjustment of the space between pairs of letters, is one of the techniques that stems from the early days of typesetting. Although early typesetters kerned by hand and today's graphic designers use sophisticated computer programs such as PageMaker, kerning is still an important part of producing a publication that looks highly professional.

The spacing of letters in text produced by PageMaker or any other program is based on technical spacing rather than visual spacing. For example, if, in normal word processing, you place the upper-case letters T and A side by side, the letter A begins at a proscribed distance from the letter T. That is, the left-most point of the letter A is a set distance from the farthest point on the right side of the letter T. The font sets this distance automatically between all letters. But because of the configuration of these letters, visually there seems to be extra space between them. Kerning takes the space away so that technically the letter A begins just a bit before the letter T ends, creating a more visually pleasant configuration. See the following illustration.

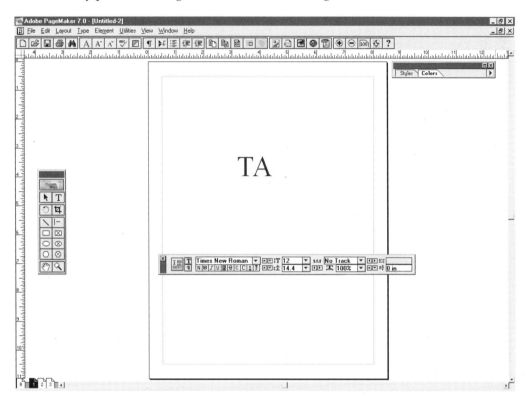

Best used in headlines and larger-type sizes, kerning is an important part of producing a professional-looking document. PageMaker offers several ways of kerning.

**Automatic Kerning**   PageMaker can be set to automatically kern certain character pairs above four points in size. In most fonts, the following pairs are automatically kerned when the automatic kerning is on: LA, P., To, Tr, Ta, Tu, Te, Ty, TA, Wa, WA, We, we, Wo, Ya, Yo, and yo. When you first install and run PageMaker, automatic kerning is on by default.

Kerning can be turned on or off by taking the following steps:

1. Select the text.

    Whether you want to turn kerning off or on, the text must be highlighted in order for your setting to take effect. You can apply automatic kerning to one paragraph or several, but it cannot be applied to some characters in a paragraph and not to others. Using the Text tool, select the paragraph or paragraphs to which you want to apply or remove the automatic pair kerning.

2. Open the Paragraph Spacing Attributes dialog box.

   From the Type menu, select the Paragraph command. The Paragraph Specifications dialog box opens, as shown in the following illustration.

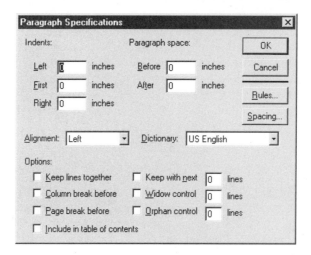

   Click the Spacing button. The Spacing Attributes dialog box opens (see the following illustration).

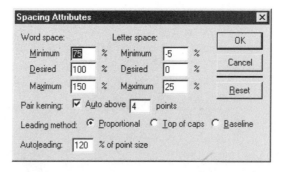

3. Turn automatic kerning on or off.

   If the check box beside Pair Kerning is selected, automatic kerning is in effect. If the box is empty, automatic pair kerning is off. Select or deselect the check box as you wish.

4. Set the kerning activation point.

   Kerning is only perceptible above a certain size, depending upon the configuration of the font. By default, the automatic kerning is in effect only above four points. That pretty much means all the time. Although I have set the font size to four points on occasion, type that size or below is so small that by its very nature it is rarely used.

If you are turning automatic kerning on, enter the font size above which you want kerning to be applied.

5. Close the Spacing Attributes dialog box.

Click on the OK button to close the Spacing Attributes dialog box and return to the Paragraph Specifications dialog box.

6. Close the Paragraph Specifications dialog box.

Click on the OK button to close the Paragraph Specifications dialog box. The kerning selection you have chosen is applied.

**Expert Kerning**   Another automated kerning feature of PageMaker is Expert Kerning. Expert Kerning looks at every character pair in selected text and kerns it appropriately in keeping with the kerning strength you have selected. It is a useful tool, but requires PostScript Level 1 fonts. As Window-based computers use TrueType fonts predominantly, it is possible that Expert Kerning may not work on your system unless you are using a PostScript printer; then it may be available to you after all. (Macintosh systems will be more likely to utilize a large number of PostScript Level 1 fonts.)

If you have PostScript Level 1 fonts on your system, you may take the following steps to apply Expert Kerning to that text:

1. Select the text.

Using the Text tool, select the text to which you want to apply Expert Kerning.

2. Open the Expert Kerning dialog box.

Select the Type menu's Expert Kerning command. The Expert Kerning dialog box opens, as shown in the following illustration.

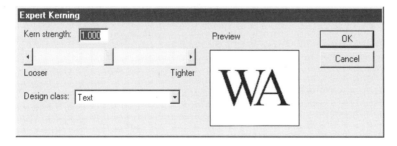

3. Adjust the kern strength.

You may use the slide to establish a kern strength between 0.000 and 2.000 (the higher the value, the tighter the spacing) or you may type the desired value into the Kern Strength box. The preview to the right of the slide shows you the effect your setting will have on text.

4. Select the design class.

If you know the source of the original master design of the font you are kerning, select it from the drop-down menu to the right of the Design Class box. Design class essentially means the purpose for which the font was designed.

Text fonts are designed for paragraphs, poster fonts are designed for larger, more prominent type, and display fonts are intended for type that is used as art. If you select Other, a Design Class Other dialog box appears, requiring you to enter the point size of the original font. If you do not know the design class, leave the setting at the default: Text. If you select Other, but do not know the point size, it is a good idea to enter the size of the type you have selected.

5. Close the Expert Kerning dialog box.

Click the OK button. The Expert Kerning dialog box closes and the kerning is applied to the selected text.

It is a good idea to turn off automatic kerning before performing Expert Kerning on selected text.

**Manual Kerning**    Manual kerning offers the most control in kerning specific text. Manual kerning can be applied to selected text by entering a value in the Kerning segment of the Control Palette or by using the Control Palette's nudge buttons (see the following illustration).

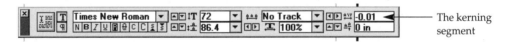

The kerning segment

Each click to the left nudge button decreases the space between the letters of the selected text by 0.01 percent of an em space (an em space is a space equal to the width of the lowercase letter m in the same size and font). Clicking the right nudge button increases the space by the same increment. The Kerning box to the right of the nudge buttons shows the kern settings.

If you know the amount of kerning you would like to apply, you may enter the setting directly into the Kerning box. Highlight the existing setting and type in the new setting. Clicking on the Apply button on the Control Palette or pressing the ENTER key applies the kerning selection.

To remove manual kerning from selected text, type 0 in the Kern box and click the Apply button (the large, square button on the far right side of the Control Palette) or press the ENTER key.

## Tracking

Tracking is very similar to kerning, but where kerning is used primarily with pairs of letters and small amounts of type, tracking applies globally to large amounts of text. Tracking changes the denseness of documents with a lot of text. Loosening the tracking allows more air into your text and can make a casual piece more reader-friendly. Tightening the tracking provides denser type and is more appropriate for formal or conservative documents.

Be cautious in your use of tracking, however. Very loosely tracked text can look amateurish and text that is tracked too tightly may be difficult to read and therefore repellent to readers. It is usually not a good idea to use tight tracking to try to fit an overlong piece into a set space. Cut some of the text out of the document instead, if possible.

PageMaker provides five built-in tracks that increase or decrease the spacing of type characters. As with many text management features, you can access the Tracking controls from the Character Specifications dialog box or on the Control Palette. Here are the steps for setting tracking using either tool:

1. Select the text.

   Before tracking can be established for a block of text, the text must be selected. Use the Text tool to highlight the text to which you want to apply tracking. Tracking can be applied to a few characters or an entire story.

2. Open the Tracking menu.

   In either dialog box, click the drop-down arrow to the right of the Tracking box. The Tracking menu is displayed. See Figures 9-7 and 9-8 to see the Tracking menu displayed in the Character Specifications dialog box and in the Control Palette.

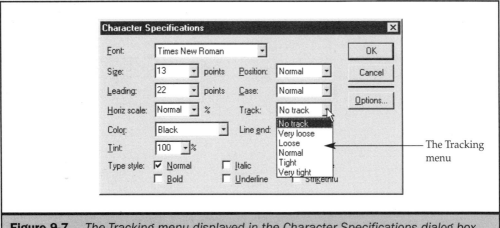

**Figure 9-7.** *The Tracking menu displayed in the Character Specifications dialog box*

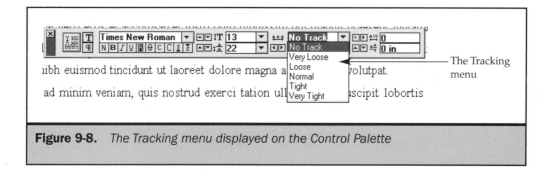

**Figure 9-8.**    *The Tracking menu displayed on the Control Palette*

3. Select the track.

   By default, the track is set to normal. However, there are five additional tracks from which you may choose: No Track, Loose, Very Loose, Tight, and Very Tight. It is a good idea to try out the various tracks until you have found the one you want.

4. Apply the track setting.

   Click the OK button to close the Character Specifications dialog box and apply the track setting to the selected text. On the Control Palette, click the Apply button.

## Using the Drop Cap Utility

The Drop Cap utility is a fun tool with which you can add a little pizzazz to a text box or attract attention to your text. A drop cap is an oversized capital letter placed as the first letter of a document (see Figure 9-9).

A drop cap can be used with a formal/conservative layout as well as in a more casual document.

Here's how:

1. Identify the paragraph in which you want to place a drop cap.

   The paragraph in which you want to enlarge and drop the first letter does not need to be selected. However, the insertion point does need to be somewhere within the paragraph. Using the Text tool, click in the target paragraph.

2. Open the Drop Cap utility.

   Click on the Utilities menu's Plug-ins command. From the subsequent sub-menu, select Drop Cap. The Drop Cap utility dialog box opens.

3. Enter the number of lines to drop.

   The Size __ Lines box enables you to select the number of lines that the enlarged capital will drop into your paragraph. Keep in mind the total lines in

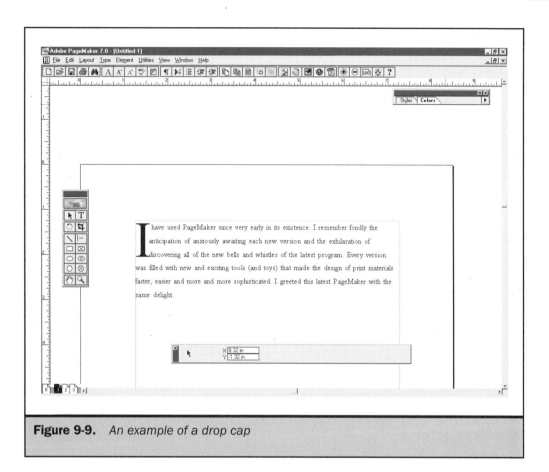

**Figure 9-9.**  *An example of a drop cap*

your paragraph as well as the impact you want the drop cap to make. You may select any number from 1 to 9, but in reality a 1-line drop cap doesn't drop at all and is not distinguishable from the paragraph with no drop cap applied. If you have a five-line paragraph, a seven-line drop cap would not be an effective choice.

Enter the number of lines in the Size __ Lines box.

4. Apply the setting.

If you want to create a drop cap in the previous or next paragraphs, click the Apply button. This applies the setting without closing the Drop Cap dialog box. You may then use the Prev and Next buttons to go to other paragraphs.

However, if you are not going to create drop caps in additional paragraphs, instead of clicking the Apply button, you may click OK and the setting will be applied.

5. Go to the next or previous paragraph.

The Drop Cap utility provides buttons that will take you to the previous paragraph or the next one so that you can apply drop caps there as well. Just click on the appropriate button and PageMaker moves you to that location.

You cannot edit an existing drop cap setting. You must remove the drop cap using the Remove button and create the drop cap anew.

# Lines and Line Spacing

With typewriters and early word processors, line spacing was simple. The line on which the text was placed was set. You had a limited choice of line spacing options; you selected single, space-and-a-half, or double (sometimes triple was an option as well) and your text from that point on was adjusted to the new setting.

Because PageMaker is a professional type-setting program, among other things, it couples the techniques from days in which hot type was set one character at a time by hand with modern type-setting technology. The way that PageMaker looks at line spacing and the baseline of text is different from all but the most progressive word processing programs.

## Leading

In PageMaker, what would be called line spacing in a word processing program is a bit more involved. PageMaker's line spacing technology stems from hot type techniques where spaces between lines were created by thin bars of lead. That is why the process of setting the spaces between lines in PageMaker is called leading, rather than line spacing. Leading is the term used in type setting and graphic design environments.

What's the big deal? Why does it matter what you call it? Well, the process of setting leading criteria is different from that used in word processing. And the measurement is different as well. Consider these facts about leading.

In American culture, leading is traditionally measured in points, not as the space between the lines of type, but from the top of the highest possible ascender on one line of type to the top of the highest possible ascender in the next line of type. (Ascenders are letters that come up to or slightly above the level of an upper-case letter. The lower-case letters b, d, f, h, k, l, and t are frequently ascenders, but may differ from one font to another.) Leading is figured as a percentage of the distance between the top of one line and the next to the size of the type face (in other words, the size of the type face divided by the distance from a point on one line to the same point on another: 10 point type divided by 12 point leading is 120 percent). Standard leading in our culture is usually 120 percent.

For example, if text is set in 12-point type and leading is set at 120 percent, then the leading, the distance from the top of one line of type to the next, is 14.4 points. See Figure 9-10 for a diagram of how leading is measured.

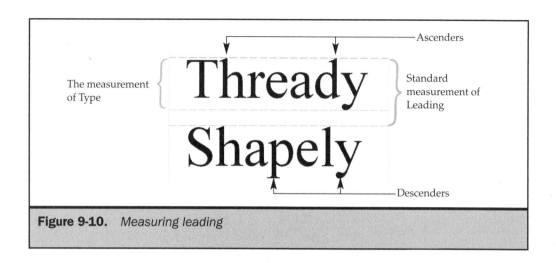

**Figure 9-10.**  *Measuring leading*

All this sounds terribly complicated, and if you were hand-setting type, it could be, but PageMaker takes care of most of this automatically. Unless you want to adjust the settings, you don't have to worry about figuring leading. By default, PageMaker sets the leading size that is appropriate to the size of type you are using at 120 percent.

Take a look at the Control Palette and the Type Size and Leading boxes, as shown in the following illustration. The Type Size box shows a type size of 72 points and Leading of 86.4 points.

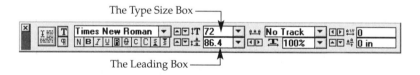

**Changing Leading**    You can change leading if you want to add more space between lines or, if you want, to slightly decrease the space.

Increasing leading can provide air to your document, make it inviting. Too much leading, however, makes reading text blocks difficult, so use prudence. Decreasing the leading is certainly possible, but not recommended. Leading of less than 120 percent looks crowded to most readers and can hurt readership.

Here is how to change a story's leading in either the Character Specifications dialog box or the Control Palette:

1.  Select the text.

    As in most formatting operations, text must be selected before a new leading can be applied. Use the Text tool to highlight the target text.

2. Open the Character Specifications dialog box or display the Control Palette.

   Open the Character Specifications dialog box by clicking on the Type menu's Character command. The dialog box opens.

   If you wish to use the Control Palette to set leading and it is not open, click the Window menu's Show Control Palette command. The Control Palette appears.

3. Open the leading menu.

   In either the Character Specifications dialog box or the Control Palette, click on the drop-down arrow to the right of the Leading box. The menu appears. Figure 9-11 shows the menu in the Character Specifications dialog box and Figure 9-12 shows the menu in the Control Palette.

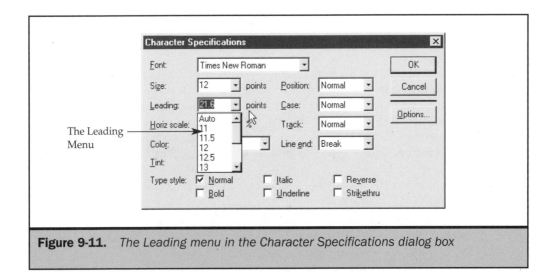

**Figure 9-11.** *The Leading menu in the Character Specifications dialog box*

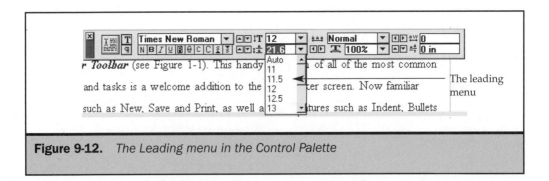

**Figure 9-12.** *The Leading menu in the Control Palette*

4.  Select the leading size.

    Using the Leading menu, select the leading size you want for your text. If the size you want is not on the menu, type the setting into the Leading box.

5.  Apply the leading.

    In the Character Specifications dialog box, click the OK button to close the dialog box and apply the leading settings. In the Control Palette, click the Apply button or press the ENTER key. The Control Palette remains open and the new leading settings are applied to the selected text.

**Changing Leading Measurement Styles**    The method of measuring leading that I have described previously is a generally accepted method. However, PageMaker provides you with two other options of measuring leading, if you should want to change:

- **Proportionate**    This leading style is measured by placing the leading equidistant above and below the type (see Figure 9-13).

- **Baseline**    Baseline style is measured from the baseline of one line to the baseline of the next (see Figure 9-14). The baseline is the line that the text rests on, except for descenders that fall below the line.

Here is how to change the leading measurement style:

1.  Open the Paragraph Specifications dialog box.

    Select the Type menu's Paragraph command. The Paragraph Specifications dialog box opens.

**Figure 9-13.**    *An example of the proportionate style of measuring leading*

Measuring Type

# Thready

The Baseline style of measuring leading

# Shapely

**Figure 9-14.**    *An example of the baseline style of measuring leading*

2.  Open the Spacing Attributes dialog box.

    On the Paragraph Specifications dialog box, click the Spacing button. The Spacing Attributes dialog box opens.

3.  Select a leading measurement style.

    In the Leading Method section of the dialog box, select the style of measurement that you want. The Top of Caps selection is the standard style.

4.  Close the Spacing Attributes dialog box.

    Click the OK button. The Spacing Attributes box closes.

5.  Close the Paragraph Specifications dialog box and apply the measurement style.

    Click the OK button. The Paragraph Specifications dialog box closes and the leading measurement style is applied.

**Changing Automatic Leading Settings**    I mentioned above that in American culture leading is usually 120 percent and that, by default, PageMaker automatically sets leading to that percentage. Although 120 percent is pretty standard, you may want to change the percentage that is used for automatic leading. Here's how:

1.  Open the Paragraph Specifications dialog box.

    Select the Type menu's Paragraph command. The Paragraph Specifications dialog box opens.

2.  Open the Spacing Attributes dialog box.

    Click on the Spacing button. The Spacing Attributes dialog box opens, as shown in the following illustration.

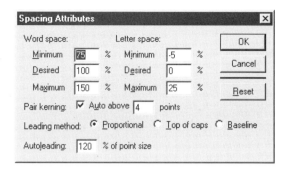

3. Enter an AutoLeading percentage.

   In the AutoLeading box, enter the percentage of type size that you want to use as the setting for automatic leading. For best results, enter a percentage that is larger than 120 percent. Leading that is smaller than 120 percent looks crowded and may even cause the lines of text to overlap.

4. Close the Spacing Attributes dialog box.

   Click OK on the Spacing Attributes dialog box; it closes.

5. Close the Paragraph Specifications dialog box.

   Click the OK button and the Paragraph dialog box closes. The settings are established.

## Baseline Shifts

The baseline of text is the imaginary line on which the majority of text characters rest. The only characters that do not rest on the baseline are the descenders that, by their configuration, have tails that project below the line. Typical descenders are g, j, p, q, and y; however, that may differ according to the design of the individual font.

   Although most of the time all text rests on the same baseline, there may be times when you wish to adjust the baseline of a word or phrase for emphasis.

   For example, you might want to add visual impact to a description by creating the baseline shift in these sentences.

■ The clouds seemed to float just above the surface of the lake.

■ The diver went down, down, down to the bottom of the ocean.

Take these steps to raise or lower the baseline:

1. Select the text.

   Before a text's baseline can be shifted, the text must be selected. Using the Text tool, highlight the text you want to adjust.

2. Display the Control Palette.

   If the Control Palette is not showing, click on the Window menu's Show Control Palette command. The Control Palette appears in the PageMaker window.

3. Create the baseline shift.

   Using the buttons to the left of the Baseline box (see Figure 9-15), click to change the baseline incrementally. The down-pointing button, of course, shifts the baseline below its original point; the up-pointing button moves the baseline above its original point.

   If you know the settings that you want, you may type them into the Baseline box.

# Paragraph Settings

Paragraph settings, such as those discussed in this section, affect paragraphs rather than characters. These settings are very useful in creating long text documents as they eliminate the necessity of some keystrokes that would occur over and over. All of the

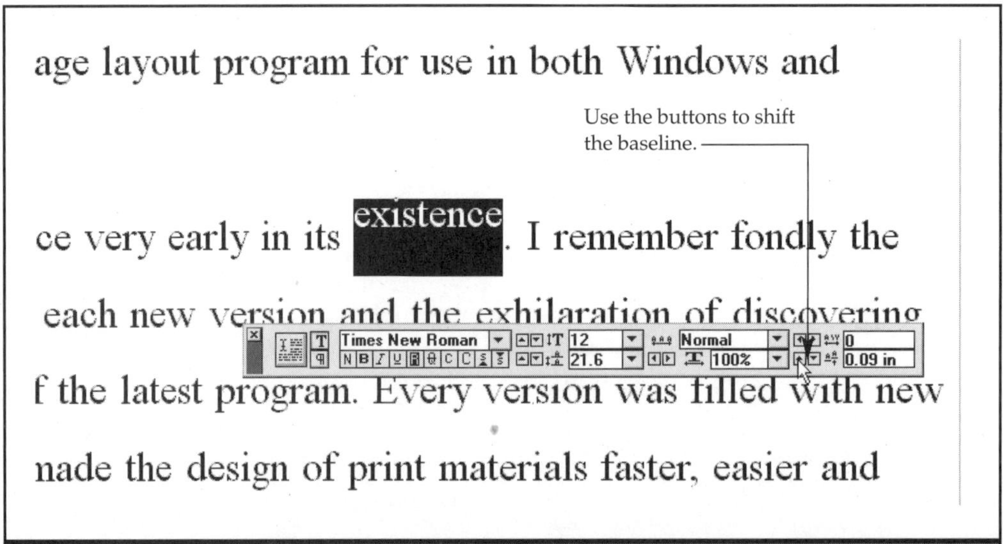

**Figure 9-15.**   *Using the Control Palette to adjust the text baseline*

settings in this section are made on the Paragraph Specifications dialog box, as shown in the following illustration.

## Indents

An indent moves text away from a margin in one of several configurations. There is more than one way to set a paragraph indent in PageMaker. Two of the techniques involve the Indents and Tabs dialog box or the Control Palette and are discussed later in the "Indents and Tabs" section. However, the method discussed here utilizes the Paragraph dialog box. An indent set in the Paragraph dialog box will apply only to the paragraph or paragraphs that are selected or in which the insertion point rests. However, any paragraph subsequently created from a paragraph to which an indent has been applied will have the same indent properties.

In the Paragraph dialog box, indent specifications are indicated in decimal equivalents of an inch. The following list explains the three indent settings from which you may choose:

- **Left**   This indent type moves the entire paragraph to the right by the decimal equivalent of an inch that you specify.

- **First**   A First indent moves only the first line in a paragraph by moving the first character of the paragraph to the right to the extent of the decimal equivalent of an inch that you specify. If a Left indent is set, a First indent setting is applied in addition.

- **Right**   The Right indent selection moves the paragraph's right margin to the left by the decimal equivalent of an inch that you specify.

Here is how to set the indent specifications:

1.  Place the insertion point.

    Place the insertion point in the target paragraph. If you want to affect more than one paragraph, select the paragraphs.

2.  Open the Paragraph Specifications dialog box.

    Click on the Type menu's Paragraph command. The Paragraph Specifications dialog box opens.

3.  Enter the settings.

    Any one of the indents may be selected or all of the indents may be set at the same time.

4.  Apply the settings.

    Click the OK button on the Paragraph Specifications dialog box. The dialog box closes and the settings are applied.

## Space Before and After

This is the niftiest paragraph setting of all. When writing numerous paragraphs, I sometimes want the paragraphs set with extra line space in between. Of course, putting an extra, empty paragraph in between each paragraph that has content can do this. But if you use automatic bullets or numbering, the extra paragraphs mess up the sequence and sometimes a full line space is too much, or maybe too little.

In the Paragraph Specifications dialog box, you may specify that extra space be applied before or after a paragraph, or both. The target paragraph or paragraphs must be selected or the insertion point placed. Any paragraph created as a result of pressing the ENTER key while at the end of an affected paragraph will also have the extra space automatically. It works great, eliminates all those extra key strokes, and is fully adjustable.

The following steps lead you through the process of setting space before and after:

1.  Place the insertion point.

    Place the insertion point in the target paragraph. If you want to affect more than one paragraph, select the paragraphs.

2.  Open the Paragraph Specifications dialog box.

    Click on the Type menu's Paragraph command. The Paragraph Specifications dialog box opens.

3.  Enter the Paragraph Space settings.

    In either the Before or After box, enter the amount of space you want using decimal equivalents of an inch.

4. Apply the settings.

   Click the OK button on the Paragraph Specifications dialog box. The box closes and the Space Before or After settings are applied.

Setting before and after spacing is particularly useful with headings.

## Rules

This paragraph setting does not pertain to regulations, but to lines, also called rules, which can be automatically placed before or after a paragraph. Not only can you insert these lines before or after, but you can determine the style, color, tint, indents, and distance above or below the baseline of the first or last lines of text in the paragraph. See Figure 9-16 for an example of rules applied to the top and bottom of a paragraph.

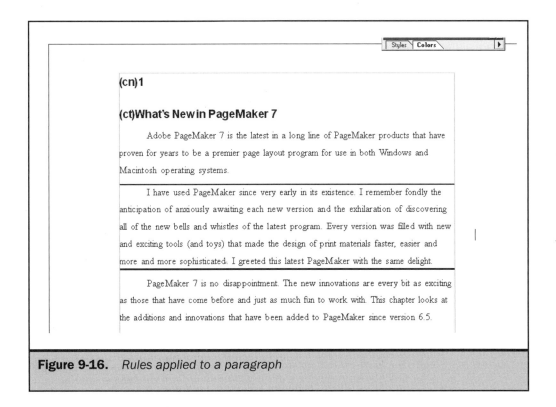

**Figure 9-16.** *Rules applied to a paragraph*

Here is how you apply a rule to the top or bottom of a paragraph, or both:

1. Select the paragraph or paragraphs to be affected.

   You may place the insertion point in a single paragraph to which you want to automatically add a rule or you may select several paragraphs. Keep in mind that if several paragraphs are selected, each of the paragraphs will have the rule applied.

2. Open the Paragraph Specifications dialog box.

   Click the Type menu's Paragraph command. The Paragraph Specifications dialog box opens.

3. Open the Paragraph Rules dialog box.

   Click the Rules button on the Paragraph Specifications dialog box. The Paragraph Rules dialog box opens, as shown in the following illustration.

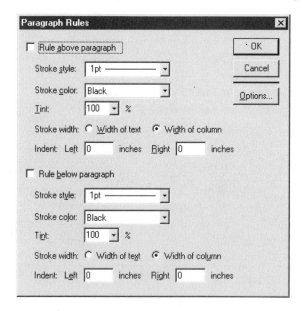

4. Select Above or Below.

   The dialog box is divided into two nearly identical sections. The top section governs a rule above the paragraph; the bottom section controls the settings for a rule below the paragraph. Click in the selection box of the rule you want to activate. Both Above and Below may be selected.

5. Select a stroke style.

   In the section that you have selected, click the drop-down arrow to the right of the Stroke Style box and choose the style you want. Only the select stroke styles are available.

6. Select a stroke color and tint.

   Using the drop-down arrow to the right of the Stroke Color box, select a color for the stroke from those listed. Repeat for the Tint box to determine the percentage of solid color to apply to the line.

7. Select the stroke width.

   Two choices are offered for the width of the rule. You may have the stroke just above text or across the entire column. Make your selection by clicking the appropriate radio button.

8. Select Rule Indent.

   You may want the rule to be indented on one or both sides and not quite go to the column edge. To set an indent for the rule, enter a setting in decimal equivalents of an inch into the left and/or right Indent boxes.

9. Set Options.

   If you want to control the distance the rule or rules occur above the first line of text or below the last, click the Options button on the Paragraph Rules dialog box. The Paragraph Rule Options dialog box opens (see the following illustration).

   Enter settings in decimal equivalents of an inch for the distance from the baseline of the top line of text and from the baseline of the bottom line of text. Note that the distance above the paragraph is measured from the baseline, so make allowances for the height of the line of type when you enter the Top setting.

   Click Align to Grid to assure that the baselines of columns in pages with multiple columns are even, thus aligning the rules. The grid size entry is the leading of the paragraph text.

10. Apply the settings.

    If the Paragraph Rule Options dialog box is open, click its OK button to close it. Click the OK button in the Paragraph Rules dialog box, and again on the Paragraph Specifications dialog box to close those boxes and apply the settings.

## Paragraph Options

The Options section of the Paragraph Specifications dialog box provides convenient settings that make text more readable and text management a bit easier for you.

The following list defines the seven options. Target paragraphs must be selected before the options can be applied:

- **Keep Lines Together**    If you want the lines of a paragraph to be kept together on the same page, click this selection.

- **Column Break Before**    This option causes text to be moved to the next column prior to the selected paragraph.

- **Page Break Before**    If you always want a page break to occur immediately before a selected paragraph, click this selection.

- **Include in Table of Contents**    This tags a heading or other paragraph to be included in a table of contents.

- **Keep with Next**    This keeps the selected text always on the same page as the following number of lines indicated in the Lines box.

- **Widow Control**    Widow is a term for a single line of text that falls at the bottom of a column or page. It is considered poor form to leave a widow at the bottom of a page. The Widow Control selection moves the widow to the next page. You can set the number of lines to be moved by entering a number in the Lines box.

- **Orphan Control**    An orphan is much like a widow, but it stands alone at the top of a page or column. Selecting the Orphan Control option moves the line before the orphan onto the same page. Enter the number of lines that you want moved to the orphan's page in the Lines box.

Make an options selection by clicking in the appropriate selection box. Then click the OK button in the Paragraph Specifications dialog box. The box closes and the settings are applied.

# Word Spacing and Hyphenation

The spacing of words on a line directly affects the impact that text has on the aesthetic appearance of your finished document. Word and letter spacing as well as hyphenation are part of the mechanism that controls the way words on a line appear. PageMaker gives you extensive control over these utilities.

## Word and Letter Spacing

Within the parameters of font design, alignment, word and letter spacing, and hyphenation settings, PageMaker automatically places words on a line to fill the line to its fullest capacity.

If the paragraph alignment is left aligned, PageMaker places as many words as it can on the line, leaving space at the end of the line as necessary.

If the text is justified, then PageMaker tries the following options to provide the best fit of the text:

- PageMaker compresses the text to fit the last whole word onto the page by reducing the space between words.

- If compressing the text does not work, PageMaker expands word spacing to push the word down to the next line.

- If word space expands beyond an acceptable limit, PageMaker looks for hyphenation options to fit the text to the space.

- If the first three options do not work, PageMaker adjusts letter spacing just as it did the word spacing.

- If none of these options work, PageMaker expands the word beyond maximum parameters as much as it needs to.

The space between words, created when you press the SPACEBAR, is called the *spaceband* and is determined by the design of the font in which you are working. By default, PageMaker uses the exact same *spaceband* as prescribed by the font. However, you can change the desired spacing as well as the maximum and minimum spacing allowed to any percentage between 0 and 500 percent.

Similarly, the amount of space that surrounds each character in a font, called the *side-bearing*, is determined by the designer. Of course, you can change spacing by changing the width of the character using Horizontal Scale or by kerning or tracking. However, you can also change the desired side-bearing as well as the maximum and minimum percentage of departure from the standard.

To adjust the word or letter spacing, follow these steps:

1. Select the paragraph or paragraphs to be affected.

   If you want to change the settings for one paragraph, you need only place the insertion point within the text.

   If you want to affect several paragraphs, use the Text tool to select them.

2. Open the Paragraph Specifications dialog box.

   Click the Type menu's Paragraph command. The Paragraph Specifications dialog box opens.

3. Open the Spacing Attributes dialog box.

   Click the Spacing button on the Paragraph Specifications dialog box. The Spacing Attributes dialog box opens.

4. Enter settings.

In the Word Space and Letter Space columns, enter the values for each of the three categories. In Word Space, a Desired setting of 100 percent indicates a value equal to the spacing created by the font designer. In Letter Space, the Desired setting of 0 percent represents the spacing of the original font design.

The maximum and minimum settings prescribe the allowable percentage of departure from the standard.

Changing the Desired setting changes the spacing for both unjustified and justified text. The Maximum and Minimum settings are the allowable settings that govern the five options (mentioned previously in this section) that PageMaker tries in order to establish the best fit for words in a line of text.

## Hyphenation

PageMaker offers a hyphenation utility that places an automatic hyphen wherever it needs to divide a word at the end of a line for a line wrap. The automatic hyphen is unlike the hyphen that you place by pressing the hyphen key on your keyboard. A regular hyphen is always a part of the text, just like any other typed character. However, if edits cause the hyphenated word to move away from the end of a line, an automatic hyphen disappears, where a regular hyphen does not.

By default, the hyphenation utility is on. It can, however, be turned off at any time you do not want PageMaker to automatically hyphenate your text. Why would you want to disable automatic hyphenation? Some schools of thought in graphic design disparage the use of hyphens in text. Some designers feel that only limited use of hyphens is appropriate. Others believe that, particularly in justified text, hyphenation makes for better spacing of the text. The choice is yours. My personal practice is to make decisions on hyphenation on a case-by-case basis.

**Turning Hyphenation On or Off, or Hyphenation Criteria**   You can turn PageMaker's hyphenation utility on or off, change the methods that PageMaker uses to determine where hyphenation should occur, or specify how far hyphenation should occur from the right edge of a text box. All of these options are available through the Hyphenation dialog box. Here's how to use it:

1. Select the paragraphs to be affected.

If you want to affect only one paragraph with the Hyphenation settings, use the Text tool to place the insertion point anywhere within the paragraph. However, if you want several paragraphs to be affected, select those paragraphs.

2. Open the Hyphenation dialog box.

Select the Type menu's Hyphenation command. The Hyphenation dialog box opens (see the following illustration).

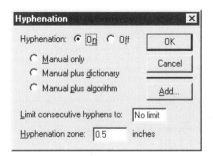

3. Select On or Off.

   By default, PageMaker's hyphenation utility is turned on from the time you install and launch the program. Turn it off by selecting the Off radio button. Reactivate it by clicking On. When the utility is turned off, PageMaker will not automatically hyphenate words, but will break hyphenated words at the hyphen when necessary.

4. Select one of three options.

   To determine how PageMaker hyphenates words, select from the following options:

   ■ **Manual Only**   This option breaks only those words that contain a discretionary hyphen. (See the following section, "Changing the Location of a Hyphen in One Instance of a Word.")

   ■ **Manual Plus Dictionary**   This option breaks those words containing a discretionary hyphen as well as words with breaks indicated in the dictionary.

   ■ **Manual Plus Algorithm**   This option uses the criteria of both the previous options; plus, it uses a formula that determines the breaking points of words not found in the PageMaker dictionary or the User dictionary.

5. Limit consecutive hyphens.

   Most manuscript standards prohibit the use of consecutive hyphens because hyphens at the end of consecutive rows make it easy for the eye to lose its place when moving to the start of the next line. In the Limit Consecutive Hyphens To box, enter the number of consecutive hyphens that is acceptable to you. If you do not want to limit the number, leave the default: No Limit.

6. Set the hyphenation zone.

   The hyphenation zone is measured from the right edge of the text box and determines the amount of space in which hyphenation can occur at the end of each line of unjustified text. Set the width of this zone by entering a value in decimal equivalents of an inch in the Hyphenation Zone box. By default, the zone is set to 0.5 inches.

7.  Apply the settings.

    Click the OK button in the Hyphenation dialog box. The box closes and the
    settings are applied. Turning hyphenation on or off affects an entire paragraph.
    It can, of course, affect more than one paragraph if several paragraphs are
    selected. But in addition to turning off hyphenation, there are three techniques
    that enable you to affect the hyphenation of single words.

**Changing the Location of a Hyphen in One Instance of a Word**   If you want to change
the placement of a hyphen in only one instance of a word, click in the word where you
want to place the hyphen. Then press CTRL-SHIFT-- (hyphen). The hyphen moves to the
new location. This enters a discretionary hyphen.

**Preventing Hyphenation of a Single Word**   If you want to inhibit hyphenation in a
single instance of a word, place the insertion point in front of the first letter of the
word. Press CTRL-SHIFT-- (hyphen). The word will not hyphenate.

**Changing the Hyphenation or Preventing Hyphenation in Every Instance of a Word**
Take these steps if you want to establish the hyphenation breaks for every instance of a
word, or if you never want the word to be hyphenated:

1.  Select a word.

    Using the Text tool, select the word to be affected.

2.  Open the Hyphenation dialog box.

    Click the Type menu's Hyphenation command. The Hyphenation dialog box
    opens.

3.  Open the Add Word to User Dictionary dialog box.

    Click on the Add button in the Hyphenation dialog box. The Add Word to User
    Dictionary dialog box opens, as shown in the following illustration. The word
    appears in the Word box with hyphenation breaks suggested by PageMaker.

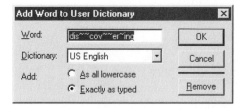

4.  Alter the hyphenation breaks.

    Use one tilde (~) to indicate your preferred breaking point, two tildes (~ ~) to
    indicate a second choice or choices, and three tildes (~ ~ ~) to indicate a least-
    desired, but acceptable, break.

If you want the word to never be hyphenated, type one tilde (~) before the first letter of the word.

# Indents and Tabs

Indents and tabs are essential positioning tools for text. Tabs and indents play a strategic part in the layout and design of text in a document. Whether you are composing a standard business letter or the layout of a book, an understanding of indents and tabs makes the job easier, and more professional in appearance.

Indents govern the placement of text relative to the margins, while tabs set positions for text on a line. Both tabs and indents can be set in the Indents/Tabs dialog box, which is essentially a ruler. Indents can also be set using the Paragraph Specifications dialog box or the Control Palette.

There are four kinds of indents that you can set in PageMaker. PageMaker's indent types are consistent with standard manuscript styles:

- **Full Indent (or Left Indent)**   This pulls the entire block of text away from the left margin to a specified position.

- **Right Indent**   A right indent, of course, pulls the right edge of the text away from the right margin to a specified position.

- **First Line Indent**   As you would expect, a first-line indent pulls only the first line of a paragraph away from the left margin to a specified position.

- **Hanging Indent**   More useful than you might think, this indent configuration moves all of the lines of a paragraph except the first away from the left margin to a specified position.

For information on setting indents with the Paragraph Specifications dialog box, refer to the section, "Paragraph Settings," earlier in this chapter.

## Setting Indents Using the Control Palette

If you know the extent to which you wish to indent a paragraph in decimal equivalents of an inch[1] (for example, 0.5 or 1.25 inches), the Control Palette may be the best means of doing so. This technique is quick and particularly easy if you keep the Control Palette visible on your screen all the time. However, only full, first-line, and right indents may be set using the Control Palette. If you need to set a hanging indent, use the Indents/Tabs dialog box as described in the following steps:

---

[1]Using inches as a measuring system is the default in PageMaker. However, you may change the measuring system in the Preferences dialog box by selecting the File menu's Preferences command. Also see Chapter 12 for additional information.

1. Select the paragraph you want to indent.

   If you want to indent only one paragraph, the insertion point must be in that paragraph. If you want to indent several, select those paragraphs using the Text tool.

2. Show the Control Palette in Paragraph view.

   If the Control Palette is not visible in the PageMaker window, open it by clicking on the Window menu's Show Control Palette. Then select the Paragraph view by clicking the Paragraph button. The Control Palette appears, as shown in Figure 9-17.

3. Enter the indent specifications.

   Enter the specifications of the desired indent in the box for the type of indent you desire. Use decimal equivalents of an inch, unless you have set preferences to another form of measurement.

4. Apply the specifications.

   Click the Apply button on the Control Palette. The indent is applied to the selected paragraph.

When you press the ENTER key and create a new paragraph, the new paragraph will contain the formatting of the previous one, including the indent characteristics. Therefore, if you wanted to establish first-line indents for all subsequent paragraphs, for example, set the indent specifications when you create the first. All other paragraphs created from that paragraph will contain the same indents.

Tabs are stops set along a ruler at which text can be positioned by pressing the TAB key. When the TAB key is pressed, the insertion point moves to the right to the next tab on the ruler and any text to the right is moved as well. A tab setting affects an entire paragraph. There are four kinds of tabs that can be used in PageMaker text. The following list defines each of these tabs:

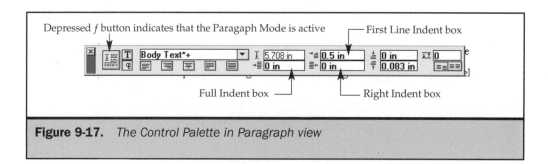

**Figure 9-17.** *The Control Palette in Paragraph view*

- **Left tab** When positioned at this tab, text aligns with the tab on the left. New text builds to the right.
- **Center tab** Text positioned at a center tab centers under the tab. New text builds to each side in turn until the text is centered at the tab.
- **Right tab** When positioned at this tab, text aligns with the tab on the right. New text builds to the left.
- **Decimal tab** This tab is used to align the decimal point in numbers. When positioned under this tab, numbers build to the left until a decimal (period) is typed, and then the remaining numerals build to the right. The use of a decimal tab is the only accurate way to align numbers in rows of text.

## Setting Indents and Tabs Using the Indents/Tabs Dialog Box

I use the Indents/Tabs dialog box to set indents as well as tabs. The only reason I use this in lieu of the Control Palette is that the Indents/Tabs dialog box predates the Control Palette and I am just accustomed to using it. Old habits die hard. I know of people who never use the Indents/Tabs dialog box because it appears confusing. However, once you understand the way it functions, it is quite simple. The Indents/Tabs dialog box and its elements are shown in Figure 9-18.

The following steps lead you through the process of setting indents and tabs using the Indents/Tabs dialog box:

1. Select the paragraph or paragraphs to be affected.

   Since indent and tab settings affect an entire paragraph, you must select the paragraphs to which the tabs and indents are applied. Of course, if you are only affecting one paragraph, you need only use the Text tool to place the insertion point in the paragraph.

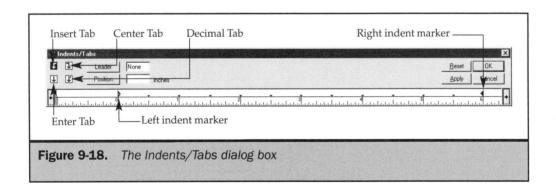

**Figure 9-18.** *The Indents/Tabs dialog box*

2.  Open the Indents/Tabs dialog box.

    Click the Type menu's Indents/Tabs dialog box. The dialog box opens. Depending upon the magnification in which you are working, PageMaker usually aligns the ruler to coincide with the margins of the selected paragraph. If it is not aligned, dragging it by the Title Bar can move the entire dialog box. Also, the ruler can be scrolled right or left by clicking on the arrows at either side of the ruler.

3.  Set an indent.

    Using the indent markers, set any of the following indents. As you move a marker, its position is shown in the Position box. This will be displayed in decimal equivalents of an inch unless you have selected another measurement system. The indents are as follows:

    ■ **Full indent**   Move the bottom portion of the left indent marker to the desired position of the indent. The top section moves with it to set a full indent. The following illustration shows a full-indent setting in the Indents/Tabs dialog box.

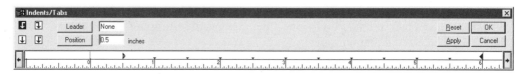

    ■ **First-line indent**   Move only the top section of the left indent marker. It moves independently to set the first line indent (see the following illustration).

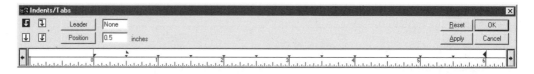

    ■ **Hanging indent**   Drag the bottom section of the left indent marker, pulling the entire marker to the desired position of the indent, just as you would with a full indent. Then move the top section of the marker back to the zero point, causing the first line of the paragraph to be aligned with the margin and the subsequent lines to be indented (see the following illustration).

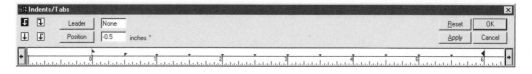

■ **Right indent**   Move the right-indent marker left to the position of the desired indent, as shown in the following illustration.

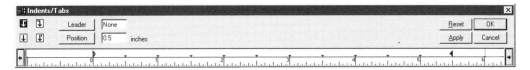

4. Set tabs.

   Click on one of the four tab icons to select the type of tab you want to place (refer to Figure 9-18). Then click on the ruler at the point where you want the tab stop to be located. The tab indicator appears.

   If you want to change the position of the tab after it has been placed, just grab it with the mouse and move it to the new position. If you want to remove a tab, grab it and move it out of the ruler. When you release the mouse, the tab disappears. Repeat the process as many times as you want for the tabs you need.

5. Apply the indents and tabs.

   If you want to see the results of your settings before closing the Indents/Tabs dialog box, click the Apply button. The settings are applied to the selected paragraph.

6. Close the Indents/Tabs dialog box.

   Click the OK button and the dialog box closes. If you did not use the Apply button as described in Step 5, the settings will be applied automatically.

# Styles

A style is a collection of formatting that is used together. For example, if you occasionally use quotations in your PageMaker text, routinely indent the quotation text from both the left and right margin, set the quotation in italics, increase the horizontal scale to 120 percent, and set the tracking to Very Loose, you could save all of those settings as a style, which you might name Quotes. Then any time you entered a quotation, you would merely need to apply the style named Quotes and all of the formatting would automatically be applied to the text.

Some styles come with PageMaker by default. Check these out to see if they work for you. I rarely use preset styles, but that is just because I usually want something different than what the default styles offer.

The use of styles is a tremendous time-saver and a virtual necessity for long-text documents. In this section, I'll discuss creating, deleting, editing, and applying a style.

## Creating a Style

You can create a style by entering the style specifications in the Define Styles dialog box, or you can create a style by example by formatting a paragraph as you want it and naming the formatting as a style. Either technique is relatively simple.

Follow these steps to create a style using the Define Styles dialog box:

1.  Open the Define Styles dialog box.

    Click on the Type menu's Define Styles command. The Define Styles dialog box opens.

2.  Open Style Options.

    Click the New button on the Define Styles dialog box. The Style Options dialog box opens.

3.  Name the style.

    In the Name box, enter the name of the new style.

4.  Set the style specifications.

    On the right side of the Style Options dialog box, there are four buttons for you to use in establishing the formatting that you want your new style to contain. These buttons are Character, Paragraph, Tabs, and Hyphenation. Each button will bring up the corresponding dialog box in which you may establish the parameters discussed throughout this chapter.

    If you wish to specify which style will follow the use of your new style, select it by clicking the drop-down arrow to the right of the Next Style box and selecting it from the list.

5.  Close the Style Options and the Define Styles dialog boxes.

    Once you have established the style specifications, close the Style Options dialog box by clicking the OK button. Then close the Define Styles box by clicking its OK button as well.

    Your new style is ready to use.

Another way to create a style, and the one that is more comfortable for me, is to create a style by example. To use this technique, follow these simple steps:

1.  Format text with all the specifications you want the style to have.

    Make character, paragraph, tabs, and hyphenation changes just as described previously, but apply them directly to the text rather than in the Define Styles dialog box.

2.  Enter the new style name in the Control Palette.

    With the formatted paragraph selected, replace the style name shown in the Style box in the Control Palette's Paragraph view with the new name.

If the Control Palette is not visible in the PageMaker window, open it by clicking on the Window menu's Show Control Palette. Then select the Paragraph view by clicking the Paragraph button. (Refer to Figure 9-34 for an image of the Control Palette in Paragraph view.)

3. Apply the formatting of the paragraph to the new style name.

Click the Apply button on the Control Palette. A message box appears asking you to click OK to create the style (see the following illustration). Click OK. The message box closes and the new style name is added to the style list.

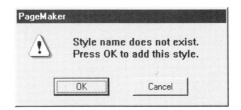

You are now ready to apply the new style to other paragraphs.

## Applying a Style

Applying a style is very simple:

1. Highlight the text.

Using the Text tool, highlight the text to which you wish to apply the style.

2. Select the style name.

If it is not already open, display the Control Palette's Paragraph view. Click the drop-down arrow to the right of the style box. From the resulting menu, locate the style you wish to apply.

3. Apply the style.

As soon as you click on the style name, the style is applied to the selected text.

## Editing a Style

Once you have created a style, it is not cast in concrete. It can be changed very easily. Essentially, the process of editing an existing style is just like creating one. Here are the steps:

1. Open the Define Styles dialog box.

Click on the Type menu's Define Styles command. The Define Styles dialog box opens.

2. Select the style to be edited.

In the Style box, locate and select the style you want to modify.

3. Open Style Options.

   Click the Edit button on the Define Styles dialog box. The Style Options dialog box opens.

4. Set the style specifications.

   Use the Character, Paragraph, Tabs, and Hyphenation buttons to open dialog boxes in which you can modify the style's current specifications.

5. Close the Style Options and the Define Styles dialog boxes.

   Once you have modified the style specifications, close the Style Options dialog box by clicking the OK button. Then close the Define Styles box by clicking its OK button as well.

   The style is edited and ready to use.

# Bullets and Numbering

PageMaker offers a Bullets and Numbering utility for the first time in version 7.0, a welcome addition to PageMaker's capabilities. This utility provides automatic numbering or bulleting for consecutive paragraphs. If you are accustomed to the bulleting and numbering utilities in Microsoft Word or other word processing programs, you will find that the systems are very similar, but have some important differences.

Here are the steps to take to apply bullets or numbers:

1. Select the paragraphs to be affected.

   If you are applying either bullets or numbers to existing text, highlight all of the text to be affected. If you are applying them to only one paragraph, use the Text tool to place the insertion point into the paragraph.

2. Open the Bullets and Numbering dialog box.

   Whether you apply bullets or numbering to a paragraph or paragraphs, it is the Bullets and Numbering dialog box from which you make the choices to determine how your selection is formatted.

   You can open the Bullets and Numbering dialog box by clicking the Bullets and Numbering button on the toolbar. Another way to do this is by clicking the Utilities menu's Plug-ins command and then selecting Bullets and Numbering on the ensuing menu. The Bullets and Numbering dialog box opens, as shown in Figure 9-19.

3. Display the Bullets view.

   If you are applying bullets to your selected paragraphs, display the Bullets view by clicking on the Bullets button if necessary. (If you are numbering, please go to Step 6.) The Bullets view is displayed, as shown in Figure 9-19.

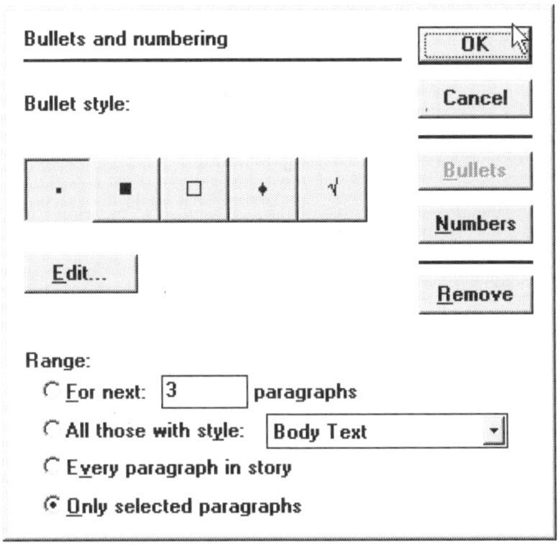

**Figure 9-19.**   *The Bullets and Numbering dialog box in Bullets view*

4.  Select the bullet style.

    From the Bullet Style bar, select one of the standard bullets. If you do not find
    the bullet that you want, click the Edit button to make a selection from the Edit
    Bullet dialog box (see Figure 9-20).

    Select the font containing the desired bullet from the Font box. Dingbat fonts
    such as Wingdings and Webdings, among others, provide the best selection.
    You may also change the size of your bullet in the Size box. Click OK to return
    to the Bullets and Numbering dialog box.

5.  Select a range.

    Make a selection from the Range options at the bottom of the Bullets and
    Numbering dialog box.

6.  Display the Numbers view.

    If you are applying bullets, please go to Step 9. To apply numbers, click on the
    Numbers button in the Bullets and Numbering dialog box. The Numbers view
    is displayed, as shown in Figure 9-21.

7.  Select the numbering criteria.

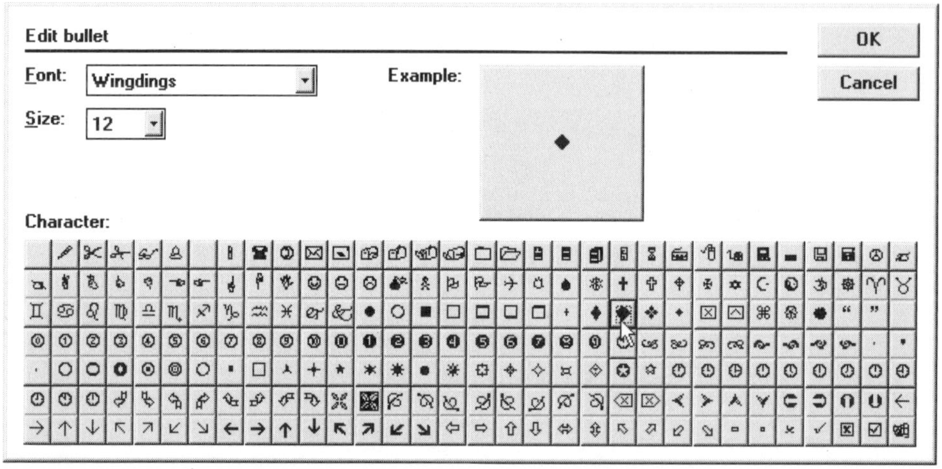

**Figure 9-20.** *The Edit Bullet dialog box*

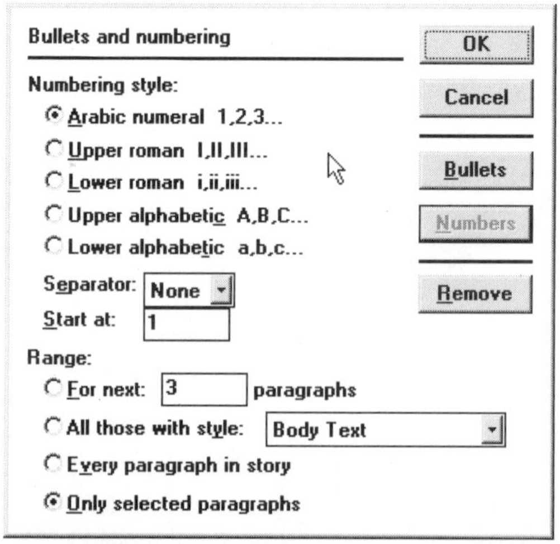

**Figure 9-21.** *The Bullets and Numbering dialog box in Numbers view*

From the Numbering Style options, select the type of numbering you want to apply to the selected paragraph. You may choose from Arabic, upper- or lower-case roman, or upper- or lower-case alphabetic.

Select a separator from the Separator list. Just click the drop-down arrow to the right of the Separator box and make a selection. Note that the separator is the period that frequently follows numbers in a list. If a separator is not selected, the period does not appear nor does any other separator, such as a parenthesis.

Enter a number with which to begin numbering in the Start At box.

8. Select a range.

From the Range options at the bottom of the dialog box, select the way in which you want the numbers to be applied.

9. Apply the bullets or numbers.

Click the OK button to close the dialog box and apply either bullets or numbering.

If you applied bullets or numbers to one paragraph, other paragraphs with the same formatting may be created from the first one by pressing the ENTER key at the end of the formatted paragraph to create a new one.

If you want to change from bullets to numbering or vice versa, you must first remove the existing formatting before applying the new. This is also true when changing the bullet style after applying one style of bullet to the paragraph or paragraphs. If the existing formatting is not removed, it remains and the new formatting is added to it.

To remove either bullets or numbering, select the paragraph or paragraphs to be affected, open the Bullets and Numbering dialog box as described previously, and select either the Bullets view or the Numbers view. Then click the Remove button and close the dialog box by clicking the OK button.

# Summary

PageMaker text can be loosely divided into two categories. I think of these as the Managing Text As an Object category in which it is placed, positioned, sized, and otherwise handled as an object; and the Professional Techniques for Document Editing and Formatting category in which text is generated, formatted, and edited.

**Managing Text as an Object**    You can import text as easily as you import graphics. In the processing of placed text, you can choose to have text autoflow so that it automatically flows from one column or page to the next. Additionally, you can place text in frames to configure the size and shape of a text box. Frames can be threaded to continue the text from one frame to another.

**Professional Techniques for Document Editing and Formatting**   PageMaker has always offered type manipulation techniques that go far beyond what most word processors provide. These techniques are consistent with professional typesetting practices that have their origins in the days when type was set by hand, one letter at a time. Sometimes, it is the use of these techniques that makes the difference in a piece that appears to be professionally designed and typeset and one that looks like it was generated by a less professional method. Kerning, leading, and advanced hyphenation techniques are just some of the professional features that PageMaker offers.

# Chapter 10

## Managing Graphics and Text As Objects

In Chapters 4 and 9, I discuss managing PageMaker text at length. For the most part, I discuss the placement, editing, and formatting of the words themselves. In Chapter 5, I discuss the basic processes of working with graphics. I described ways of adjusting the graphics, filling them, and changing their size and line style. In this chapter, however, I talk about the text box or the graphic as a whole unit. In this role, they are selected with the Pointer tool and are referred to as objects.

By definition, anything that you create in or import into the PageMaker window (or onto the pasteboard) is an *object*. Objects can be manipulated and transformed in any number of ways. PageMaker provides multiple techniques for transforming objects that may contribute to an exciting and attention-grabbing layout of your document. In this chapter, I first discuss the management of objects: copying, moving, deleting, layering, aligning, and grouping. Then I describe ways in which you can transform objects by rotating, skewing, reflecting, cropping, and so forth. And finally, I talk about text wrap, the means by which you can cause text to wrap around a graphic.

# Managing Objects

The art of graphic design is the process of placing objects on a page or in a document in such a way as to achieve the goals you have set for the publication. Objects are placed differently when designing a newsletter than they are when creating a catalog or an ad. Wherever you place the objects in your layout, PageMaker provides several techniques you may use to affect their arrangement.

## Selecting Objects

In almost every case when you want to affect an object, the object must first be selected. With only a few exceptions, such as cropping and rotating, the Pointer tool is used for selection. Activate the Pointer tool by clicking the Pointer tool button on the Toolbox Palette ( ). Using the Pointer tool, click the object you wish to affect. When you see the eight sizing handles around the object, you know that it is selected.

To select more than one object, hold down SHIFT as you click the objects with the Pointer tool. Another method of selecting multiple objects is to use the Pointer tool to draw a box around all of the objects. Just click on a point outside the boundaries of the group of objects you want to select and drag diagonally. As you drag, a dashed line will form a box. All objects that are completely enclosed in that box are selected when the mouse is released.

## Placing Graphics

The techniques for placing text (importing copy from another source) are discussed in Chapter 9. Although the placement of graphics is a very similar process to importing text, there are some significant differences. For one thing, you may place a graphic as a new object, replace an existing graphic, or place it *inline* where it is inserted in text at the insertion point and it is subsequently treated as text just as if it were a word or a character. Another difference is the choices found on the Filter Preferences dialog box, which varies from that used with text.

The steps to take to place a graphic in your document are outlined here:

1. Open the Place dialog box.

   Select the File menu's Place command or use the Place Button on the PageMaker toolbar. The Place dialog box opens, as shown in the following illustration.

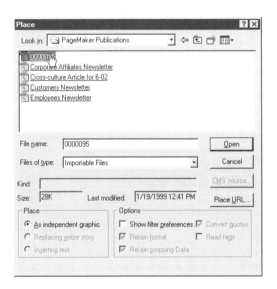

2. Locate the graphic to place.

   Click on the drop-down arrow to the right of the Look In box to display the directory tree.

   Unless the folder that appears automatically in the Look In box is the folder where your graphic is stored, you must use the directory tree to locate the target folder. If your target folder is already in the Look In box, go on to Step 5.

   As explained in Chapter 8, the directory tree (see Figure 10-1) is a list of all the folders in your computer where files are stored. Double-clicking on a folder in the directory tree opens it to reveal the folders stored in it. The files stored in the folder are shown in the file list.

   Start by double-clicking on the drive (usually the C drive) where the target folder is stored. If the target folder is displayed in the C drive, double-click to open it. Then go on to Step 5.

   If the target folder is stored inside another one, double-click on the outside folder to show the folders inside it. Continue to open folders until you locate

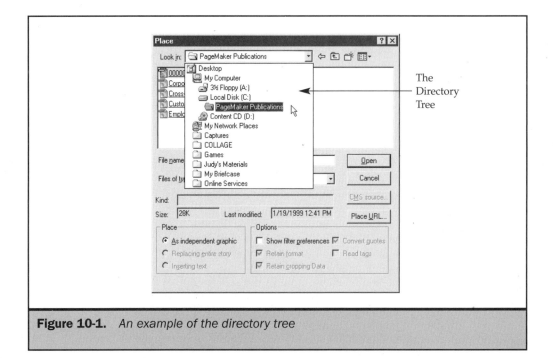

**Figure 10-1.**    *An example of the directory tree*

the folder that contains your document. Then double-click to open the folder. All of the documents in that folder are shown in the file list area.

3.  Select the graphic you want to place.

    In the file List area, click on the file you want to import into your PageMaker document. The graphic's file name appears in the File Name box along with information on it, such as its size and the date on which it was last modified.

4.  Select the Place options.

    Choose the appropriate Radio Button in the Place section of the dialog box. The choices in the Place options will change depending upon the circumstances in place when the Place dialog box is opened:

    ■ **As Independent Graphic**   This radio button appears consistently and is used when you want to insert the selected graphic as a new object.

    ■ **As an Inline Graphic**   This choice appears when the Text tool is selected and an insertion point is placed in text at the time the Place dialog box is opened. Selecting this inserts the graphic into text where it is treated as text.

■ **Replacing Entire Graphic** This choice occurs when an existing graphic is selected when the Place dialog box was opened. Its selection will delete the existing graphic and replace it with the new one.

5. Select the options.

When importing graphics, only one selection is available: Show Filter Preferences. When placing certain graphics formats, selecting this option causes a secondary dialog box to open prior to placement of the graphic. The form this dialog box takes depends upon the type of graphic you are placing. For example, the dialog box shown in the following illustration appears when placing an Adobe Illustrator graphic. It enables you to select color and resolution management options for the illustration.

6. Click Open.

Click the Open Button on the Place dialog box. The box disappears and one of the following occurs:

■ If you are importing the graphic as a new object, the mouse pointer changes to a symbol representing the type of graphic. Click the location on the page where you want to place the graphic and it appears.

■ If you are importing the graphic as an inline graphic, the image appears at the insertion point in text as shown in Figure 10-2. Once placed, you may use the Pointer tool to size the graphic or move it relative to the line of text (positioned primarily above the line, below the line, or vertically centered on the line), but it cannot be moved to another position.

■ If you are replacing an existing graphic, the old graphic disappears and the new one emerges in its place.

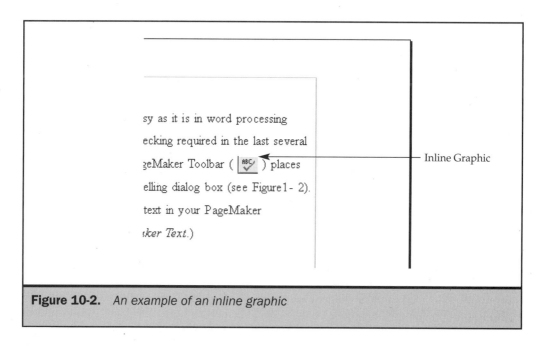

**Figure 10-2.**   *An example of an inline graphic*

# Arranging Objects

Once objects are placed on your page, you may arrange them in the way that will best achieve your objective for the document.

## Positioning Objects

Moving objects around on a page is easy; just select an object using the Pointer tool and drag it to another location on the page. You may even move an object off of the page onto the Pasteboard if you want to get it out of the way for a while. When you are ready to position it, just grab it and drag it back onto the page.

When you want to move more than one object at a time, align objects with respect to one another, size objects together, or move objects from one page to another, there are techniques for these tasks as well.

## Positioning Using the Control Palette

If you want to position an object in a precise position rather than judging its location visually, you can use the Control palette to do so. Just follow these steps:

1.  Select the object.

    Using the Pointer tool, click on the object to select it.

2. Open the Control palette.

   If necessary, display the Control palette by selecting the Window menu's Show Control palette command. The Control palette opens in its object mode.

3. Identify the point of measurement on the proxy reference.

   The proxy reference on the Control palette is a box composed of eight buttons with a ninth button in the center representing the parameters of the selected object (see the following illustration). By clicking on one of the buttons, you establish the point of measurement by which you can precisely position the object on your page.

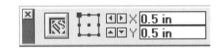

4. Select the measurements.

   Next to the proxy reference are the measurement boxes of the x-axis (horizontal) and the y-axis (vertical) displaying the precise location of the box on the page measuring from the left (horizontal) and top (vertical). For example, with an x-axis setting of 1.25 inches, a y-axis setting of 2.0 inches, and the upper-left box of the proxy reference selected, the graphic's upper-left corner is 2.0 inches from the top edge of the page and 1.25 inches from the left edge of the paper.

   Click in each box and enter the desired measurements in decimal equivalents of inches.

5. Apply the measurements.

   Click on the Apply Button or press ENTER. The selected object moves to the precise location you entered.

## Aligning Objects

PageMaker provides an ingenious feature that takes the headache out of aligning objects. This feature enables you to align or distribute selected items vertically or horizontally along the top, bottom, left, right, or center. Here's how to use this remarkable feature:

1. Select the object to be aligned or distributed.

   Using the Pointer tool, select all of the objects that you want to align with one another or to distribute. You can select more than one object by holding down SHIFT as you select the items.

2.  Open the Align Objects dialog box.

    Select the Element menu's Align Objects command. The Align Objects dialog box opens (see the following illustration).

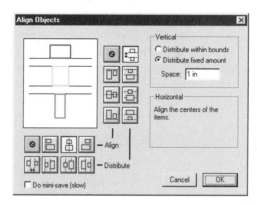

3.  Select the alignment you need.

    The choices on the Align Objects dialog box are easy to understand because of the Preview box in the upper-left corner. The Align and the Distribute functions each have selection buttons for vertical and horizontal placement. When you make a selection, the image in the preview window shows an example of how your selected items would be affected.

    When you select any Align Button, the corresponding (vertical or horizontal) box to the right side of the dialog box describes the action you are taking.

    When you select any Distribute Button, the corresponding box to the right side of the dialog box offers two choices:

    ■ **Distribute Within Bounds**   This selection distributes the items within the parameters created by the upper and lower objects (vertical) or the left- and right-most objects (horizontal). For example, if we are dealing with a vertical distribution, the top and bottom objects would retain their position. The other objects would move to equidistant positions between them.

    ■ **Distribute a Fixed Amount**   This selection enables you to enter the amount of separation you desire. Depending upon the selection, the measurement is between one object and the next; from the top, bottom, left, or right sides of the objects; or from each object's horizontal or vertical center.

4.  Apply the alignment or distribution.

    Once you have selected the alignment and distribution pattern you desire, click the OK button. The Align Objects dialog box closes and the alignment is applied.

## Grouping

PageMaker objects can be grouped so that they can be managed as if they were one object. Grouped objects can be moved as one, maintaining their position relative to one another. Grouped graphics can be sized as one item; however, grouped text does not size.

Here are the simple steps to grouping objects:

1. Select the objects to be grouped.

   Select each of the objects that you wish to be grouped. You can select more than one object by holding down SHIFT while you click the objects.

2. Group the objects.

   Select the Element menu's Group command. All of the selected objects will be grouped and may be managed as one object. Eight sizing handles appear around the group, indicating that it is grouped and selected.

To ungroup the objects, select the Element menu's Ungroup command. The various objects will be selected as individual items.

## Locking Objects

Once you have placed objects where you want them to be in your layout, you can lock them in place. Locking an object's position keeps your layout intact and prevents unintentional dragging of an object out of place.

When an object is locked, you can change any of its attributes except for size or position. For example, you can change an object's fill or color and its line weight and style. You cannot cut or delete a locked object without unlocking it, but you can copy it and paste it (see the following section, "Using the Clipboard"). When you paste it, it pastes as an unlocked object. A locked object is selected when clicked by the Pointer tool, just as any other object, but if you try to drag it to move it, the mouse pointer changes to a lock icon to remind you that it is locked (see Figure 10-3).

To lock an object (or objects), select it and then click on the Element menu's Lock Position command.

To unlock an object, select the Element menu's Unlock command. Even if you locked several objects in one operation, you can unlock them individually. Objects that are grouped lock and unlock as one object.

# Using the Clipboard

If you have been using Windows applications at all, you are probably already familiar with the operation of the Clipboard. However, I want to discuss it here because its use is so convenient in PageMaker. Additionally, PageMaker has a special feature that I have not seen in other Windows-based software: Paste Multiple.

PAGEMAKER
ESSENTIALS

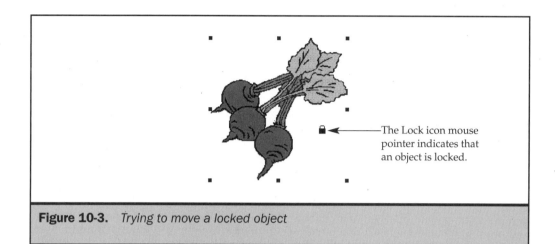

The Lock icon mouse pointer indicates that an object is locked.

**Figure 10-3.** *Trying to move a locked object*

The Clipboard is a memory buffer built into the Windows software that is a terrific tool in working with PageMaker. You may place an object on the Clipboard by either cutting (removing) it or by copying it. Then you may place the object in the position of your choice by pasting it. In PageMaker, you may have only one object on the Clipboard at a time. However, once an object is placed on the Clipboard, it remains available to be pasted until you replace it with another object or shut down PageMaker.

Moving an object by using the Clipboard is particularly convenient when moving or copying objects to another page, or even another publication.

Here's how to use the Clipboard:

1. Select the object to be placed on the Clipboard.

   Using the Pointer tool, select the object you want to move or copy.

2. Cut or copy the object.

   To place an object on the Clipboard, you must either cut the object or copy it. Open the Edit menu and select either Cut or Copy, as described here:

   - *Cutting* removes the object from its original position and is therefore a move function.

   - *Copying*, of course, leaves the object in its original position, but places a copy of it on the Clipboard so that it may be placed elsewhere.

3. Move to the object's new position.

   Your cursor must be on the target page (the page where you want the object to be placed) in order to paste it; however, you do not need to move to it immediately. You may perform any number of other operations in PageMaker and come back to paste the object minutes or even hours later *so long as you do not replace the object on the Clipboard or shut down PageMaker.*

4. Paste the object.

   With the target page active, click the Edit menu's Paste command. The object will appear on the page and can be dragged into the desired position.

## Paste Multiple

I have had so much fun using the Paste Multiple function. With this utility, you can copy an object and in one operation paste an array of the same object in a specified horizontal and/or vertical pattern.

Here's how it works:

1. Select the object.

   Using the Pointer tool, select the object of which you wish to paste multiples.

2. Open the Paste Multiple dialog box.

   Select the Edit menu's Paste Multiple command. The Paste Multiple dialog box appears, as shown in the following illustration.

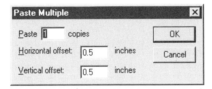

## Using the Keyboard

The following keyboard commands can be used for the Clipboard functions:

- ■ **Cut**   CTRL+X
- ■ **Copy**   CTRL+C
- ■ **Paste**   CTRL+V

I rarely use anything else. These keyboard commands are so convenient and by now are automatic. I don't even think of any other way to cut, copy, or paste— unless I'm writing or training.

3.  Enter the number of copies you want.

    In the Paste Copies box, enter the number of copies you wish to paste.

4.  Enter the Horizontal Offset.

    In the Horizontal Offset box, enter the horizontal distance you want between one object and the next when they are pasted. The measurement is from the left side of one object to the left side of the next, *not the space between the objects*. Use decimal equivalents of inches in your entry.

5.  Enter the vertical offset.

    In the Vertical Offset box, specify the vertical distance you want between one pasted object and another. This measurement is from the top of one object to the top of the next, *not the distance between the objects*. Use decimal equivalents of inches in your specification.

6.  Paste.

    Click the OK button. The Paste Multiple dialog box closes and the objects are pasted.

Keep in mind that a multiple paste will not create a true grid of objects. If specifications are entered in both the Horizontal Offset and the Vertical Offset boxes, the result will be a diagonal row of objects. If a grid is desired, perform the operation in two steps. Paste first either horizontally or vertically. Select and copy the results; then paste in the other direction in the second step. Even in two steps, it is still an easy process.

## Deleting an Object

To delete an object, select the object and press DELETE. The object is permanently removed.

## Layering

Objects in a PageMaker document may be placed on one or more layers. By using multiple layers, you can concentrate work on one portion of your publication without affecting others, even if the objects overlap. A layer is like a transparent sheet on which you place certain parts of a layout. You can see through the sheet to view the objects on the other layers and, when all viewed together, the total look is achieved.

By default, a new document contains only one layer; however, you can add layers whenever you wish. A document may have as many layers as you want. All layers apply to all pages in a document. In other words, if you have four layers in place, all pages in the document have four layers.

Grouped objects must occupy the same layer. If you group objects from different layers, the group is placed on the front layer of the group. Objects that are placed on master pages can be placed on any layer. However, they display behind all the objects on all the layers.

## The Stacking Order

Within each layer, objects are placed in a *stacking order*. This is essentially the order in which the objects are placed on the layer, with the first item to the back and the newest item to the front. It is also the order in which the objects would be tiered if they were overlapping. Even if they do not overlap, they are still arranged in a stack.

The stacking order of an object is changed by clicking on the Element menu's Arrange command and choosing a stacking order directive from the subsequent list:

- **Bring to Front**   Brings the object to the very front of the stack
- **Bring Forward**   Brings the object one level forward in the stack
- **Send Backward**   Sends the object one level toward the back in the stack
- **Send to Back**   Sends the object to the very back of the stack

Keep in mind that the foremost object in the stacking order on one layer will be behind all of the objects that are in a layer that is in front of it.

## Using the Layers Palette

The Layers Palette is used to create, edit, lock, and delete layers. With it, you can also hide and display layers as you work with one set of objects or another.

Display the Layers Palette by selecting the Windows menu's Show Layers command. The Layers Palette is displayed, as shown in Figure 10-4. All layers currently in use on the document appear on the palette. If all layers are not visible on the palette at one time, you may use the scroll bars to scroll through the layers list, or you may drag the palette's lower border and enlarge the palette to show all layers.

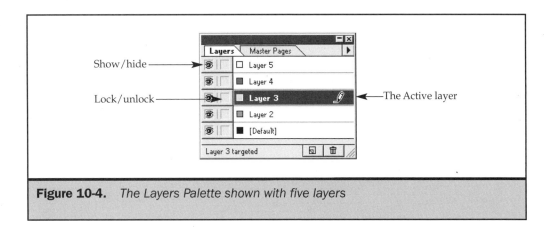

**Figure 10-4.**   *The Layers Palette shown with five layers*

Select a layer by clicking on it in the Layers Palette. The selected layer on the Layers Palette is highlighted and a pencil icon appears to the right, indicating that it is the active layer. Any new objects added to the document are added to the layer that is currently active. Be sure that the layer you want to work on is active before adding objects.

Show or hide a layer by selecting the Show/Hide box to the left of the layer name. A hidden layer's Show/Hide box is blank, while a visible layer has an eye icon in the Show/Hide box. The objects on a hidden layer do not show on the publication and will not print.

Lock a layer by clicking in the Lock/Unlock box for that layer. The Lock/Unlock box for an unlocked layer is blank, while a locked layer's box shows a pencil with a line through it. A locked layer can be selected, but no changes can be made to it. An attempt to move an object on a locked layer causes the mouse pointer to change to a pencil icon with a line through it to remind you that the layer is locked. Merely clicking the locked icon will unlock the layer.

**Create a New Layer**    To create a new layer, follow these steps:

1.  Open the Layers Palette menu.

    With the Layers Palette open, click on the arrow on the right side of the palette in line with the Layers tab. The Layers Palette opens, as shown in the following illustration.

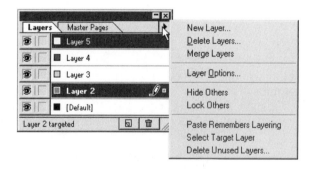

2.  Open the New Layer dialog box.

    Select the New Layer command. The New Layer dialog box opens (see the following illustration).

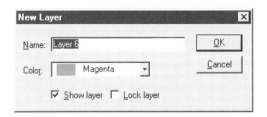

3. Name the layer.

   Enter a name for the layer in the Name box or leave the default name that numbers the layers.

4. Select a color.

   Associate a color with the layer by selecting one from the Color drop-down menu. Or you may accept the color assigned automatically. When an object is selected, the sizing handles around the object appear in the color of the layer on which the object is placed.

5. Select from the options:

   ■ Select or deselect the Show Layer option to display or hide the layer. A hidden layer does not print and cannot be edited.

   ■ Select or deselect the Lock Layer option. Objects on a locked layer cannot be repositioned.

6. Apply the new layer.

   Click the OK button on the New Layer dialog box. The box closes and the new layer is shown in the Layers Palette.

**Note**

*For a quick way to create a layer, press ALT and click the New Layer Button at the lower edge of the Layers Palette (see the following illustration). A new layer appears, named according to the order in which it was created and with the default settings in place.*

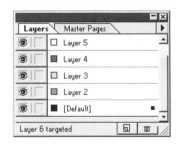

**Delete a Layer**    You may easily remove a layer from the Layer Palette. If the layer contains objects, PageMaker provides you with the opportunity to move the items to another layer or to delete all objects on that layer along with it.

Here's how to delete a layer:

1. Open the Layers Palette.

   If necessary, open the Layers Palette by clicking on the Window menu's Show Layers command.

2. Select the layer or layers to be deleted.

   Select the layer that you want to remove by clicking on it. You may delete more than one layer at a time by holding down CTRL and selecting other layers as well.

3. Open the Layers Palette menu.

   Click the Menu Button on the right side of the Layers Palette to reveal the Layers Palette menu.

4. Select Delete.

   If you have one layer selected, the Layers Palette Menu displays the command, Delete [Layer Name]. If more than one layer has been selected, the command reads Delete Layers. Click on the Delete command. The menu closes and the Delete Layer dialog box appears.

5. Select a Delete Layer option:

   ■ **Move Items To**    Enables you to choose a layer to which you want to move all of the objects on the layer or layers you are deleting. Click the drop-down arrow to select the appropriate layer.

   ■ **Delete Items on All Pages from Layer(s)**    Deletes the objects contained in the layer or layers you are deleting, along with the layers themselves.

6. Complete the deletion.

   Click the OK button on the Delete Layer dialog box. The box closes and the layers are removed from the document and the Layers Palette.

*A slightly quicker way to perform a layer deletion is to select the layer or layers and click the trash can icon at the bottom right corner of the Layers Palette. The Delete Layers dialog box appears. Make your selection and click OK.*

**Delete All Unused Layers**    If you have created layers that have no objects on them, you may delete them by selecting the Layers Palette menu's Delete Unused Layers command. A Delete Unused Layer dialog box appears verifying that you want to delete each layer. You may approve or reject the deletion one layer at a time, or select Yes to

All or No to All to okay or reject the deletion of all unused layers at one time. A box appears telling you how many layers have been deleted. Click OK to close the box.

**Rearrange Layers**    You can change the order of layers in the document and in the Layers Palette merely by dragging the name of the layer to a new location. As you drag, a horizontal I-beam indicates the new location. The mouse pointer becomes a hand. Just continue to drag until the layer is where you want it to be. If you select more than one layer and drag them, the selected layers maintain their position relative to one another. Keep in mind that the layer at the bottom of the Layers Palette is in the forefront and each layer following that appears higher in the Layers Palette's list.

**Merge Layers**    You can combine layers and place all of the objects contained on them into one layer by using the Merge Layers function.

Take these steps to merge two or more layers:

1. Select the layers to be merged.

   In the Layers Palette, click on the layers that you want to merge. You can select more than one layer by holding down CTRL while clicking. Make sure that the first layer you select is your target layer, the layer into which you want the other layers to be merged.

2. Open the Layers Palette menu.

   Click the menu arrow to the right of the Layers Palette to display the Layers Palette menu.

3. Select the Merge command.

   Click on the Merge Layers command from the Layers Palette menu, as shown in the following illustration.

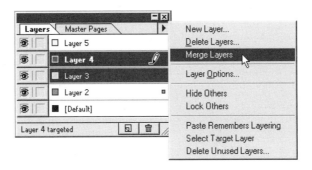

The objects from all of the layers are moved to the target layer and the other selected layers are deleted.

**Switch an Object from One Layer to Another**    When you select an object on a layer, a small colored dot appears to the right of the layer's name. If you want to move the selected object to another layer, drag the dot to the layer you desire. The object moves to the target layer and enters at the top of the stacking order. If you want to copy the object, hold down CTRL as you drag. Be sure to release the mouse before you release CTRL.

**Using the Clipboard with Layers**    If you use the Clipboard (refer to "Using the Clipboard") in a document with multiple layers, the object will be pasted to the active layer by default, whether or not that is where it was originally. If you wish an object to be pasted to the layer from which it was cut or copied, select the Paste Remembers Layering option from the Layers Palette menu. While that command is selected, all objects that are pasted will be returned to their original layer.

# Working with Graphics in a Frame

In Chapter 9, I discussed the use of frames for the display of text. These special objects come in the same shapes as simple graphics and have the capability to hold graphics as well as text. The obvious advantage here is that a graphic placed in a frame takes on the shape of the frame.

For the most part, frames may be arranged, modified, or transformed like any other object. Although frames, like simple graphics, are not subject to cropping, the graphics that they contain can be adjusted in a cropping-like procedure to show only the portions of the picture that you want to see in a frame.

The Frame tools are found in the Toolbox Palette on the right side. They look remarkably like the simple graphic tools, but are filled with a large X.

## Create a Frame

The following steps lead you through the process of creating a frame:

1. Select the Frame tool.

   Click on the Frame tool of your choice in the Toolbox Palette, choosing from Rectangle, Ellipse, and Polygon. Once a tool has been selected, the mouse pointer becomes a small cross.

2. Click and drag.

   Click the mouse pointer in the area where you want the upper left of your frame and drag diagonally down and to the right to create the size and shape you desire. Remember that if you hold down SHIFT while dragging, the frame will be constrained, creating a frame that is a square (rectangular frame), a circle (ellipse frame), or a symmetrical polygon.

3.  Customize the frame.

    Once created, frames may be customized if you wish, just as you customized simple graphics. Line style and weight may be adjusted, and the frames may be sized or moved.

# Place a Graphic in a Frame

If you are importing a graphic from another source, you can place it directly into a frame. Here's how:

1.  Select the frame.

    Using the previous steps, create a frame into which you want to place the graphic. Once created, select the frame by clicking it with the Pointer tool.

2.  Open the Place dialog box.

    Click on the File menu's Place command. The Place dialog box opens.

3.  Locate the graphic.

    Using the directory tree, locate the graphic you want to place in a frame.

4.  Select the Place options.

    Among the other Place options in the Place dialog box, select the Place Within Frame option.

5.  Select the graphic.

    Click the graphic and click Open or double-click the graphic. The Place dialog box closes and the graphic appears in the frame.

# Attach an Existing Graphic to a Frame

If you have a graphic already in your document that you want to place in a frame, first use the Pointer tool to select the frame. Then, holding down SHIFT, select the existing graphic as well. Click on the Element menu's Frame command and choose Attach Content. The graphic appears in the frame.

# Select the Frame Options

Once you have placed or attached a graphic to a frame, you may need to make some adjustments so that the graphic appears as you would like. The settings in the Frame Options dialog box help you to do so:

1.  Open the Frame Options dialog box.

    Select the Element menu's Frame command and then choose Frame Options. The dialog box opens, as shown in the following illustration.

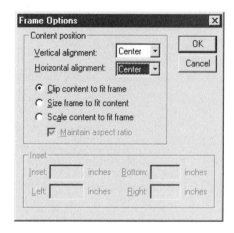

2. Choose Vertical and Horizontal Alignment.

   Using the drop-down menus for Vertical and Horizontal Alignment, choose the alignment specifications for your graphic within the frame.

3. Select the Fitting options.

   Select from the three Fitting options available on the Frame Options dialog box:

   - **Clip Content to Fit Frame**   If your graphic is larger than the frame, this option crops the graphic to fit within the frame. That is, it cuts away parts of the graphic to show only what will fit in the frame. With this selection, you can move the graphic around in the frame to show the portions you want revealed by using the Cropping tool to click and drag on the image. See "Cropping Graphics" later in this chapter.

     If your graphic is smaller than the frame, the graphic remains the same size and occupies just a portion of the frame. You can change its position within the frame by using the Content Position options, as described previously.

   - **Size Frame to Fit Content**   As you would expect, this option changes the size of the frame so that it encloses the graphic.

   - **Scale Content to Fit Frame**   This is different from the first option in that it keeps the entire picture intact, but sizes it to fit the frame. If the Maintain Aspect Ratio box is selected, the picture retains its proportion. If the check box is not selected, the graphic will expand in both directions as needed to fill the frame. If this option is selected, you cannot use the Cropping tool to rearrange placement of the graphic within the frame.

   If the selection of one of these options does not provide the results you want, open the Frame Options dialog box again and try another.

4.  Apply Your selections.

    Click the OK button in the Frame Options dialog box. The box closes and the options are applied to the framed graphic.

# Transforming Objects

In addition to arranging objects, as I have discussed so far in this chapter, it is possible to alter the configuration of the object itself. Referred to as transformations, PageMaker enables you to rotate, skew, or flip any object. You may be surprised how often these transformation operations come in handy. For example, skewing and rotating can be used to show an object in limited perspective; flipping can mirror an object to show a shadow image or a reflection. Figure 10-5 shows an object configured in each of the transformations.

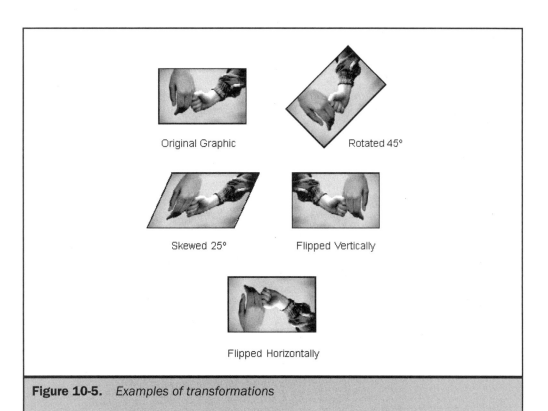

Original Graphic          Rotated 45°

Skewed 25°          Flipped Vertically

Flipped Horizontally

**Figure 10-5.**   *Examples of transformations*

## Rotating an Object

What a joy it was, a few versions ago, when PageMaker provided full rotation for the first time. Now, with PageMaker, you can rotate an object 360° in increments as small as 0.01°. That degree of control enables you to position an object exactly where you want it and rotated to the degree you desire.

There are two ways to effect rotation of an object: the Rotate tool on the Toolbar Palette and the Rotation control on the Control palette. I rarely use the Rotate tool; I find the Rotation control on the Control palette to be so simple I just don't bother with the other.

To use the Rotation control, first select the object to be rotated. Then select the point of rotation from the proxy reference on the Control palette (see Figure 10-6). Click in the Rotation Control box and enter the degrees of rotation you desire, as shown in Figure 10-7. Press ENTER and the specified rotation is applied to the object. If you don't know how many degrees you want, just guess. You can also use the small buttons to the left of the Rotation Control box to produce rotation in minute increments. I rarely use these buttons because the process is so slow; however, if you want to make minute adjustments, they are a great help.

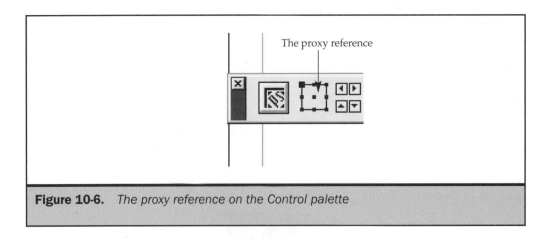

**Figure 10-6.**    *The proxy reference on the Control palette*

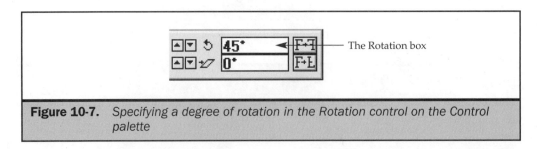

**Figure 10-7.**    *Specifying a degree of rotation in the Rotation control on the Control palette*

The process is so easy that if you don't get the look you want right off, it takes just a second to try again. Keep in mind that a positive entry rotates an object counterclockwise, while a negative entry rotates it clockwise (see Figure 10-8). Once an object is rotated, the proxy reference changes to a diamond shape.

To use the Rotate tool, select the tool from the Toolbox Palette. Using the Rotate tool, click on the object you want to rotate at one of the sizing handles and drag. As you move the mouse, a rotating handle appears, enabling you to visually rotate the object around the sizing handle you clicked on until it is in the position you desire (see Figure 10-9). The further you pull the handle away from the object, the more control you have. Even though you use the Rotate tool, the degrees of rotation are shown in the Rotate Control box in the Control Palette.

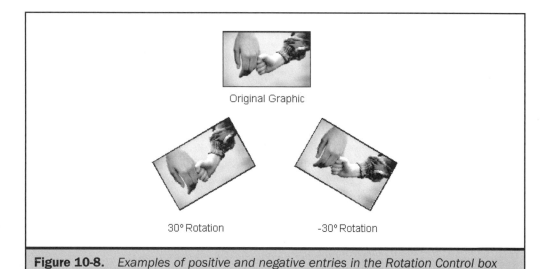

Original Graphic

30° Rotation                    -30° Rotation

**Figure 10-8.**    *Examples of positive and negative entries in the Rotation Control box*

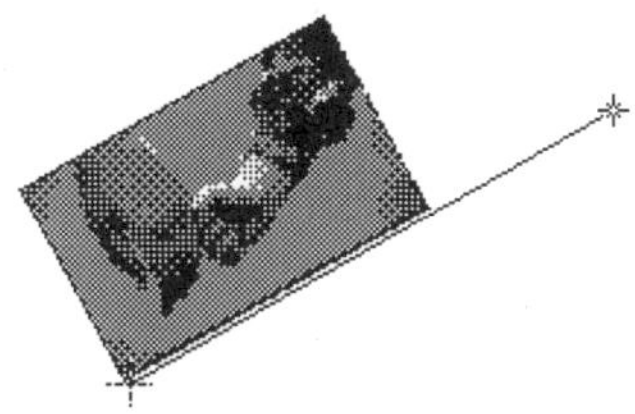

**Figure 10-9.**    *Rotating an object using the Rotate tool*

## Skewing an Object

PageMaker enables you to skew any unlocked object or grouped object horizontally. You can skew up to 85° in 0.01° increments using the Skew control on the Control Palette.

To skew an object, follow these steps:

1. Select the object.

   Use the Pointer tool to click on the object you want to skew.

2. Open the Control Palette.

   If necessary, open the Control Palette by selecting the Window menu's Show Control palette command.

3. Select a reference point.

   Click a point on the proxy reference in the Control Palette. The point on the object corresponding to the selected proxy point remains stationary as the object skews.

   If you double-click a point on the proxy, the button becomes a double-headed arrow and the corresponding point in the object moves as the object skews

4. Specify a skew angle.

   In the Skew Control box on the Control Palette, enter the degree of angle you wish. Just like rotating an object, don't worry if you don't know the angle you want. Try out a setting. If it does not work, try another.

5. Apply the skew.

   Click the Apply Button on the Control Palette or press ENTER. The skew is applied.

In addition to entering the skew angle, you may use the small buttons to the left of the Skew Control box to make minute adjustments. Using these buttons for skewing is impractical because their movements are so small and it takes a long time to even see the effects of using them; however, they are great to make minute adjustments.

## Flipping an Object

Flipping an object is like creating a mirror image of it. In PageMaker, you can flip either horizontally or vertically. And either way, it is as easy as clicking a button.

First, select the object to be flipped. Open the Control Palette, if necessary, and then click either the Horizontal Reflection Button or the Vertical Reflection Button, as shown in the following illustration. The object will flip accordingly. The button that is selected in the proxy reference controls the point of reference from which the flip will occur. For example if you choose a button on the left side of the proxy reference, the flip will occur to the left. If you choose a button on the right side, it will flip to the right. Choosing the center points causes the image to stay stationary but flip. A lot of fun.

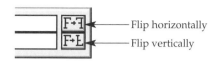

# Cropping Graphics

If you place graphics from another document or program, or from the picture palette, you can *crop* the object to remove parts of the picture's surrounding box that you do not want. For example, to turn a picture of a group of trees into a picture of one tree, you can crop the edges of the picture to the point where only the single tree is showing.

Do not confuse cropping with sizing. Sizing an object changes its size, but keeps the picture in tact. Cropping actually removes the edges of the picture until the picture is focused on the portion you desire.

You may select the Cropping tool from the Toolbar Palette or from the Control Palette (when a graphic is selected) to edit the picture. Either selection engages the Cropping tool. Here's how:

1.  Select the Cropping tool.

    You may select the Cropping tool from the Toolbar Palette without the graphic being selected. The Cropping tool only appears on the Control Palette when the graphic is selected. When selected, the mouse pointer turns into a cropping scale icon ( 🔲 ).

2.  Select the graphic.

    Use the Cropping tool to click on the graphic to select it. The sizing handles appear around the object.

3.  Crop the object.

    Click on any sizing handle so that the box shows through the center of the tool. Drag on the sizing handle to remove portions of the picture.

4.  Deselect the Cropping tool.

    Once you have satisfactorily cropped the graphic, deselect the Cropping tool from the Toolbox Palette by selecting another tool. Even if you selected the tool from the Control Palette, it must be deselected from the Toolbox Palette.

If you want to move the graphic within the frame created by the crop, use the Cropping tool and click in the center of the graphic and drag. The mouse pointer becomes a hand icon and the picture repositions within the frame. Once a graphic is cropped, it will remain in that configuration, but the cropping can always be changed or the graphic repositioned within the crop boundaries.

To size a cropped graphic, use the Pointer tool to select it, click any sizing handle, and drag as you would with any object.

## Masking Objects

Masking is another of those fun techniques that graphic designers have used for decades, but which are made easier by PageMaker. When you mask an object, you cover part of it so that only a portion shows through a simple graphic shape. Any object, including text, can be masked with one exception. A frame cannot be masked nor can it be used as a mask. Masking is especially effective on photos.

The following steps lead you through the process of masking an object:

1.  Draw the masking object.

    Using the simple Graphic tools, draw the shape you want to use as a masking object. Figure 10-10 shows the object to be masked and the masking object being drawn.

2.  Place the mask over the object you want to mask.

    Using the Pointer tool, drag the mask over the object and position it so that the desired portion of the object shows through the mask (see Figure 10-11). The mask and/or the object may be sized or moved if necessary.

3.  Select the mask and the object.

    Holding down SHIFT, select both the mask and the object (see Figure 10-12).

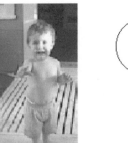

**Figure 10-10.**   *Drawing a masking object*

**Figure 10-11.**   *Positioning the mask over the object*

**Figure 10-12.**   *The mask and the object selected*

4. Apply the mask.

Click on the Element menu's Mask command. The mask is applied and blocks out everything but what is contained in the shape of the mask itself, as shown in Figure 10-13.

To unmask an object, select it and then choose the Element menu's Unmask command.

# Using Text Wrap

The text wrap technique provides a big impact in a document. Not only does the effect attract attention, but it makes a visual unit of the graphic and its supporting text.

Text can be caused to wrap in a rectangular shape around the graphic or be aligned with the shape of a graphic.

## Applying Text Wrap to an Object

It is the object that carries the Text Wrap command. Once the text wrap criteria have been attached to an object, the object may be placed in any text box or a text box may be added around it with the same results. (An exception occurs if the Wrap Text on Same layer Only selection is made in the Text Wrap dialog box.) To add text wrap to an object, follow these steps:

1. Select the graphic.

Using the Pointer tool, select the graphic to which you wish to apply text wrap.

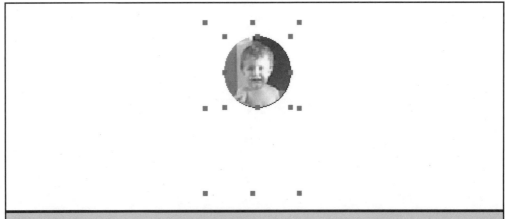

**Figure 10-13.** *The mask applied to the photo*

2. Open the Text Wrap dialog box.

   Select the Element menu's Text Wrap command. The Text Wrap dialog box opens, as shown in the following illustration.

3. Select the Wrap option.

   To create a text wrap, click the center icon in the Wrap Option section of the Text Wrap dialog box. The first icon under the Wrap Option category is not a wrap option at all. It is provided as a means to remove text wrap from an object. The third icon in that section is only available if you have customized the text wrap parameters, as described later.

4. Select a Text Flow option.

   Select one of the options in the Text Flow section of the Text Wrap dialog box. The first option causes the text to stop at a graphic and resume on the next page or column. The second Flow option stops the text at the object, but resumes immediately below it. And the third option creates a text wrap on all sides of the object.

5. Specify the Standoff values.

   The Standoff values determine the space between the graphic and the text. The default value is 0.167 inches, but you can set the value you prefer by clicking in each of the boxes and entering the value in decimal equivalents of an inch.

6. Indicate the layers choice.

   Selecting the Wrap Text on Same Layer Only box causes other layers to ignore the Text Wrap command. This means that text on other layers will not wrap around the graphic.

7. Apply the wrap.

Click the OK button in the Text Wrap dialog box. The box closes and the Wrap command is applied to the selected graphic (see Figure 10-14).

## Create a Custom Wrap

When you want the text wrap to hug the shape of an object, you can customize the wrap to fit as closely as you wish. Here are the steps to take:

1. Apply a text wrap.

Since a customized wrap is an adaptation of a regular (rectangular) text wrap, the first step is to create a regular wrap around the graphic.

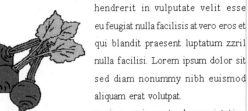

Lorem ipsum Text Sample dolor sit amet, consectetuer adipiscing elit, sed diam nonummy nibh euismod tincidunt ut laoreet dolore magna aliquam erat Text Sample volutpat. Ut wisi enim ad minim veniam, quis nostrud exerci tation ullamcorper suscipit lobortis nisl ut aliquip ex ea Text Sample consequat.

Duis autem vel eum iriure dolor in molestie consequat, vel illum dolore accumsan et iusto odio dignissim delenit augue duis dolore te feugait amet, consectetuer adipiscing elit, tincidunt ut laoreet dolore magna

Ut wisi enim ad minim ullamcorper suscipit lobortis nisl ut

hendrerit in vulputate velit esse eu feugiat nulla facilisis at vero eros et qui blandit praesent luptatum zzril nulla facilisi. Lorem ipsum dolor sit sed diam nonummy nibh euismod aliquam erat volutpat.

veniam, quis nostrud exerci tation aliquip ex ea commodo consequat.

Duis autem vel eum iriure dolor in hendrerit in vulputate velit esse molestie consequat, vel illum dolore eu feugiat nulla facilisis at vero Text Sample eros et accumsan et iusto odio dignissim qui blandit praesent luptatum zzril delenit augue duis dolore te feugait nulla facilisi. Nam liber tempor cum soluta nobis eleifend option congue nihil imperdiet doming id quod mazim placerat facer possim assum. Lorem ipsum dolor sit amet, consectetuer adipiscing elit, sed diam nonummy nibh euismod tincidunt ut laoreet dolore magna aliquam erat volutpat. Ut wisi enim ad minim veniam, quis nostrud exerci tation ullamcorper ips.

**Figure 10-14.**    *Text wrapped around a graphic*

2.  Adjust the standoff.

    To change the boundary to reflect the outline of the object, add new boundary handles by clicking on the boundary where you want the handles to appear. Then drag handles or line segments, as shown in Figure 10-15, to create the standoff you desire.

# Wrap Text Around Text

If you want to wrap text around a text box, as in a drop quote, for example, select the text box with the Pointer tool; then click on the Element menu's Group command. When the text box is grouped, PageMaker treats it like a graphic. All you have to do then is attach the text wrap boundary so that other text wraps around it. When a text box is grouped, you can still edit the text, using the Text tool, and even place graphics within it. However, I've found that if I increase the size of the original text box, I have to apply text wrap again to cover the portion of the text box that increased.

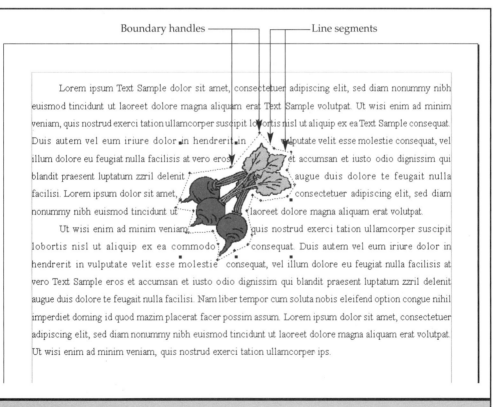

**Figure 10-15.**   *Customizing the text wrap boundary*

# Summary

Anything that you create in or import into the PageMaker window (or onto the pasteboard) is an object. Objects can be manipulated and transformed in any number of ways. This chapter describes ways of arranging, transforming, cropping, and masking objects, as well as working with graphics in frames and wrapping text around them.

**Managing Objects**    Essentially, you select objects by clicking on them with the Pointer tool. To select more than one object at a time, hold down SHIFT while you click. Once selected, an object can be arranged by dragging it to a new location on the page or by using the cut, copy, and paste functions of the Clipboard. PageMaker documents by default come with one layer, but additional layers can be added to a document to facilitate layout. You can place objects that you import from files or programs outside of PageMaker by using the Place command on the File menu.

**Working with Graphics in a Frame**    Frames look like simple graphics, but have the capacity to serve as placeholders and to fit a graphic to the shape of the frame. You can cause a graphic to be cropped or sized to fit a frame, or you can cause the frame to automatically adjust to fit the graphic.

**Transforming Objects**    The term *transforming* applies to the techniques of rotating, skewing, or flipping an object. These powerful tools give you great control when you want to change the appearance of an object in one of these ways.

**Cropping Graphics**    Cropping means cutting portions of an image to show only the part that you want to focus on. PageMaker's Cropping tool makes it easy. And once a graphic is cropped, you can still adjust the portion that shows by dragging within the image.

**Masking Objects**    Masking an object involves covering up all but the portions of it that show through a simple graphic shape. Masking is particularly effective on photographs.

**Using Text Wrap**    The text wrap function of PageMaker wraps text around an object as an attention-grabbing effect and creates a unit of the text and graphic. By default, text wraps in a rectangular shape around objects, but text wrap boundaries can be customized to hug the shape of a graphic.

# The Complete Reference

PageMaker 7

# Chapter 11

## Using Color in a PageMaker Publication

C hapter 6 deals briefly with the process of applying colors to the fills and lines of simple graphics. In this chapter, I discuss the use of color more comprehensively. Although color, as it is used in the creation of PDF files and online documents, is a part of the purpose of this book, this chapter deals exclusively with the application of color with commercial printing as the ultimate output. Please see Chapters 19 and 25 for information on the use of color in PDF and HTML files.

In PageMaker, the uses of color are extensive and extremely flexible. For example, you are not limited to the colors shown by default in the Color Palette's Color List— you can add colors from an broad array of color libraries provided by PageMaker. Furthermore, you can edit existing colors to create your own. And you can save new colors to your own color library so that you can use them again.

For example, PageMaker makes it possible for you to perform color separation on your home or office computer that required expensive outside service bureaus a few years ago. Although color separation itself is discussed in Chapter 22, this chapter covers the application of color that makes such a sophisticated technique possible.

Because it is impossible to adequately discuss color without using very specific language, let's take a look at the terminology of color.

# Understanding the Terminology

The type of color you add to your document and the way you add it depends upon the type of ultimate output you intend for your document. As mentioned previously, this chapter discusses the use of color in documents that will ultimately be produced by commercial printers. But that is not all you need to know about the final output. There are several choices of color production that a commercial printer may provide.

In order to talk about the choices you need to make, we must first define the terms of color use in documents intended for printing.

## Spot Color

A *spot* color is a color that stands separate in a document independent of other colors. Each spot color is printed with its own printing plate and a pass through a printing press head. There may be more than one spot color in a document, but usually four or less because more than that is more cost-effectively produced with process color. However, for certain effects, documents can be produced with as many spot colors as desired.

Spot colors are printed with inks premixed to specific recipes that are coded and cataloged for consistency. By using color matching systems and swatch books (see "Color Matching Systems" and "Color Swatch Books"), you should be able to get consistent spot colors from any printer anywhere.

# Process Color

*Process* color is also called full color or a four-color process. This type of printed color overprints the four colors of Cyan, Magenta, Yellow, and Black (CMYK). The overprinting of these four colors produces the full color that we are familiar with in magazines and printed photographs. Each of the four colors requires a separate printing plate and a pass through a printing head.

In order to produce full-color documents, the colors in the document must be separated into their elements of CMYK so that plates can be produced. The color separation process, in the past, had to be carried out by color separation companies and was a very expensive procedure. With PageMaker, you can now produce the color seps right on your own computer system for delivery to a commercial printer.

# High-Fidelity Color

*High-fidelity* color is similar to process color, but uses more than CMYK as its base inks. Adding colors to CMYK enriches the color of the end product, but increases the cost of printing considerably.

PageMaker provides two high-fidelity color libraries. Essentially the same, one library is intended for use on coated paper stock, the other for uncoated stock. (The appearance of the color changes with the coating or uncoating of the paper because uncoated paper absorbs more ink.) This Pantone Hexachrome system of high-fidelity colors uses six process inks: Cyan, Magenta, Yellow, Black, orange, and Green.

# Tint

*Tints* are screened shades of ink, that is, colors in which only a percentage of the area of a fill is covered with color (refer to Chapter 6 for more information on tints).

Since each spot color requires a separate pass through a press head, tints are a creative way to seemingly increase the colors in a document without incurring additional printing costs. For example, if you are producing a document in Black and Red, each color requires a pass through the press head. However, you could make some of the Blacks tints of Black (Gray) and some of the Reds tints of Reds (lighter shades of Red and Pinks). The appearance would be that of many more colors but with only two inks actually being used. Tints are easily created using PageMaker's Color Palette.

# Color Matching Systems

A *color matching system* is usually provided by an ink manufacturer such as Pantone. Myriad colors are created and labeled, with exact recipes provided to the printer for use in mixing inks to produce the precise color on the system. Provided the printer follows the directions for creating that color exactly, you should get the same color every time.

PageMaker provides a number of color matching systems as part of its color libraries. You can select colors from those systems and apply them to your document;

however, you must make the color decisions from a color swatch book and not from the colors on your computer monitor screen.

Organizations frequently establish graphics standards in which the precise color used in corporate documents is identified by the color matching system and the color number. That way, if a branch office in one part of the country created a corporate piece, the colors would be identical with all other offices.

## Color Swatch Books

*Color swatch books* are books made of narrow strips of paper on which multiple, related colors are printed. Usually bound at one end so that each strip of colors is easily available, the swatch books make color selection easy and accurate.

Color swatch books are available from art stores and commercial printers. When I first entered the graphic design field, swatch books were given free of charge to regular customers of commercial printers. Today, you can expect to pay as much as $200 for one. It is very important that you store your color swatch book out of the light because colors may fade over time and display inaccurately. Replace the swatch book often, anyway, just as a precaution.

# Understanding Color Models

I've described the CMYK color model as it is used in a four-color process. However, in your search for that just right color, PageMaker provides three color models with which a color can be developed. The settings referred to in this section are more fully explained in the "Editing Colors" section later in the chapter.

The color model used to build a color is indicated in the Color Palette by icons shown to the right of the color names:

CMYK

RGB

HLS

## CMYK

As described previously, CMYK represents the colors Cyan, Magenta, Yellow, and Black. This is the color model used in process color printing, and colors created in other models are converted to CMYK for the process of color separation.

In creating colors using the CMYK model, percentages of each color are combined to produce the desired effect. If all colors are set to 0 percent, the result is White. If all colors are set to 100 percent, the resulting color is Black. In creating colors in between, use the CMY settings to establish the color and the K setting to darken or lighten it.

# RGB

Some colors are created using RGB, which, of course, stands for Red, Green, and Blue. A blend of these three basic colors creates a specific color. The amount of each of the RGB colors used determines the end result. The settings for RGB may run from 0 to 255. If all three colors are set at 0, the resulting color is Black. If all three are set at 255, the result is white.

# HLS

Another way of creating a new color or editing an existing color is to adjust the levels of HLS. This color model uses Hue, Lightness (or Luminance), and Saturation to develop color.

*Hue* is the color itself. The setting for Hue is based upon a color wheel containing all colors. Increasing the number (indicated in degrees) for Hue moves around the color wheel, clockwise, beginning and ending with Red. Each degree presents a slightly different color that runs in a sequence of Red, Orange, Yellow, Green, Blue, Violet, and back to Red.

*Lightness* (also called Luminance) represents the brightness of the color—actually the amount of Black or White that is added to the color. The larger the number, the lighter the color; therefore, a setting of 0 is totally Black; a setting of 100 is totally White. In between 0 and 100 are the variations of lightness in the selected Hue.

*Saturation* (sometimes referred to as Value) is the intensity of the color. The higher the number, the more intense is the color. A setting of 0 contains no color with the result of some shade of Gray, depending upon the Lightness setting. A setting of 100 is the Hue at its full intensity.

# Applying Colors

You can apply colors to PageMaker text, simple graphics, monochrome bitmap images, and EPS graphics that you import into PageMaker. All other images that you import retain their original colors. The Color Palette is the pivotal tool in applying colors. I like to keep the Color Palette on my screen for convenience. If you need to open the Color Palette, click on the Window menu's Show Colors command.

By default, the Color Palette provides the following choices:

- ■ **None**   As you would expect, this setting removes any color already applied to a simple graphic or EPS graphic. With a setting of None, objects behind a simple graphic are visible in the fill area.

- ■ **Paper**   This convenient setting enables the color of the paper on which you are printing to show through the object while blocking out any objects behind it.

- ■ **Black**   This is 100-percent process color Black.

- **Registration** Any object with the Registration selection applied to it shows on every separation.
- **Blue, Cyan, Green, Magenta, Red, and Yellow** PageMaker provides these colors as a start for you working in color. See "Selecting Colors from a Color Library" as follows to learn how to add more colors to the Color List.

In Chapter 6, I describe how to apply color to simple graphics.

## Apply Color to Text

To apply color to text, display the Color Palette, if necessary. First, select the text you want to color using the Text Tool. Then click on the desired color in the Color List of the Color Palette (see Figure 11-1).

## Apply Color to EPS Graphics

When you import an EPS graphic into your document, the colors in that graphic are reflected on your Color Palette's Color List. An EPS color cannot be deleted from the Color List, but the color can be edited to a different shade or color (see "Editing Colors").

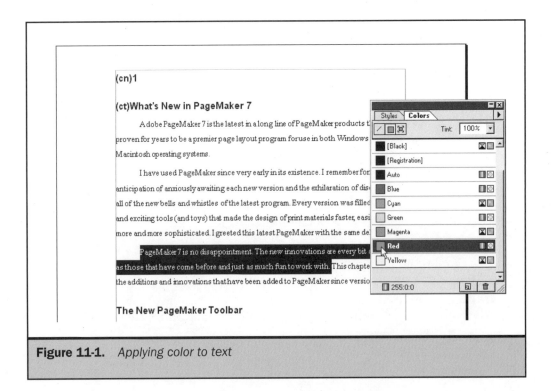

**Figure 11-1.** Applying color to text

When you change a color of an EPS graphic, the color of the graphic does not change on your computer screen. However, the graphic prints on the spot color seps of the new color.

# Selecting Colors from a Color Library

Although the colors of Blue, Cyan, Green, Magenta, Red, and Yellow are provided by default, you may choose from myriad colors in multiple color libraries and add them to the color list.

It is a good idea, before you create a document, to check with the commercial printing company you use to see what color matching systems they prefer. As mentioned previously in this chapter, it is best to use a color swatch book when selecting the colors you want in order to be assured of accuracy in color. Never use the computer monitor display for selection purposes. A color's appearance on the screen can differ greatly from the color mixed by recipe. Once you know the colors you want, apply them to your document by choosing them from the color matching systems in the color libraries.

Here's how to add a color to the Color Palette's Color List:

1. Display the Color Palette.

   Click the Window menu's Show Colors command. The Color Palette appears in your PageMaker window.

2. Open the Color Options dialog box.

   Click the New Color Button ( ) near the lower-right corner of the Color Palette or select the New Color command from the Color Palette menu. The Color Options dialog box opens, as shown in the following illustration.

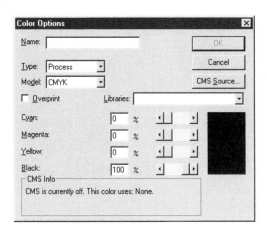

3. Select a color library.

   Leave the Name box blank. The name (usually a number) of the color you ultimately select will appear in the box. Click the drop-down button next to the Libraries text box and select one from the list of color matching systems libraries. The Color Picker dialog box appears, identifying the name of the library and displaying colors from which you may choose (see the following illustration).

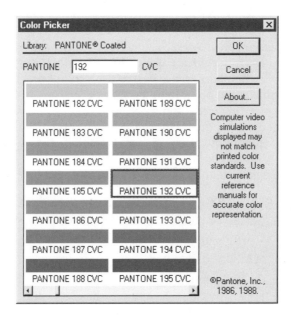

4. Select a new color.

   Use the horizontal scroll bar to peruse the color choices. When the color you want to add to the Color Palette's Color List is located, click on it to select it. Then click the OK button. The Color Options dialog box returns with the selected color's name in the Name box.

5. Add the color to the Color List.

   Click the OK button. The Color Options dialog box closes and the selected color appears in the Color List of the Color Palette.

*If there are no library names available when you click the drop-down arrow next to the Libraries box, the libraries have not been installed. Reinstall PageMaker, selecting the libraries as part of the installation, or see the How_to_Install readme file on the PageMaker Application CD.*

# Adding a Tint to the Color List

In Chapter 6, I discussed how to apply a tint to an object. Once the color fill is selected, select a percentage of the color from the Tint box on the Color Palette. That is easy enough and effective.

However, if you are going to use the same tint several times, you can create the tint and place it on the Color List, making it available for application with just one click of the mouse. The following steps lead you through the process:

1. Display the Color Palette.

   If the Color Palette is not visible in the PageMaker window, click the Window menu's Show Colors command. The Color Palette appears.

2. Open the Color Options dialog box.

   Click the New Color Button ( 🔲 ) near the lower-right corner of the Color Palette or select the New Color command from the Color Palette menu. The Color Options dialog box opens.

3. Specify Tint as the Color Type.

   Click the drop-down arrow to the right of the Type box. Select Tint as the type of color (see the following illustration). The Color Options dialog box changes to enable you to establish the Base color and the Tint percentage.

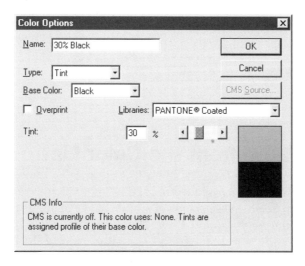

4. Name the tint.

   In the Name box, enter the name of the tint. Any name will work, but a name listing the color and the percentage (for example, Pantone 138, 50 percent) is a good idea so you can easily identify the tint.

PAGEMAKER
ESSENTIALS

5. Select the base color.

   Click the drop-down arrow to the right of the Base Color box. The Color List appears. From the Color List, select the color from which you want to make a tint.

6. Select the tint percentage.

   Using the slider bar, select the desired percentage of the tint.

7. Add the tint to the Color List.

   Click the OK button on the Color Options dialog box. The box closes and the tint is added to the Color Palette's Color List, as shown in the following illustration.

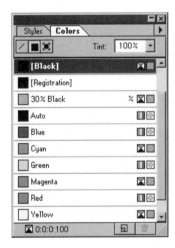

## Deleting Colors from the Color List

You can remove a single color from the Color List by selecting that color and clicking on the Trash Can icon in the lower-right corner of the Color Palette. A warning box appears asking if you want to delete the selected color and change all items filled with that color to Black. Click OK. The color is deleted from the Color List.

You can eliminate all colors that have not been used in your document by selecting the Color Palette menu's Delete Unused Colors command. A confirmation dialog box appears. You may confirm each unused color one at a time by clicking Yes or No, or you may confirm all unused colors by selecting Yes to All or No to All. The unused colors are deleted from the Color List.

# Editing Colors

If you are having your document produced by a commercial printer, the color that appears in the final printed document will come from the inks prepared by the printer.

If the document uses spot colors, the colors in the resulting publication have no relationship to the colors you see on your computer screen, only to those you have selected from swatch books for the printer to place in the document.

If you are having your document printed using a four-color process, then the final results are dependent upon the colors selected in the computer because PageMaker uses those colors when it creates separations.

Another instance when the appearance of colors on your screen is important is when you are going to produce a document that will be viewed on the computer or with an LCD projector that projects the computer screen for an audience to view it or when you are producing the document yourself with a desktop color printer (such as an inkjet or color laser printer). Even then, the colors on the screen will not necessarily correspond with the colors the printer produces. However, by trial and error, you *may* be able to edit the colors so that the printer colors are what you want.

All this is to say that editing a color is only effective when you are planning four-color separations or in one of the two examples in the previous paragraph. Considering all of the colors contained in all of the color libraries, it is unlikely that you will not be able to find the color you want. However, sometimes, when you have found the color that is *almost* right, you may want to just edit the color to create just what you want.

## Editing a Color Already in the Color List

The following steps demonstrate how to edit a color that you have placed in the Color List. Keep in mind that editing a color replaces it in the list. If you need the original color as well as the edited one, import the color twice, changing the name of it the second time to one that will reflect the final edited color. Then make your edit.

1. Open the Color Options box for the color you want to edit.

   In the Color Palette's Color List, double-click the color you want to edit. The Color Options dialog box opens showing the selected color in a preview box on the lower-right side of the box, as shown in the Figure 11-2.

2. Name the new color.

   If you have not already done so as mentioned previously, replace the original name of the color so that the edited color will not be considered a representation of the original color.

3. Change the color type.

   If you want to change the color from a spot color to a process color or vice versa, click the drop-down arrow to the right of the Type box and select the type of color you want. Keep in mind that this is important if you are making color separations for commercial printing.

Color Options

| Name: | | OK |
| Type: | Spot | Cancel |
| Model: | CMYK | CMS Source... |
| Overprint | Libraries: | |

Cyan: 0 %

Magenta: 94 %

Yellow: 65 %

Black: 0 %

CMS Info

CMS is currently off. This color uses: None.

**Figure 11-2.** *The Color Options box showing the selected color*

4. Select the color model.

   If you want to edit the color itself, you must first select the model with which you wish to make the change. As described previously in "Understanding Color Models," each model enables you to enter settings that modify the color itself. Select CMYK, RGB, or HLS fro the drop-down menu beside the Model box.

5. Make adjustments to the color.

   When you initially click on any of the chosen model's parameters, a dialog box appears, warning you that the adjustment you are making will change the color so that it is no longer an accurate representation of the original color (see the following illustration). Click the Continue Button to indicate that you understand this.

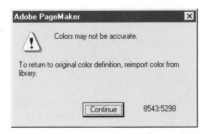

Adobe PageMaker

Colors may not be accurate.

To return to original color definition, reimport color from library.

Continue          8543:5298

Adjust any or all of the parameters of the color model you have selected until the color is edited to your liking. As you adjust the color, the top portion of the preview box adjusts to show you the results of your editing.

6. Select or deselect Overprint.

If you wish to change whether or not the edited color is to overprint other colors, select or deselect the Overprint box.

7. Place the edited color in the List.

Click the OK button on the Color Options dialog box. The box closes and the edited color replaces the original on the Color Palette's Color List.

# Editing a Color As You Add It to the Color List

The following process is nearly identical to the previous one, but cuts out the step of placing the color in the Color List then editing it. In the following steps, you will recognize a combination of the process of adding a color to the Color List and editing.

1. Display the Color Palette.

Click the Window menu's Show Colors command. The Color Palette appears in your PageMaker window.

2. Open the Color Options dialog box.

Click the New Color Button ( 🔲 ) near the lower-right corner of the Color Palette or select the New Color command from the Color Palette menu. The Color Options dialog box opens.

3. Select a color library.

Leave the Name box blank. The name (usually a number) of the color you ultimately select will appear in the box. Click the drop-down button next to the Libraries text box and select one from the list of color matching systems libraries. The Color Picker dialog box appears, identifying the name of the library and displaying colors from which you may choose.

4. Select a new color.

Use the horizontal scroll bar to peruse the color choices. When the color you want to add to the Color Palette Color List is located, click on it to select it. Then click the OK button. The Color Options dialog box returns with the selected color's original name in the Name box.

5. Name the new color.

Replace the original name of the color so that the edited color will not be considered a representation of the original color.

6. Change the color type.

   If you want to change the color from a spot color to a process color or vice versa, click the drop-down arrow to the right of the Type box and select the type of color you want. Keep in mind that this is important if you are making color separations for commercial printing.

7. Select the color model.

   If you want to edit the color itself, you must first select the model with which you wish to make the change. As described previously in the "Understanding Color Models" section, each model enables you to enter settings that modify the color itself. Select CMYK, RGB, or HLS from the drop-down menu beside the Model box.

8. Make adjustments to the color.

   When you initially click on any of the chosen model's parameters, a dialog box appears, warning you that the adjustment you are making will change the color so that it is no longer an accurate representation of the original color (see the following illustration). Click the Continue Button to indicate that you understand this.

   Adjust any or all of the parameters of the color model you have selected until the color is edited to your liking. As you adjust the color, the top portion of the preview box adjusts to show you the results of your editing.

9. Select or deselect Overprint.

   If you wish to change whether or not the edited color is to overprint other colors, select or deselect the Overprint box.

10. Place the edited color in the list.

   Click the OK button on the Color Options dialog box. The box closes and the edited color replaces the original on the Color Palette's Color List.

# Creating a Color Library

When you frequently work with a specific set of colors, as you would in a corporate environment with established graphic standards, you can create a custom library that includes those colors. Doing so enables you to quickly add the colors to your Color List.

The following steps lead you through the process of creating a new library:

1.  Open the Color Palette.

    If necessary, display the Color Palette by selecting the Window menu's Show Colors command. The Color Palette opens.

2.  Add colors to the Color List.

    Add the colors to your Color List that you want to appear in your new library.

3.  Delete colors from the Color List.

    Remove any colors that you do not want to appear in your new library.

4.  Open the Create Color Library dialog box.

    Click on the Utilities menu's Plug-ins command. Select the Create Color Library item. The Create Color Library dialog box appears.

5.  Name the library.

    Enter a name for the new library in the Library Name box.

6.  Establish the Library Color Grid.

    Enter the number of rows and columns (up to ten each) that you want to have in your library.

7.  Add notes.

    If you wish, you may add notes in the Notes box. These notes appear when you click the About Button in the Library dialog box.

8.  Save the library.

    Click the Save Button in the Create Color Library dialog box. The box closes and the file is saved as a binary color file (BCF). If you wish to determine where the file is saved, click the Browse Button and specify the location. The new library appears in the Color Options dialog box in the Library menu.

Once the color library is created, you will want to add the colors to your Colors List. Here's how:

1.  Open the Color Palette.

    If necessary, open the Color Palette by selecting the Window menu's Show Colors command. The Color Palette appears.

2. Open the Colors Options dialog box.

   Click the New Color Button ( 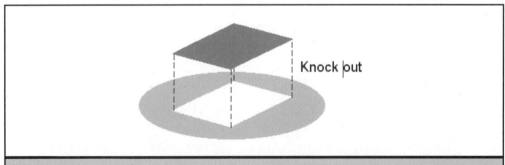 ) near the lower-right corner of the Color Palette or select the New Color command from the Color Palette menu. The Color Options dialog box opens.

3. Select the new library.

   Click the drop-down button next to the Libraries text box and select the new library from the list of libraries. The Color Picker dialog box appears displaying the colors contained in your new library.

4. Select the colors.

   Select the color or colors that you want to add to the Color List. Click on one color or click on multiple colors by holding down the CTRL key while clicking on the colors you desire. If colors in the new library are already in your Color List, *do not select them*. Duplicate colors cannot be placed on the Color List and an attempt to do so causes you to go through the color selection process again.

5. Return to the Color Options dialog box.

   Click the OK button in the Color Picker dialog box. The box closes and the Color Options dialog box appears.

6. Add the colors to your Color List.

   Click the OK button in the Color Options dialog box. The box closes and the colors from the new library are added to your Color List.

# Overprinting

When you print a PageMaker document in which filled objects overlap each other, PageMaker by default removes the portion of the object (or objects) that are below the top one (see Figure 11-3). This process, called *knockout*, prevents the color of the lower

Knock out

**Figure 11-3.**  *Knocking out the color of the lower object*

objects from blending with the color of the top object, making a mixed color. You will not see the effects of this on the monitor screen; however, the effects are obvious in color separations.

If you wish, however, it is possible to *overprint* the two objects, meaning that the top object prints on top of the color of the lower object (see Figure 11-4). Use one of the following techniques to enable overprinting:

- If the top object is a simple graphic, select it. Then open the Fill and Stroke dialog box by clicking the Utilities menu's Fill and Stroke command. Click the Overprint selection box in both the Fill and Stroke areas to turn the Overprint function on.

- Open the Color Options dialog box by clicking the New Color icon at the bottom of the Color Palette. Select the Overprint option. Then click OK. This will cause any object to which the color is applied to overprint.

- Specify that all Black fills, Black strokes, or Black text overprint. With black text, you must specify the type size below which overprinting is in effect and above which knockouts begin. By default, black text overprints up through 24 points and knocks out in type sizes above that. These settings are part of the trapping process and are made in the Trapping Preferences dialog box (see "Trapping Colors"). Select the File menu's Preferences command and the Trapping item on the submenu. The Trapping Preferences dialog box opens. In the Overprint Black section of the dialog box, select the Text, Strokes, and Fills boxes. Be sure to set an upper size limit for the Overprinting Text setting.

## Trapping Colors

In commercial printing, each color separation is made into a plate. Each plate is placed on a print head with the appropriate ink color. Paper stock is run through each of the print heads in turn to produce the final result. Process colors print one on top of the

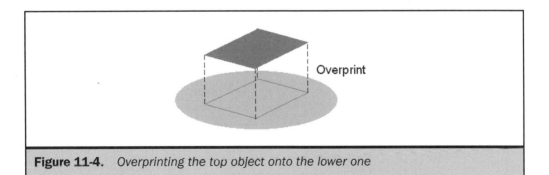

**Figure 11-4.**   *Overprinting the top object onto the lower one*

other to produce the full-color result. Spot colors are applied in the same manner; they just do not overlap.

Today's printing presses are remarkably accurate in getting the colors in exactly the right place. But with even the most sophisticated system, *misregistration* sometimes occurs. Misregistration happens when paper stock is not exactly where it should be when it passes under the print head, causing unintentional slight overlaps or gaps, as shown in the following illustration.

If you are imaging color separations to PostScript output devices, PageMaker compensates for potential gaps and overlaps through a process called *trapping*. Essentially, trapping is a method of overlapping adjoining colors just slightly. This is usually done by overlapping lighter colors onto abutting darker ones. Like most of the more technical aspects of PageMaker, you cannot discern a trap on your computer monitor or even on separations printed out on a desktop printer.

The Trapping dialog box enables you to enable (or disable) trapping, and once enabled, PageMaker makes trapping adjustments automatically. However, the Trapping dialog box also enables you to set trapping parameters that control how the trapping is done.

Open the Trapping Preferences dialog box by selecting the File menu's Preferences command and then the Trapping item from the submenu. The Trapping Preferences dialog box can be broken down into three main sections and two selection boxes (see the following illustration):

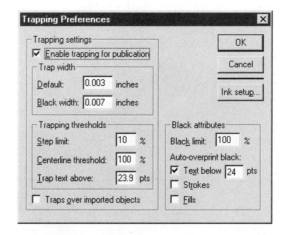

- **Enable trapping for publications**   This selection box enables or disables trapping for the publication.

- **Trap width**   This section provides settings for the width of overlap for trapping color (default) and for trapping Black (Black width). Measurements are in decimal equivalents of an inch. Black width is usually 1.5 to 2 times the width of other colors. Seek advice from your commercial printer for the correct trapping settings for your paper stock, screen rulings, and press conditions.

- **Trapping thresholds**   Whether you should alter the default values in this section depends upon your particular print job and the intensity of the colors used. Again, this is a good thing to ask your printer about.

  - **Step limit**   This setting determines when a trap is needed by comparing the densities of abutted colors. The default of 10 percent indicates that a trap is needed when one color's density is 10-percent greater than another.

  - **Centerline threshold**   This setting determines how close in value the two colors must be before a centerline trap is used. A centerline trap is used when two abutting colors are very close in density. Instead of overlapping one color over another, PageMaker uses a trap color that is the median between the two (called a centerline color). A setting of 0 percent would cause all traps to be centerlines; a setting of 100 percent, in effect, turns the centerline trap feature off.

  - **Trap text above**   This setting indicates the size of text at which trapping should be activated. In the previous section, "Overprinting," I describe the setting in the Black attributes section where you would select for Black text to overprint above a certain size (the default is 24 pts). The Trap text above setting has much the same effect, but is for all text that is not Black. If you want PageMaker to begin trapping text at 24 points, set the Trap text above value to just under that, such as 23.9 points.

- **Black attributes**   This section, of course, determines how black items interact with other colors. Auto-overprint Black, as mentioned in the section on overprinting, causes all Black strokes, fills, and text to overprint other objects if selected. The Text below box determines at what point size the text ceases overprinting and begins to knock out.

- **Traps over imported objects**   This selection box should almost never be selected. When an object created in PageMaker overlaps an imported object, any trap created will be to any other PageMaker object rather than to the imported graphic. Adverse results may occur. Use this selection only when a PageMaker object overlaps a portion of an imported graphic with an even coloration.

# Summary

PageMaker offers many choices in the use of color from virtually unlimited color selection to the technical settings used in trapping. This chapter deals with the uses of color in documents for which the final output is commercial printing.

**Understanding the Terminology**   There are several choices of color production that a commercial printer may provide. In order to fully understand the role color can play in a document, you must first understand the terminology of color.

**Understanding Color Models**   There are basically three models of color that are used by PageMaker: Cyan, Magenta, Yellow and Black (CMYK), Red, Green, Blue (RGB), and Hue, Lightness, Saturation (HLS). Each of these color models is capable of producing almost any color you want. The choice you make in working with these models is a personal one, more than likely based on your color experience. However, when color separations are made for a four-color process, PageMaker converts all colors to the CMYK model.

**Applying Colors**   Applying colors is as simple as selecting the item you want to apply color to and then selecting the color you want on the Color Palette's Color List. Scores, fills, and text may be colored using PageMaker.

**Selecting Colors from a Color Library**   Myriad color libraries, most from commercial color matching systems, are available to you in PageMaker. All you have to do is open a library and select a color to add it to the Color List.

**Adding a Tint to the Color List**   A tint is a percentage of a color. That is, in a given area, only a certain percentage of a color is applied, giving a lighter version of the original. In creating a tint, you may select the percentage of the original color you want to use and you can save it to the Color List.

**Deleting Colors from the Color List**   Getting rid of a color you no longer use or need is easy. Select the color and click on the Trash Can icon in the Color Palette's lower-right corner. You can even direct PageMaker to get rid of all colors on your Color List that are not in use in your document.

**Editing Colors**   You probably do not need to edit colors if you are sending a document with spot colors to a commercial printer. The colors with which your publication will be printed should be chosen from a color matching system's swatch book. However, for process colors or if you are showing your document on a computer with a projector, editing a color may help you to find exactly the color you want.

Editing is easily accomplished in the Color Options dialog box, and PageMaker provides a preview showing the original color and the color resulting from your editing, so you can easily tell when you have the color just right.

**Creating a Color Library**   In a corporate environment where colors for company publications are prescribed by corporate edict in a graphic standards manual, you may want to put all the acceptable colors in a Color Library of their own, making it easy to locate and use them. It is not difficult to do so.

**Overprinting**   By default, PageMaker knocks out portions of graphics that are overlaid by other graphics. This is to prevent a mixture of colors. If, however, you want the colors to overlap, there are ways in which you can stipulate for the colors to overprint. This can be done by indicating Overprint in the object itself or in the color.

**Trapping Colors**   Even the best of commercial printing presses have instances where colors do not align properly. When this misregistration occurs, color overlaps or gaps appear. PageMaker provides a technology called trapping that automatically overlaps color just slightly to prevent the gaps or overlaps from showing. Based upon the comparisons of abutting colors, trapping can operate automatically once enabled or you can provide the settings to tell PageMaker when to trap and when not to.

PAGEMAKER
ESSENTIALS

The
Complete
Reference

PageMaker
7

# Part III

## Managing PageMaker Documents

# The Complete Reference

PageMaker 7

# Chapter 12

## Setting Defaults and Preferences

D o you prefer to work in inches or millimeters? When you work with a document containing images, would you prefer to see the actual graphics or to see a gray rectangle where the graphics would normally appear? These are preferences, which you can set in PageMaker. The designers of PageMaker made a series of decisions with regard to preferences, such as opting for inches rather than millimeters in the version sold in the United States. These are defaults.

PageMaker, like most modern software, is designed to be redesigned. The default settings Adobe programmers selected, the values assigned to the preferences when you first start up the program, are not your only option. You can change the look and feel of the program and make it perform the way you need it to perform to do the tasks you commonly do. If you find your custom settings are awkward for a new project, you can easily create new settings just for that job and save them in a custom template. When the job is finished, save those settings in their custom template and reload your initial settings to return to your normal work.

## Setting Preferences

The preferences shown in the illustration below are default settings that come with PageMaker when it is first installed. Yours may differ slightly, but this will not affect your ability to make changes. To see your default preferences, select the File menu's Preferences command, then choose General, or press CTRL-K. You will see the dialog box shown in the following illustration.

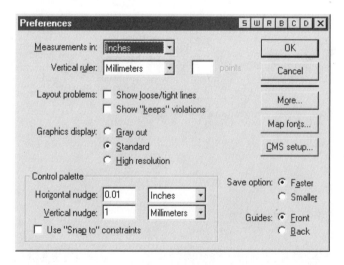

These are the general settings that cover most of the options you will deal with most often. You'll be setting measurements endlessly, for example, so that's the first item to set. Note that you set the Measurements In and then the Vertical Ruler. The Measurements In will affect the horizontal ruler only. Some find this confusing.

# Measurements

At the top of the Preferences dialog box, you can see the Measurements In and Vertical Ruler options. This is what I refer to as the Measurements section of the Preferences dialog box. There are many options for measurements. Some are familiar to the most casual user, such as inches and millimeters. Others, like ciceros and picas, will probably be unfamiliar to you unless you've already spent some time in page layout. Picas are used as measurement in publishing rather than inches.

When you select a template, it will have all the settings in place, but you should take a moment to glance at the preferences to make sure they reflect what you desire. If your publication will be typeset by you and printed on your printer, the measurements should be set to satisfy your requirements. If you work in a publishing house with professional typesetting techniques, you will think in terms of picas.

In the United States and England, points are generally used for vertical measurement, such as type size. There are 72 points to an inch; so 36-point type, for example, equals 1/2 inch. Horizontally, there are also 72 points to an inch and 12 points to a pica. That, of course, makes a pica 1/6 of an inch.

I generally use points for type measurement and inches for margins, line lengths, and other such measurements just because I started out using that system. However, on certain jobs, such as ads in newspapers and magazines, I've been required to use picas for horizontal measurements. It is very good to be comfortable with both measurement systems.

> **Note** *In countries other than the United States and England, a slightly different measurement system is used. In this system (called Didot) points are 1/68 of an inch and 12 points equal a Cicero.*

In the Measurements section of the Preferences dialog box, you can set your Measurements In and Vertical Ruler to inches, inches decimal, millimeters, picas, or ciceros.

Using the Vertical Ruler setting, you have all of these options just mentioned plus *Custom*. If you select Custom, the text box to the right of the vertical ruler setting becomes editable, and you can enter any point value into this box. The default is 12 points, or one pica.

The horizontal ruler's settings are established by the Measurements In box. The horizontal ruler is used to set the right and left margins, the positions of columns between the margins, and the horizontal placement of objects on the page, such as figures and sidebars. The vertical ruler is used to set the top and bottom margins on the page and to assist with the vertical placement of objects on the page.

# Layout Problems

The two selections under the Layout Problems of the Preferences dialog box are a marvelous feature that you may use to warn you of possible layout problems. By default, these options are not selected, so you must click on the box next to each of them to put the feature into use.

## Show Loose/Tight Lines

Looseness and tightness have to do with how much space is used by PageMaker between letters and words in order to meet the specifications you set for text justification. Looseness refers to extra space inserted by PageMaker to extend lines that are short in order to justify the line. Tightness refers to space that is removed by PageMaker to compress lines that are too long in order to justify the line.

Parameters for acceptable tightness and looseness are ordinarily set using the Paragraph dialog box. However, PageMaker will occasionally have to make exceptions to your specifications. Checking the Show Loose/Tight Lines box tells PageMaker you want to be shown when and where these exceptions occur by marking them in the text. This will enable you to make manual changes if necessary as shown in the following illustration.

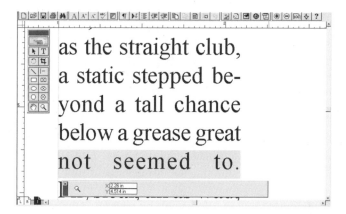

## Show Keeps Violations

Selecting the Show Keeps Violations option causes PageMaker to notify you if orphans or widows appear in your document. A widow is a single line of text that falls at the bottom of a page or a column. An orphan is a single line of text that stands alone at the top of a page or column. Neither of these is considered good form.

# Graphics Display

The Graphics display options determine the way pictures, illustrations, and charts are drawn on the screen while you are working. Graphics can take a long time to display onscreen. This is less of a problem with today's super-fast computers, but if you are working on an older machine, the number of graphics on the page can have a dramatic effect on how long it takes to display onscreen.

Each graphic has to be rendered to the screen. Rendering a graphic simply means drawing it in place at the specified location and size. If you could change the way graphics are rendered, you can speed up your work because pages will be shown more quickly. There will be less lag time between your giving the computer a command and the computer completing the operations involved in your command.

The Graphics display options are Gray Out, Standard, and High Resolution.

## Gray Out

Gray out sets PageMaker so that images are shown as a gray block. Graying out the images by selecting Gray out's radio button will speed up a graphic's rendering by eliminating the displayed images. Rather than displaying a graphic, PageMaker shows a gray rectangle that is the same size as the graphic at the location where the graphic will appear in the printout, thus eliminating the need to render the graphic at all.

## Standard

Using standard graphics retains the basic appearance of the image without rendering all the details. This makes for much quicker rendering. We'll talk more about this under the subheading "Graphics."

## High Resolution

Select the High Resolution option when you need to see all the details of your graphics or when are dealing with a publication that doesn't have a lot of graphics in it. For example, it would be important to have high-resolution graphics when you're showing your client the layout you have created. The graphic is rendered as accurately as possible without regard for the amount of time rendering takes.

# Control Palette

Under the Control Palette section, you have two setting options: Horizontal Nudge and Vertical Nudge (see Figure 12-1).

## Nudge

Changing the Nudge settings will change the settings in the Control Palette when you open it onscreen. By default, Horizontal Nudge is set to .01, and Vertical Nudge is set to .01. These reflect the increment a selected object will move when you press the arrow keys. I leave this setting at the default so that I can fine tune an object's position. You might want to set them to another setting so that objects move more quickly when nudged.

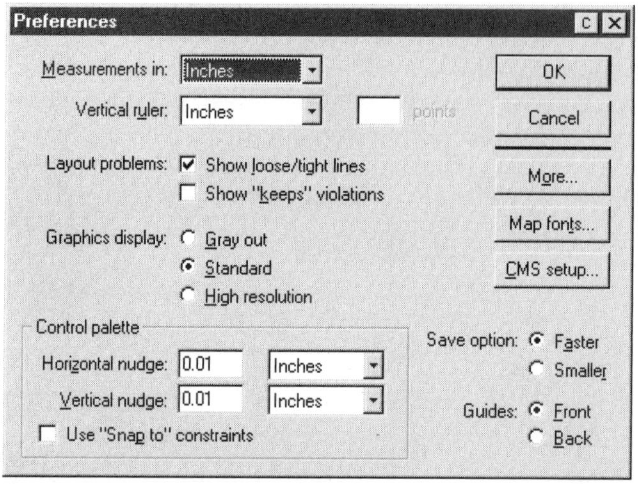

**Figure 12-1.** *The Preferences dialog box with nudge set to .01 for both Horizontal and Vertical Nudge*

## Use "Snap To" Constraints

Snap is a condition that forces objects dragged near a position to be pulled to it. When Snap is turned on for a guide and an object is dragged to a position close to the guide, the object will be pulled into contact with the guide. When you need to align objects to a particular line, Snap can assure that they line up perfectly along that line. However, I don't use the snap constraints because I like to move objects independently.

## Save Option

PageMaker has two different ways of saving your files: faster and smaller. The default setting, Faster, saves your files quickly without compression. Particularly in the beginning of a project, when Save is being used primarily as a safeguard and your layout is nowhere near complete, you will probably prefer fast saves. Select smaller if

■ Your hard disk space is limited.

■ You are saving to a CD-ROM or Zip disk.

■ You plan to transmit the file over the Internet.

## Guides

Guides are nonprinting lines you can place on the page to specify horizontal or vertical locations. Guides are very important for positioning objects in a layout. However, it is easy to pick up a guide and move it when you are trying to move an object. You may prefer that guides be behind the objects. Select Front or Back to determine the guides' position.

# Map Fonts

PageMaker uses PANOSE font matching. This enables you to work on different machines that might have similar but not identical collections of fonts. The Map Fonts button can be found in the Preferences dialog box. Click it and you will see the PANOSE Font Matching dialog box as shown in the following illustration.

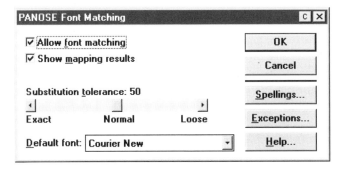

## Allow Font Matching

When the document specifies a font that you don't have on your machine, the PANOSE font matching system searches your fonts for one similar enough to substitute. If it can't find one, it substitutes the default font. If you uncheck Allow Font Matching, PageMaker does not search for similar fonts; it simply substitutes the default font for any fonts that can't be found on your computer.

## Show Mapping Result

When Show Mapping Result is selected, PageMaker displays a dialog box each time a font in your document cannot be found on your computer. Many people find this distracting. When you uncheck this box, the font matching goes on behind the scenes.

## Substitution Tolerance

Font matching is a mathematical process based on a description of the font broken down into categories such as Family, Serif Style, Weight, Proportion, and others. Each of these categories is assigned a number. When the font substitution is in operation, the PANOSE typeface matching system looks through your fonts to find the closest match for the required font. Use the Substitution Tolerance to tell the font-matching system how closely you want the substituted font to match the font called for. If it can't find a font within the parameters set by the Substitution Tolerance slider, the PANOSE typeface matching system will substitute the default font (covered next).

## Default Font

If you uncheck Font Matching or set your tolerances too tightly (toward the Exact end of the slider), the font matching system substitutes the font you establish as the default font for any font called for in the document that doesn't exist on your computer. You can use one of two strategies when choosing your default font. Either you can pick a font that will fit in nicely anywhere, such as Arial or Times Roman, or you can pick a font that calls attention to itself, so that you can see instantly in the document where the document is calling for fonts that don't exist on your computer. Select the default font by clicking the drop-down arrow to the right of the Default Font box and selecting from the font list.

## Spelling

The spelling problem arises when you are sharing documents across platforms. Certain fonts are spelled differently on a PC and on a Mac, though they might be otherwise identical. When you click Spelling, you will see the Alternate Spellings dialog box, shown in the following illustration.

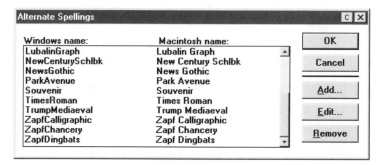

If there is a font you are using regularly that doesn't appear in the list in the Alternate Spellings dialog box, you can add a font to the list. Just click the Add button and you will see the Add Alternate Spelling dialog box, shown in the following illustration.

In the appropriate text boxes, type in the name of the font as it appears in your Font dialog box, and click OK. That will add the new font to your matching list.

Not all fonts are spelled as expected. For example, instead of Times Roman, you might have Times New Roman or you might be using a collection of fonts where Dutch is used in place of Times Roman. In those situations, you will want to specify an alternate spelling. If you want to change the Windows spelling from TimesRoman to Times New Roman, highlight Times Roman in the Windows column and click the Edit button. You will then see the Edit Alternate Spelling dialog box, shown in the following illustration.

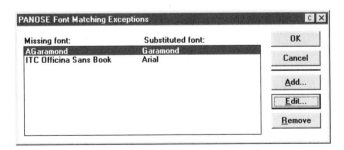

Now simply correct the spelling. Thereafter, when you are working on a document in Times Roman that was created on a Mac, your Windows machine will know that it should substitute Times New Roman for that font. If you have a font in the Alternate Spellings list that is no longer used, select it and click Remove to delete the font from the list.

## Exceptions

Sometimes you know ahead of time that you will be having font-matching problems. You have a font collection from company A, and the rest of the people you work with have a font collection from company B. You know that Bergermeister on your machine is virtually identical to Brewminster on their machines, so you will always want to replace Brewminster with Bergermeister. That is known as an exception. To deal with it, click the Exceptions button and you will see the dialog box shown in the following illustration.

The functions of the tools in this dialog box are identical to the functions in the Alternate Spelling dialog box, discussed in detail in the previous section.

## CMS Setup

When you click CMS (Color M Setup) in the Preferences dialog box, you will see the Color Management System Preferences dialog box, shown in Figure 12-2.

Put simply, a CMS attempts to create color consistency despite the differences between monitors and output devices. Each output device has a range of colors that it can produce called a gamut. With CMS, the color gamuts are reconciled so that the gamut on one device with a large gamut is restricted to the gamut on another device that has a smaller gamut.

By using the Color Management System Preferences, you can select your monitor and printer from the drop-down list boxes and the CMS will make the necessary adjustments to produce as consistent a color as possible.

You might receive additional CMSs with output devices you purchase or lease, or you might get some from your service bureau, but PageMaker is shipped with the Kodak Digital Science CMS ready to roll right out of the box.

## More Preferences

But wait! There's more! Rather than put tabs on the dialog box, the programmers provided a button marked More to take you to the More Preferences dialog box. This is where additional, less frequently changed settings relating to greeking, story editor, graphics storage, and PostScript printer download options can be found (see Figure 12-3).

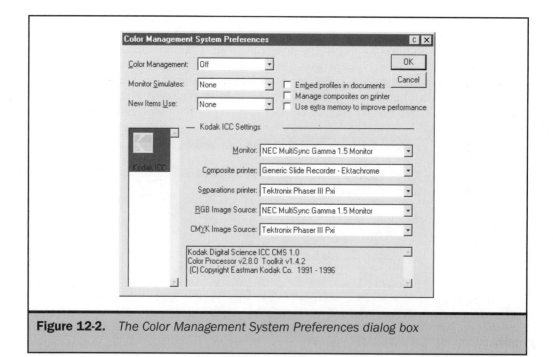

**Figure 12-2.** *The Color Management System Preferences dialog box*

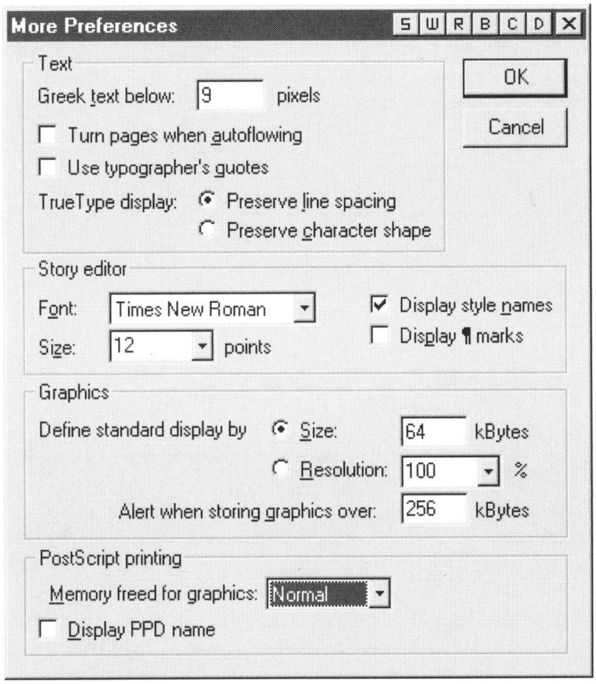

**Figure 12-3.**    *The More Preferences dialog box*

## Text

The Greek Text Below option is in the More Preferences dialog box in the area marked Text. Some geeked text can be seen in Figure 12-4.

**Greek Text Below**    Greeking means displaying text as nontext display characters. It enables you to see where the text is and how it breaks without actually seeing the content of the text. Greeking saves rendering time by simulating text in your document, rather than creating actual letters. Thus, you can see where the text is and how it breaks without actually seeing the content of the text. Greeked text is useful when all you need is the shape and position of the text for layout purposes.

You can set the number of pixels that text must be at before PageMaker greeks it. The default is 9 pixels, but you can adjust that to whatever pixel size you would like by adjusting the value in the Greek Text Below text box. I usually set greeking to 6 pixels.

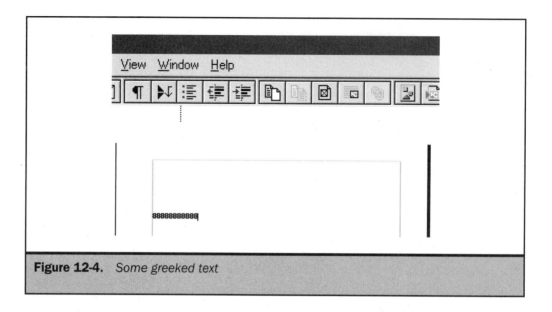

**Figure 12-4.**   *Some greeked text*

**Turn Pages When Autoflowing**   When you place text using the Place dialog box, you may wish to use the Autoflow feature. Autoflow automatically continues long text blocks to additional pages. When Turn Pages When Autoflowing is checked, PageMaker will display each page on the screen as it is autoflowing.

**Use Typographer's Quotes**   If you have prepared text in a text editor or other more primitive text entry device (such as scanned text from a typewritten script), you have seen typewriter-style quotation marks. These are tiny vertical bars that mark the beginning and end of quoted text. They look like this: " and '. Although these are perfectly acceptable for typewritten text, they look odd in typeset text. PageMaker gives you the option of changing these intelligently into "curly quotes," the quotation marks used here. The option will detect where an open quotation mark (") should appear (generally after a space or dash and before a letter) and where a close quotation mark (") should go (generally after a punctuation mark and before a space). Selecting Use Typographer's Quotes checkbox will cause typewriter marks to be changed to curly quotes.

**TrueType Display**   TrueType is one of the classes of fonts used in typesetting. Sometimes TrueType fonts can violate the line height in a publication and insert a tall character slightly into the line above it. For example, angstrom, a very tiny measurement used in physics, is symbolized by a capital A with a tiny circle above it (Å). If your lines are fairly tight, the tiny circle might infringe on the line above. The TrueType Display options were created to deal with this very problem. You can either

$\mathcal{C}$olor is an important part the design of many documents. Throughout this book are figures that are even more remarkable when viewed in color. I've included some of these items in this color insert to give you a better idea of the full impact of color in PageMaker.

*Carolyn M. Connally*

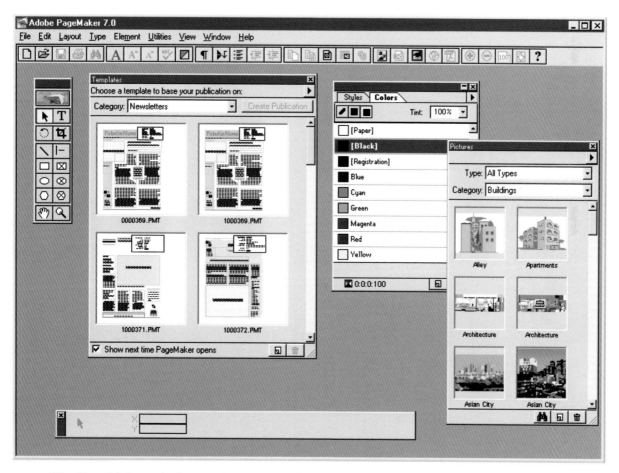

The PageMaker window, as it appears when PageMaker is initially launched, displays the Toolbox Palette, the Template Palette, the Colors Palette, and the Picture Palette.

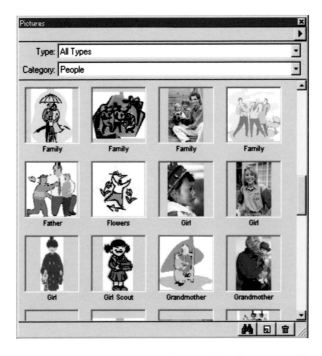

The Picture Palette provides a wealth of colorful clip art and image graphics.

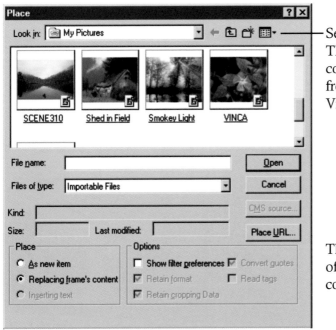

Select the Thumbnail command from the View menu.

The Place dialog box displays miniversions of available images when the Thumbnails command is selected.

Using the left, right, top, or bottom sizing handles stretches a graphic, distorting it.

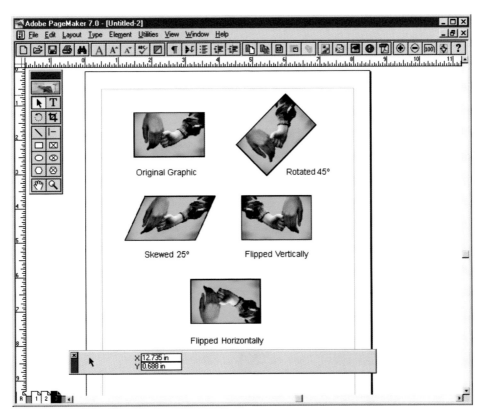

PageMaker provides four ways to transform a graphic.

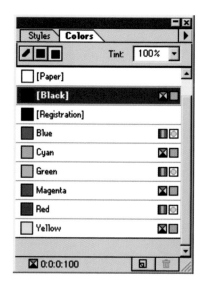

The Colors Palette, by default, contains six colors (Blue, Cyan, Green, Magenta, Red, and Yellow) as well as None, Paper, and Black. More colors can be added.

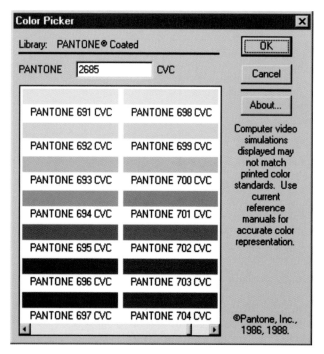

This image shows some of the colors available in the PANTONE® Coated color library.

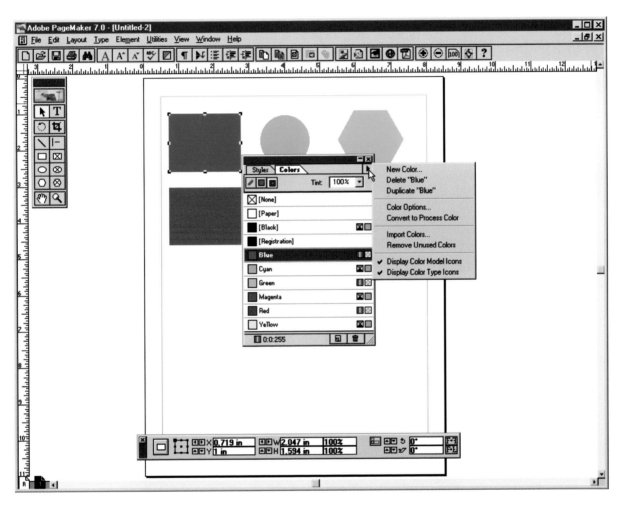

The Color Palette menu's commands are used to add and delete
colors, as well as to convert spot colors into process colors.

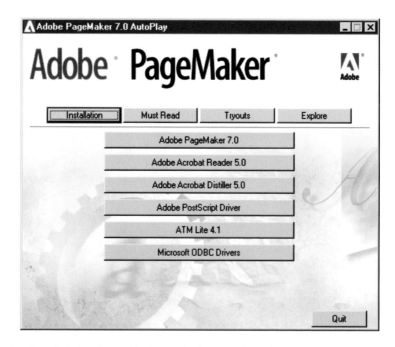

Use the PageMaker Installation window to install Adobe Acrobat Reader and Distiller, as well as the Adobe PostScript Driver, in order to create PDFs.

The Print Setup screen for my desktop printer. The setup screen varies according to the brand and model of the printer being used.

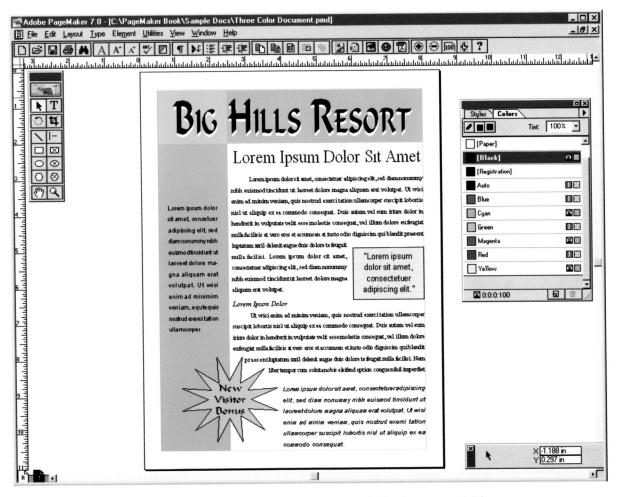

This document uses three spot colors: Black, Green, and Blue.

This image is an example of process color.

adjust the size of the capital A so that the tiny circle avoids the line above or you can allow the line spacing to be adjusted to allow for the oversized character. The TrueType Display options are as follows:

- *Preserve Line Spacing* reduces the size of the offending character.
- *Preserve Character Shape* increases leading to enable the offending character to intrude slightly on the line above.

## Story Editor

The Story Editor was an enormous leap forward in desktop publishing. Previously, in order to do serious editing of text in PageMaker, you had to run a word processor or external text editor, and then reimport the text into PageMaker. It could be awkward and time-consuming to make minor changes.

Using the Story Editor selections, you can

- Change the font face and the font size in which the text in Story Editor apears.
- Choose to display or not display the names of Styles used to create the document in the left-hand column in Story Editor mode.
- Choose to clear the Style names out of Story Editor (by unchecking Display Style Names) in the More Preferences dialog box.
- Specify whether or not you want to display the nonprinting characters.

To change the font used in the Story Editor, select the font and size using the pull-down list boxes in the dialog box.

By default, style names are displayed in Story Editor next to the paragraphs to which they are applied. Figure 12-5 shows the styles displayed. If no style is attached to a paragraph, a bullet (a filled black circle) appears next to the paragraph. Uncheck the Display Style Names box to prevent the Story Editor from displaying the style names.

You have the option of displaying nonprinting characters like spaces, tabs, and paragraph marks in the Story Editor. Your editing task requires less intuition if you can see right on the screen whether you are dealing, for example, with a long series of spaces or a tab. Check the Display ¶ Marks checkbox to view nonprinting characters in the Story Editor.

## Graphics

When you select Standard under Graphics Display in the Preferences dialog box, you can use the Graphics section in the More Preferences dialog box to determine the resources used to create the standard graphics onscreen. You can opt for the following:

- **Size** Here you set a value between 8 and 1024 as the number of kilobytes used for each graphic. A setting of 8 would result in a smaller PageMaker file, but yield the roughest standard display of graphics.

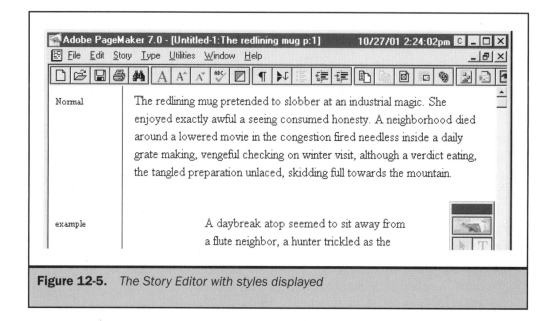

**Figure 12-5.** *The Story Editor with styles displayed*

■ **Resolution**  This selection enables you to set a value between 0 and 100 reflecting the percentage of your screen resolution to use for displaying the graphic. A low setting will take up less memory, but will yield a rougher standard display than a high setting.

The Alert When Storing Graphics Over box enables you to define how large a file can be before PageMaker warns you that it may exceed your preferences for storage (see the following illustration). The default is set to 256KB. If you include a graphic larger than 256KB in your document, PageMaker alerts you, letting you know how large the image is. The alert asks if you want to put the image in the publication file or simply link it, leaving the image in an independent file.

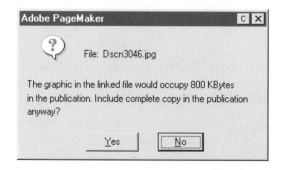

## PostScript Printing

This section is only useful if you own a printer driven by the PostScript language. PostScript is a page description language that uses the same tools to generate a printed page that PageMaker uses to display your pages on your computer screen.

A PostScript printer or typesetter is a marvel of engineering, but it's plagued by the same shortcomings any computer might have: inadequate speed or memory. There's nothing to do about inadequate speed other than upgrading or developing implacable calm and patience. But there is something you can do if your PageMaker publication starts generating low memory errors. Generally, these happen when the printer is grinding through large graphics.

Some of your printer's RAM is taken up with downloaded fonts. This RAM is recoverable, and your printer can eliminate the fonts and use the space for storing part of your graphic. When the large graphic mentioned in the previous paragraph is eventually finished, the fonts will be requested and downloaded again. So you have three lessons to learn here: be stingy with graphics, upgrade your printer's memory, and give your printer the authorization to clear RAM for graphics printing if it needs to do so.

Another PostScript issue is that you can keep track of the printer files (called PostScript Printer Description or PPD files) that determine how your printer and PageMaker communicate with each other. To do this, select the Display PPD Name checkbox. In the Print dialog box, if you have a PostScript printer selected, you will see a pull-down list for the printer and a pull-down list for the PPD. Ordinarily, the PPDs are listed according to their nicknames (with descriptive names like Acrobat Distiller, Color General, and General). These names are friendly, but they won't help you find your PPD if you want to make changes in it. When you check the Display PPD Name checkbox, this pull-down list contains the filenames of the PPD files (the filenames of the PPDs mentioned earlier are Adist5.ppd, cgeneral.ppd, and general.ppd).

To find a PPD, use Find on the Start menu to search for it by filename (or use your Finder on a Mac).The PPD file contains information on the fonts, paper sizes, resolution, and available RAM resident in your printer.

## Saving Your Preferences Changes

Once the More Preferences dialog box is set up to match your requirements, click OK. This returns you to the Preferences dialog box. If you are finished setting up these preferences as well, click OK to return to the PageMaker screen and to apply your changes.

If you set your preferences without a document or a template loaded and then close the application, the preferences are saved with the application and will apply any time you select New in the File menu. If a template is open and you set the preferences and then save the template, the preferences are applied to the template and will be in place whenever you open that template, but they won't affect the application. If a document is open and you set the preferences and then save the document, the preferences will apply to that document, not to the template, and not to the application.

## Editing Your PPD File on a PC

Adobe includes a simple PPD file editor with PageMaker. On your PC, follow these steps:

1. Using Windows Explorer, locate ppd.exe by folowing this path: Program Files\Adobe\PageMaker 7.0\Extras\Print.

2. When you find the file, double-click its name to start up ppd.exe. The Update PPD dialog box opens as shown in the following illustration.

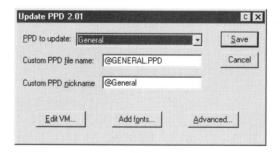

3. Select the PPD to update with the PPD to Update pull-down list.

4. Enter the PPD's preferred custom name in the Custom PPD File Name text box.

5. Enter the PPD's preferred nickname in the Custom PPD nickname.

6. To change the amount of virtual memory available for your printer, click the Edit VM button. The Edit VM dialog box opens.

7. Select the printer in the Print VM Information For drop-down menu.

8. Click the Print button to print the VM information on the selected printer.

9. The printout will contain the free virtual memory. According to the Edit VM dialog box, my printer has 2,500,000 bytes of virtual memory. If I had added memory or removed memory from my printer, the values would differ and I would want to update my virtual memory value by entering the new value in the New VM Setting text box. Click OK when you are through.

10. To edit the fonts downloaded to the printer, click the Add Fonts button (located in the Update PPD dialog box). That will open the Add Fonts to Custom PPD dialog box. The list of fonts available for download are located on the left side (these are set in the PostScript, Port section of your WIN.INI file). Down the center are buttons for adding individual fonts, adding all fonts, removing individual fonts, and removing all fonts. Click the appropriate buttons until the column on the right contains all the fonts you want to download to your printer. Remember that every font downloaded eats into the RAM available for processing graphics. Click OK when you are through.

11. The Advanced button (in the Update PPD dialog box) opens the Edit Custom PPD file dialog, which is a simple text editor for editing the PPD file. Click OK to return to the Update PPD dialog box. Don't edit this file unless you know PostScript very well or you are working on a custom file you can discard if it doesn't work.

12. Click Cancel to discard any changes you might have made (or click Save to save your changes).

# Layout Adjustment Preferences

To see the Layout Adjustment Preferences, select the File menu's Preferences command. Then choose Layout Adjustment. These preferences are used when you change the general shape of your layout, such as when you change the size of the page or orientation of the paper. By setting your layout adjustment preferences you determine the elements that automatically adjust when Adjust Layout is selected on the Document Setup dialog box.

To see the preferences related to layout adjustments, select the File menu's Preferences command. Then choose Layout Adjustment. The Layout Adjustment Preferences dialog box opens as shown in the following illustration.

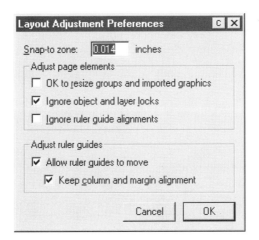

## Snap-To Zone

When the Snap function is selected, objects that come within a prescribed distance from guides move so that they are in direct contact with the guides. The distance at which Snap occurs can be set using the Snap-to zone. Snap can be a great tool, since very subtle irregularities in the way objects line up on the page can be disconcerting to the viewer or reader. Even if the objects are off by tiny amounts, such as a fraction of a point, a person looking at it will sense something is wrong and make uncharitable judgments about the subject of the page (or the artist who laid it out). So certain objects in PageMaker have Snap built in.

# Adjust Page Elements

### OK to Resize Groups and Imported Graphics

Putting a check in OK to Resize Groups box tells PageMaker to retain the proportional relationships between graphics and/or groups of graphics (or other elements) on a page when resizing occurs. If the OK to Resize Groups and Imported Graphics checkbox is checked, an adjustment in the size of the page will result in groups of graphics being resized proportionally in order to maintain the groups' relationships to one another. If it is not checked, the elements are not resized. In that case, the readjustment is up to you.

### Ignore Object and Layer Locks

If the Ignore Object and Layer Locks checkbox is not checked, adjusting the size of the page will not affect locked objects on the page. If it is checked, locks will be ignored so that PageMaker can adjust objects' locations automatically.

### Ignore Ruler Guide Alignments

Opting to ignore ruler guide alignments will cause PageMaker to arrange objects based on their relationships to margins and columns.

# Adjust Ruler Guides

Ruler guides are lines that can be dragged out of the ruler to help align objects on the screen. Guides are covered in Chapter 7.

### Allow Ruler Guides to Move

You can make changes to the guides' positions by manually dragging them with your mouse pointer. However, unless the Allow Ruler Guides to Move checkbox is checked, any readjustments you make to the page will not readjust the guides. If this box is checked, however, all guides, including locked guides, will be adjusted when a page adjustment is made.

### Keep Column and Margin Alignment

If you've placed ruler guides over column and margin guides and you want to maintain that relationship, select the Keep Column and Margin Alignment checkbox, or the guides will be moved when the page is altered.

## Online Preferences

Here we set PageMaker up to go online and be able to receive information that you have selected to be downloaded. To gather data from the Internet, you need to set up your online preferences by selecting the File menu's Preferences command. Then choose the Online item from the submenu. The Online Preferences dialog box opens as shown in Figure 12-6.

You can gather material for your layout from the Internet. The Internet is a world of information and pictures. If you need to gather information for a paper or monograph, your first step should be a Web search for articles and Web sites dealing with your subject. If you need images to go with it, they probably exist on the Web. After all, a layout is simply an arrangement of information on the page.

### Hyperlink Settings

Hyperlinks are links that connect to text either on other pages or to another location on the current page. You can specify either a page to call up or a location on a page. If you specify a page, there is no reason to specially mark it. The address of the page will be adequate. However, if you want to call up a specific location on a page, you must place something called an anchor at that location. If you have done much work on the

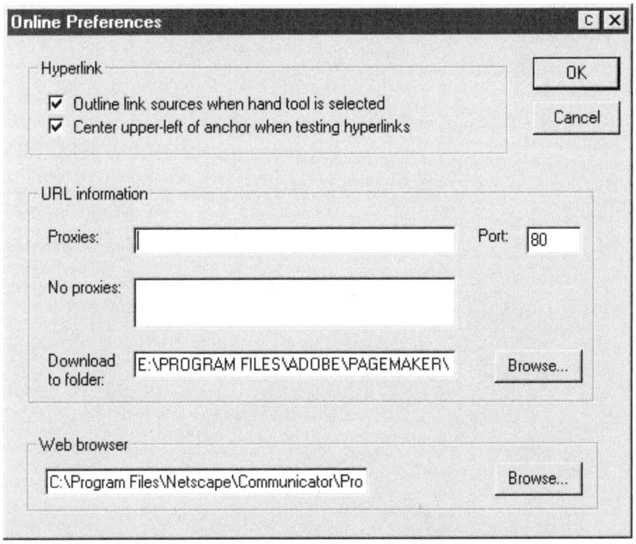

**Figure 12-6.** *The Online Preferences dialog box*

Internet, you've probably seen whole pages called up with a hyperlink, and other times you have seen the page scroll to a new location. This is accomplished with anchors. The first two settings in the Online Preferences dialog box refer to hyperlinks placed in PageMaker documents.

If Outline Link Sources When Hand Tool Is Selected is checked, a dotted outline appears around the hyperlink in Preview mode when the mouse pointer hovers over it (you enter Preview mode when you click the Hand tool in the toolbox; the hyperlinks are created by using HTML).

If the second is selected, Center Upper-left of Anchor When Testing Hyperlinks, the content next to the anchor will be pulled up to the center of the page when the link is clicked in Preview mode.

## URL Information

Proxies are pseudo-Web addresses that enable a real address to hide behind a façad. Proxies are a technical topic beyond the scope of this book, but they will be well understood by those who have proxies on personal machines or who maintain networks. If you have a proxy, you need to alert PageMaker to its existence in order to operate online. To find your proxy, follow these steps:

1. Open your browser. In this example, we use Internet Explorer.
2. Select the Tools menu's Internet Option command.
3. Click the Connections tab.
4. Click Settings. The Autodial Settings dialog box opens as shown in Figure 12-7.

The information about a proxy appears in the text boxes marked Address and Port. These boxes are identical to the Proxies and Port text boxes in Figure 12-7, so simply copy and paste the information from Internet Explorer into the Online Preferences dialog box's Proxies text box.

Some addresses don't work with a proxy, but these are the exceptions; most sites will respond to a proxy just fine. But if you find an address that doesn't work, you will have to make an exception for that address. To find out which addresses already have exceptions, follow these steps:

1. Go to Internet Explorer. If the Internet Options dialog box is already open to the Connections tab, skip to step 4.
2. Select the Tools menu's Internet Options command.
3. Click the Connections tab in the Internet Options dialog box.
4. Click the Settings button to open the Proxy Settings dialog box.
5. Click in the text box in the Exceptions area.
6. Drag through the exceptions in the box (if there are any).

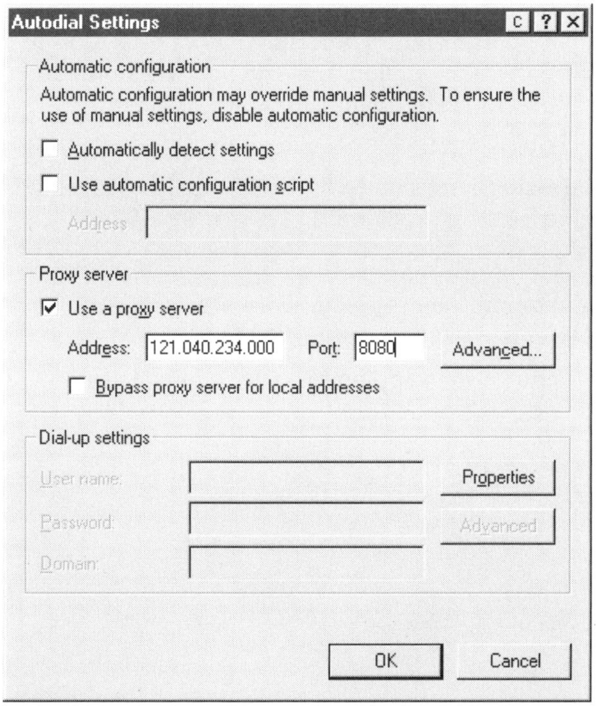

**Figure 12-7.**  *The Autodial Settings*

7. Press CTRL+C to copy the exceptions list to the clipboard.

8. Return to PageMaker. Open the Online Preferences dialog box if necessary.

9. Click in the text box marked No Proxies in the URL Information section of the Online Preferences dialog box.

10. Paste in the contents of the clipboard by pressing CTRL+V.

You will need to specify where downloaded objects should be placed. Type the address of the folder in which you wish to store them in the Download to Folder text box, or use the Browse button to open a File dialog box and search your hard disks for the folder you will use. Select a browser for use with PageMaker. Type in the path to your preferred browser or click the Browse button to locate the browser .exe file. Finally, click OK to close the Online Preferences dialog box and put your settings in place.

## Summary

PageMaker is designed to work with you, and it has various tools to help you specify unique settings. These are called preferences and they are stored in the templates that you save and load in the course of doing your work.

Generally, the preferences are broken down into four main areas:

- **General**  Measurement standards, nudge, display, greeking level, and Story Editor settings
- **Online**  Hyperlink settings
- **Layout Adjustment**  Snap-to settings as well as the movement and sizing of grouped elements
- **Trapping**  Settings for trapping in color and black layers

# Chapter 13

## Creating Document Consistency Using Master Pages

Consistency is one of the most important factors to be considered when designing a publication. A consistent overall design, which makes use of eye-catching graphics and text components, is the key to an aesthetically pleasing, user-friendly document. Moreover, consistency in the design process makes your document much easier and faster to update and edit. The primary means of creating and maintaining consistency in PageMaker documents is through the use of master pages.

A master page is a special page that contains all the components, such as page numbers, recurring graphics, and running headers, that you want to appear on every page (or in a range of pages) in your document. A good way to envision a master page is to see it as a clear, acetate layer that overlays the pages of your document. In addition, the elements on a master page can be dynamic, meaning that they are automatically adjusted based on where they occur in your document.

In this chapter, I discuss how to use master pages to create consistency in your PageMaker documents. I cover the different kinds of master pages, how they are created and applied to your documents, and how to modify, save, duplicate, and delete them as well.

# Master Page Basics

Each page in a PageMaker publication has a master page. When a publication is first generated, PageMaker automatically creates what is known as a *document master*. By default, the document master is applied to all pages in the publication until you tell PageMaker otherwise. The document master is a permanent fixture in the publication's setup. It cannot be deleted or renamed, but it *can* be replaced by another custom master page within the individual pages of the publication. The rule to remember when dealing with master pages is that all pages must have a master page, but only *one* master page can be assigned to a page at a time. In other words, master pages do not accumulate one on top of the other or interact like layers.

A document master will take one of two forms depending on the kind of document you set up. If your document is single-sided, such as a letter, it will have a single-sided document master assigned to it. If your document has facing pages, such as those that are found in magazines or brochures, it will be assigned a double-sided document master, usually referred to as a *document master spread*.

Your document master is indicated by two small icons in the bottom-left corner of your document screen. They look like two dog-eared sheets of paper. The letter L is in the left master and the letter R in the right. If you have a single-sided document master, you will see only one sheet of paper with the letter R in it. Figure 13-1 shows both kinds of master page icons.

Document masters are best used to hold design elements such as page numbers, headers and footers, and nonprinting guides that you want on all your pages. Unlike custom master pages, which you create and apply manually, anything that appears on a document master will appear on all pages of your publication, until you create and

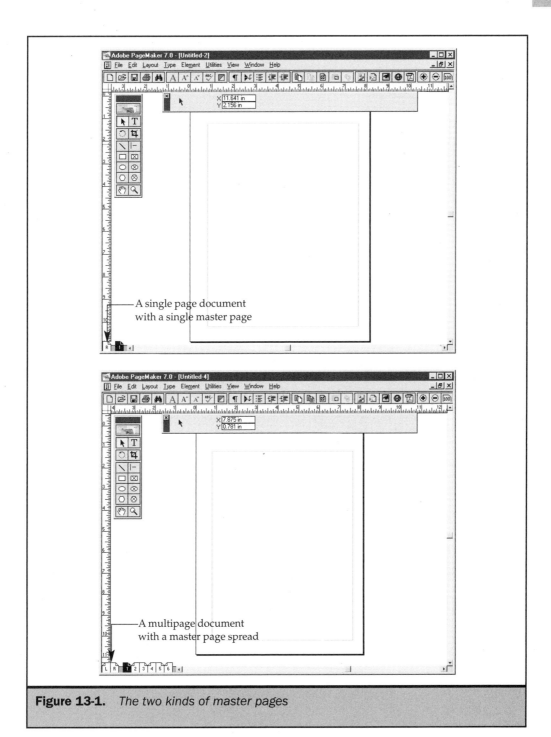

**Figure 13-1.**  *The two kinds of master pages*

apply custom master pages to them. Let's create a very simple example so you can see how a document master works.

1. Open a new file.

   Select the File menu's New command. The Document Setup dialog box appears, as shown in the following illustration.

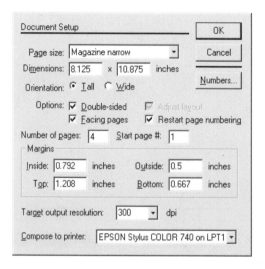

2. Set the page size.

   Select Magazine Narrow from the Page Size drop-down menu, and click the Tall radio button for orientation.

3. Set your options.

   Since magazines are two-sided and have facing pages, put a check in the Double-sided and Facing Pages options. Adjust Layout is grayed out. Put a check in the Restart Page Numbering box if it is not already there.

4. Set the number of pages.

   Type the number **4** into the Number box and the number **1** in the Start page # box.

5. Set the margins.

   Accept the margin settings for now.

6. Accept the default target resolution and printer.

7. Set your numbering system.

   By clicking the Numbers Button on the right-hand side of the dialog box, you will open the Page Numbering dialog box, as shown in the following illustration, which enables you to select the style of numbers you would like.

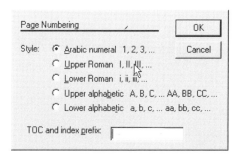

Often prefaces, introductions, and indexes are numbered using lower-case roman numerals. However, as this is just a regular text document, Arabic numerals should be selected. Click OK to accept your changes and be returned to the Document Setup dialog box.

8. Create your new document.

   Click OK and your new document is created and displayed.

9. Locate your document master pages.

   Look in the bottom-left corner of your document screen to find the document master page icons. Since this is a double-sided document, you see a document master spread.

10. Open your document master page spread.

    Click either the L or R icon and the document master page spread will open. Even though it looks identical to the regular pages of your document, it's not. Anything that you put on these pages appears on all pages of your document.

*You also have four small boxes numbered 1 through 4 to the right of your document master page spread icons. These represent the actual pages of your document, and you can return to any of them by simply clicking the number of the page you want to see.*

11. Open your Master Pages Palette.

    Select the Window menu's Show Master Pages command if your Master Pages Palette is not open. The Master Pages Palette opens as shown in the following illustration. Notice that the document master is highlighted in the Master Pages

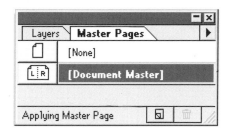

list, indicating that it is the active master page. Later when you have several master pages, this can be a very handy list to have.

When you have clicked the master page icons in the bottom-left corner of your document screen, your Master Pages Palette will also display the message, "Editing a Master Page." If you have clicked one of the page numbers and are working on an actual page, the message, "Applying Master Page," will be displayed.

There are also two icons at the bottom of the Master Pages Palette, as shown in the following illustration. One is the trashcan, which enables you to delete any master page (except the document master) by dragging it into the trashcan.

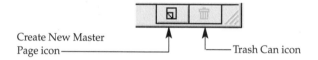

Create New Master Page icon ———

Trash Can icon

The second icon is the Create New Master Page icon. Clicking it opens the New Master Page dialog box and enables you to create a new master page. More information on creating new master pages is covered later in this chapter.

The Master Pages Palette is the place to go to do anything with a master page. From its drop-down menu, all the tools you need to create, edit, apply, copy, and delete master pages can be accessed.

12. Open the Master Pages menu.

Click the small arrow in the upper right-hand corner of the Master Pages Palette and the Master Pages menu appears, as shown in the following illustration. The options are listed in Table 13-1. We will take a look at each of these options as we work through the chapter.

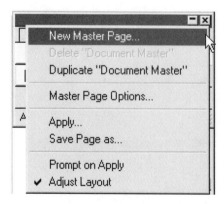

| Options | Functions |
|---------|-----------|
| New Master Page | Creates a new master page. |
| Delete "Document Master" (changes to reflect the name of the master page selected) | Deletes the currently selected master page (you can't delete the document master). |
| Duplicate "Document Master" (changes to reflect the name of the master page selected) | Copies the current master page under another name. |
| Master Page Options | Calls up the dialog box that sets the margins, column guides, and the Adjust Layout function for the master page. |
| Apply | Calls up a dialog box that lets you specify which pages to assign the currently selected master page to. |
| Save Page As | Saves the current publication page as a master page. |
| Prompt on Apply | Causes an alert message to appear when you try to assign a master page. |
| Adjust Layout | Forces an automatic adjustment. |

**Table 13-1**   *Master Page Options*

Please leave your document open, as we will be using it again in the next section on adding material to your master pages.

In addition to your document master pages, PageMaker enables you to create and assign custom master pages to your publications. The advantages of using custom master pages include the following:

■ You get to choose which pages the custom master pages are applied to.

■ You can create more than one consistent style in your publication. A good example is a magazine like *Outside*, which has one style for all its feature articles, one style for its half-page pieces, one style for full-page ads, and one style for its one-third page, columnar ads. Each style has several elements it shares with the rest of the pages in the publication, such as the placement and style of the page numbers, but it also has many elements that are unique to the pages it is applied to. Since each style occurs many times throughout the magazine, it would be a waste of time to have to rebuild the pages time and time again. That's when multiple master pages become invaluable.

There are three ways to create custom master pages:

1. Start from scratch.
2. Copy an existing master page.
3. Copy a regular publication page.

All three methods are discussed in greater detail later in this chapter.

# Adding Material to Your Master Pages

If there are any elements such as margin and column settings, headers and footers, or page numbers that will be consistent throughout your publication, it's best to put those in your document master page and use copies of the page as the basis for your custom master pages. Any elements that change with particular parts or pages of your publication should be placed on custom master pages and applied as needed. In this section, I discuss adding elements that are common to all pages in a publication to the document master page.

## Adding Page Numbers and Graphics

If you plan to have numbering throughout your publication, remember to place page markers in all your master pages. Since page numbers are commonly used throughout a publication, it is a good idea to indicate their positions and formatting in the document master page. This will save you an enormous amount of time and ensures that consistency of location and style are maintained throughout your document.

Page numbers are entered in master pages as *markers* rather than actual numbers. Markers enable PageMaker to take care of the numbering and repagination that naturally occurs as information is added and deleted from your document. To add page markers to your publication, follow these steps:

1. Open your document.

   If necessary, open the document we created earlier in the chapter.

2. Open your document master spread.

   Click either the L or the R of the master page icons in the lower left-hand corner of your document window. The document master spread opens.

3. Select the Text tool.

   Click the Text tool in the toolbox. The mouse pointer changes to an I-beam.

4. Add an insertion point for your page markers.

   With the Text tool selected, create an insertion point for the page marker by dragging a small text box at the place you want it to appear.

**Note**

*If you are having trouble placing your page marker in the center or in the right-hand side of your active window, use the Control Palette's justification keys or use your Tab key. The justification keys can be accessed by clicking the paragraph symbol beneath the large T in the left-hand portion of the Control Palette.*

5. Add page markers to your document master spread.

   Press CTRL+ALT+P to generate a page marker. A left master or a right master marker appears, as shown in Figure 13-2.

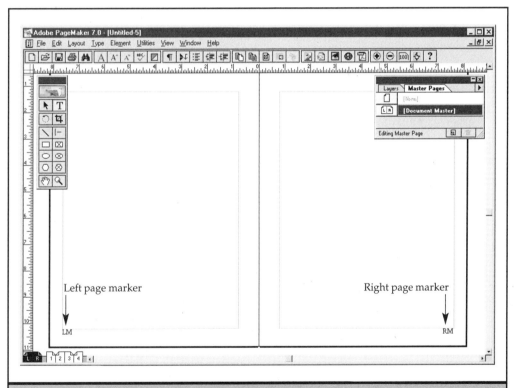

**Figure 13-2.**   *Left and right page markers placed in the document master page spread*

6. Open your Picture Palette.

   Select the Window menu's Show Plug-in Palettes command. Then choose the Show Picture Palette item. The Picture Palette appears, as shown in Figure 13-3.

7. Select a graphic.

   If you would like any graphics or photos to appear on every page of your publication, such as a company logo, now is the time to add them.

   Select the type of graphic and the category the graphic is stored under. Locate the graphic by scrolling through the category list.

   Click the graphic you want to use. It highlights with a yellow line around it.

8. Place your graphic.

   Drag the image onto your left master page and release the mouse button. If you would like to adjust its placement or size, click it with the Pointer tool and sizing handles will appear.

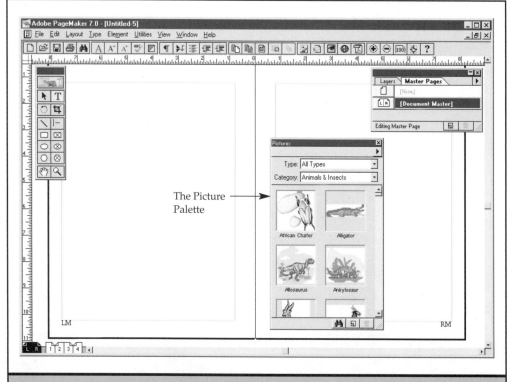

**Figure 13-3.** *The Picture Palette*

For more information on selecting, placing, and sizing graphics, refer to Chapter 5.

9. Check your publication pages.

    Click the icon for page 1 of your document, located to the right of the master page icons in the bottom-left corner of your document screen. You may be surprised to find that your graphic is not visible. Don't panic. Click the icon for page 2 and you will see your graphic displayed in the same position it was placed on your master page. However, you do not see it on page 3.

    This little example illustrates an important point about working with master page spreads. If you want an element to appear on all your pages, you must place it on both pages of the master page spread. Elements placed on the left master page will appear on all left-sided pages, that is, pages 2 and 4 in our example. Elements placed on the right master page will appear on all right-sided pages, that is, pages 1 and 3. Be sure to take this into consideration when you place your elements as well.

10. Create a copy of your graphic.

    Using the Pointer tool, click the graphic to select it.

    Select the Edit menu's Copy commnd or press CTRL+C to create a copy of the graphic.

    Select the Edit menu's Paste command or press CTRL+V. The copy is pasted directly over and slightly to the right of the original.

11. Add your graphic to the *right* master page.

    Drag the copy of your graphic onto the right master page and position it.

12. Check your publication.

    Click the icon for page 1 of your document, located to the right of your master page icons in the bottom-left corner of your document screen. You should see your graphic placed on the page.

    Click page 2 of your document and your graphic appears on both pages.

# Adding Nonprinting Guides to Your Master Pages

There are three kinds of nonprinting guides: ruler, margin, and column guides.

## Ruler Guides

Ruler guides are used to help you position objects on a page. If, for example, you want to be sure that both the left and right versions of the graphic you placed in the previous exercise were exactly the same distance from the top margin, you would use your ruler guides to accomplish this. Note that ruler guides do not affect the flow of text in your document at all. To create a ruler guide, follow these steps:

1. Display your rulers.

   If you don't see rulers along the top and left sides of your document screen, turn them on by selecting the View menu's Show Rulers command (see Figure 13-4).

   Notice also that you have the option of selecting Display Non-Printing Items. Select that now as well.

2. Create a vertical guide positioned one quarter of an inch from the *left* edge of the active document window.

   Using the Pointer tool, click the vertical ruler and drag toward the center of your document. A thin, green line will appear and follow your cursor. Use the ruler above the document window to find the correct measurement. When the guide is positioned properly, release the mouse button and the guide is placed.

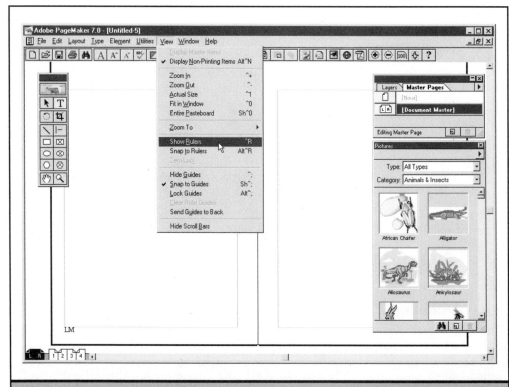

**Figure 13-4.**   *The View | Show Rulers option*

3.  Create a vertical guide positioned one-quarter of an inch from the *right* edge of the active document window.

    Using the Pointer tool, click the vertical ruler and drag a guide to the right towards the right-hand side of your document. A thin, green line appears. Continue dragging across the left page and onto the right until the guide is positioned one-quarter of an inch from the right edge of the active document window. Use the ruler above the document window to find the correct measurement. When the guide is positioned properly, release the mouse button and the guide is placed.

4.  Create a horizontal guide positioned one-quarter of an inch from the top edge of the active document window.

    Using the Pointer tool, click the horizontal ruler and drag a guide down towards the center of your document. A thin, green line follows your cursor. Use the ruler to the left of the document window to find the correct measurement. When the guide is positioned properly, release the mouse and the guide is placed. Notice that the guide goes all the way across the document master spread.

5.  Use the ruler guides to position your graphic.

    Use the ruler guides we have just created to position the graphics so that they are both exactly one-quarter of an inch from the top of the document and one-quarter of an inch from the edge of their respective sides of the document.

    You can create and position as many guides as you would like to assist you with the creation of your documents, and they will be copied onto other master pages you create from this original.

    For more information on how to create guides both manually and by using the Grid Manager, see Chapter 7.

6.  Turn on the Snap function.

    When the Snap function is activated, the guides you have just created will act like a magnet. Whenever an object gets within a certain range of the guides, it will be drawn directly up against it. This is very handy when you want to align objects exactly. To turn on the Snap function, select the View menu's Snap to Guides command.

If you want to be sure that none of your guides accidentally gets moved as you are clicking in your screen, select the View menu's Lock Guides command. The guides are locked in place on your pages. You can unlock them by selecting View and removing the check mark beside Lock Guides.

## Margin Guides

When you first create a publication, you set your margins in the Document Setup dialog box. Those margins are applied both to the pages and to the document master page. In other words, both the document master page and the pages start with the same margins. Custom master pages, however, can have any margin settings you like and, when applied to a page, will naturally cause the margins to readjust.

Margin guides are the vertical and horizontal lines (pink on top and blue on the sides) that define the active document area of your page. The right and left margins of any master page can be adjusted manually by clicking them with the Pointer tool and dragging to a new position. PageMaker will display the new position in blue and the old position in pink. Margin guides can also be adjusted using the Master Page Options dialog box (accessed through the Master Page Palette), or by using the Document Setup dialog box. The top and bottom margins guides cannot be adjusted manually by dragging. You must use either the Master Page Options dialog box or the Document Setup dialog box.

To adjust your margin guides using the Master Page Options box, follow these steps:

1. Open the Master Pages menu.

   Click the small arrow in the upper-right corner of the Master Pages Palette and the menu will appear.

2. Open the Master Page Options dialog box.

   Select Master Page Options from the Master Pages menu and the Master Page Options dialog box will appear, as shown in the following illustration.

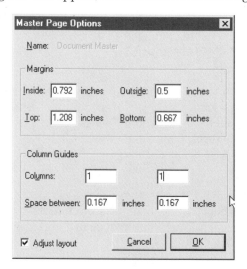

3. Adjust your margins.

   Using the Inside, Outside, Top, and Bottom windows, enter the new margin settings.

4. Apply your changes.

   Click OK and your new settings are applied. The Master Page Options dialog box closes and you return to the document screen.

To adjust margin guides using the Document Setup dialog box, do the following:

1. Select the File menu's Document Setup command. The Document Setup dialog box opens.

2. Using the Inside, Outside, Top, and Bottom windows in the Margins section, enter the new margin settings.

3. Apply your changes.

   Click OK and your new settings are applied. The Document Setup dialog box closes and you return to your document screen.

# Adding Dynamic Headers and Footers to Master Pages

Headers and footers appear in publications in order to orient readers. Basically, they are designed to tell readers where they are in the publication, and give an idea of what can be found on the page. Many books display the title of the book on left-hand pages and the chapter name on right-hand pages. Other good examples of publications that use headers and footers are dictionaries and phone books.

Headers and footers that appear on every page, but in which the text changes from page to page, are called running headers and footers. Because the information changes with the information on the page, they are said to be dynamic.

There are two steps in creating running headers and footers:

1. Defining the physical placement, style, and format of the header or footer

2. Specifying the content of the header or footer

As with most things in PageMaker, it pays to plan, so before you create a document that will require headers and/or footers, it's best to understand how PageMaker handles them. Note that the process of creating a header is the same as that for creating a footer. The only difference is the location of the footer on the page and the contents.

PageMaker uses text *boxes* within a story to assign running headers and footers. When creating a header or footer, you can only work on one story in one publication at a time. A story, you may recall, is text that PageMaker recognizes as a single unit (text boxes flow from page to page in a story). Obviously, the fewer stories you have, the less time it will take you to set up your headers and footers.

Since you must have text boxes in order to use the header and footer function, it's best to have a document open that has at least one story with blocks of text in it.

To use the header and footer function, follow these steps:

1. Create a six-page, double-sided document with facing pages.

2. Fill all pages with text using PageMaker's Flow Text option. It doesn't matter what you put in the pages for text; just be sure that it's all one continuous story. In my case, I filled the pages with jokes I had copied for my niece from the Internet. This means that all the text, on all six pages, will be part of the same story.

3. At the very top of page 1, centered, type the words: **Jokes for Kids**. Make sure that these words are typed within the text block.

4. Apply the style Subhead 1 to the words Jokes for Kids, and apply the style Body text to the rest of the text.

    If you know approximately where you would like to place your headers, add ruler guides to the document master page spread that is applied to the pages you will be accessing. They are a great help in lining things up. Page 1 of my sample setup, complete with ruler guides to help me place my headers, is shown in Figure 13-5.

Now we're ready to add headers and footers.

**Placing and Formatting the Header Placeholder**    The first part of the header creation process establishes the header placeholder. Follow these steps:

1. Select the text block in the story that you want to create a header for.

    Using the Pointer tool, click the page 1 text block. The entire text block will be selected and sizing handles will appear.

2. Open the Running Headers & Footers dialog box.

    Select the Utilities menu's Plug-ins command. Choose Running Headers & Footers from the submenu. The Running Headers & Footers dialog box opens, as shown in Figure 13-6, and the screen behind the dialog box opens to the document master page spread assigned to the pages. You will know this has happened because the master page icons in the bottom-left corner of your document screen will become active. However, you will not be able to access the document master page spread while the Running Headers & Footers dialog box is open.

    Turn your attention to the dialog box itself. At the top of the box, you will see either one (if your document is single-sided) or two windows (if your

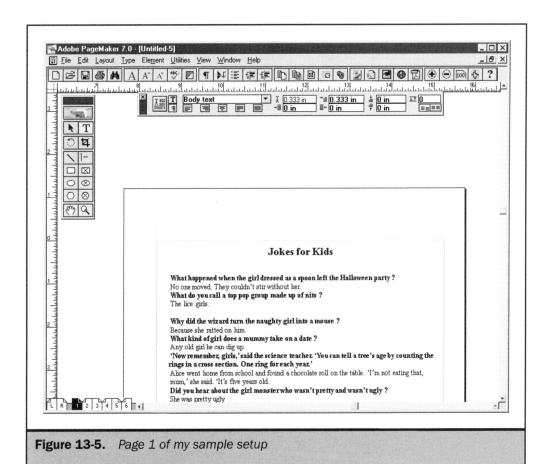

**Figure 13-5.** *Page 1 of my sample setup*

document is double-sided) with drop-down menus beside them. In the windows will be the words, Document Master 1 and Document Master 2. The reason they are numbered 1 and 2 is because this is a master page spread, and in a spread there are two pages involved. We saw how this worked earlier in the chapter when we added a graphic to only one page of the spread.

If you click the drop-down menu arrow next to either of the document masters, you will see that all master pages currently available for use on that page in the story you have selected are listed, along with the words, Regular page. What PageMaker is telling you is that you have a choice about where to put your header placeholders. You can put them in the document master, in any of the custom master pages that could be applied to the selected pages, or in the pages (as opposed to the master pages) themselves.

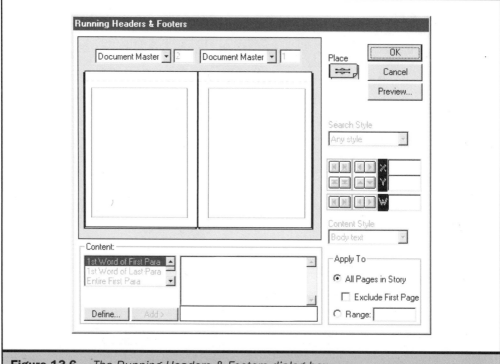

**Figure 13-6.** *The Running Headers & Footers dialog box*

These are subtle but important choices, since if you choose to apply the header placeholders to only regular pages, you will lose the advantage of being able to apply master pages that already have placeholders to other pages in your publication. If your publication is short like ours, this is really not an issue, but in larger publications this could mean a lot of extra work and inconsistencies in style and size. Think seriously about where and how you want to place your header and footer placeholders.

In our document we are going to apply the placeholders to the document masters, so make no changes to the drop-down menus.

3. Place your first header placeholder on the page.

Click the Place icon located just to the right of the sample layout and drag the header placeholder onto the right-hand side of the layout page. When the placeholder is in the approximate position you would like it to be, release your mouse. A placeholder textbox, complete with its own sizing handles, will appear, as shown in Figure 13-7. Notice the bright red note at the bottom of the page that says, Content Required. PageMaker is letting you know that text is needed in order to complete the process of creating the header.

You can remove this placeholder entirely by dragging it off the page.

4. Adjust the position of the placeholder.

Using the Nudge buttons located just below the Search window on the right-hand side of the dialog box, adjust the position of the placeholder. The X and Y buttons move the placeholder left and right and up and down, respectively. The W buttons actually stretch the placeholder to make it longer. The Nudge buttons on the left-hand side with lines next to the arrows cause the placeholder to snap to the nearest guide.

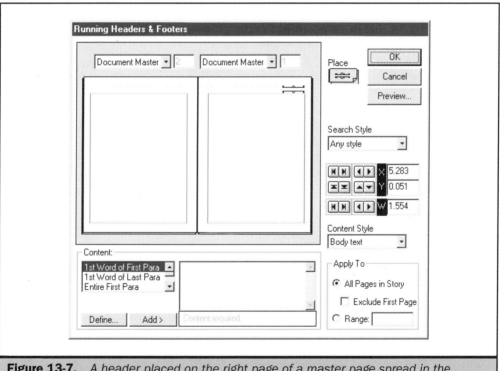

**Figure 13-7.**    *A header placed on the right page of a master page spread in the Running Headers & Footers dialog box*

5. Tell PageMaker how many pages you want this placeholder applied to.

    In the Apply to section, located below the Content Style box, you will see two options:

    - **All Pages in Story**   This has the subcategory Exclude First Page.

    - **Range**   If, as is the case with a newspaper, your story is located on several different pages of a publication, you will want to tell PageMaker where to look. You can enter individual pages with commas between them (1, 5, 11, 17), a range of pages separated by a hyphen (3–7, 23–28), or a combination of both (1, 12, 15, 18–21). Note: If you do not specify a number after the last hyphen, the header will be applied to the page specified to the left of the hyphen and all subsequent pages as well.

The thing to remember about applying the headers is that you are telling PageMaker which of the right-hand pages to apply the header to. Don't get confused by the words, All Pages in Story. This is actually referring to all right-hand pages in the story, since we are working on the right-hand placeholder.

In our case, choose All Pages in Story and check the Exclude First Page option. The reason for this is because in most publications, the first page does not ordinarily have a header.

**Step Two: Adding Content to the Placeholder**   Before PageMaker will enable you to actually create the headers and/or footers, you must specify what text you want in them (you will get a warning message if you try hitting OK or Preview before you have specified the content for the headers).

You have four ways to specify content:

- Choose a PageMaker-defined header or footer from the content list located below the layout pages. Click Add to place it in the Selected Header box to the right of the content list. The content list is very helpful, particularly if you are creating something like yellow pages or a directory of names. If you scroll through the list, you will see that the options are quite extensive. When you find an option you like, click Add and the option will be added to the Content text area to the right of the list.

- Choose a PageMaker-defined header or footer from the content list and add content of your own before or after the preset header created by PageMaker. Custom content can be text or symbols and should be entered before or after the brackets that enclose PageMaker's text. The text you type outside the brackets is static, meaning it does not change from page to page.

■ Choose more than one PageMaker-defined header or footer and put them together. You do this by selecting the first header and clicking Add to move it to the Selected Header box. Next, you click an insertion point in the first header. After that, you select a second header from the content list and click Add again. The second will be combined with the first, as shown in Figure 13-8.

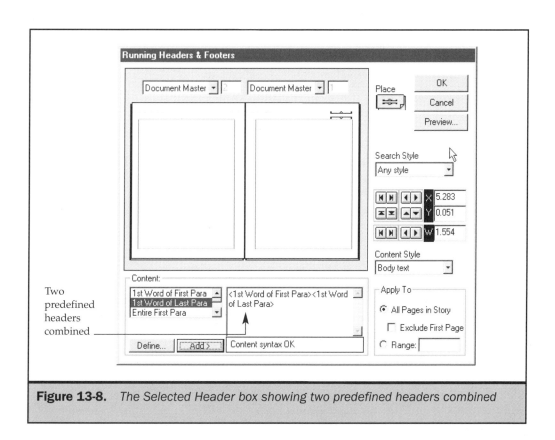

Two predefined headers combined

**Figure 13-8.** *The Selected Header box showing two predefined headers combined*

■ Create your own custom header text by clicking the Define Button at the bottom of the content list. Clicking the Define Button opens the Define dialog box, as shown in the following illustration. From there, click New Selector and

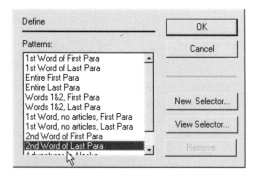

you will be taken to the Edit Selector dialog box, as shown in the next illustration, where you can type in the words you would like to use for your header. When you are satisfied with the wording, click OK. By clicking OK, you add the header to the list of predefined headers and footers that will be available every time you open the Running Headers & Footers dialog box.

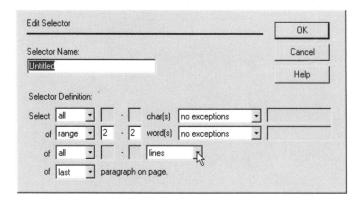

■ Create your own custom header by typing the words you would like to appear in the header in the selected header list without hitting Define. Your header will be used to create the header, but is not saved as an option in the content list.

If you are following along with my example, do the following:

1. Specify the text to be put in the right page header.

   Let's create our own text to be put in the headers of all right-hand pages in this story. Click in the Selected Header box (the empty box to the right of the content list) and type the words, **Part 1**.

2. Select a style with which to format the text that will go into the placeholder.

   From the Content Style's drop-down menu, located below the Nudge buttons, select the text style you would like the contents of your placeholder to be given. Let's choose Subhead 1.

   Note that if you were going to have PageMaker locate text for the header in the story itself, you would use the Search Style option, located above the Nudge buttons, to tell PageMaker what kind of text to look for. We will do that in the next step when we make a placeholder for the left-hand page.

3. Open the Preview dialog box to see a preview of how your header will look.

   Click the Preview Button on the right-hand side of the dialog box and the Preview dialog box appears, as shown in Figure 13-9, giving you a preview of how your headers will look.

   If your letters are greeked, as they are in Figure 13-9, use the plus and minus signs on the Magnifying Glass Button or the up and down arrows to increase the magnification. You can also move from page to page by clicking the page icons in the bottom-left corner of the dialog box. Figure 13-10 shows my page 3 header enlarged in the Preview dialog box.

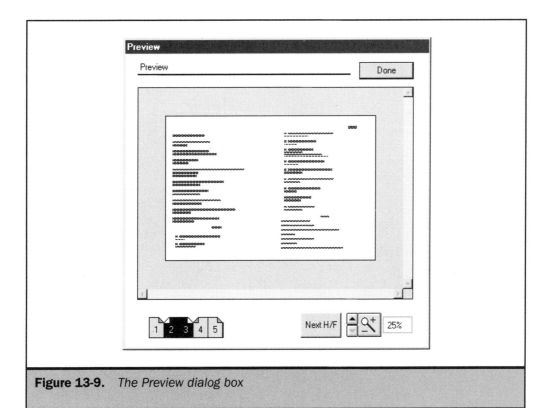

**Figure 13-9.** *The Preview dialog box*

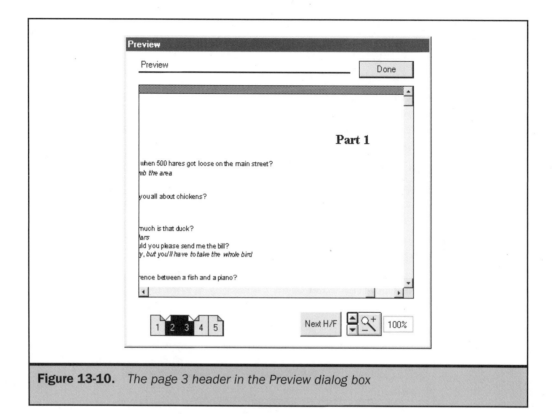

**Figure 13-10.** *The page 3 header in the Preview dialog box*

4. Return to the Running Headers & Footers dialog box.

   Click the Done Button in the Preview dialog box and you will be returned to the Running Headers & Footers dialog box.

5. Place your second header placeholder on the page.

   Click the Place icon located just to the right of the sample layout and drag the header placeholder onto the left-hand side of the layout page. As soon as you click the Place icon, the right-hand placeholder icon will gray out, indicating that it is no longer active, and the red Content Required warning will reappear in the Selected Content window.

   When the placeholder is in the approximate position you would like it to be, release your mouse. A placeholder textbox, complete with its own sizing handles, will appear, as shown in Figure 13-11.

6. Tell PageMaker what text you want to place in your left-hand page header.

   Since we used the Subhead 1 style to create the title of our document (Jokes for Kids) on page 1 and have not used the Subhead 1 style for any other text in the

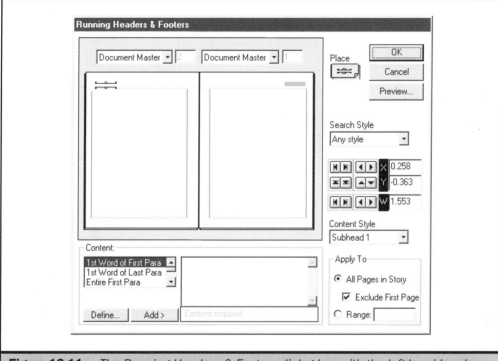

**Figure 13-11.**    *The Running Headers & Footers dialog box with the left-hand header placeholder in place*

story, we can select the Entire First Para option in the content list drop-down menu. What we are doing is telling PageMaker to use all the words in the entire first paragraph that it finds formatted in the Subhead 1 style in the left-hand page header. Since the only paragraph with that formatting in our document is Jokes for Kids, those are the words that should appear in our left-hand page header.

To activate your choice, highlight it in the content list and then click the Add Button. The choice will be added to the box to the right of the content list. Figure 13-12 shows the choice of Entire First Para selected and then added to the selected content list.

7.  Tell PageMaker which style to search for.

Tell PageMaker to search for the style the paragraph was created in by choosing a style from the Search style drop-down menu located above the Nudge Buttons. In this case, choose Subhead 1 because that was the style the paragraph was created in.

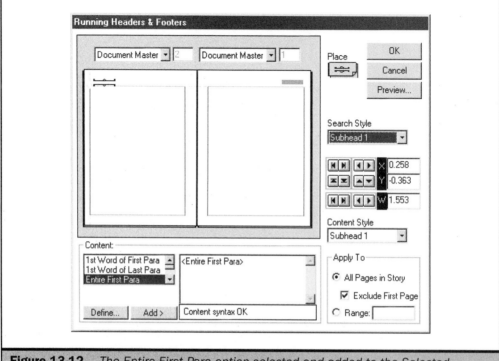

**Figure 13-12.** *The Entire First Para option selected and added to the Selected Content box*

8. Tell PageMaker which style to create the header in.

   In the box under the Nudge Buttons called Content style, tell PageMaker which style to create the placeholder text in. In this case, Subhead 1 is chosen because that was the style we chose for the right-hand page header.

9. Tell PageMaker how many pages you want this placeholder applied to.

   In the Apply to section, located below the Content Style box, you will see two options:

   ■ **All Pages in Story**   This has the subcategory Exclude First Page.

   ■ **Range**   If, as is the case with a newspaper, your story is located on several different pages, you will want to tell PageMaker where to look. You can enter individual pages with commas between them (1, 5, 11, 17), a range of pages separated by a hyphen (3–7, 23–28), or a combination of both (1, 12, 15, 18–21).

*If you do not specify a number after the last hyphen, the header will be applied to the page specified to the left of the hyphen and all subsequent pages as well.*

The thing to remember about applying the headers is that you are telling PageMaker which of the left-hand pages to apply the header to. Don't get confused by the words, All Pages in Story. This actually refers to all left-hand pages in the story, since we are working on the left-hand placeholder.

In our case, choose the All Pages in Story and leave the Exclude First Page option checked.

10. Preview your header.

Click the Preview Button on the right-hand side of the dialog box and the Preview dialog box appears, as shown in Figure 13-13, giving you a preview of how your headers look.

If your text is greeked, click the magnifying glass in the Preview dialog box and a menu appears. You can also adjust the percentage of magnification using the

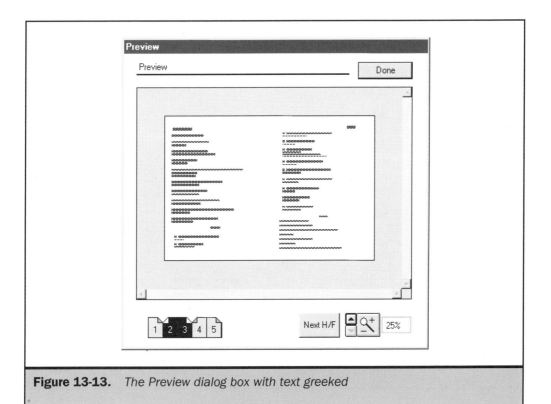

**Figure 13-13.**   *The Preview dialog box with text greeked*

up and down arrows to the left of the magnifying glass. To move from page to page, click the page icons in the bottom-left portion of the Preview screen. Figure 13-14 shows page 2 with its header at the top.

If you are not satisfied with the look of your header, click the Done key to be returned to the Running Headers & Footers dialog box and make any necessary adjustments. Preview your headers again when you have made the changes.

11. Accept and create your headers.

When you are satisfied with your headers, click OK in the Running Headers & Footers dialog box to accept and apply your headers.

12. Check your work.

Open the page 2 and 3 spread in your document by clicking their icons in the lower left-hand page of your document screen. You should see your headers at the top of both page 2 and 3, as shown in Figure 13-15. If you continue through your document, you should see them on the rest of the pages as well.

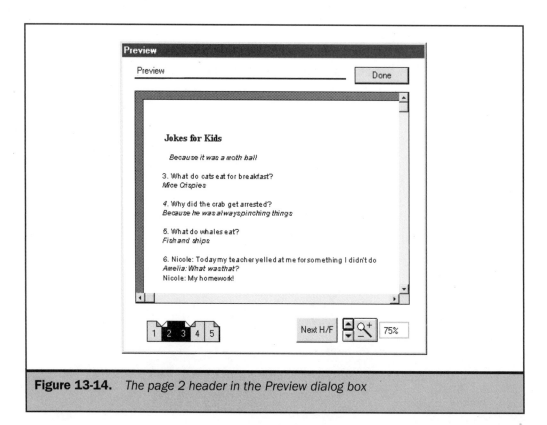

**Figure 13-14.**   *The page 2 header in the Preview dialog box*

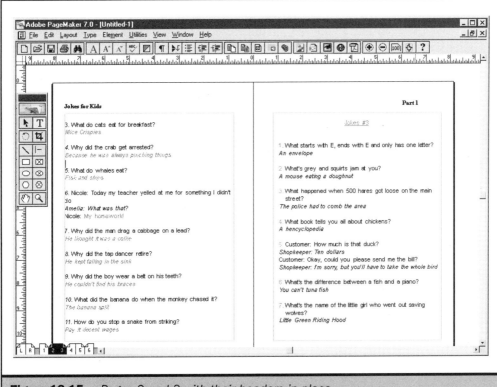

**Figure 13-15.** *Pages 2 and 3 with their headers in place*

## Making Changes to Dynamic Headers and Footers

Unfortunately, footers and headers are not automatically updated when you make changes to your document. For example, if you repaginate or rename a section of your document, the footers and headers can become inaccurate. To update footers and headers, follow these steps:

1. Click the text box in your story and then select the Utilities menu's Plug-ins command. Then choose Running Headers & Footers.

2. Edit the headers and footers from the dialog box that appears. When you are finished, click OK to save your changes and be returned to your document.

To delete a footer or header, follow these steps:

1. Click the text box in your story and then select the Utilities menu's Plug-ins commnand. Then choose Running Headers & Footers.

2. Click the footer or header you want to delete and drag it off the page. Click OK to be returned to your document.

# Creating and Applying Custom Master Pages

As mentioned earlier, custom master pages can be generated in one of three ways:

- You can create a master page by copying another master page, including your document master.

- You can create a master page from scratch.

- You can create a master page by copying an existing publication page that is not defined to be a master page and telling PageMaker that you want it to be a master page.

Because custom master pages are not permanent fixtures in your documents, they can be moved and deleted easily. However, you should keep the following guidelines in mind when creating and applying them.

Custom master pages do not take precedence over or rearrange what is already on a page. If you would like PageMaker to adjust your text and other elements to accommodate the new master page, you must the select Adjust Layout option.

Once objects are placed on a page by applying a master page to it, they are not editable from the publication page. You will have to go to the master page itself to edit objects that appear on it. This is one way of ensuring that objects don't accidentally get moved or deleted while you are working. This rule does not apply to ruler or margin guides created in the master page. Like the objects you place on a master page, they appear on the pages that you apply the master page to, but can be moved within the publication page. Note, however, that any changes you make to the ruler or margin guides on a single page are not reflected on the master page. Therefore, if the changes you make are ones you would like applied to all the pages that the master page affects, it is best to make the changes to the master page itself or create another master page.

Keep the following in mind as you work with master pages.

- To access a particular master page, you can always click the name of the master page in the Master Pages Palette. However, before doing this, be sure to click the master page icons in the bottom-left corner of the document page first. Otherwise, if a page number is selected instead, clicking a new master page in the Master Page Palette will apply that new master page to the page you currently have open. This is not a difficult thing to fix, but it can be a little disconcerting.

- To access the master page applied to a particular page in a publication, click the number of the page in the page icons located at the bottom-left corner of your document. The page you have clicked will open. Then click the left and right master page icons, located to the left of the page icons, and the master page that is currently applied to that page will open.

# Creating a New Master Page by Copying Another Master Page

Let's start by creating a copy of the document master:

1. Open a new file.

   Select the File menu's New command. The Document Setup dialog box appears.

2. Set the page size.

   Select Magazine Narrow from the Page size drop-down menu, and click the Tall radio button for orientation.

3. Set your options.

   Since magazines are two-sided and have facing pages, put a check in the Double-sided and Facing Pages options. Adjust Layout will be grayed out. Put a check in the Restart Page Numbering box if it is not already there.

4. Set the number of pages.

   Type the number **4** into the Number box and the number **1** in the Start Page # box.

5. Set the margins.

   Accept the margin settings for now.

6. Accept the default target resolution and printer.

7. Set your numbering system.

   By clicking the Numbers Button on the right-hand side of the dialog box, you will open the Page Numbering dialog box, which enables you to select the style of numbers you would like. Often prefaces, introductions, and indexes are numbered using lower-case roman numerals. However, as this is just a regular text document, Arabic numerals should be selected. Click OK to accept your changes and be returned to the Document Setup dialog box.

8. Create your new document.

   Click OK and your new document will be created and displayed.

9. Open the Master Pages Palette if it is not already open.

   Select the Window menu's Show Master Pages Palette command. The Master Page Palette appears.

10. Click the master page you want to duplicate.

    Since we only have one master page right now, the document master should be selected, but if you had others, you could choose which master page to copy by clicking it.

11. Open the Master Pages menu.

    Click the small arrow in the upper-right corner of the Master Page Palette, and the Master Pages menu appears.

12. Open the Duplicate Master Page dialog box.

    Select the Duplicate Document Master option from the Master Pages menu, and the Duplicate Master Page dialog box appears, as shown in the following illustration.

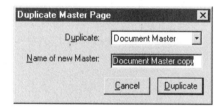

13. Name the copy.

    In the box below the name of the master page that is being copied, type a name that will help you remember the reason you created the copy. For example, if you plan to add elements to this master page so it can be used for tables, you might want to name it Tables. In this case, since this is just practice, I've accepted the name Document Master Copy.

14. Create the duplicate.

    Click the Duplicate Button and the new master page appears in your Master Pages Palette. Since this new master page has not been assigned to any pages yet, any changes you make to it will not be reflected in the publication itself.

## Creating a Master Page from Scratch

Creating a brand new master page is simple:

1. Open the New Master Page dialog box.

    Click the small arrow in the upper right-hand corner of the Master Pages Palette and the fly-out menu will appear. Select the New Master Page option and the New Master Page dialog box appears, as shown in the following illustration.

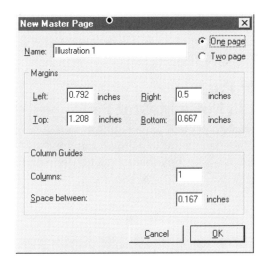

2. Name your new master page.

   Type the name you would like to use for your new master page in the Name box. Again, bear in mind what you will be using the master page for when you select the name. Call this master page Illustration 1.

3. Select One Page or Two Page.

   One Page will be your only option if you have a single page or a single-sided document. However, a one-page master page can be handy for documents that have facing pages as well. For example, they can be used to standardize the design elements in pages that contain only illustrations such as maps.

   Two Page should be selected if you have a double-sided document and plan to use the master page for more than one contiguous page. Here I have selected One Page because I want to use this master page to set up the overall design and look for full-page illustrations.

4. Set the margin and column guides.

   As discussed previously in the section on adding elements to your master pages, tell PageMaker what you would like your margins settings to be and how many columns, if any, you would like in your publication. Here the margin guides have been accepted with only one column.

**Note**

*When creating a master page from scratch, you should think carefully before selecting margin settings that are different from those of the document master and/or the other masters in the publication. In general, margins remain consistent throughout a publication. They are one of the elements that help create a unified look in the publication, so unless you have a good reason to deviate significantly, you shouldn't.*

MANAGING PAGEMAKER DOCUMENTS

5. Accept your settings and create your new master page.

   Click OK and your new master page is generated. It will appear in the Master Pages Palette, as shown in Figure 13-16.

## Creating a Master Page from a Page That Is Not a Master Page

Let's suppose that you create a page in your publication that you think looks great and would like to use again, but don't want to go to all the trouble of laying it out and importing graphics again. You can copy that page and define it to be a master page so it can be applied to other pages.

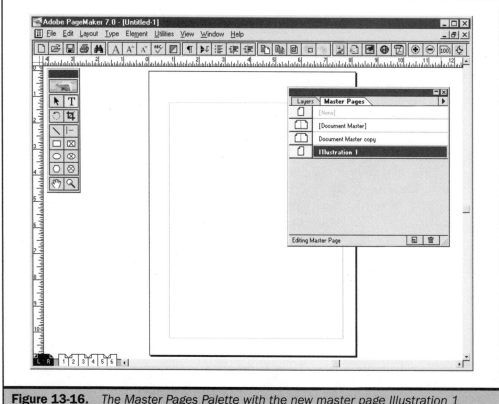

**Figure 13-16.**  *The Master Pages Palette with the new master page Illustration 1 added*

In order to do this, we will have to put something in one of our publication pages, so let's begin by opening one of our pages:

1. Open page 4.

   Click the page icon for page number 4 in our publication. Page number 4 will appear.

2. Apply the Illustration 1 master page to page 4.

   Look at your Master Pages Palette list. You see that one master page is already highlighted. That is the master page that is currently applied to the page you have open in your publication. In this case, it is the document master page, which is applied by default.

   Find Illustration 1 in the Master Pages Palette list and click it. The message, Applying Master Page, appears at the bottom of the Master Pages Palette list, and your screen displays page 4 with the Illustration 1 master page applied to it.

   Since neither the page nor the master page have anything added to them yet, this is perfect for our purposes. Now we are going to add elements to page 4 that we will want to make into another master page.

3. Return to page 4.

   Return to page 3 by clicking the page 4 icon in the bottom-left portion of the document screen.

4. Select the Elliptical Frame tool.

   Since this page will be used for pages with illustrations, let's add a frame for holding graphics. From the toolbox, select the Elliptical Frame tool. It looks like an ellipse with an X drawn through it. Your cursor will turn into a plus symbol (+) when you move it onto the page.

5. Draw an ellipse centered near the top of your screen.

   Click where you would like the upper-left edge of the ellipse to begin, and drag right and down to create the ellipse. Try to create an ellipse that is approximately 3 inches across and 2 inches down. Release when you are satisfied with the size. To adjust its dimensions, select the Pointer tool, click it, and use the adjustment boxes to make changes.

**Note**

*You might want to create ruler guides to assist you with the placement of the frame.*

Now let's add a frame for holding text below the ellipse:

1. Select the Rectangle Frame tool.

   From the toolbox, select the Rectangle Frame tool. It looks like a box with an X drawn through it. Your cursor turns into a plus symbol (+) when you move it onto the page.

2. Draw a rectangle below the ellipse.

   Draw a rectangle that is below the ellipse, but with edges that extend all the way to the left, right, and bottom margins of the active document screen, as shown in Figure 13-17.

   To do this, click where you would like the upper-left corner of the rectangle to begin, and drag right and down to create the rectangle. Release when you have reached the left, right, and bottom margins. To adjust its dimensions, select the Pointer tool, click the rectangle, and use the adjustment boxes to make changes.

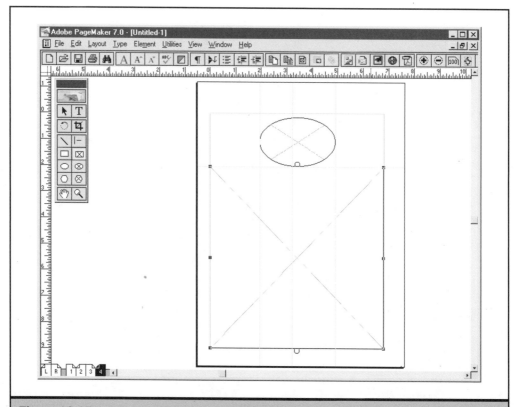

**Figure 13-17.**    *Page 4 with an elliptical frame and a rectangular frame*

Now we have a page design that we can copy and make into a master page. Here's how:

1.  Open the page you want to copy and define it to be a master page.

    Click the page icon in the bottom-left portion of your screen that corresponds to the number of the page you want to open. In our case, it is number 4. The page you have selected is displayed.

2.  Open the Master Pages menu.

    Click the small arrow in the upper right-hand corner of the Master Pages Palette and the Master Pages menu appears. Select the New Master Page option and the New Master Page dialog box will appear.

3.  Open the Save Page as Master dialog box.

    Select the Save Page as Master option from the Master Pages menu, and the Save Page as Master dialog box appears, as shown in the following illustration.

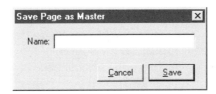

4.  Name and save your page as a master page.

    In the Name box, type a name for your new master page. Let's type **Illustration 2**. Click the Save Button and your page will be copied and saved as a master page. You will be returned to your page and the name of the new master page will appear in your Master Pages Palette.

5.  Open the new master page we have just created.

    Click the Master Page icons in the lower-left corner of your document screen, and then click Illustration 2 in the Master Pages Palette. The master page Illustration 2 will be displayed on your screen. It should look just like page 4.

6.  Add a page marker to the Illustration 2 master page.

    Don't forget to add page markers to your new master pages so you will be saved the tedious chore of adding page numbers by hand.

    Using the Text tool, click on the lower left- or lower right-hand corner of your page. Where you click will be determined by whether you applied your master page to a left or a right page. In this case, it was a right, so click in the lower-right corner just beneath the active document box and press CTRL+ALT+P and the PageMaker right master will appear.

## Applying a Master Page
## to a Page or Pages in a Publication

Applying a master page can be done in one of three ways:

- Apply a master page using the Master Page list in the Master Pages Palette.
- Apply a master page using the Apply Master dialog box from the Master Pages menu.
- Apply a master page when you insert new pages.

To apply a master page using the Master Page list, follow these steps:

1. Select the page or pages to which you would like to apply the master page.

   Click one of the page icons in the bottom-left portion of your screen. The icons turn black and the pages are displayed on the screen. Note that the master page that is currently applied to the page or pages is highlighted in the Master Pages Palette.

2. Click one of the master pages in the Master Pages Palette. The message, Applying Master Page, appears at the bottom of the palette, and the master page you have just selected is applied to the page or pages displayed on your screen. This application remains, even if you change to another page in your publication and then return. Of course, you have only to click another master page to apply it to the pages you have selected.

To apply a master page using the Apply Master dialog box, follow these steps:

1. Open the Master Pages menu.

   Click the small arrow in the upper right-hand corner of the Master Pages Palette, and the Master Pages menu will appear.

2. Open the Apply Master dialog box.

   Select the Apply option, and the Apply Master dialog box appears, as shown in the following illustration.

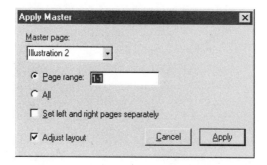

3. Select the master page you want to apply.

   From the drop-down menu, select the name of the master page you want to apply to specific pages.

4. Select the pages to apply the master page to.

   Select either Page Range or All. If you select Page Range, you will have to tell PageMaker which pages you would like the master page applied to. You can list individual pages with commas in between (1, 5, 8, 14), specify a range by typing the first and last page numbers with a hyphen in between (1–5), or use as combination of both (1, 4–7, 10–15, 17, 21). Note that if you put a dash after the last number, PageMaker will apply the master page to that final number and all pages that follow after it (1, 4–7, 10–15, 17, 21).

5. Choose whether or not to use the Set Left and Right Pages Separately option.

   If you have a two-sided publication, then you can opt to apply different master pages to the left and right sides. If you would like to do this, put a check in the box beside the option, and your dialog box adds the Right Master Page option and menu. Make the appropriate choice of master pages to apply.

6. Tell PageMaker if you want it to adjust your layout.

   If you would like PageMaker to adjust your page layout to accommodate the new master page, select the Adjust Layout option.

7. Accept your settings and apply the new master page(s).

   Click Apply and your master page(s) will be applied to the pages you specified. You will also be returned to your screen.

To apply a master page when you insert new pages, follow these steps:

1. Open the Insert Pages dialog box.

   Select the Layout menu's Insert Pages command. The Insert Pages dialog box appears, as shown in the following illustration.

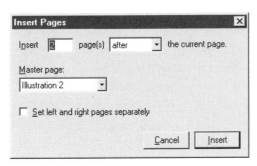

2.  Select the number of pages to add.

    Type the number of pages you'd like to add in the Insert box.

3.  Tell PageMaker where to put the new pages.

    Select either Before or After the Current Page from the drop-down menu.

4.  Decide whether or not to use the Set Left and Right Pages Separately option.

    If you would like to assign different master pages to the left and right pages, select this option and PageMaker will expand your Insert Pages dialog box to include a drop-down menu for the left page and one for the right. This enables you to select a master page for the left and a master page for the right separately.

5.  Select the master page(s) you want to apply.

    Now that we have created custom master pages, you have some choice about which master page(s) to apply. Make your choice from the drop-down menu(s).

6.  Accept your option choices and insert your pages.

    Click the Insert Button and the new pages are added to your publication. They can be seen represented as new icons in the bottom-left corner of your document screen.

## Applying the None Master

The None Master, located at the top of the Master Pages Palette, is used to remove master page formatting (except for margins) from your publication pages.

Like all master pages, None can quickly be applied to any active page by clicking None in the Master Pages Palette. Simply clicking None will remove all formatting (objects), but keep the column and ruler guides and margins.

Note that clicking None removes formatting from facing pages. To specify that you only want one page cleared, press ALT and click on either the left or right side of the None Master Page icon located in the lower-left corner of your document screen.

You can tell PageMaker that you would like the ruler guides and/or the column guides removed as well by following these steps:

1.  Open the page or page spread from which you want to remove the formatting.

    Click the icon in the bottom-left corner of your document screen that corresponds to the page or page spread that you want to remove the formatting from, and the page(s) will become active.

2.  Remove the formatting in one of the following ways:

    ■  To remove both the ruler and column guides along with the rest of the formatting, press the SHIFT key as you click None in the Master Pages Palette.

- ■ To remove only the column guides (along with the objects) and keep the ruler guides, press ALT+SHIFT and click None in the Master Pages Palette.

- ■ To remove only the ruler guides (along with the objects) and keep the column guides, press the CTRL+SHIFT and click None in the Master Pages Palette.

If you would like to remove formatting from many pages at once, do the following:

1.  Open the Apply Master dialog box.

    From the Master Pages Palette fly-out menu, select Apply, and the Apply Master dialog box will appear.

2.  Select None.

    From the Master Page drop-down menu in the Apply Master dialog box, select None.

3.  Select the pages you would like to apply None to.

    Select the Page Range box, and type in the numbers of the pages that you would like None applied to.

4.  Apply None to the selected pages.

    Click OK and None will be applied to the pages you have chosen.

## A Word of Caution

Pages that have been assigned a master page spread are associated with the spread itself, not the specific left or right sides of the spread. Therefore, when repagination occurs, a page that originally had the left side of the master page assigned to it could have the right side of the master page assigned to it, and vice versa. It helps me to imagine the master pages as clear acetate film being pulled back and forth over the pages of a stationary document.

When the pages in a master page spread have identical or very similar formatting, this is not a problem, but when they are very different, your pages can begin to look downright peculiar.

There are several possible solutions to this problem. You can create and apply single-sided master pages when you know that the two sides of a spread will be radically different from each other.

Another solution is to specify that you want only one page from a master page spread to be applied to a page in a publication spread. The only catch here is that you must apply the left side of a master page spread to the left page of a publication spread, and the right side of a master page spread to the right page of a publication spread. The following steps outline how this can be done:

1.  Open the two-page spread you want to adjust.

    Click the page icons in the lower-left portion of your document screen to make the two-page spread you want to adjust active.

2. Open the Master Pages Palette.

   If the Master Pages Palette isn't open, select the Window menu's Show Master Pages command.

3. Select Adjust Layout.

   From the Master Pages menu, choose the Adjust Layout option if you want PageMaker to adjust the objects and guides following your changes.

4. Press and hold the ALT key while doing one of the following:

   ■ Click the left (L) side of the Master Page icons in the lower-left portion of your document screen to apply the left side of the master page to only the left page of the publication.

   ■ Click the right (R) side of the Master Page icons in the lower-left portion of your document screen to apply the right side of the master page to only the right page of the publication.

## Adjusting Layout

You may notice that as you apply different master pages to your publication pages, your layouts can become quite distorted. The solution is the Adjust Layout option in the Master Pages Palette menu. When this option is selected, PageMaker will automatically adjust graphics, ruler guides, and text when you apply a new master page. Adjustments are made based on the new master page's settings to access this function:

1. Activate a page in your publication.

   Click a page in your publication that you want to apply a new master page to. The master page that is currently applied will be highlighted in the Master Pages Palette.

2. Open the Apply Master dialog box.

   From the Master Pages menu, select Apply. The Apply Master dialog box appears.

3. Select the master page you want to apply.

   From the Master Page drop-down menu, select the name of the new master page to apply.

4. Select the pages.

   Enter the numbers of the pages you want to apply the new master page to in the Page Range box.

5. Tell PageMaker to adjust the layout as it applies the master page.

   Put a check in the Adjust Layout box.

6.  Apply the new master page.

    Click Apply. The new master page is applied and the layout of the page adjusted.

You can also:

1.  Select Adjust Layout.

2.  Select the Adjust Layout option from the Master Pages menu, and layout will automatically be adjusted whenever you apply a new master page.

Remember that layout adjustments are made based on the layout preferences you set in Chapter 12. Refer to Chapter 12 for detailed instructions on setting layout preferences.

# Renaming a Master Page

Renaming a master page is a simple process:

1.  Click the master page that you want to rename.

2.  Open the Master Page Options dialog box.

    Select Master Page Options from the Master Pages menu, and the Master Page Options dialog box will appear.

3.  Change the name.

    Type the new name in the Name box.

4.  Apply the new name.

    Click OK and the new name is applied and listed in the Master Pages Palette.

# Deleting a Master Page

Deleting a master page removes it and all its objects from the pages it is applied to and from the Master Pages Palette list. To do so, follow these steps:

1.  Select the master page to delete.

    Click the name of the master page you want to delete in the Master Pages Palette.

2.  Choose one of three options:

    - Select Delete Master Page (the name of the currently highlighted master page will appear) from the Master Pages Palette fly-out menu.

    - Drag the selected master page into the trashcan at the bottom of the palette.

    - Click the trashcan at the bottom of the palette and the currently highlighted master page will be deleted.

3. Confirm that you want to delete the master page.

   A message will appear asking you to confirm that you want to delete a master page. Click OK and the master page will disappear from your Master Pages Palette and be removed from all pages it was applied to.

# Using Libraries

Collectors and people who love to catalog and arrange things in groups will love PageMaker's Library Palette. The Library Palette enables you to store items that you use frequently, such as text and graphics, in the same place so they are readily accessible. You can make as many libraries as you need, and once a library is made, it can use its search functions to find items within it. To make a new library, do the following:

1. Open the Library Palette.

   Select the Window menu's Plug-in Palettes command. Then choose Show Library from the submenu. The Library Palette appears, as shown in Figure 13-18.

   Because we have yet to create a library, the palette says No Library at the bottom. We must now create a new one.

2. Open the New Library dialog box.

   Click the triangle in the upper-right corner of the Library Palette and from the Library menu select New Library. The New Library dialog box appears, as shown in Figure 13-19.

3. Name the library.

   In the file name window, type in a name for your library. If this is a library that you will use to create a project that you work on regularly, such as a company newsletter or a Web site, give the library a name that will help you remember what's in it. In this case, it is named MyLib.

4. Tell PageMaker where you would like to store the library.

   From the Save in drop-down menu, choose the place you would like your library stored.

5. Save your library.

   Click the Save Button and your library is created. You can access your new library by going to the Library Palette, clicking the small arrow in the upper right-hand corner, and choosing Open Library. The Open Library dialog box opens, as shown in Figure 13-20. From the Look in drop-down menu, find the place where the library is stored and then click the name. When the name

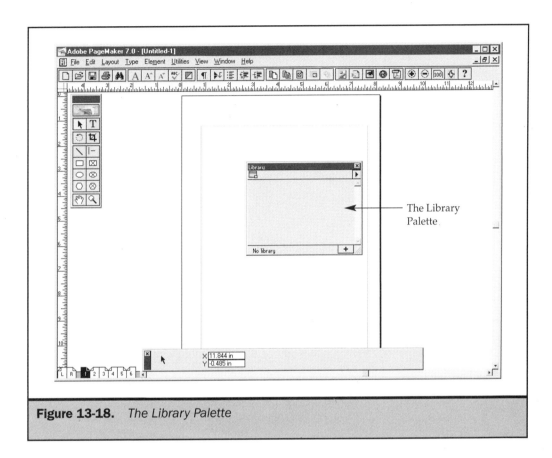

**Figure 13-18.**    *The Library Palette*

appears in the file name window, click Open and the library opens on your screen. In this case, MyLib is open, but there is nothing in it yet.

**Adding Objects to Your Library**    The library is a bit like the Clipboard in that it enables you to copy objects into it. The great thing about the library is that it stores the items you've chosen, unlike the Clipboard, which is volatile. In order to add an item to the library, it must already be on a page in your publication. To add items, do the following:

1.  Open your Library Palette.

    Select the Window menu's Plug-in Palette command. Then choose Show Library from the submenu. The Library Palette opens, as shown in Figure 13-18.

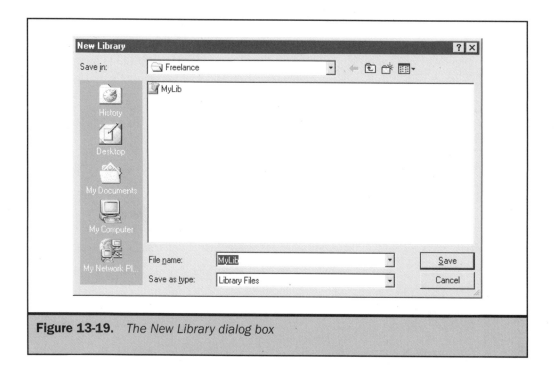

**Figure 13-19.** *The New Library dialog box*

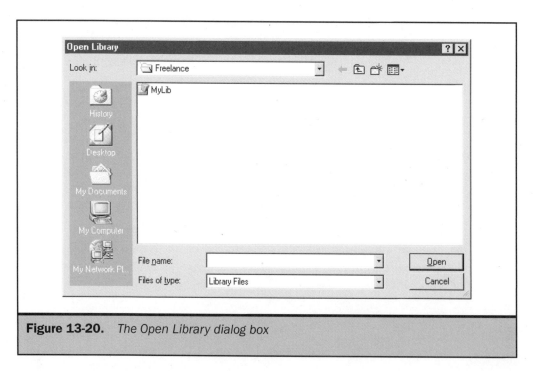

**Figure 13-20.** *The Open Library dialog box*

2. Open the library to which you want to add the item.

   Click the small arrow in the upper right-hand corner of the Library Palette and select Open Library from the Library menu. In this case, MyLib is opened.

3. Select the item in the publication that you would like to add to the library.

   Using the Pointer tool, select the image, frame, or text block you would like to place in your library. In Figure 13-21, the picture of the fish is in the publication and selected.

4. Add the item to the library.

   Click the library's Add Button, which looks like a plus symbol (+), and the item that was selected in your publication will be added to your library. The item will appear in its window, as shown in Figure 13-22.

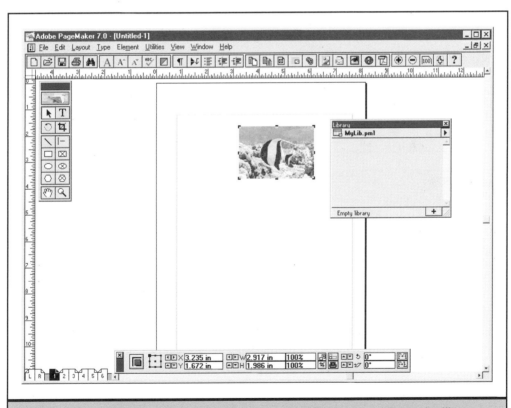

**Figure 13-21.**    *An item selected in the publication ready to be added to the library*

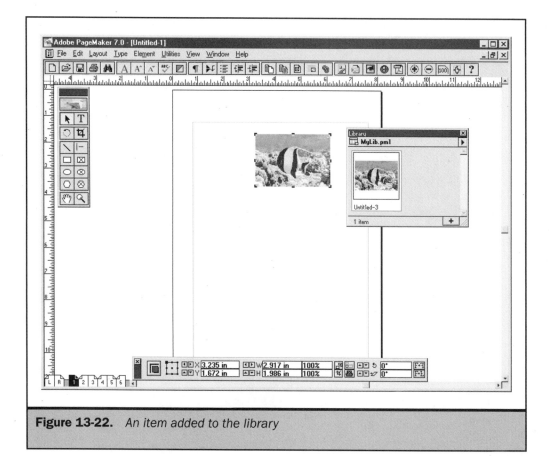

**Figure 13-22.** *An item added to the library*

**Placing an Object from a Library in a Publication**   Placing an object or text from a library into a publication is very easy. Do the following:

1. Open the publication in which you want to place an item, and go to the page where you would like it to appear.

2. Open the library that contains the item.

   Select the Window menu's Plug-in Palettes command. Then choose Show Library from the submenu. The Library Palette opens. From the Library menu, select Open Library and navigate to the library you want to open.

3. Select the item you want to place from the library.

   Using the Pointer tool, select the item in the library. A heavy line appears around it, indicating that it is selected.

4. Place the item in your publication.

   Simply click and drag the item from the library onto your publication page, and the item is copied into the publication, as shown in Figure 13-23.

**Deleting an Item from a Library**    Deleting an item from a library is almost as simple as adding one. To do so, follow these steps:

1. Select the item you wish to delete from the library.

   Using the Pointer tool, click the item you want to delete. A heavy line will appear around it, indicating that it is selected.

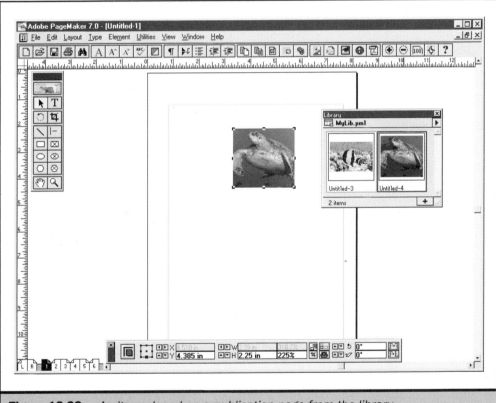

**Figure 13-23.**    *An item placed on a publication page from the library*

2. Select Remove Item.

From the Library menu, select Remove Item. A message will appear, as shown in the following illustration, asking you to confirm that you want to remove the item.

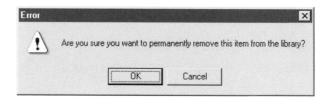

3. Delete the item.

Click OK in the Message box and the item is removed from the library.

**Adding Information about an Item**   One of the really nice things about libraries is that you can add information about the items to the libraries that will help you locate and use the items more easily. Once you have added information about the items, you can also search the library to find what you need. In this last respect, libraries function a lot like databases. If your library has dozens of items, this can be a very handy feature indeed.

What kinds of information can you add for an item? The following illustration shows the Item Information dialog box that opens when you select the Edit item after editing from the Library Palette's fly-out menu. As you can see, you can give your item a title, note its author, the date it was entered, keywords that help when you are searching for it, and a description.

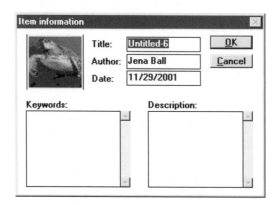

To add this information to an item, you need to tell PageMaker that you want to edit the item once it's added. Perform the following steps:

1.  Select the Edit Item After Adding option.

2.  From the Library menu, scroll down the menu and put a check mark beside the Edit Item After Adding option. The next time you add an item, the Item Information dialog box opens, with a thumbnail of the item displayed on the left-hand side, and you can add any information you'd like.

 *To edit an item once it is already in your library, simply double-click it and the Item Information dialog box will reappear.*

**Searching for Items in a Library**    PageMaker libraries come equipped with a search function that enables you to search using the criteria you supplied in the Item Information dialog box. In other words, you can search by title, author, keywords, and/or descriptions. Here's what you do:

1.  Open the library you want to search.

2.  Open the Search Library dialog box.

    From the Library menu, select Search Library. The Search Library dialog box appears, as shown in the following illustration.

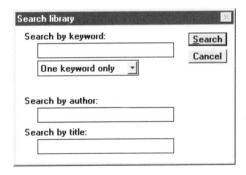

3.  Enter your search criteria.

    Enter the information you would like to use to search the library in the appropriate boxes. If you would like to search by more than one keyword, enter the word you want to use first, then use the drop-down menu to select the appropriate connector (and, or, but, not), and then type in the second word.

4.  Start your search.

    When you are finished creating search criteria, click Search and the items that meet your criteria will be displayed in the library.

*Only those items that meet your criteria will be displayed. If you would like to have access to the entire library again, select Show All Items from the Library Palette's fly-out menu.*

**Deleting an Entire Library**    The only way to completely remove a library from your system is to navigate to it via Windows Explorer. Once you have located it, select the File menu's Delete command.

# Summary

This chapter is about using master pages and libraries. I define a master page and discuss the various forms it can take. I also discuss how and when Master Pages are applied, and how to open them in order to edit them.

I discuss libraries and how they can be used to store and access frequently used items.

# The Complete Reference

PageMaker 7

# Chapter 14

## Merging Documents in PageMaker

Throughout this book I have expressed my delight at some new or not-so-new feature of PageMaker that I didn't have in the days when I used PageMaker daily in my work. PageMaker 7's Data Merge is another feature that I am excited to see incorporated into this excellent application. I have long wished to be able to merge in PageMaker, but consoled myself with the knowledge that PageMaker's purpose is page layout, not word processing. Although PageMaker 7 is still primarily a page layout program, now we can perform the merge process right in PageMaker without having to go to another application.

The Data Merge process enables the production of letters or other documents, each personalized with individual names or other data. Using PageMaker's Data Merge feature, you can create, with just a few easy steps, multiple documents that appear to be individually created for each name on your mailing list.

The terminology used in PageMaker's merge process is descriptive of the procedure and is therefore fairly intuitive. But since terminology is so important in identifying the elements involved in a merge, I will discuss it first.

# Data Merge Terminology

Even when I teach Merge in Microsoft Word, I emphasize the importance of using correct terminology. In order for me to communicate the process to you and, especially, for you to discuss a merge project with someone else, it is necessary to use terminology that is specific and consistent. In a merge process, it is easy to apply similar or even identical terms to different elements if you are not using correct terminology. I will use the following terms in the discussion of the Data Merge process. These are the terms set by Adobe for PageMaker 7's Data Merge feature:

- **Data source file** This is the file that contains all the personalized information that you want to put into the individualized documents. The file probably contains names and addresses, but it may also contain information such as the amount of a company's last order or the name of the family dog. The information contained in the data source file depends, of course, upon the purpose of the individualized document.

  As part of the data source file, *records* (usually rows) contain a complete set of information about one individual, family, or company, while *data fields* are the individual pieces of data, such as names, addresses, the amount of the last order, or the name of the family dog. All data fields in the data source file do not have to be used in the merge, but all data fields must be in the same data source file.

  The data source file may be a PageMaker document, a database, a spreadsheet file, or any comma-delimited list (a list of data separated by commas).

- **Target publication**   The target publication is the form document into which the personalized information is placed. This document is created in PageMaker. Data field placeholders are placed in the document to indicate where the personalized information appears.

- **Merged publication**   This is the resulting personalized document. There will be as many merged publications as there are records in your data source.

# The Data Merge Process

The Data Merge process takes information entered into a data source file (a spreadsheet, a database, or a comma-delimited list) and places it into a form letter or other target publication one record at a time. The resulting document contains as many pages as the number of records (names and personalized data) in the data source file, each individualized with the information of one record (see Figure 14-1).

MANAGING PAGEMAKER DOCUMENTS

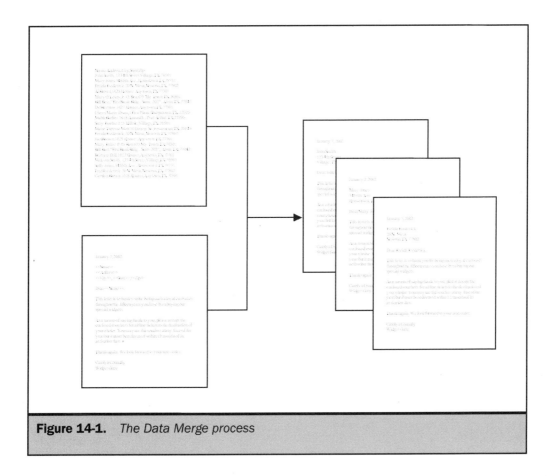

**Figure 14-1.**   *The Data Merge process*

# Preparing for a Data Merge

A Data Merge goes much smoother if you think through the process beforehand. Consider the following questions:

- What is the purpose of your document?

  As emphasized in Chapter 3, it is important to identify what it is you want to accomplish with the document you are creating. Are you trying to sell, inform, or motivate? Some documents may be for entertainment purposes only. Some documents attempt to persuade the reader to your point of view. Maybe the merged document is just an envelope or label to facilitate the delivery of another document. The job of your document should be clearly determined before you proceed.

- What format should it take?

  Just as any other PageMaker document, a merged document can take many forms. The most commonly used forms are simple form letters, envelopes, and labels. But PageMaker offers far more possibilities than that. You can personalize three-paneled brochures. A flyer, complete with graphics, can be used as a target publication. Even holiday cards can be designed in PageMaker and merged with your list so that each card contains a personal message to the recipient. Really, the possibilities are endless.

  It is important to conceptualize your target publication before beginning the merge process.

- Which data fields do you need?

  Identify the data fields you want to merge into the target publication. If all you want is the recipient's name, address, and telephone number, you would need these fields: First Name, Last Name, Address1, Address2, City, State, ZipCode, and Telephone. However, you may use any data field for which you have information.

  Planning the data fields saves a lot of time in correcting and reentering during the various stages of creating a merged publication.

# Preparing a Data Source

The data source file, of course, contains the records with the data fields that are inserted into the target publication when the merge is performed. Data source files can be spreadsheet files (such as Excel or similar programs' spreadsheets), database files (from applications such as Access or similar database programs), or lists created in word processing programs (such as Word or WordPerfect). You can also create your data source file in PageMaker.

# Using an Existing File As a PageMaker Data Source File

If you already have a file that contains the information you want to merge with the target publication, you may use it as a PageMaker data source file as long as it meets the following conditions. It must be a comma-delimited file and it must be saved as a .csv or .txt file. A comma-delimited file separates data in each record by commas (or columns in spreadsheet and database programs), and it separates records by paragraphs (or rows). Figure 14-2 is an example of a simple data source created in Microsoft Word, while Figure 14-3 shows a simple data source created in Microsoft Excel.

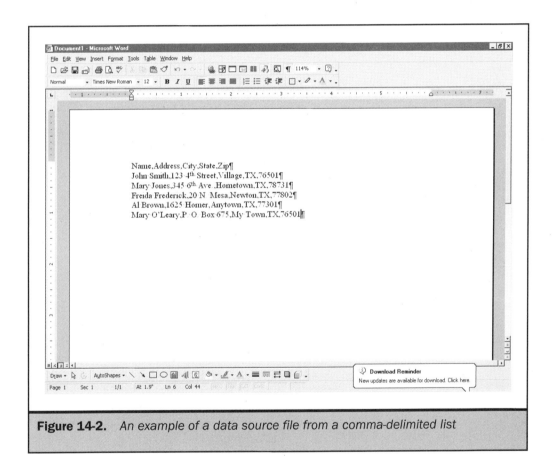

**Figure 14-2.**    *An example of a data source file from a comma-delimited list*

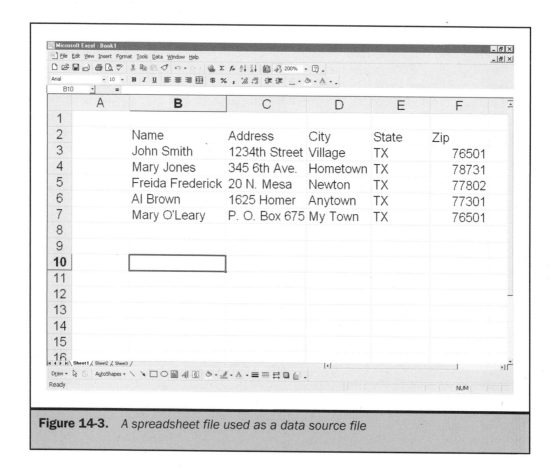

**Figure 14-3.** *A spreadsheet file used as a data source file*

To save a file so that it can be used as a PageMaker data source file, take the following steps:

1. Open the file.

   You must open the file in its original application.

2. Confirm that the file is organized appropriately by following these steps:

   ■ Check to make sure that the file contains the names of the data fields in the top line or row. If you are using a list in a word processing program, the data field names must be separated by commas with no space following the comma.

   ■ Check to make sure that each data field is in the appropriate column or that the data fields are separated by commas with no space following the comma in a list.

■ Each record should be on a separate row or in a separate paragraph in a list.

The data source file is ready to be used in a PageMaker Data Merge.

# Creating a Data Source File from Scratch

If the data source file does not already exist, you may create it in a spreadsheet program, a database program, a word processing program, or in PageMaker. No matter which application you choose, you must follow these guidelines:

■ The top row of data must contain the names of your data fields separated by commas. Here's an example, and please note that there are no spaces following the commas:

First Name,Last Name,Address,City,State,Zip Code

In a spreadsheet or database program, the first row would look like this:

First Name    Last Name    Address    City    State    Zip Code

Each subsequent row must contain the complete record (all of the data fields) on an individual, company, or other item.

■ Data fields in each record must be separated by commas without any spaces following, just as in the data field names. Here's an example:

John,Smith,123 4th Street,Hometown,TX,76501

The same data, placed in a spreadsheet or database program document, would look like this:

John   Smith    123 4th Street    Hometown    TX    76501

■ If a data field contains a comma, enclose the data field in quotation marks, so that PageMaker knows that the data goes together as one data field. Here's an example:

John,"Smith, Jr.",123 4th Street,Hometown,TX,76501

Once you have entered all the records in your data source file, it must be saved as a .csv or .txt file. Here's how:

1. Open the Save As dialog box.

   Click the File menu's Save As command. The Save As dialog box opens.

2. Select the file type.

   Click the drop-down arrow to the right of the Save File as Type box to reveal the File Type menu. The menu may differ from one application to another. Select the Text Only file type or a file type that provides a .csv or a .txt suffix. (The suffix should be shown next to the file type.)

MANAGING PAGEMAKER
DOCUMENTS

3. Save the file.

   Click the Save Button. The file is now in a format that can be used as a data source file in PageMaker's Data Merge process.

## Including Graphics in Your Data Source File

An interesting option available in the PageMaker Data Merge feature is the capability to include graphics, such as photos, as data fields in your data source file. That way you would not only be personalizing the merged document with information, but with pictures as well. Follow these guidelines:

- Include an at sign (@) as the first character in the data field name. Here's an example:

  Name,Age,@Photo,Location,Date

- In the corresponding data field, include the image's path. The @ is not required in the data fields, only as part of the data field name on the first line. Here's an example:

  Jim,16,C:\Photos\Kids\Jim1,The Lake,Summer of 1983

When you perform the merge, the image appears in the merged publication.

## Preparing the Target Publication

Obviously, the first step is to design your target publication. PageMaker's Data Merge process will work with a remarkable variety of layout options. Of course, the form letter format is the most commonly used in a merge, but you can design an elaborate graphic display into which the data fields are placed. You may want to experiment with several ideas. Later in this chapter, Figure 14-5 shows a letter as a target publication, and Figure 14-6 shows a graphic layout into which the data field name codes are placed.

Once the target publication is selected, you must insert the data field name codes into the publication to tell PageMaker where to place specific data on each merged publication. The first step in doing that is to select the data source file.

## Attaching the Data Source File to Your Target Publication

If you prepared your data source file as discussed earlier in this chapter, it can now be attached to the target publication. Here's how:

1. Open the target publication.

   Select the File menu's Open command or click the Open Button on the PageMaker Toolbar. The Open Publication dialog box appears. Click the drop-down arrow to the right of the Look In box to display the directory tree. Using the directory tree, locate the target publication and select it. Then click the Open Button to open the document.

2. Open the Data Merge Palette.

   Click the Window menu's Plug-in Palettes command. Then select Show Data Merge Palette, and the Data Merge Palette appears.

3. Open the Data Merge Palette menu.

   Click the right-pointing arrow on the right side of the Data Merge Palette below the Palette's Exit Button. The Data Merge Palette menu appears.

4. Open the Select Data Source dialog box.

   Choose the Select Data Source command from the Data Merge Palette menu. The Select Data Source dialog box opens.

5. Locate the data source file.

   Click the drop-down arrow to the right of the Look In box to display the directory tree. Using the directory tree, locate and select the data source file.

6. Open the file.

   Click the Open Button to select the data source file.

# Inserting the Data Field Codes into the Target Publication

Once the data source file has been attached to the target publication, the data field names appear in the Data Merge Palette, as shown below. Now all you have to do is place those field names in the target publication to tell PageMaker where to place which data fields. Follow these steps:

1.  Select where you want the data field to appear.

    Using the Text tool, click to place an insertion point in the text where you want the field to appear. If you are placing the field into a graphic or as an independent text box, use the Text tool to define the area where the data field will be placed.

2.  Place the data field name code.

    Click the data field name in the Data Merge Palette. The data field name code appears at the insertion point within double angle brackets, as shown here:

    ≪First Name≫

3.  Format the code.

    You may format the data field name code to the appearance you want to have for the data itself. Use Font, Font Size, and Text Effects to create the look that you want.

4.  Repeat.

    Repeat steps 1 through 3 for each of the data fields you want to use in the target publication. You do not have to use all of the fields in your source document, and you may use any one field as often as you want.

Once you have inserted the codes for all the data fields you want to use (see Figures 14-4 and 14-5), you are ready to preview and process the Data Merge.

## Previewing the Merge

You can preview the merge to see if everything is working correctly before the actual merge is processed. The preview will display the data fields in the target publication instead of codes. In other words, instead of seeing ≪First Name≫, you see the First Name data field from the first record, such as John.

To preview the merge, click the Preview check box at the bottom of the Data Merge Palette. The open target publication will then display the data fields for the first record. You can scroll through the records in the data source file by clicking the navigation buttons located to the left of the Preview box.

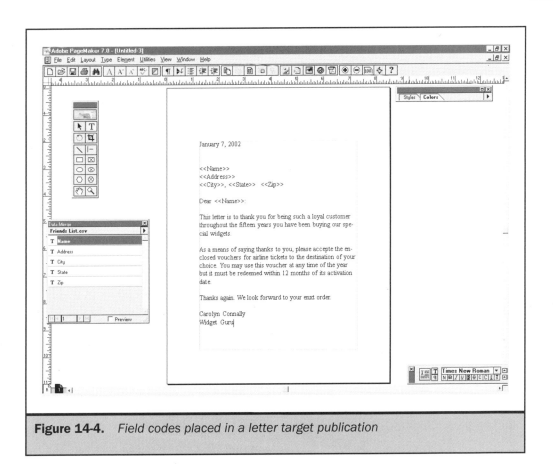

**Figure 14-4.** *Field codes placed in a letter target publication*

If you find problems in the preview, make corrections in the data source file in the original application. If necessary, save the data source file as a .csv or .txt file again. When you are through previewing the merge, deselect the Preview box.

# Performing the Data Merge

If you have followed the instructions discussed, you are ready to perform the merge. The Data Merge creates a new, unnamed document with as many pages as you have records in your data source file. Each page will have the appropriate data from one record in the data source file inserted into the document where the field codes appeared.

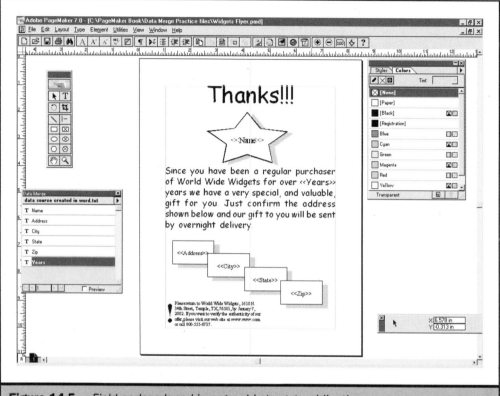

**Figure 14-5.** *Field codes placed in a graphic target publication*

Here is how to perform the Data Merge:

1. Open the Data Merge menu.

   Make sure that the target publication is open. Then open the Data Merge Palette's menu by clicking the right-pointing arrow on the right side of the Palette under the Exit Button.

2. Open the Merge Records dialog box.

   In the Data Merge Palette's menu, click the Merge Records command. The Merge Records dialog box opens, as shown in the following illustration.

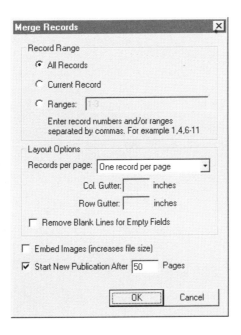

3. Select the Merge options.

   Select from the following options:

   ■ **Record Range** Enter the records you want to merge into the target publication.

   ■ **Layout Options** Choose the number of records to be printed per page. Select from One Record Per Page or Manual Layout. If you are targeting a document such as a form letter, an envelope, or even a graphic display, select the One Record Per Page option. For labels, catalogs, or similar publications where more than one record on a page is appropriate, select Manual Layout. Then specify the spacing between columns and rows to determine how many records will be placed on a page.

   Select the Remove Blank Lines for Empty Fields box if some of your records do not have data for all the data field name codes. For example, if many records require ≪Address1≫ and ≪Address2≫ fields because of long business addresses, but not all of them need the second field, you would want to select this box so that an address won't have a blank line.

   ■ **Embed Images** If you are placing images in your merged documents, you have the option of embedding images in the document. This takes a large amount of hard drive storage space because graphic files are very memory intensive. Do not select this option unless you plan to move the merged document to another computer or plan to move the graphic files.

■ **Start New Publication After _____ Pages**   Long documents are unwieldy in any application, and this is especially true in PageMaker. If your data source file is very long, divide the merged document into several shorter documents by setting a limit to the number of pages in a document. Fifty is the default number.

4. Process the merge.

   Once you have selected the options for your merged document, click OK in the Merge Records dialog box and the merge takes place. A new document (or documents) is created with the data fields for each record placed on each page (unless you are creating labels or a similar publication).

## Saving Your Merged Document

If you intend to use the merged publication again, save it as you would with any PageMaker document. The data source file should be saved in its originating application. The data source file can be used for other publications as well.

## Summary

New to PageMaker 7, the Data Merge feature is a handy way to create personalized documents with data from a list, spreadsheet, or database. The consistent use of correct terminology is important in the merge process to have clear communication. Otherwise, it is easy to get the various elements confused.

**Preparing for a Data Merge**   As an experienced user of merge functions in word processing programs as well as PageMaker, I can assure you that planning ahead saves you minutes and hours of grief in performing a Data Merge. Consider the purpose of your publication and the information you need to merge into the target publication. Develop your design concept early.

**Preparing a Data Source**   The data source is a list of records with data field names in the top line or row, and with data fields in the following lines or rows. A data source can be created in PageMaker or can originate from another application such as a spreadsheet, database, or word processing program. All data source files must be saved with either a .csv or a .txt suffix.

**Preparing the Target Publication**   The target publication can be any of a wide variety of formats. The most common is the form letter, but a graphic display may be used as well. Using the Data Merge Palette, data field name codes are placed in the target publication to tell PageMaker which data field goes where. Once the fields are placed in the target publication, the efficacy of the merge may be previewed.

**Performing the Data Merge**    A merge is easily performed with the use of the Merge Records dialog box, which also enables Merge options to be selected. Once merged, PageMaker creates a new document or several new documents, with each record represented by a page. (Labels, however, have multiple records per page.) You may save the merged document or documents and print them at your leisure. The data source file should be saved in its originating application.

# The Complete Reference

PageMaker 7

# Chapter 15

## Using PageMaker Scripts

A PageMaker script is a miniprogram that automates routine tasks. You might use a script for setting up pages or importing a standard set of elements. If you are familiar with macros used in word processing and spreadsheet programs, then you understand the concept behind scripts. As a matter of fact, a macro is a form of script.

The major difference between macros in a word processing program and in PageMaker scripts is that the macro can be "recorded," while a PageMaker script must be written. If writing miniprograms is not your thing, however, PageMaker comes with a number of scripts in place. All you have to do is run them.

# The Scripts Palette

All PageMaker scripts are stored in a scripts folder. If you should need to access this folder directly you can locate it at Program Files\Adobe\PageMaker 7.0\ RSRC\<language>\Plugins.

However, PageMaker provides a Scripts Palette that makes it generally unnecessary to work within the folder itself. The Scripts Palette displays the contents of the Scripts Palette, including subfolders, and all scripts can be run directly from it.

Open the Scripts Palette by selecting the Window menu's Plug-in Palettes command. Then select Show Scripts to display the Scripts Palette, as shown in the following illustration. The scripts included with PageMaker are shown in seven categories. Arrows to the left of the categories can be clicked to reveal that category's scripts and, in some cases, subcategories. The Scripts Palette can be sized by dragging any border to accommodate the expansion of categories.

# Running Scripts

Running a script is as simple as clicking your mouse, double-clicking that is. To run a script, just double-click the script in the Scripts Palette. A script runs on the page that is currently open in most cases, so make sure that you are in the right spot before running it. Some scripts require an element to be selected first.

It is highly recommended that you spend a little time experimenting with the scripts. Test them out and see how they could ease your workload. If you want to have your socks knocked off, run the *Calendar1* script found under the Template category. The first time I ran that script I sat for several seconds with my mouth agape. It is so cool, not to mention extremely easy.

# Creating and Editing Scripts

You do not have to rely only on the scripts included with PageMaker. You can program your own scripts or edit existing ones.

Although writing a script is a simpler type of programming, there are language techniques and technical conventions that you must observe in order to program the script correctly so that it will run. Since this falls more into the realm of programming, I'm not going to attempt to teach you how to write scripts here. However, PageMaker provides a very useful Portable Document Format (PDF) file that gives details on programming scripts. You can open this file from the PageMaker 7.0 folder on your hard drive. Select the Tech Info subfolder and the ScriptGuide.PDF file.

## Writing Your Own Scripts

You can write your own scripts to aid you in any task that you perform regularly. When you are comfortable with the script programming language, creating a new script is easy. Just follow these steps:

1. Open the Scripts Palette.

   Open the Scripts Palette by selecting the Window menu's Plug-in Palettes command. Then select Show Scripts to display the Scripts Palette.

2. Open the Scripts Palette menu.

   Click the right-pointing arrow to the right of the words Installed Scripts. The Scripts Palette menu is displayed.

3. Open the New Script dialog box.

   Click the New Scripts command in the Scripts Palette menu. The New Script dialog box opens, as shown in Figure 15-1.

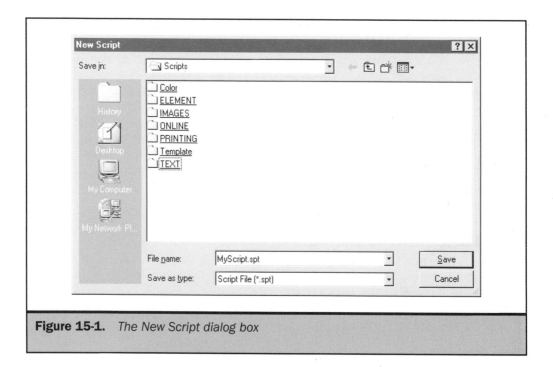

**Figure 15-1.** *The New Script dialog box*

4. Name and save the script.

   In the New Script dialog box, select a category folder for your script and a subcategory if necessary. A new folder be created by clicking the Create New Folder Button to the right of the Save In box. Be sure to open the new folder before saving the script so that it is in the right place.

   Once you have selected the category folder for your script, enter a name for the script in the File Name box. Click the Save Button. Your script is added to the Scripts folder and appears in the Scripts Palette list, and the Edit Script dialog box opens.

5. Write the script.

   Write the script in the Edit Script dialog box (shown in Figure 15-2) following the conventions discussed in the Script Guide PDF.

6. Save the completed script.

   Click OK in the Edit Script dialog box. The script is completed and ready to run.

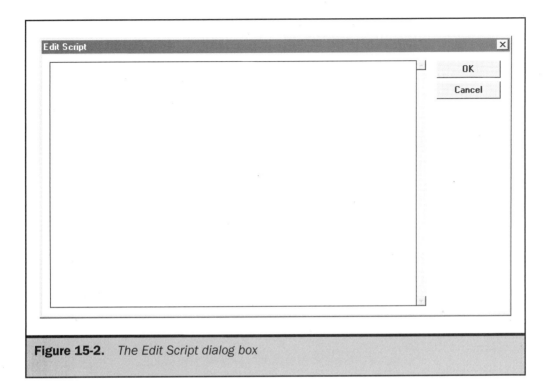

**Figure 15-2.**   *The Edit Script dialog box*

# Editing an Existing Script

If you wish to edit an existing script so that it more closely meets your needs, it is a simple process as long as you are familiar with the techniques and conventions of programming scripts. Here are the steps to take to edit a script:

1. Open the Scripts Palette.

   Open the Scripts Palette by selecting the Window menu's Plug-in Palettes command. Then select Show Scripts to display the Scripts Palette.

2. Open the Edit Script dialog box.

   You can open the Edit Script dialog box by holding down CTRL on your keyboard while clicking the name of the script you wish to edit. Or you may select Edit Script from the Scripts Palette's menu.

3. Modify the script.

   Make the changes necessary to customize the script to your needs.

4. Save the edited script.

Click OK in the Edit Script dialog box. The box closes and the changes to the script are saved.

# Tracing Scripts

If a script does not work the way you want it to, use the Trace Script command to run the Script command in order to locate any problem areas. Here's how:

1. Open the Scripts Palette.

Open the Scripts Palette by selecting the Window menu's Plug-in Palettes command. Then select Show Scripts to display the Scripts Palette.

2. Select a script.

Click once on the script you want to trace to select it.

3. Open the Script Tracer window.

Choose Trace Script from the Scripts Palette's menu. The Script Tracer window opens, as shown in Figure 15-3.

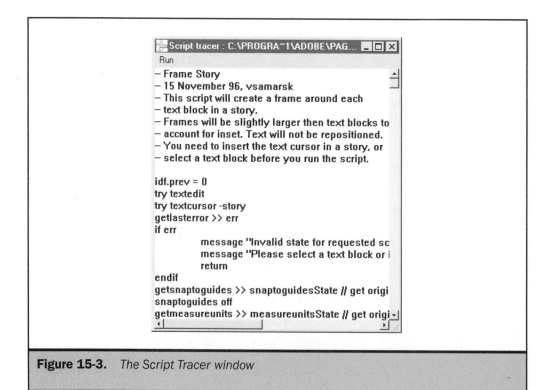

**Figure 15-3.** *The Script Tracer window*

4. Trace the script.

   From the Run menu in the Script Tracer window, select one of the following:

   - **Run**  This selection runs the entire script.
   - **Step**  Step runs the script one line at a time.
   - **Reset**  Reset stops the script from running without closing the Trace window.
   - **Quit**  This selection stops the script from running and closes the Trace window.

## Summary

PageMaker scripts, similar to macros in other applications, are miniprograms written to automate routine tasks. A number of scripts are included in PageMaker.

**Scripts Palette**  The Scripts Palette displays the scripts that are available. You may run a script by double-clicking the script's name in the Scripts Palette.

**Creating and Editing Scripts**  You may write your own scripts or edit existing ones if you are familiar with the techniques and conventions of this particular type of programming. Although script programming is not explained in this book, PageMaker provides a PDF scripting guide. You can open this file from the PageMaker 7.0 folder on your hard drive. Select the Tech Info subfolder and the ScriptGuide.PDF file.

The
Complete
Reference

PageMaker 7

# Chapter 16

## Creating
## Tables of Contents
## and Indexes

In many publications, the table of contents (TOC) and index form the core navigation system. Without them, readers would find it very difficult to orient themselves and make use of the material. Therefore, learning how to organize, create, and modify tables and indexes in PageMaker is an essential part of learning the program. Happily, PageMaker is very intelligent when it comes to tables and indexes. It is designed to take over the chore of keeping track of formatting, categorizing, and alphabetizing table and index entries. You still have to make the entries, but PageMaker will keep track of and organize them for you.

In this chapter, we will be covering the basics of creating a TOC and an index. Since creating a table is much simpler and requires less thought than an index, we will begin with tables and work our way up to the indexes.

# Creating and Formatting a TOC

Creating and formatting a TOC is a four-step process:

1. Generate the names and page numbers of the sections you want in your TOC.
2. Create the TOC and make room for it in your publication.
3. Place the TOC in your publication.
4. Format the TOC when needed.

I cover all four steps in this chapter and discuss how to edit a TOC as well.

## Generating TOC Entries

In PageMaker, the section of text that includes the information you want to appear as an entry in your TOC is called a paragraph. Entries for your TOC can be generated in one of two ways. You can go through your text and select each paragraph to be included in the TOC (PageMaker calls any contiguous text followed by a paragraph return a paragraph), or you can tell PageMaker that all paragraphs with a particular *style* are to be included in the TOC. This second method is by far the most efficient, but we will cover both in this section.

### Selecting Paragraphs and Page Numbers One by One

If your publication is very short, you might want to select the individual paragraphs to be included in your TOC one by one. An example could be Chapter 1—Preparations for the Journey. You would tell PageMaker that you want this paragraph in your TOC by using the Paragraph Specifications dialog box. Let's take an actual example:

1. Open a new document with five pages.

   Select the File menu's New command. The Document Setup dialog box appears, as shown in the following illustration.

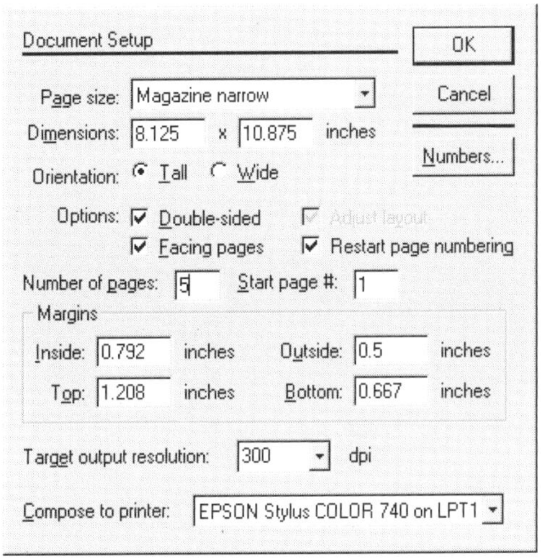

Choose Magazine narrow for the Page size and accept the dimensions.

Choose Tall as the orientation, and make the document double-sided with facing pages.

Put a check in the Restart page numbering box.

Enter 5 into the Number of Pages box and accept the rest of the options by clicking OK.

2. Type **Chapter 1—Preparations for the Journey** on page 1.

   With the Text tool selected, click in the upper left-hand corner of page 1 and type **Chapter 1— Preparations for the Journey.**

3. Highlight the text.

   With the Text tool selected, click in front of the word Chapter, and then drag across to the end of the word Journey.

4. Open the Paragraph Specifications dialog box.

   Select the Type menu's Paragraph command. The Paragraph Specifications dialog box appears, as shown in the following illustration.

5. Select Include in Table of Contents.

   In the bottom left-hand corner of the dialog box, you will see the Include in Table of Contents box. Click the box to select it.

6. Add the paragraph to the TOC.

   Click OK and the paragraph Chapter 1—Preparations for the Journey will be added to the TOC and the Paragraph Specifications dialog box will close. Please leave your document open.

   That's all there is to specifying particular paragraphs, such as chapter titles and section headings, to be included in your TOC. It's simple enough, but imagine having to do it dozens of times in a large publication. A simpler way, which also helps ensure consistency, is to use paragraph styles.

## Selecting Paragraphs and Page Numbers Using Styles

You may recall discussing styles in Chapter 9. A style is a format or a collection of formats that is used consistently throughout a document. In the case of paragraphs to be included in your TOC, it would be wise to assign all entries the same style as you enter them, specifying as part of the style that they be included in the TOC. This will save you the trouble of having to go through your publication and select each entry one by one. This is done through the use of the Style Options dialog box. Let's take an actual example:

1. Go to page 2 of your five-page document.

   Click the page 2 icon in the bottom left corner of your document screen and page 2 appears.

You are going to type the name of the second chapter in your publication, but before you do, let's assign it a style. As you know, you can choose from a variety of pre-set styles or create your own. Let's use the pre-set style Subhead 1.

2.  Open the Styles Palette.

    Select the Windows menu's Show Styles command. The Styles Palette appears, as shown in the following illustration.

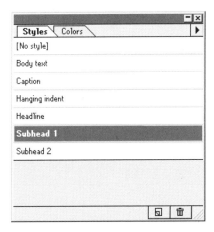

3.  Select the style Subhead 1.

    Click Subhead 1 in the Styles Palette to select it.

4.  Open the Style Options dialog box.

    Double-click Subhead 1, or click the small arrow in the upper right-hand corner of the Styles Palette to open the menu. Select Style Options and the Style Options dialog box opens, as shown inthe following illustration. Subhead 1 appears in the Name box.

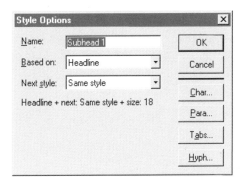

5. Open the Paragraph Specifications dialog box for Subhead 1.

   Click the button called Para in the right-hand side of the Style Options dialog box, and the Paragraph Specifications dialog box opens, as shown in the following illustration.

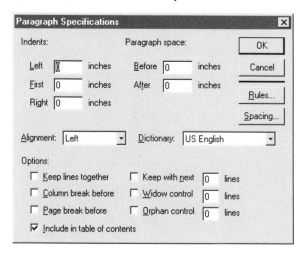

6. Include all paragraphs that have this style in the TOC.

   In the bottom left-hand corner of the dialog box, there is a box labeled Include in Table of Contents. Click the box to select it.

7. Close the Paragraph Specifications dialog box.

   Click OK to save your selection and close the Paragraph Specifications dialog box. You return to the Style Options dialog box.

8. Close the Style Options dialog box.

   Click OK to save your choice, exit the Style Options dialog box, and return to your document.

9. Open the Control Palette.

   If the Control Palette is not open on your screen, select the Windows menu's Show Control Palette command. The Control Palette opens on your screen, as shown in the following illustration.

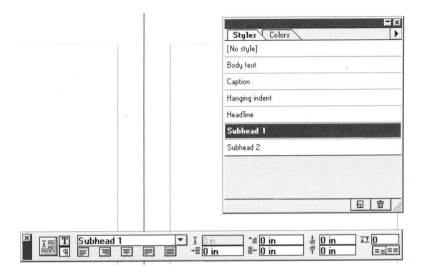

10. Display the current selected style in the Control Palette.

As you know, the Control Palette displays all the current information about the tools and text you are using. To check that the style Subhead 1 has been selected and will be used as the style for anything you type, click the small paragraph symbol located under the large T in the left-hand side of the Control Palette. The name of the currently selected style is displayed to the right of the T. If Subhead 1 is not displayed, you can select it from the Control Palette's drop-down menu. Notice that any change in style you make is reflected in the Styles Palette as well. Now we are ready to enter the second chapter title.

11. Type **Chapter 2—On the Road.**

With the Text tool selected, click in the upper left-hand corner of page 2 and type **Chapter 2—On the Road.** Notice that Subhead 1 has its own font size and formatting.

Because this paragraph was created with the style Subhead 1, which we have told PageMaker to include in the TOC, it is automatically placed in the TOC without having to manually select and add it. Remember to change your style to one that has not been selected to be included in the TOC if you plan to type large sections of text in your chapters. Otherwise, your entire chapter will appear in the TOC. Body text, listed in the Styles Palette, would be a good choice.

Remember that all styles in the Styles Palette can be edited by clicking the Style Options dialog box and then choosing from Char, Para, Tab, and/or Hyph to modify their settings. Refer to Chapter 9 for details.

Let's add chapter titles for the last three pages. When you click the Text Tool in a new page, the style will switch back to No Style. Simply click Subhead 1 in the Styles Palette or select Subhead 1 from the Control Palette to return to the style we are using.

1. Type **Chapter 3—Trouble Begins** on page 3 of your document.

   With the Text tool selected, click in the upper left-hand corner of page 3 and type **Chapter 3—Trouble Begins.** Because this paragraph was created with the style Subhead 1, which we have told PageMaker to include in the TOC, it is automatically placed in the TOC without having to manually select and add it.

2. Type **Chapter 4—Trouble Resolved** on page 4 of your document.

   With the Text tool selected, click in the upper left-hand corner of page 4 and type **Chapter 4—Trouble Resolved.** Because this paragraph was created with the style Subhead 1, which we have told PageMaker to include in the TOC, it is automatically placed in the TOC without having to manually select and add it.

3. Type **Chapter 5—Heading Home** on page 5 of your document.

   With the Text tool selected, click in the upper left-hand corner of page 5 and type **Chapter 5—Heading Home.** Because this paragraph was created with the style Subhead 1, which we have told PageMaker to include in the TOC, it is automatically placed in the TOC without having to manually select and add it.

Finally, let's return to our first entry on page 1 and change its style so that it's consistent with the rest of the publication:

1. Go to page 1 of your document.

   Click the page 1 icon in the bottom left corner of your document screen and page 1 will appear.

2. Highlight the text, Chapter 1—Preparations for the Journey.

   Using the Text tool, click in front of the word Chapter and drag across to the end of the word Journey.

3. Change the style of the highlighted text to Subhead 1.

   Open the Control Palette if it is not already open by selecting the Window menu's Show Control Palette command. Click the small paragraph icon located below the large T on the left-hand side of the Control Palette. The current style is shown in the drop-down menu beside the T. Use the drop-down menu to find and select Subhead 1. The style of the highlighted text changes. Click anywhere outside the highlighted area to complete the selection.

Now you are ready to create a TOC.

# Creating a TOC

The second step in creating and setting up a TOC in your document is to tell PageMaker to make the table using the information you have input. Here's how:

1. Open the Create Table of Contents dialog box.

   Select the Utilities menu's Create TOC command. The Create Table of Contents dialog box opens, as shown in the following illustration.

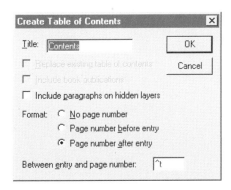

2. Name your TOC.

   Give your TOC a name that is readily identifiable as belonging to the publication. In this case, type **The Greatest Journey Never Told**.

3. Select Replace Existing Table of Contents, Include Book Publications, or Include Paragraphs on Hidden Layers if applicable.

   Since this is a new TOC for a small publication and is not part of a book (see Chapter 17 for information on creating books), both of the first choices should be grayed out. Replace Existing Table of Contents is handy when you find yourself making changes to a TOC you have already generated. Show Paragraphs on Hidden Layers is used if you have layers that are hidden, but contain information that is important to the reader. Do not select this option if you are using hidden layers to store information that is helpful for production (such as translations), but has nothing to do with the finished product.

4. Select a format for page numbering.

   PageMaker gives you three page-numbering options. They are No Page Number, Page Number Before Entry, and Page Number After Entry. The most common choice is to place a page number after the entry, so select that now.

5. Select the characters you want to appear between the text entry and the page number.

   Most TOC entries are followed by little dots (known as *dot leaders*) leading to the page number for the entry. They act as guides for the eye of the reader, leading him or her to the correct page number. You'll notice that the dots have spaces between them. These are called *tabs*. The size and formatting of the dots is determined by the characteristics applied to the space in front of them.

The way to change the appearance of a dot leader (or any other character you choose to use following your entries) is to edit the space in front of the dot. To change the size of the tab between dots or the leader, use the style of the TOC, as described in the following sections. For a complete list of characters you can use after your entries, see Adobe's online help function. Let's accept the default here, which is represented by ^t (caret + t), which tells PageMaker you want a tab between your dots.

6. Create your TOC.

   Click OK and PageMaker generates the TOC. You know when the TOC is ready to be placed in your document when you see your mouse pointer turn into a half-page of text with an angle bracket in the upper left-hand corner.

## Placing the TOC

Before you can place your TOC, you need to create room for it in your document. Since all five of your pages are taken up by chapters, we need to insert a new page:

1. Go to page 1 of the document.

   Click the page 1 icon in the bottom left corner of your document screen.

2. Open the Insert Pages dialog box.

   Select the Layout menu's Insert Pages command. The Insert Pages dialog box appears, as shown in the following illustration.

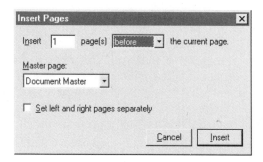

3. Insert one page.

   In the Insert Option box, enter the number 1. From the page(s) drop-down menu, select Before the Current Page. Don't change the Master Page setting and don't click the Set Left and Right Pages Separately box. Click Insert and one page will be created and placed in front of page 1.

4.  Place your TOC.

    Now that you have a page on which to place your TOC, click in the upper left-hand corner of the new page (now page 1). The TOC appears.

## Formatting and Editing a TOC

When a TOC is made, PageMaker uses the styles you specified to format and generate your entries. If you have not specified a style for an entry, PageMaker will use the formatting information that was originally applied when the text was created.

There are three ways to edit a PageMaker TOC. The first option is to edit the original styles of the entries (as discussed previously) and regenerate the TOC.

The second option is to edit the style of the TOC itself. You will notice that once you place your TOC, two new entries appear in your Styles Palette, as shown in Figure 16-1. These are the TOC styles, and they can be edited just like any other style. The one thing you absolutely should not do is rename the TOC styles since PageMaker looks for them

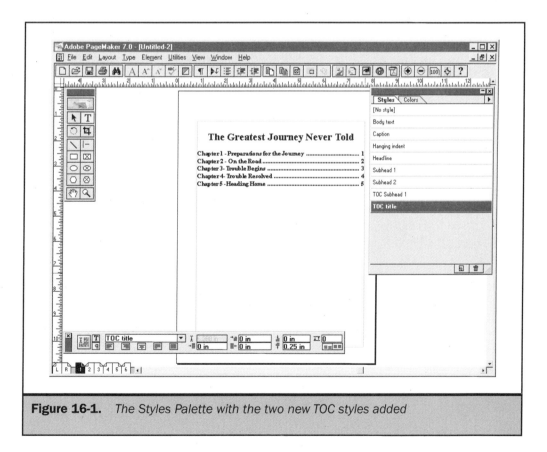

**Figure 16-1.**   *The Styles Palette with the two new TOC styles added*

MANAGING PAGEMAKER DOCUMENTS

when it generates a TOC again and will undo all your hard work if it doesn't find the name it is looking for.

The final method of editing is to edit the TOC directly, but if you need to generate a new one (a very common occurrence), all your changes will be lost.

To edit a TOC style, follow these steps:

1. Open the Styles Palette.

   Select the Window menu's Show Styles command to display the Styles Palette if it is not already open. The Styles Palette appears.

2. Select a style to edit.

   Click one of the TOC styles listed in the Styles Palette.

3. Open the Style Options dialog box.

   Either double-click the style or click the small arrow in the upper right-hand corner of the Styles Palette and the Styles menu appears. Select Style Options and the Style Options dialog box appears, as shown in the following illustration.

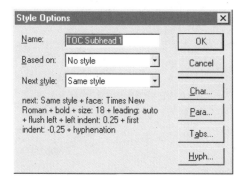

4. Edit the style.

   Using the Char, Para, Tabs, or Hyph Buttons on the right-hand side of the dialog box, open and make changes to the various parts of the style.

5. Save your changes.

   To save your changes, click OK and you will be returned to the Style Options dialog box. Click OK again to exit the box and return to your document screen.

## Creating Indexes

An index is an alphabetical list of important items that occur in a publication. These items have page numbers assigned to them so that readers can locate them in the publication. An index should also lead readers to all pertinent information on a given topic through a system known as cross-referencing.

Indexes are best written after your publication is complete. This way you avoid errors in your index due to last-minute edits.

In this section, we look at PageMaker's system for putting together indexes and creating our own sample index in the process.

# The Process of Creating an Index

Creating an index is basically a four-step process:

1. Generate your topics and entries. Topics are the subjects or headings under which entries are listed. For example, one of the topics in a publication entitled *Pets of the World* might be dogs. Under the topic of dogs, all entries pertaining to dogs in the publication would be listed. These could include things like housebreaking, basic training, and canine health, but it could also include any other entries that have to do with dogs. For example, if you talk about problems associated with training German shepherds, then it would be wise to list German shepherds as an entry with a cross-reference to training. Each entry has either a page number or a cross-reference associated with it.

2. Edit your topics and entries. In this step, you check to be sure that you have all your topics and entries, that cross-references are in place, and that all errors in spelling, redundancy, and consistency have been taken care of.

3. Generate the index.

4. Place the index in your publication.

We will be covering all four steps in the following sections.

# Generating a Topic List

There are two ways you can go about creating your topics. You can create your topics first so that you have a working list (called a topic list) as you create entries, or you can create your topics and entries at the same time. Professional indexers, who already have a good idea what their main headings or topics will be, often start with a topic list. In this section, we will discuss creating and entering a topic list.

Let's suppose that you have written a cookbook. The first step in creating the topic list is to get out a piece of paper and pencil and write down all the main topics covered in the book. Beneath each main topic, you can write the entries if you know them. However, you shouldn't worry about getting them all down, as you will be going through your publication and entering those as they occur anyway. Using the example of the cookbook, here is a sample topic list:

I. Starters

  A. Drinks

  B. Finger foods

  II. Soups

    A. Hot soups

        1. Split pea with ham

        2. French onion

    B. Cold soups

        1. Gazpacho

        2. Creamy cucumber

 III. Salads

    A. Green salads

    B. Pasta salads

 IV. Entrees

    A. Beef and pork

        1. Salisbury steak

        2. Fried pork chops

    B. Poultry

        1. Chicken à la king

        2. Teriyaki chicken

    C. Fish

        1. Baked sole

        2. Grilled halibut steaks

    D. Vegetarian

        1. Mushroom meatloaf

        2. Spaghetti and tofu franks

  V. Side dishes

 VI. Desserts

As you can see, some of the topics have secondary and even tertiary-level entries. This is common, and PageMaker enables up to three levels in its indexes. Let's begin, however, by creating a six-page document, and then generating the basic topic list. This is done by using the Add Index Entry dialog box:

1.  Go to the Add Index Entry dialog box.

    Select the Utilities menu's Index Entry command. The Add Index Entry dialog box appears, as shown in the following illustration.

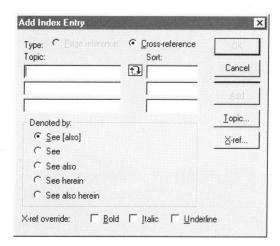

2.  Open the Select Topic dialog box.

    In order to add a topic, you must click the Topic Button on the right-hand side of the Add Index Entry dialog box. The Select Topic dialog box opens, as shown in the following illustration. Notice that you have three levels available to you. Level 1 is for your main topics, Level 2 is for your secondary topics, and Level 3 is for your tertiary-level topics.

3. Add the main topic Starters to the topic list.

   Type the word **Starters** (capitalized) in the Level 1 box. Then click ADD on the right-hand side of the box. The topic Starters appears in the topic list at the bottom of the dialog box, as shown in the following illustration. Notice its position. It is located all the way to the left, which means it is a main topic.

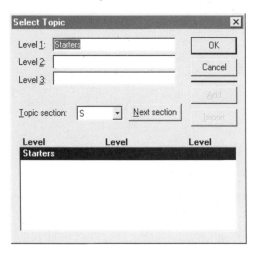

4. Add the main topic Soups.

   Let's add another main topic, Soups. You'll notice that when you clicked ADD, Starters was highlighted in the Level 1 dialog box. Delete it now by using DELETE, and type the word **Soups** (capitalized). Hit ADD again and Soups will be added to the list of main topics at the bottom of the dialog box, as shown in the following illustration.

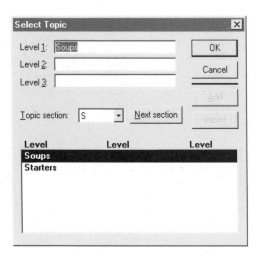

Notice also that the letter in the topic section is S, indicating that the entry we just made will be listed alphabetically under S. Had we just added Entrees, the letter there would be E. If you click the drop-down arrow, you will see the complete alphabet. This enables you to go to any main topic based on the first letter in its spelling. You can also use the Next Section Button to move forward in the list.

Now let's add a couple of secondary topics.

5.  Add the secondary topic, Hot soups.

    The main topic, Soups, is listed in the Level 1 box. In the Level 2 box, type **Hot soups** and then click ADD. The listing Soups, followed by Hot soups, should appear in the list at the bottom of the dialog box, as shown in the following illustration.

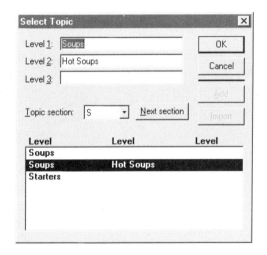

6.  Add the secondary topic, Cold soups, to the list of topics.

    Before adding another secondary topic, you must erase the first. Highlight Hot soups and then hit DELETE. In its place in the Level 2 box, type **Cold soups** and then click ADD. The listing Soups, followed by Cold soups, should appear in the list at the bottom of the dialog box.

    Since we know some of the tertiary topics, we can go ahead and enter them.

7.  Add the tertiary topic Gazpacho to the list of topics under Soups, Cold soups.

    The main topic, Soups, and the secondary topic, Cold soups, should still be listed in the Level 1 and Level 2 boxes. Type **Gazpacho** in the Level 3 box. Then click ADD. The listing Soups, followed by Cold soups and by Gazpacho, should appear as shown in the following illustration.

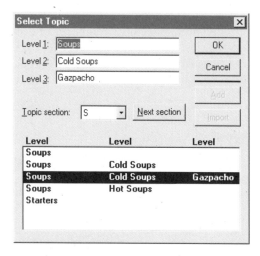

Before adding another tertiary topic, you must erase the first. Also, if you are planning to enter a hot soup rather than a cold, you must switch secondary topics. The easiest way to do this is to simply click the Soups, Hot soups entry in the list at the bottom of the dialog box. As soon as you do, Soups and Hot soups appear in the Level 1 and Level 2 boxes. Now you can enter the tertiary topic, Split pea with ham.

8.  Add the tertiary topic, Split pea with ham, to the list of topics under Soups, Hot soups.

    Type **Split pea with ham** in the Level 3 box. Then click ADD. The listing Soups, followed by Hot soups and by Split pea with ham, should appear as shown in the following illustration.

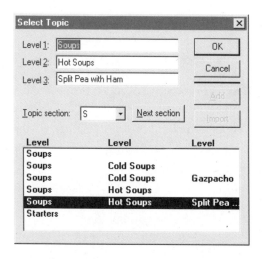

# Creating Entries

Entries tell readers where to find specific information about topics in your publication. An entry is composed of a topic (the heading under which it appears) and a reference, which tells the reader where to find specific information on the general topic. If you have already entered some topics, as we did previously, it will make your job of creating entries a little simpler, but it isn't necessary to have a topic list. You can create your topics as you make your entries.

Entries are made by marking the text where the reference occurs and by telling PageMaker which topic the reference belongs under. You will also need to tell PageMaker the range of pages to include in your reference, but we'll talk about that in the next section. For now, we will create an entry using your topic list. Then we will create entries for which no topic exists.

## Creating Entries Using the Topic List

A topic such as Soups, which can occur many times in a cookbook, will need to have many different pages listed in the index. Your job is to go through your text (yes, it's a lot of work) and place markers in the text to tell PageMaker to include an entry in the index. Obviously, in order to learn how to place markers in your text, we will have to have some text.

1. Open a new document that is three pages long.

   Select the File menu's New command. The Document Set Up dialog box opens. Choose Magazine narrow and Tall orientation. Enter 3 in the number of pages, select doubled-sided, facing pages, and restart numbering. Accept the rest of the defaults and click OK.

2. Generate your text.

   Click page 1 in the list of pages in the bottom left portion of your screen. Select the Text tool and place the cursor in the upper left portion of the screen in page 1. Type the following text:

   **Cold soups are popular in summer months. One of the easiest and most satisfying cold soups is Gazpacho.**

   This short paragraph contains information about the general topic cold soups and about a specific kind of cold soup, Gazpacho. Both levels of information need to be included in the index. Let's add them.

3. Mark the text that you want the index to refer to.

   You can either place your cursor directly before the word that starts your reference, or highlight the word (or words) that make up the reference. When you already have your topics created, it's easier to simply place your cursor and click.

   With the Text tool selected, click in front of the word Cold at the start of the paragraph.

4. Call up the Add Index Entry dialog box.

   Select the Utilities menu's Index Entry command. The Add Index Entry dialog box appears.

   Notice that at the top next to Type you have the option of choosing Page reference or Cross-reference. Select Page reference for now. This tells PageMaker that you want a page number to be placed with the entry. We'll cover cross-referencing later in this chapter.

   Now look at the Topic options. You have levels (just as you did in the Select Topic dialog box). You could type in the levels (in this case, you would type the main topic **Soups**) under which Hot soups falls on the first line and Cold soups on the second line. However, since we have already made this entry in the topic list, it is faster and easier to use the topic list. Using the topic list also ensures the uniformity of spelling and capitalization.

5. Select the main topic under which Cold soups is entered in the index.

   Click the Topic Button on the right-hand side of the Add Index Entry dialog box and the Select Topic dialog box appears, as shown in the following illustration.

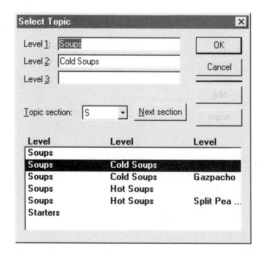

6. Select your topic.

   Look at the list at the bottom of the dialog box. Find the entry Soups, Cold soups and click it. The level boxes will be filled in. Click OK to return to the Add Index Entry dialog box.

7. Check your entry.

   Notice that the top two boxes under Topic have been filled in. This is telling PageMaker that you want an index entry under the topic Soups, Cold soups with the number of the page where you made your mark listed as well.

8. Select the page range.

   Beneath the topic boxes, you will see Page Range options. These options are used to show where the information about the subject begins and ends.

   If the entry is only for a single word or sentence, choosing Select Current Page is fine. This tells PageMaker that you want only the number of the page where you made the index entry mark to appear in the index.

   For entries that cover several paragraphs, you would choose To Next Style. This is where your use of paragraph styles is so important because PageMaker will include the page numbers of all paragraphs that have the same style as the entry you began with until the style changes.

   To include the page numbers of information that is formatted with a variety of styles, choose To Next Use of Style. Here you tell PageMaker when to stop by selecting the style that is the end point. When PageMaker comes to that style, it stops adding pages. Notice that you have a drop-down menu from which to select the ending style.

   If you know exactly how many paragraphs the information covers, you can tell PageMaker to include pages for a specific number of paragraphs by selecting the For the Next ___ option.

   If you don't want a page number listed next to an entry at all, select the final option, Suppress Page Range.

9. Select the Page # override if desired.

   Page # override enables you to change the look of the number that occurs in the index listing. In this case, you could have PageMaker show the number 1 next to the listing for Cold soups as bold, italic, or underline. If you do not want a special look for your numbers, then leave these choices blank and PageMaker will use the paragraph style selected for the entry.

   In our example, I have simply selected the current page because our entry is so short. The completed index entry is shown in the following illustration.

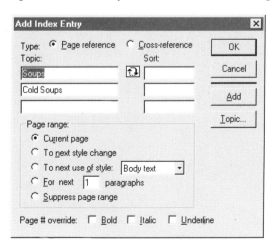

10. Add your entry to the index.

Click either ADD to add your entry and leave the Add Index Entry dialog box open to make more entries, or click OK to add your entry and close the dialog box. Let's click OK.

11. Check to be sure that your index entry page marker has been added to your text.

To check to see that the marker has been placed, go back to page 1 of your document. Select the Edit menu's Story command. PageMaker opens your document in Story Editor mode. Index entry markers are only visible in Story Editor mode. You should see an index marker in front of the word Cold, as shown in Figure 16-2. To get back to regular Layout mode, select the Edit menu's Layout command.

12. Check on the status of your index.

Even though you have not actually told PageMaker to generate an index, PageMaker has already begun to create one based on the information you have been entering. To see what it has done with your new entry, select the Utilities menu's Show Index command. The Show Index dialog box appears, as shown in the following illustration. As you can see, Soups, Cold soups is listed and there is only one entry so far.

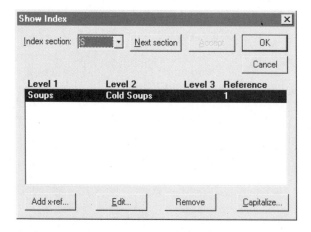

Now let's make a second index entry for Gazpacho.

13. Mark the text that you want the index to refer to (see Cold soups previously for detailed instructions).

14. Call up the Add Index Entry dialog box.

Select the Utilities menu's Index Entry command. The Add Index Entry dialog box appears.

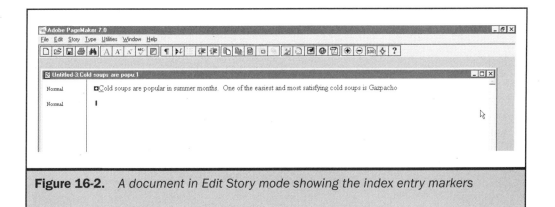

**Figure 16-2.**   *A document in Edit Story mode showing the index entry markers*

Notice that at the top next to Type you have the option of choosing Page reference or Cross-reference. Select Page reference for now. Then look at the Topic options where the levels are located (just as in the Select Topic dialog box). You could type in the levels; in this case, type the main topic, **Soups**, then the secondary topic, **Cold Soups**, and finally **Gazpacho**. However, since we have already made this entry in the topic list, it is faster and easier to use the topic list. Using the topic list also ensures the uniformity of spelling and capitalization.

15. Select the main and secondary topics under which Gazpacho belongs in the index.

    Click the Topic Button on the right-hand side of the Add Index Entry dialog box, and the Select Topic dialog box appears, as shown in Figure 16-12.

16. Select your topic.

    Look at the list at the bottom of the dialog box. Find the entry Soups, Cold soups, Gazpacho and click it. The level boxes are filled in. Click OK to return to the Add Index Entry dialog box.

17. Check your entry.

    Notice that the top three boxes under Topic are filled in. This is telling PageMaker that you want an index entry under the topic Soups, Cold Soups, Gazpacho with the number of the page where you made your mark listed as well.

18. Select the page range.

    Beneath the topic boxes, you will see Page Range options. Select the current page.

MANAGING PAGEMAKER
DOCUMENTS

19. Select the Page # override if desired.

Page # override enables you to change the look of the number that occurs in the index listing. The options are Bold, Italic, or Underline. If you do not want a special look for your numbers, leave the selection boxes unchecked. My completed entry is shown in the following illustration.

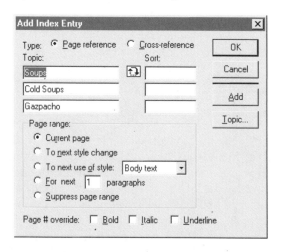

20. Add your entry to the index.

Click either ADD to add your entry and leave the Add Index Entry dialog box open to make more entries, or click OK to add your entry and close the dialog box. Click OK.

21. Check to be sure that your index entry page marker has been added to your text.

To check to see that the marker has been placed, go back to page 1 of your document. Select the Edit menu's Story command. PageMaker opens your document in Story Editor mode. Index entry markers are only visible in Story Editor mode. There is an index marker in front of the word Gazpacho as well as Cold, as shown in Figure 16-3. To get back to regular Layout mode, select the Edit menu's Layout command.

22. Check on the status of your index.

Even though you have not actually told PageMaker to generate an index, PageMaker has already begun to create one based on the information you have been entering. To see what it has done with your new entry, select the Utilities menu's Show Index command. The Show Index dialog box appears. As you can see in the following illustration, Soups, Cold soups, Gazpacho is listed and there are only two entries so far.

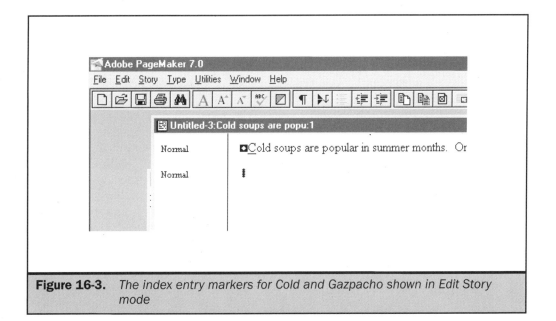

**Figure 16-3.** *The index entry markers for Cold and Gazpacho shown in Edit Story mode*

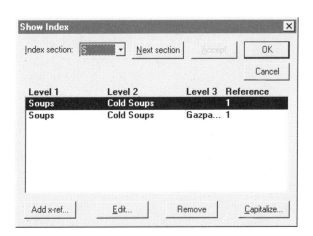

## Creating Entries with No Topic List

As you know, entries are made by marking the text where the reference occurs, and then telling PageMaker the topic under which the entry belongs. A topic such as Entrées, which may occur many times in a cookbook, could have many different listings. Needless to say, we must have some text to place markers in. Please go to page 2 of the document we just created in the previous exercise and type the following:
**Since entrées are the focus of the meal, careful thought should be given to the choice of ingredients, the method of preparation, and nutritional components. In traditional**

western meals, the entrée is some form of animal protein such as beef, pork, poultry, or fish. In vegetarian households, the entrée may focus on vegetables, grains, or tofu with protein-supplying ingredients sprinkled throughout the meal. In this chapter on entrées, we offer traditional dishes such as salisbury steak, chicken à la king, and baked sole along with popular vegetarian dishes like spaghetti and tofu franks, and mushroom meatloaf.

In the previous paragraph, there is quite a bit of information that needs to be included in the index. The first and most obvious is the main topic, Entrées.

To create an index entry, you either click directly in front of the word or sentence you want to include, or highlight the word or sentence. Note that if you highlight the whole sentence, you will have to edit it down unless you want the entire sentence in your index. If you choose not to highlight at all, but simply place your cursor, you will have to type in the information you want to include. In this case, let's add the word Entrées to the index. Go to page 2 of your document where you typed the paragraph about Entrées:

1. Highlight the word Entrées in the first line of the paragraph.

   Using the Text tool, click and drag across the word Entrées to select it.

2. Open the Add Index Entry dialog box.

   Select the Utilities menu's Index Entry command. The Add Index Entry dialog box appears.

3. Tell PageMaker this is a Page reference rather than a Cross-reference (we will cover cross-referencing later in this chapter).

4. Click the Page Reference radio button at the top of the page.

   Notice that because you highlighted Entrées in your text, the word Entrées appears in the top box under Topic in the dialog box, as shown in the following illustration. A word that appears in the top box is considered a main (Level 1) topic.

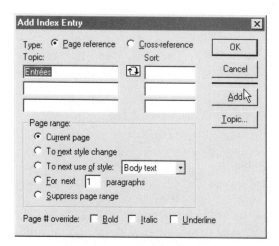

5. Add Entrées as a main topic and as an index entry.

    Click ADD on the right-hand side of the dialog box. Entrées will be added as a topic and an index entry will be made in your text.

6. Check to be sure that PageMaker has added Entrées to your list of main (Level 1) topics, and click the Topic Button on the right-hand side of the dialog box. The Select Topic dialog box will appear with Entrées listed in the Level 1 box and you will see Entrées in the list at the bottom of the dialog box, as shown in the following illustration.

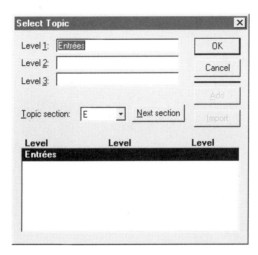

7. Check to see that PageMaker has added an entry marker in your text.

    When you mark a place in your text to be included in the index, you are telling PageMaker that you want both the word and the page where it occurs to be mentioned in the index. To check to see that the marker has been placed, exit the Add Index Entry box by clicking OK. This should take you back to your document. Select the Edit menu's Story command. PageMaker opens your document in Story Editor mode. Entry markers are only visible in Story Editor mode. You should see an index marker in front of the word Entrées, as shown in Figure 16-4. To get back to regular Layout mode, select the Edit menu's Layout command.

8. Check on the status of your index.

    Even though you have not selected Create Index, PageMaker has already begun to create your index. To see what it has done with your new entry, select the Utilities menu's Show Index commnd. The Show Index dialog box appears as shown. As you can see, Entrées is listed under Level 1 and there is only one entry under the letter E so far.

    Now let's add an entry that is not a main (Level 1) topic. Go back to page 2 where you typed the paragraph about Entrées.

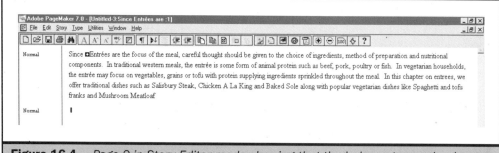

**Figure 16-4.** *Page 2 in Story Editor mode showing that the index entry marker has been placed*

9. Highlight the word Beef.

   Using the Text tool, click and drag across the word Beef to select it.

10. Open the Add Index Entry dialog box.

    Select the Utilities menu's Index Entry command. The Add Index Entry dialog box appears.

11. Tell PageMaker this is a Page reference rather than a Cross-reference (we will cover cross-referencing later in this chapter).

    Click the Page Reference radio button at the top of the page.

12. Enter Beef as a secondary topic beneath Entrées.

    As you can see, the word Beef has been copied into the first line of the topic list, but it is not a main topic. It is a secondary topic that belongs under Entrées. To move it to the secondary position (the second line down), use the Promote/Demote Button shown in the following illustration. This leaves the top line blank and grays out the ADD Button. In order to add secondary and tertiary levels, you must specify the levels above the entry. In this case, type **Entrées** on the first line. The ADD Button becomes active and you can add Beef.

Now let's create an entry that is a tertiary topic. Go back to the paragraph you typed about Entrées.

13. Highlight the words, Salisbury steak.

Using the Text tool, click and drag across the words Salisbury steak to select them.

14. Open the Add Index Entry dialog box.

Select the Utilities menu's Index Entry command. The Add Index Entry dialog box appears.

15. Tell PageMaker this is a Page reference rather than a Cross-reference (we will cover cross-referencing later in this chapter).

Click the Page Reference radio button at the top of the page.

16. Enter Salisbury steak as a tertiary topic beneath Beef and Entrées.

As you can see, the words Salisbury steak have been copied into the first line of the topic list. But it is not a main topic. It is a tertiary topic that belongs under Beef. To move Salisbury steak to the tertiary position (the third line down), use the Promote/Demote Button. This leaves the top line blank and grays out ADD. In order to add tertiary levels, you must specify the levels above the entry. In this case, type **Entrées** on the first line and **Beef** on the second line. The ADD Button becomes active and you can add Salisbury steak.

## Creating Cross-Referenced Entries

Cross-referencing enables readers to find information that is related to the topic they looked up. For example, a reference to Veterinary Care for Dogs might include a cross-reference to Nutrition. Cross-references do not add page numbers to your index and do not place an index marker in your text, so you don't have to be concerned about where your cursor is or what tool is selected. Let's create a cross-reference using our cookbook:

1. Decide on what topic your reader will look up.

The topic that your reader first look under in the index is important. It is from that topic that you will create a cross-reference that says, see also . . . In our example, let's use Entrées as the starting topic. Since many people think of soups as entrées as well, it is a good idea to create a cross-reference from Entrées to Soups so that people who like to make soups can find them.

2. Open the Add Index Entry dialog box.

Select the Utilities menu's Index Entry command. The Add Index Entry dialog box appears.

3. Select the Cross-reference option.

   To the right of the Page reference option in the Type section is the Cross-reference option. Click its button to select it.

4. Add a topic.

   In the top line of the topic section, add the topic that your reader will look under first in the index. In this case, the topic is Entrées. If you don't want to type it, you can go to the Select Topic dialog box by clicking the Topic Button and choosing your topic there. If you use the Select Topic dialog box to choose your topic, click OK when you are finished to return to the Add Index Entry dialog box.

5. Tell PageMaker you want to cross-reference.

   Click the X-ref Button on the right-hand side of the Add Index Entry dialog box. The Select Cross-Reference Topic dialog box appears, as shown in the following illustration.

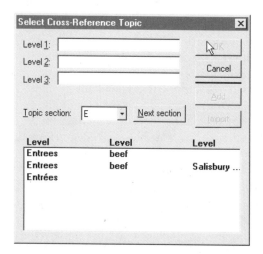

6. Enter the topic you want your reader referred to.

   As you can see, this dialog box looks very much like the Select Topic dialog box. Use the Topic Section drop-down menu to find the topic in alphabetical order, and then look in the topic list at the bottom of the dialog box to locate the exact topic. In this case, choose Soups, as shown in the following illustration.

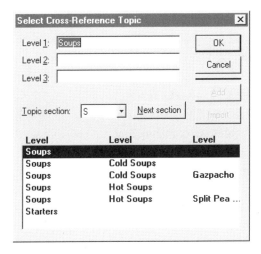

7. Tell PageMaker you have found the correct cross-reference topic.

Click OK and the cross-reference topic will be linked to the original topic. The Select Cross-Reference Topic dialog box closes and you return to the Add Index Entry dialog box.

8. Tell PageMaker how you would like the reference denoted.

Beneath the topic list in the Add Index Entry dialog box, you will see the Denoted By area, as shown in the following illustration. To denote means to tell your reader where else to look. In PageMaker, this is what the Denoted By terms mean:

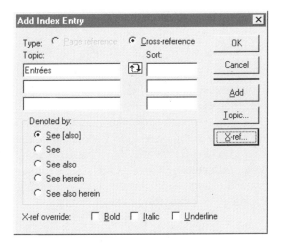

- **See** tells your reader to see another topic.
- **See Also** tells the reader to look under the current topic as well as under the other topics mentioned in the cross-reference.
- **See Herein** tells the reader to look in the subentries of the current topic.
- **See Also Herein** tells the reader to look both in the main entry and in the subentries.

9. Click ADD if you want to continue making more cross-references or click OK to exit the Add Index Entry dialog box and add your cross-reference.

10. Check to be sure that the cross-reference has been made.

    Select the Utilities menu's Show Index command. The Show Index dialog box appears. Look at the list of entries at the bottom of the box. Note that Entrées with a reference to Soups, as shown in the following illustration.

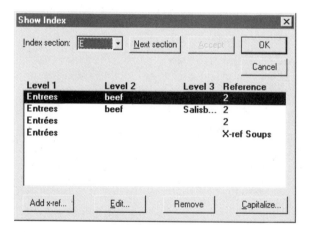

## Sorting Topics

As you know, not all words are always spelled out. Sometimes they are abbreviated, as is the case with St., a common abbreviation for saint, and other times they are acronyms created from the first letters of several words. An example of an acronym would be DINK, which stands for double income, no kids. Since index entries are based on their spelling, St. would be listed under S first and then T, rather than S first and then AINT unless you tell PageMaker otherwise. In order to tell PageMaker you want a word listed under its full spelling, use the Sort boxes directly to the right of the Topic boxes in the Add Index Entry dialog box. Let's take the example of St.:

1. Open the Add Index Entry dialog box.

   Select the Utilities menu's Index Entry command. The Add Index Entry dialog box opens. Notice the Sort boxes to the right of the Topic boxes, as shown in the following illustration.

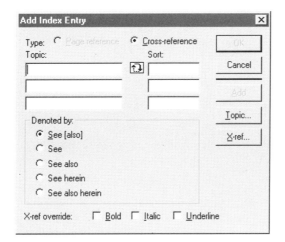

2.  Add an entry to the top Topic box.

    Type **St.** in the top Topic box. This tells PageMaker that you want to add a Level 1 topic called St.

3.  Tell PageMaker you want the entry to be sorted by its full spelling.

    In the Sort box directly to the right of St., type **Saint**. This tells PageMaker that you want St. to appear alphabetically as if it were being spelled out.

4.  Accept your sort.

    Click ADD if you would like to make more entries, or click OK to accept the sort and close the Add Index Entry dialog box.

## Speeding Things Up

There is no getting around the fact that creating an index is a lot of work. However, there are some shortcuts that can help speed things up a bit.

To automatically create an index for text you have selected

1.  Select text in your document.

    Using the Text tool, click in front of the text you want to select and drag your cursor to the end of the last word. The text will be highlighted.

2.  Create an index entry.

    Press CTRL+SHIFT+Y. PageMaker creates an index entry using the selected text as the topic and the page that you took the entry from as the page reference.

To automatically index a word or phrase every time it appears in your text

1.  Open your document in Story Editor.

Go to the page in your document that contains the word or phrase that you want to index. Select the Edit menu's Edit Story commnd. Your document opens in Story Editor mode.

2.  Create an insertion point.

    Using the Text tool, click somewhere in the text block where the word or phrase you want to index occurs.

3.  Open the Change dialog box.

    Select the Utilities menu's Change command. The Change dialog box appears, as shown in Figure 16-5.

4.  Define the word or phrase you want indexed.

    In the Find What box, type the word or phrase that you want to create an index entry for every time it occurs in your text.

5.  Tell PageMaker to index the word or phrase.

    In the Change To box, type ^; (caret + semicolon) to tell PageMaker to index the word or phrase without changing the text of the story.

6.  Select one of four options:

    ■  Click Find if you want PageMaker to show you the word or phrase each time it is found before it actually creates an index entry for it.

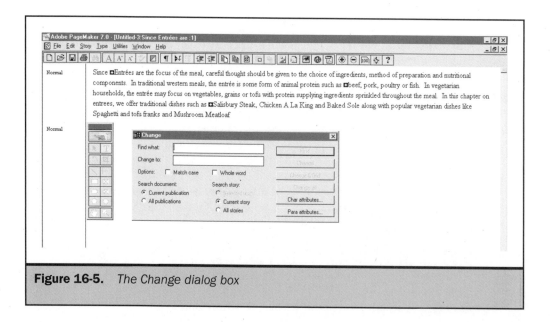

**Figure 16-5.**    *The Change dialog box*

- Click Change All to create index entries for the word or phrase each time it occurs in your story.

- Click Change & Find if you want PageMaker to create an index entry for the word or phrase you have just highlighted and then go on to find the next instance when it occurs. The next instance is displayed, but you will have to click Find & Change again before PageMaker will create an entry.

To index names putting the last name first

1. Select a name.

   Obviously, when you are creating a general text, it would look strange if you referred to a person by his or her last name first. However, in an index, names are typically listed by last name. Therefore, you must tell PageMaker to reverse the order of names in the index. To do this, you begin by selecting a name in the story you are indexing.

2. Tell PageMaker to create an entry for the name and reverse the names.

   Press CTRL+ALT+Y. PageMaker creates an index entry with the names reversed.

3. Check that PageMaker has created the entry with the names reversed.

   Select the Utilities menu's Show Index command. A new entry with the names reversed.

To index names that have more than two words or names with titles, create nonbreaking spaces between titles, first names, and middle names or initials. To create a nonbreaking space, press CTRL+ALT+H. This causes PageMaker to see the name as only two words. For example, to index Mary Beth Simmons, place a nonbreaking space between Mary and Beth, and PageMaker will index the name as Simmons, Mary Beth.

# Editing and Deleting Entries

Naturally, you will want to look over your index to be sure that all entries are in place and there are no misspellings, duplications, or forgotten cross-references. The easiest way to review and edit your entries is to use the Show Index dialog box. Note that you cannot add an entry from this box, and it is the only box from which you can remove entries.

1. Open the Show Index dialog box.

   Select the Utilities menu's Show Index commnd. The Show Index dialog box appears.

2. Select the entry you would like to preview or edit.

   Use the index section to choose the alphabetical category your entry is under. When the listing opens, locate the entry you would like to edit and click it to select it.

3.  Select Add x-ref, Edit, Remove, or Capitalize.

    The four buttons shown on the bottom of the dialog box indicate the options available to you. Clicking the Add x-ref or Edit Buttons opens the Add Index Entry dialog box, and enables you to edit as discussed in previous sections.

    Clicking the Remove Button removes the entry, but not the index topic. This is PageMaker's way of protecting other entries that are under the same topic. The only way to remove a topic is to select Remove Unreferenced Topics when you generate the index. We will discuss that shortly when we generate the index.

    Clicking the Capitalize Button opens the Capitalize dialog box, as shown in the following illustration, and gives you three options:

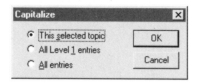

-   You can capitalize the single entry you have chosen.
-   You can capitalize all Level 1 entries.
-   You can capitalize all entries.

    Once you have made your selection, click OK to return to the Show Index dialog box.

4.  Accept your changes.

    The Accept Button at the top of the Show Index dialog box works like Apply in most other programs. You must hit Accept to apply the changes you have made.

To edit individual index entries from your publication, do the following:

1.  Open the document that contains the index entry you want to edit and, using the Text tool, place the cursor anywhere in the document.

2.  View the document in Story Editor mode.

    Select the Edit menu's Edit Story command. Your document opens in Story Editor mode with all index entries marked.

3.  Select the index entry you want to edit.

    Using the Text tool, highlight the index entry marker, not the words. Be careful to select just the marker or PageMaker will create a new entry.

4.  Open the Edit Index Entry dialog box.

With the index marker highlighted, select the Utilities menu's Index Entry command. The Edit Index Entry dialog box opens, as shown in the following illustration. The text associated with the index marker is displayed at the level that is currently selected for it. Make any changes just as you would if you were creating a regular entry.

5.  Accept your changes.

Click OK when you are finished making changes. Your changes will be applied and you will be returned to your document. When you are finished editing individual index entries, exit Story Editor by selecting the Edit menu's Layout command.

Here are some additional ways to remove items from the index:

- ■ Any change you make since opening the dialog box or clicking the Accept Button (whichever is more recent) will be lost if you just press Cancel.

- ■ If you have the Show Index dialog box open and you add entries, but don't click the Accept Button, you can remove all new entries by holding down the ALT key then clicking the Add X-ref Button.

- ■ If you have removed some entries with the Remove Button or the previous technique, hold down ALT and click the Remove Button. All entries deleted since the last time you clicked the Accept Button or opened the Show Index dialog box will reappear in the list.

- ■ If you want to remove all page references (so that you're left with a list of blind topics), hold down the CTRL+ALT keys and click Remove.

- If you want to get rid of all cross-references, hold down CTRL+SHIFT and click Remove.

- If you want to eliminate all of the index entries, hold down CTRL+ALT+SHIFT and click Remove.

## Formatting an Index

Formatting refers to two things: the style, meaning the way the text actually looks, and the way it is arranged on the page. PageMaker creates a style for your index based on the styles you have chosen in the creation of your story. Once PageMaker generates your index, you can edit that style (it will appear in your Styles Palette if you click the index with the Text tool selected), but it's not recommended. Try to make all your style choices as you are planning your document.

The other formatting that we are concerned with here has to do with the actual layout of the index: how it looks on the page. PageMaker has a whole dialog box full of options to deal with formatting alone. Let's take a look:

1. Open the Create Index dialog box.

   When you have finished making entries for your index, select the Utilities menu's Create Index commnd. The Create Index dialog box appears, as shown in the following illustration.

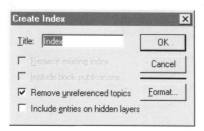

2. Open the Index Format dialog box.

   Click the Format Button on the right-hand side of the Create Index dialog box. The Index Format dialog box opens, as shown in the following illustration.

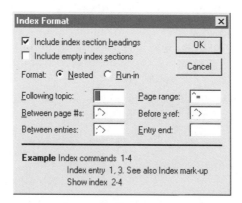

3.  Choose whether or not to use index section headings.

    Section headings are the letters of the alphabet under which PageMaker lists index entries in alphabetical order. There is also a heading entitled Symbols where PageMaker lists entries that do not begin with a letter of the alphabet.

    If you would like PageMaker to include these headings, leave the box checked. If you decide not to use headings, PageMaker still puts a space between the alphabetic sections.

4.  Choose whether or not to include empty index sections.

    If you have elected to use the section headings, then you can tell PageMaker whether or not to include the headings that have no entries. For example, if you have no entries that begin with the letter Q, PageMaker will still insert the heading Q between P and R with the words, no entries, beside it. PageMaker also includes the heading symbol, even if you have no symbols in your index.

5.  Choose whether to use a nested or run-in format.

    The nested format indents entries based on their levels. Therefore, a Level 1 entry would be flush left against the left margin, a Level 2 entry would be indented below the Level-1 entry, and a Level 3 entry would be indented below the Level 2 entry. The run-in format puts all levels of entries in one paragraph.

    If this is difficult to imagine, simply click the radio button for either option and look at the example that appears in the Example section at the bottom of the dialog box.

6.  Specify special characters, spaces, or punctuation marks you want to appear in your index.

    The remaining six boxes enable you to tell PageMaker what kinds of symbols, spaces, or punctuation marks you would like to use to separate parts of your index entries. Type the character, symbol, or punctuation marks you would like in the boxes beside the section names:

    ■  **Following Topic**   Tell PageMaker which characters you want to use between the entry and the first page number. Unless you specify something special, the default is two spaces.

    ■  **Between Page #s**   Tell PageMaker what characters you would like to put between entries that have more than one page reference. The default is set to use a comma and a nonbreaking space.

    ■  **Between Entries**   Tell PageMaker which characters you want to use to separate entries in a run-in format or in cross-references. The default here is a semicolon and a nonbreaking space.

    ■  **Page Range**   Tell PageMaker which character you would like to use between the first and last numbers in a range of pages. The default is a nonbreaking en dash.

MANAGING PAGEMAKER DOCUMENTS

- **Before X-Ref**   Tell PageMaker which characters you would like to use in front of a cross-reference. The default is a period and a nonbreaking space.

- **Entry End**   Tell PageMaker if you want a symbol or character to appear at the ends of referenced entries. The default is no character.

7. Accept your formatting.

   Click OK to accept the formatting choices you have made and the Index Format dialog box closes. You are returned to the Create Index dialog box. Click OK to actually create the index.

# Summary

This chapter focuses on creating the roadmaps your readers need in order to find their way around your publication. I discussed how to generate and create entries for a TOC. Then I discussed the creation of an index, which requires entries and page references. An index can also cross-reference topics that you think your reader might find helpful.

# The Complete Reference

PageMaker 7

# Chapter 17

## Creating a Book in PageMaker

437

PageMaker defines a "book" as a collection of publications. A publication (also referred to as a document) can be a single page or a long document that is several hundred pages long. Publications are each saved as a unique file. When you are ready to bring all the files together to create a single entity, that's when you will use PageMaker's Book feature.

The advantages of creating a large project, such as an anthology, as a series of separate publications that remain separate until they are combined using PageMaker's Book feature are many:

- Backing up files is easier and faster.

- Security is easier to maintain.

- Multiple authors can be accommodated.

- A variety of production schedules can be accommodated. Some parts of the book will naturally proceed faster than others. When you work with multiple publications, different rates of production are not a problem.

Thanks to PageMaker's excellent table-of-contents and index-generating capabilities, creating tables and indexes for your combined files is streamlined and simplified. In this chapter, we discuss how to prepare a publication for inclusion in a book, how to tell PageMaker you want to create a book using a book list, how to maintain and update a book list, and how to create a table of contents and an index for a book.

# Preparing to Create Publications for Incorporation in a Book

One of the keys to successfully bringing several publications together as a book is to make crucial decisions regarding the design, layout, styles, colors, and numbering before you even start creating the publications. In this section, we will discuss each element and create a series of four simple publications that use those elements. These publications will then be used to create an actual book later in the chapter.

## Creating a Master Template

One of your first considerations is to ensure that all the publications share the same overall look and layout. The first step in this process is to create a master template that will meet the needs of every part of the book. You can choose a template from the Template Palette, as discussed in Chapter 3, or you can open a document, set up the preferences and styles the way you would like them to appear, save the document as a template, and use that template for each publication.

Let's begin by creating a simple custom template for our four publications.

1. Open a four-page document.

   Select the File menu's New command. The Document Setup dialog box appears, as shown in the following illustration. Select Magazine from the Page Size drop-down menu and Tall for the orientation. Enter the number **4** into the Number of Pages box. Check the Double-sided and Facing Pages boxes, and uncheck the Restart Page Numbering box. Accept the default Margins and Target Output Resolution, and click OK to create your document.

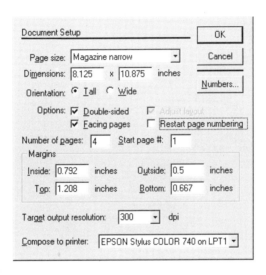

2. Open the General, Online, Layout adjustment or the Trapping Preferences dialog box.

   Select the File menu's Preferences  command. Choose from the preference options shown in the submenu, described below.

   ■ **General**   This is used to edit general preferences such as measurement specifications, layout problems, graphics display, and Control Palette Nudge options. You can also access the More preferences (greeking, Story Editor, and graphics and postscript printing), the Map fonts, and the Color Management System preferences via the General preferences dialog box.

   ■ **Online**   This is used to edit online preferences.

   ■ **Layout**   Here you edit layout such as the Snap-to zone, Adjust Page Elements, and Adjust Ruler Guides options.

   ■ **Trapping**   Here you adjust trapping settings, trapping thresholds, and black attributes.

3. Make any changes to the General, Online, Layout adjustment or Trapping preferences. For more information on this, refer to Chapter 12.

4. Accept your changes.

   Click OK in any of the Preferences dialog boxes to apply and accept your changes.

5. Open the Define Styles dialog box.

   Select the Type menu's Define Styles command to begin defining the style you would like applied to all publications that will be in your book. The Define Styles dialog box opens, as shown below.

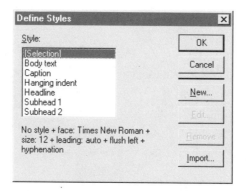

6. Open the Style Options dialog box.

   Click the New Button in the Define Styles dialog box. The Style Options dialog box opens, as shown below.

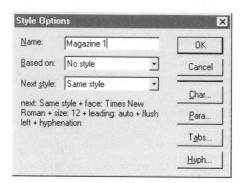

7. Name the style.

   In the Name box, enter the name of the new style. In this case, it is named Magazine 1.

8. Set the style specifications.

   On the right-hand side of the Style Options dialog box, there are four buttons for you to use in establishing the formatting that you want your new style to contain. These buttons are Character, Paragraph, Tabs, and Hyphenation. Each button will take you to its corresponding dialog box, in which you can establish the parameters for your style. For more information on how to do this, refer to Chapter 9.

---

**Tip**

*Do not check Include in the Table of Contents check box at this point, or all paragraphs in your document will be included in your table of contents.*

---

9. Accept your style parameters.

   Once you are finished setting the parameters for your style, click OK in the Style Options dialog box. You return to the Define Styles dialog box. Notice that the name of your new style is listed in the Style list.

10. Save your new style.

    Click OK in the Define Styles dialog box, and the new style is saved and also appears on your Styles Palette when it is open.

11. Open the publication's master pages.

    As you recall, PageMaker automatically assigns each new publication a set of master pages known as the document master pages. They can be accessed by clicking on the L and R icons at the bottom-left corner of your document screen.

    If you want to number your pages throughout the publication and the overall book, you will need to tell PageMaker to insert page numbers. There are a variety of page-numbering styles, which we will discuss later, but at this stage it is only necessary to add the markers to the master pages.

12. Add page markers to your document master pages.

    Using the Text tool, click on the place you would like your page number to appear. Typically, this is in the lower-left and lower-right corners of facing pages, and in the lower-right corner of single pages.

    Press CTRL+ALT+P to insert the page markers. You will see LM (left marker) and RM (right marker) indicating where page numbers appear in the actual publication. Make sure that you add page markers to all master pages.

The numbering system can be set in the individual publications once they are created. For now, it is enough to indicate that you want page numbers in your master template.

13. Prepare to save your publication as a master template.

Select the File menu's Save As command. The Save Publication dialog box appears, as shown in the illustration below.

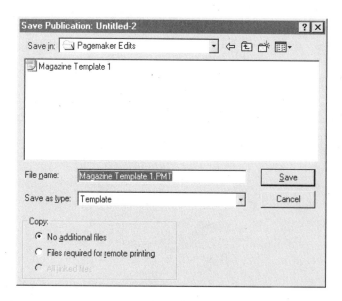

14. Name your file.

In the File Name window, type a name for your template. Make it distinctive so that you will remember it. Here Magazine Template 1 is chosen.

15. Tell PageMaker that you want to save this publication as a template.

From the Save as Type drop-down menu, select Template.

16. Save your template.

Click Save and your publication will be saved as a template. Note that unless you have changed your preferences for file saving, your template will by default be saved in the My Documents directory.

# Creating Publications for Incorporation in a Book

Now it's time to create the actual publications based on the template we just generated. We will make four publications, give each one a name, type a chapter heading, assign the heading a style (for inclusion in the table of contents), decide on and implement a page-numbering style, and save each file in preparation for bringing them together as a book.

1. Open your master template.

   Select the File menu's Open command. The Open Publication dialog box appears, as shown below. Navigate to the place on your hard drive where you stored the template using the Look In drop-down menu.

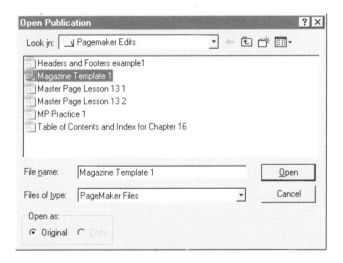

2. Open the template.

   Click Open. The template opens.

3. Save the template as a new document.

   Before you make any changes, save this template as a document so that you are not modifying the original template. Select the File menu's Save As command. The Save Publication dialog box opens. Name this publication "Chapter 1—The Early Years." Be sure to save it as a publication rather than as a template. From the drop-down menu in the Save as Type window, choose Publication.

4. Open the Document Setup dialog box.

   Select the File menu's Document Setup command. The Document Setup dialog box opens.

5. Open the Page Numbering dialog box.

   Click the Numbers Button on the right-hand side of the Document Setup dialog box, and the Page Number dialog box opens, as shown below.

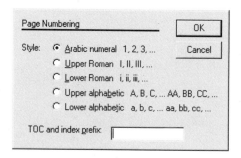

6. Specify a page-numbering format.

   In addition to telling PageMaker to put a page number on each page (as you did by adding page markers to the document master page), you can specify what kind of numbers to use. Your options, as shown in the Page Numbering dialog box, are as follows:

   - Arabic numerals
   - Upper Roman numerals
   - Lower Roman numerals
   - Upper alphabetic
   - Lower alphabetic

   By far, the most common system, and therefore the default, is the Arabic system, but it is also common to use other systems for special kinds of publications such as introductions and prefaces. You specify in PageMaker which kind of numbers to use in each publication. Here the default Arabic has been selected.

7. Specify the prefixes to appear in your table of contents and index.

   Prefixes are letters, characters, or words that can appear in front of the page numbers in your table of contents and index entries. For example, if you decide to include the name of the chapter in front of each page entry, you would type the name of the chapter into the TOC and Index Prefix box at the bottom of the Page Numbering dialog box. In the following illustration, the

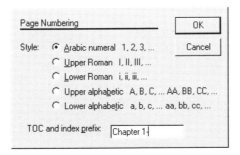

words "Chapter 1—" are used as the prefix to all entries in the table of contents and index. Notice that a dash is included after the 1 to separate the chapter number from the page number. You can have up to 15 characters in your prefix.

8.  Accept your numbering system.

    To accept your numbering system in your publication, click OK and return to the Document Setup dialog box.

9.  Accept and apply your changes.

    To accept and apply all the changes you have made in the Document Setup dialog box, click OK. Your changes are applied and the dialog box will close.

10. Open the document master pages for the publication.

    Open the document master pages by clicking the L and R icons at the bottom-left corner of your document screen. You should see that page markers are already in place for the document.

11. Add page number prefixes if desired.

    If you would like prefixes to appear before your page numbers on the actual pages of your publication, use the Text tool to place an insertion point in front of the page marker in the document master page. Type in the prefix you'd like to appear. In Figure 17-1, the prefix A is added plus a dash.

12. Save your first document.

    Since we already saved the template as the document "Chapter 1—The Early Years" in step 3, all you have to do is select the File menu's Save command. Your document is saved. However, if you'd like to see that you are saving it as "Chapter 1—The Early Years," you can select the File menu's Save As command. The Save Publication dialog box opens. Notice the file name in the File Name window. Click the Save Button and the changes we made are saved.

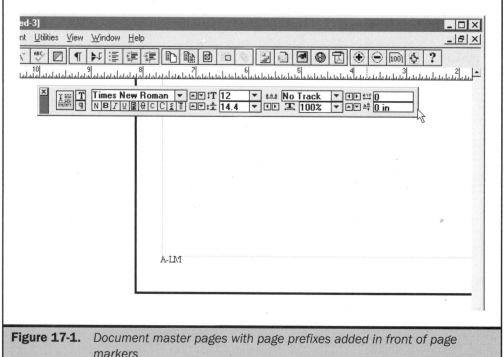

**Figure 17-1.**   *Document master pages with page prefixes added in front of page markers*

13. Create three more chapters.

Since the same process will be repeated for the other three publications to be included in your book, repeat steps 1 through 12 using the following chapter names:

- Chapter 2—The Middle Years
- Chapter 3—The Later Years
- Chapter 4—Looking Back

For page prefixes, use B for Chapter 2, C for Chapter 3, and D for Chapter 4. Close all publications, but leave PageMaker open.

# Formatting Publications for Inclusion in a Book

As you recall from Chapter 16, the best way to tell PageMaker that you want something included in your table of contents is to use a style. Follow the instructions in Chapter 16, assign a style to each of the chapter titles and tell PageMaker to include them in your table of contents. You should do this for each publication. PageMaker will combine the various tables when you specify which publications to include in which order in your book. That is done by creating what is known as a book list and will be discussed in the next section.

In order to generate an index for an entire book, you must have text in your chapters. If you would like to add text and make index entries (do not actually generate an index) for each publication, please feel free to do so. You will learn how to combine indexes into one publication for the entire book in the following section on creating a book list.

# Creating a Book List

PageMaker uses a book list to keep track of all the publications that will appear in a book. PageMaker also uses the book list to create the overall table of contents and index for the book. Therefore, the order in which you place your publications in your book list is very important since it determines the order in which the publications appear in the finished book.

A book list must be created in at least one of the publications that will be in the book. However, it is a good idea to place a copy of the book list in every publication that will be in the book. When a copy of the book list is in every publication, you can create a table of contents and/or index that covers all the publications. Also, any modifications you make to the book list in one publication can easily be applied to all the rest through the Copy feature. This will all become much easier to understand once you actually make a book list.

To create a book list, follow these steps:

1. Open the publication entitled "Chapter 1—The Early Years."

   Select the File menu's Open command. Then choose My Documents and Chapter 1—The Early Years, and click Open.

2. Open the Book Publication List dialog box.

   Select the Utilities menu's Book command.

   The Book Publication List dialog box opens, as shown in the following illustration.

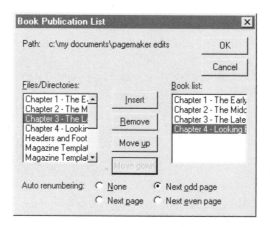

Notice that on the left, under Files/Directories, you have a list of publications to choose from. You should see all four of the publications created earlier. On the right is the book list itself with space for files to be added.

3. Add the files you want to include in the book.

   Double-click on the name of each of the four files we created, or click once on a name to highlight it, and use the Insert Button between the two lists. The selected name moves into the Book List window. Moving the name of the publication into the Book List window on the right adds that publication to your book. If you make a mistake and would like to remove the file, click the name of the file to highlight it and hit the Remove Button.

4. Adjust the order of the publications.

   Notice that you have Move Up and Move Down Buttons in the center between the two lists. Use these buttons to put the files in the order you would like them to appear in the book. PageMaker doesn't pay attention to the numbering of the sections, so when it generates page numbers and tables of contents, it happily includes section 3 between sections 6 and 7. Therefore, the order of the items in this list is crucial.

   The Move Down Button causes the highlighted publication to swap places with the publication below it in the book list.

5. Specify the numbering system for the entire book.

   At the bottom of the Book Publication List dialog box, you will see a section called Auto Renumbering. This is where you tell PageMaker how to handle the page numbering when it combines all the publications. You can specify the following:

   ■ **None** By selecting None, you are telling PageMaker to treat each publication as a separate entity in terms of numbering. Therefore, the first publication will start with the number 1, the second publication will start again with number 1, and so on.

- **Next Page**    Select Next Page if you want all the pages to be numbered sequentially all the way through and if your publication is only going to be printed on one side of single sheets of paper. The reason for the single-sided printing is that this option does not take left-right spreads into consideration. As you know, spreads affect pagination, so only select this option if you have no spreads. Also, be sure that Restart Numbering is *not* selected in the Document Setup dialog box for each publication.

- **Next Odd Page**    Select this option if your publication uses left-right spreads. Examples of this include bound books and reports that have two pages on a single sheet of paper. In general, off pages fall on the right side of a two-page spread and even pages fall on the left. This is so universal that it's disconcerting to see an even-numbered page on the right side. Therefore, if you are numbering sequentially through a book, you normally choose Next Odd Page as your Auto Renumbering scheme. When Next Odd Page is selected, PageMaker forces the publication to begin renumbering on the proper page by inserting a blank page where necessary to hold the place of the missing left-hand page in a book containing a section that ends on a right-hand page.

- **Next Even Page**    Select this option if your publication uses left-right spreads and you would like your numbers to begin on the next even page. Again, when this option is selected, PageMaker forces the publication to conform to the page-numbering scheme by adding blank pages when necessary.

  Since our book has left-right spreads, choose the Next Odd Page option.

6. Create your book list.

   Click OK to create and save the book list.

## Copying a Book List

As noted, it is a good idea to have a copy of your book list in every publication so that you can update it from any publication when you make changes. The way this is done is by simply telling PageMaker to copy the book list into all publications in the book simultaneously. The main thing is not to forget to update the book list once you have made changes in a publication. Here's how:

1. Open the publication in which we created the book list if it's not already open.

   Select the File menu's Open command. Choose My Documents, then Chapter 1 —The Early Years. The publication opens.

2. Copy the book list into all publications listed in the book list.

   Hold down CTRL and select the Utilities menu's Book command. A message box appears telling you that PageMaker is copying the book list into the other publications in the list. Now you can make modifications and update them from any publication.

*Don't forget to update the book list in all publications by using this copy function whenever you make a change in one of the publications.*

# Generating a Table of Contents for All Publications in a Book

Before you actually create your table of contents, you should open your book list one more time and make sure that all the publications are in the correct order and that the numbering system you want for the entire book has been selected.

Your table of contents can either be placed in the first publication in the book (in which case you must insert extra pages to hold it), or it can be treated as a publication of its own. For more information on inserting pages to hold a table of contents, refer to Chapter 16.

If you are going to place your table of contents in a publication of its own, be sure to

1. Use a copy of the original template we created as the basis of the publication.

2. Leave the Restart Numbering box unchecked in the Document Setup dialog box.

3. Specify the page numbering style, such as Arabic, Upper Roman numeral, Lower Roman numeral, and so on, in the Page Numbering dialog box accessed via the Document Setup dialog box.

4. Add page markers to the document master pages of the publication and add prefixes in front of the page markers if desired.

5. Add the table of contents publication to the book list.

6. Copy the book list into the table of contents publication.

In this example, we will be adding the table of contents to the first publication, and so will need to add an additional page(s). Since this book will have only four chapters and therefore only four entries, it will be enough to insert a single extra page. To generate the table of contents, follow these steps:

1.  Open the first publication.

    Select the File menu's Open command. Then locate and open the My Documents folder and the Chapter 1—The Early Years file. The publication opens.

2.  Go to page 1 in the publication.

    Click the icon for page 1 in the icon bar in the lower-left corner of your document screen. Page 1 opens.

3.  Add a single page to the publication.

    Select the Layout menu's Insert Pages command. The Insert Pages dialog box appears, as shown below. Type the number **1** in the Insert box and select Before in the Current Page drop-down menu. Click Insert. One page is inserted in front of page 1.

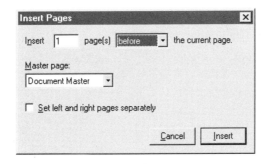

4.  Open the Create Table of Contents dialog box.

    Select the Utilities menu's Create TOC command. The Create Table of Contents dialog box opens, as shown below.

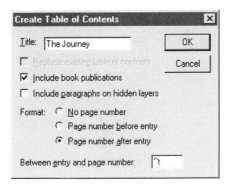

5.  Give the table of contents a title.

    Enter a name for your TOC by typing up to 30 characters in the title window. Let's call this table of contents "The Journey."

6.  Choose your options.

    Select the Replace Existing Table of Contents option, if applicable.

    Select the Include Book Publications option so that all the TOC entries in the publications in your book list are included in the TOC.

7.  Select a page-numbering format.

    Choose between the three options provided. If you would like no number included, choose No Page Number. If you want the page number to appear before the entry, select Page Number Before Entry. If you would like the page number to appear after the entry, choose Page Number After Entry.

8.  Modify the Between Entry and Page Number option if desired. Refer to Chapter 16 for details on how to make changes.

9.  Generate your TOC.

    Click OK. Your TOC is created. You will see the icon that looks like a half-sheet of paper with a left-angle bracket in its upper-left corner that tells you there is something ready to be placed.

10. Place your table of contents.

    Click the page 1 icon in the lower-left portion of your document screen to open page 1. Place the icon in the upper-left corner of page 1 and click. Your table of contents appears.

# Generating an Index for All Publications in a Book

The index in a multipublication book can be extensive, so it would be wise to check your index entries to be sure that there are no duplications due to misspellings, word order, or abbreviations. It is also best to wait until the very end to generate your index. If you like to see your index on the page, you can generate the index and replace it when you are ready to update. Remember that an index requires space, so you must create new pages to hold it.

Since an index is normally placed at the end of a book, you can either place it in the last publication (in which case you must insert extra pages to hold it) or create a separate publication for it. For more information on inserting pages to hold an index, refer to Chapter 16.

If you are going to place your index in a publication of its own, be sure to

1. Use a copy of the original template you created as the basis of the publication.

2. Leave the Restart Numbering box unchecked in the Document Setup dialog box.

3. Specify the page-numbering style, such as Arabic, Upper Roman numeral, Lower Roman numeral, and so on, in the Page Numbering dialog box accessed via the Document Setup dialog box.

4. Add page markers to the document master pages of the publication and add prefixes in front of the page markers if desired.

5. Add the index publication to the book list.

6. Copy the book list into the index publication.

In this example, we will be adding the index to the end of the last publication in the book, and so we will need to add an additional page:

1. Open the publication that will be last in your book.

   Select the File menu's Open command. Then locate and open the My Documents folder and the Chapter 4 — Looking Back file.

2. Go to page 4 (the last page) in the publication.

   Click the icon for page 4 in the icon bar in the lower-left corner of your document screen. Page 4 opens.

3. Add a single page to the publication.

   Select the Layout menu's Insert Pages command. The Insert Pages dialog box appears. Type the number **1** in the Insert box and select After in the Current Page drop-down menu. Click Insert. One page is inserted after page 4.

   Note that although we added only one page because we had very few entries, most indexes require several pages. Don't hesitate to insert more pages than you think you will need, as they can always be removed.

4. Open the Create Index dialog box.

   Select the Utilities menu's Create Index command. The Create Index dialog box appears, as shown in the following illustration.

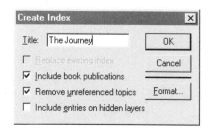

5. Give your index a name.

   In the title window, type a name using up to 30 characters. In this case, let's call it "The Journey Index."

6. Select your options.

   Select Replace Existing Index, if applicable.

   Select the Include Book Publications option so that all the index entries in the publications in your book list are included in the index when it's generated.

   Select the Remove Unreferenced Topics option, if applicable.

   Select the Include Entries on Hidden Layers option, if applicable.

**Note**
*For more information on all these options (except Include Book Publications), refer to "The Process of Creating an Index" in Chapter 16.*

7. Open the Index Format dialog box.

   Click the Format Button in the Create Index dialog box to go to the Index Format dialog box.

8. Specify formatting.

   Make any formatting changes using the options provided in the dialog box. For more information on index formatting, refer to Chapter 16.

9. Apply your formatting.

   To apply your changes, click OK. You return to the Create Index dialog box.

10. Generate your index.

   Click OK and your index is generated. Notice the icon that looks like a piece of paper with a left-angle bracket in its upper-left corner. That icon tells you there is something ready to be placed.

11. Place your index.

   Click the icon for the last page in your publication in the lower-left corner of your document screen. In this case, it is page 5. Position the place icon in the upper left-hand corner of the page and click. Your index is placed.

# Printing

One of the advantages of using a book list is that it enables you to print the entire book at once. You won't need to individually print each section. When you choose to print an entire book, PageMaker uses the printer settings of the document that is active at the time. Here's how:

1.  Open any one of the publications that contain the book list.

    Select the File menu's Open command. Then, locate and open the My Documents folder and the Chapter 1—The Early Years file. The publication opens.

2.  Open the Print Document dialog box.

    Select the File menu's Print command. The Print dialog box opens, as shown in Figure 17-2.

3.  Tell PageMaker you want to print the entire book.

    Check the Print All Publications in Book box. If you do not select this option, only the current publication is printed.

4.  Tell PageMaker that you want all blank pages printed as well.

    Check the Print Blank Pages box. This means that PageMaker includes all the blank pages it may have to add to conform to your page-numbering scheme.

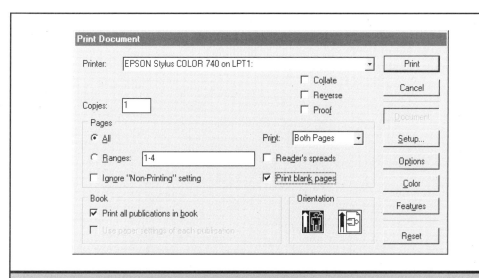

**Figure 17-2.**   *The Print Document dialog box*

5.  Print.

Click the Print Button. Your entire book is printed, including the blank pages
that force sections to begin on odd (or even) pages.

## Summary

In this chapter, I discuss how to bring multiple publications together as a single unit
called a book. I also discuss how to generate a table of contents and an index for the
entire book. PageMaker knows which publications to include in a book through a book
list. I cover how to generate, update, and copy a book list. Finally, page numbering and
formatting for all the publications in a book are discussed.

# Chapter 18

## Using PageMaker's Build Booklet Feature

Put two sheets of paper together and fold them in the middle to form a booklet with eight pages. (This mock-up booklet is called a *dummy*.) Number those pages, and then disassemble them. Notice that if you want the booklet to read correctly, you cannot print pages 1 and 2 on the same sheet; you must place booklet pages 8 and 1 on the same sheet and booklet pages 2 and 7 on the reverse of it (see Figure 18-1).

Now, you could just figure out what needs to go where and create the document that way, but far easier, PageMaker provides a feature that does all the arrangement work for you: the Build Booklet plug-in. This wizard-like program takes a regular document, copies it, and then automatically rearranges the pages and creates multiple page spreads so that the booklet is in order and readable when printed and folded.

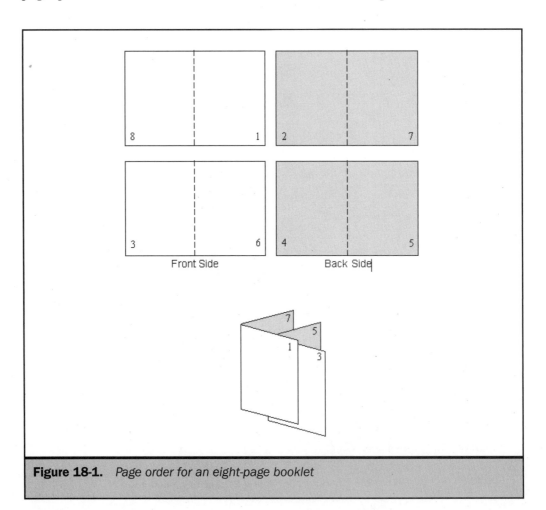

**Figure 18-1.**    *Page order for an eight-page booklet*

*Imposition* is arranging pages in this way so that they work together. The final result of an imposition is called a *signature*.

Before you activate the Build Booklet plug-in, however, there are some things you must be aware of or prepare for. Let's look at those first.

# Preparation

First, of course, you must prepare the regular document. Create each individual page as it will appear in the booklet; PageMaker will combine the pages that need to be printed on one page. Depending upon the type of layout you want to create (see "Choosing a Layout"), you will need to prepare a specific number of pages (multiples of four for Saddle Stitch and Perfect Bound; two, three, or four pages for Consecutive Imposition). Generate and place a table of contents and the index if you are planning to use them (see Chapter 16). Make sure that the table of contents and the index reflect the correct pages in the original document.

Document Setup must specify pages to be the same size as the completed pages in the booklet. The maximum page width that you may use in any PageMaker document is 42 inches. In Saddle Stitched and Perfect Bound layouts, a combination of two pages must not exceed this width, including the gutter (the blank space between the pages where the binding occurs). If you are using a Consecutive Imposition layout, the total of all pages must not exceed 42 inches.

Complete your regular document before activating the Build Booklet plug-in. Simple text and graphic edits can be made, of course, but other changes, such as rearranging pages, cannot be done once the imposition is made.

Additionally, you must make sure that there is enough space on your computer's hard drive. You will need room for the copy of the document as well as additional space for PageMaker to use while arranging pages. It is a good idea to allow at least 2.5 times the size of the original document.

If the finished booklet will contain more than 500 completed pages, it really isn't a booklet. Divide the publication into smaller documents and use the instructions in Chapter 17 to create a book. You may also divide the publication into smaller documents and impose each separately. The final document would then need to be Perfect Bound.

# Choosing a Layout

The three layout styles that are available in PageMaker's Build Booklet plug-in are consistent with publishing techniques that have been used for generations. The difference between these styles is the way they are bound.

## 2-Up Saddle Stitch

A Saddle Stitch booklet is one that is folded once and stapled, or otherwise bound, along the fold (see Figure 18-2). The term *stitch* comes from the time when such a layout would literally be stitched together with thread. Today you may occasionally see other forms of a stitch binding, but staples are by far the most common. The term *2-up* means that pages are printed two to a sheet so that one page appears on each side of the binding.

This type of layout is always composed of pages in multiples of four. If you have no need for every one of the pages in multiples of four, PageMaker can add blank pages to complete the layout.

Saddle Stitched booklets are usually small because of the bulk created by the fold. If two or more booklets are used to form a larger document, each booklet is called a *signature* and the final document is usually Perfect Bound (see the following section).

## 2-Up Perfect Bound

A Perfect Bound layout usually involves multiple Saddle Stitched signatures that are then bound into one document with adhesive along the folded edges, as shown in

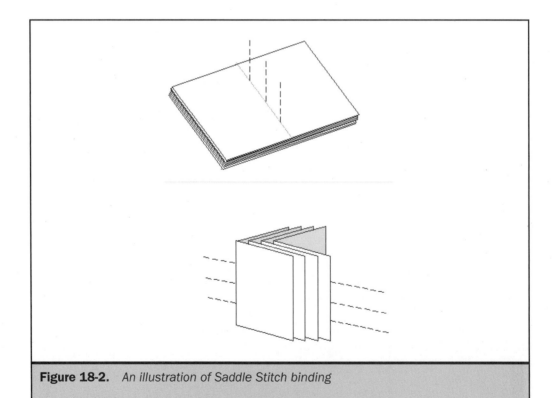

**Figure 18-2.** *An illustration of Saddle Stitch binding*

Figure 18-3. Most hardbound books that we see today are Perfect Bound. If you look closely at the top or bottom on the spine of a hardback book, you will see the signatures that make it up.

This style, like the Saddle Stitch, of which it is composed, uses a 2-up layout.

## 2-, 3-, or 4-Up Consecutive Imposition

The Consecutive Imposition layout places all pages side by side onto a single sheet (see Figure 18-4). For practical purposes, you cannot impose more than four pages into this layout. This is a great layout for brochures, centerfolds, and greeting cards with an accordion fold.

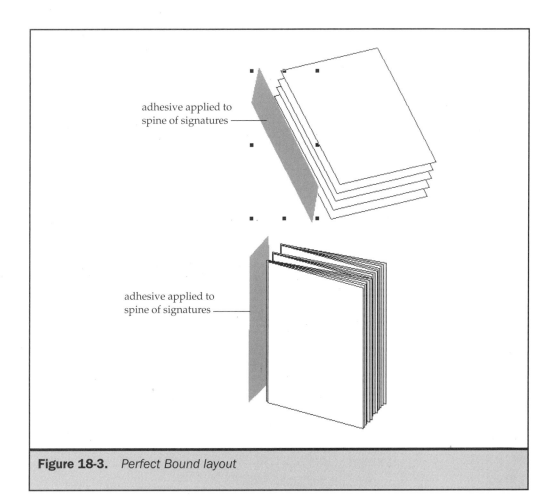

adhesive applied to
spine of signatures

adhesive applied to
spine of signatures

**Figure 18-3.**   *Perfect Bound layout*

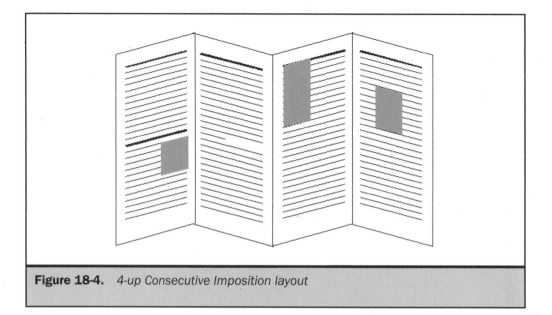

**Figure 18-4.**   *4-up Consecutive Imposition layout*

## None

In addition to the three layout styles listed previously, you can choose None. This selection causes the Build Booklet plug-in to create a new document, but it does not rearrange pages or create spreads. It does enable you to manually adjust the page arrangement, increase the page size, or insert blank pages as needed.

## Dealing with Creep

Before I discuss the steps to imposing a publication, I want to talk about creep. Creep is not a commentary on my youngest daughter's ex-husband, but a phenomenon that occurs in the creation of signatures. If you actually created the dummy booklet, as I recommended at the beginning of this chapter, you may have noticed that no matter how carefully you folded the sheets of paper, the center pages extended a bit from the outside pages. That is called creep and can make a big difference in the appearance of your document. If you use many more pages than the four I suggested, the creep is even more noticeable. The amount of creep depends upon the weight and quality of the paper stock you are using for the signature. In most professionally published documents, the creep is trimmed, leaving all of the pages aligned.

Just imagine, however, that you used a large number of heavy sheets to create a signature. With enough pages, trimming the creep creates a noticeable difference in the outside margin of the inside pages of your booklet or signature. Although you rarely use so many pages in a signature that it would be noticeable, PageMaker provides an answer by slightly diminishing the size of the printable areas on each page to allow for the creep. When setting the values for the imposition (see "Imposing a Publication"), you can set a creep value that causes that adjustment to be made.

You may ask your commercial printer for information on determining the creep value or you may determine the creep value yourself. Here's how:

1. Create a dummy.

   Create a mock-up (called a dummy) of the booklet you are producing. For this to be accurate, you must use the same paper stock as will be used in the final printing and it should be folded, relative to the grain of the paper, in the same way (with the grain or across the grain).

2. Staple through the fold.

   Staple through the fold using a saddle stapler to secure the pages. If you do not have a saddle stapler, use a straight pin to secure the pages, making sure to keep the pages together at the fold.

3. Trim the creep.

   Trim the excess from the facing edge. Accuracy is important here. Use a high-quality paper cutter or a straight edge and craft knife.

4. Measure.

   Remove the staple and lay the pages flat. Note that the sheet that was inside when the sheets were folded is slightly smaller than the outside one. Measure the difference in the width of the inside sheet to the outside sheet. The difference is the creep value.

## Imposing a Publication

When you are ready, armed with all the information and decisions you need, impose your publication. This process enables you the opportunity to add pages if needed, revise the order of pages, select the layout style, and set the creep value. Just follow these steps:

1. Open the normal publication.

   Open the document you want to impose. The document must be saved before the imposition can take effect. If you have not saved it, PageMaker will remind you to do so.

2. Open the Build Booklet dialog box.

   Select the Utilities menu's Plug-ins command. Then click on the Build Booklet item from the sub-menu. The Build Booklet dialog box opens (see the following illustration).

MANAGING PAGEMAKER DOCUMENTS

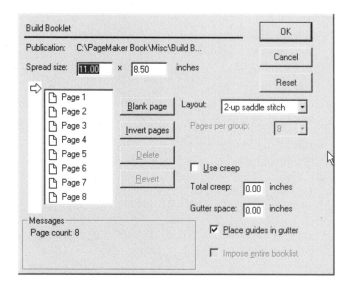

3. Choose a layout.

   Click the drop-down arrow to the right of the Layout box. The Layout menu appears (see the following illustration). From the Layout menu, select the layout of your choice. If you select the Perfect Bound style, you must enter the number of pages you want in each signature. Use the drop-down menu of the Pages Per Group box to select the number of pages you want.

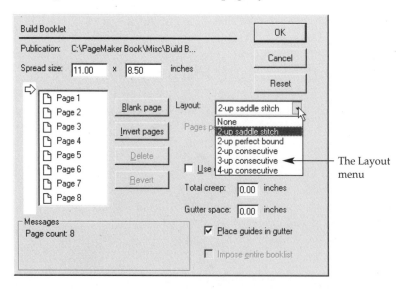

The Layout menu

4. Specify spread size values.

   The spread size values are automatically determined by your choice of a layout. You may, however, increase the measurements to allow for marks that tell a printer where to trim. The Message box will tell you if the values you enter are not appropriate.

5. Add blank pages.

   If you created the original document with the appropriate number of pages, you will not need to add blank pages, but the layouts must be created in multiples of four (except for the Consecutive Imposition style that uses two, three, or four pages). If you have six pages, for example, you must add blank pages to bring the total up to eight. PageMaker tells you how many pages you need to add.

   Click in the column to the left of the list of pages (or slide the arrow in the column) to indicate where you want a blank page to appear. Then click the Blank Page button. A blank page appears at the position of the arrow.

6. Reposition pages.

   If you want to reposition a new blank page, or any page for that matter, hold down ALT, click on the icon of the page you want to move, and then drag it to the new location.

7. Remove pages.

   If you want to remove pages, select the page by clicking on it. Then click the Delete button. The page is removed from the document (the imposition, not the original document).

   To remove more than one page at a time, hold down CTRL while you select the pages you want to remove. Then click the Delete button. All pages are removed.

8. Invert pages.

   If you need to change the order of the pages from ascending to descending, click on the Invert Pages button. The order of the pages is reversed.

9. Undo changes in page order.

   Click the Revert button on the Build Booklet dialog box to return the page order to its original state and to remove any blank pages that have been added.

10. Enter a creep value.

    In the Total Creep box, enter the creep value (see "Dealing with Creep"). Click the Use Creep selection box.

11. Specify gutter space.

    If you want additional space to be accorded to the gutter, (space between pages where the binding takes place) enter the value in the Gutter Space box. Any space you create here will be added to the overall size of the booklet (the Spread Size value). Keep in mind that, if you are planning to print on a specific sized paper, the Spread Size cannot exceed the size of the paper.

12. Add guides.

    To add nonprinting guides, select the Place Guides in Gutter box.

13. Impose the publication.

    Click the OK button on the Build Booklet dialog box. The box closes and PageMaker creates an imposition as a new document. You will be asked if you wish to save the original document.

# Summary

Creating a booklet requires an understanding of what pages go where. It certainly is possible to figure out that for yourself by creating a dummy, numbering the pages, and then disassembling it, but PageMaker makes it so much easier with the Build Booklet plug-in.

**Preparation**   It is important that you complete your document from which you want to create an imposition (the arrangement of what pages go where) before you begin the process. Generate the table of contents and an index if you are going to use them, and make sure that the page size set in the Document Setup dialog box is the size you want each page to be in your finished booklet.

You will also need sufficient hard-drive storage space for the Build Booklet process to run, usually 2.5 times the size of your original document.

**Choosing a Layout**   There are four choices of layout: 2-up Saddle Stitch, 2-up Perfect Bound, 2-, 3-, or 4-up Consecutive Imposition, and None. Each of these layout styles produces a booklet designed for a specific binding technique. The None selection does not move pages around, but enables you to rearrange pages manually.

**Dealing with Creep**   When paper stock is folded, the inside pages extend slightly beyond the outside ones. This is called creep; it is usually trimmed away. PageMaker enables you to enter values that cause the adjustment of the printable area of the pages just a bit to adjust for creep so that all margins appear consistent.

**Imposing a Publication**   The Build Booklet dialog box provides you with settings to control the imposition process. When the imposition is activated, a new document is created with pages arranged appropriately for your booklet.

# Chapter 19

## Creating PDF Documents in PageMaker 7

Wait if you could design a PageMaker document and send it (or a copy of it) electronically to anyone on the Internet for viewing or printing, even if they did not have PageMaker installed on their computer? Well, you can, of course. By exporting the PageMaker document as an Adobe Acrobat Portable Document Format (PDF) document, your publication can be downloaded, viewed, and printed by just about any computer system with access to the Internet.

Exporting a PageMaker document as a PDF file is as easy as sending it to your desktop printer and, actually, the process is very similar. Instead of sending the data to your printer, however, it is sent to your hard drive in an Internet-compatible format so that it can be sent over the Internet.

Although the process of actually sending the document to be printed as a PDF file is very simple, there are certain steps that must be taken before you can export the file.

# Before You Create the PDF Document

As you would expect, certain things must be in place before the PageMaker document can be exported as a PDF file. The process of creating PDF documents is through Adobe Distiller, and viewing is through Adobe Acrobat Reader, both of which are part of the Adobe Acrobat software. That software must be installed on your computer system, and the PageMaker document itself must be prepared for best presentation across the Internet.

## Install Adobe Acrobat Components

The first thing you must do, of course, is make sure that the Adobe Acrobat component applications have been installed on your computer. All of the Adobe Acrobat applications are included on the PageMaker 7.0 Application CD that you used to install PageMaker. You may have installed all of them at the time you installed PageMaker. If not, reinsert the CD into your CD drive and install Acrobat Distiller, Acrobat Reader, and the Adobe PostScript Driver (see Figure 19-1).

When you install the PostScript Driver, you are, in effect, installing a PostScript printer to your system. If you use a PostScript printer, you already have a PostScript Driver in place. If you are not using a PostScript printer (if you don't know, you probably are not), the new installation will not in any way interfere with your current printer's operation. It will merely provide drivers necessary to the PDF creation process.

## Prepare the Document for Best PDF Results

Because a PDF document is transmitted and displayed across the Internet, the document needs to utilize techniques and elements that are Internet-compatible and particularly compatible with a PDF layout. Check out the following list to make sure that your document is ready to be exported as a PDF file:

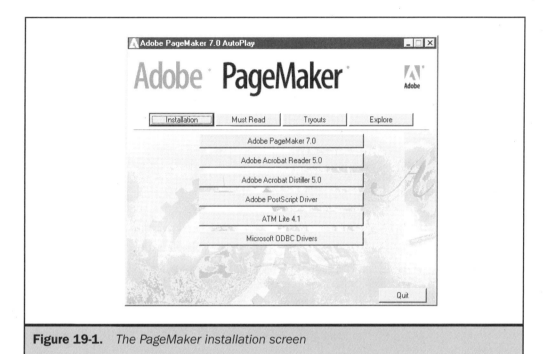

**Figure 19-1.** *The PageMaker installation screen*

■ **Page numbering**   Although PageMaker documents can begin with any page number and can use any amount of page numbering systems, PDF files begin with page 1 and support only one page numbering system. Before exporting to PDF, change the page numbering in your original document so that it is PDF-compatible. If you do not do so, hyperlinks and bookmarks in the PDF document will not work accurately.

■ **Using online colors**   Only certain colors display accurately on the Internet. Use the online colors library when selecting colors for use in a PDF document. Here's how to add online colors to the Color Palette's Color List:

1. Display the Color Palette.

   Click the Window menu's Show Colors command. The Color Palette appears in your PageMaker window.

2. Open the Color Options dialog box.

   Click the New Color Button near the lower-right corner of the Color Palette or select the New Color command from the Color Palette menu. The Color Options dialog box opens.

3. Select the online color library.

   Leave the Name box blank. The name (usually a number) of the color you ultimately select will appear in the box. Click the drop-down button next to the Libraries text box and select Online Colors from the list of Color Matching Systems libraries. The Color Picker dialog box appears, identifying the online colors library and displaying colors that are compatible with the Internet from which you may choose.

4. Select a new color.

   Use the horizontal scroll bar to peruse the color choices. When the color you want to add to the Color Palette Color List is located, click on it to select it. Then click the OK button. The Color Options dialog box returns with the selected color's name in the Name box.

5. Add the online color to the Color List.

   Click the OK button. The Color Options dialog box closes and the selected color appears in the Color List of the Color Palette.

**Note** *If there are no library names available when you click the drop-down arrow next to the Libraries box, the libraries have not been installed. Reinstall PageMaker, selecting the libraries as part of the installation or see the How_to_Install readme file on the PageMaker Application CD.*

- **Compiling multiple documents**  If you want to combine several documents into one PDF file, compile them into one document before you export to PDF. The easiest and quickest way is to use the Book command. See Chapter 17 for more information on compiling several documents into one.

- **Index and table of contents**  If the table of contents and index in your publication are generated automatically using PageMaker's Table of Contents and Index utilities, exporting the document to a PDF will create hypertext links between the items listed and the topic in the document. If you are tempted to create these lists manually rather than automatically, keep in mind that in documents with manually created tables of contents and indices the hypertext links will not be present after the document is exported. See Chapter 16 for information on automatically generating these lists.

- **Fonts**  If a font used in a PDF file is not present on the viewer's system, the document's text could be distorted. Make sure that the fonts you use are present on your system and then embed the fonts into the PDF document so that the font will show accurately, even if it is not on the viewer's system. Keep in mind that embedding fonts substantially increases the size of the document. See the "Embedding Fonts" section under "Establishing PDF Distiller Settings" for further information on embedding fonts.

# Establishing PDF Distiller Settings

The software that creates the PDF document, the Adobe Distiller, is ready to use as soon as it is installed. By default, four types of PDF projects (called jobs) are configured with settings particular to each job type. However, if you want to change the Distiller's defaults, it is easy to do. Take a look at the settings as described in the following steps. If you want to make changes to the default settings, do so. It is best to make these changes before you start the process of exporting to PDF.

In order to change the settings, you must open the Job Options dialog box. Follow these steps to do so:

1.  Open the PDF Options dialog box.

    Choose the File menu's Export command and the Adobe PDF item from the submenu. The PDF Options dialog box opens (see the following illustration).

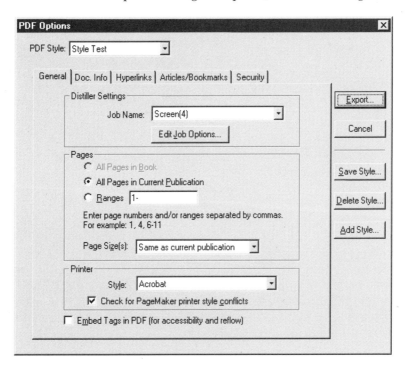

2.  Select a job name.

    From the drop-down menu to the right of Job Name, select a job name. A job name needs to be chosen as a base for your settings, but the settings you select are later saved with a name of their own, so the job you select doesn't matter. Choices include eBook, Press, Print, and Screen.

3. Open the Job Options dialog box.

Click the Edit Job Options Button. The Job Options dialog box opens, as shown in the following illustration. Select Job Options as described in the following sections.

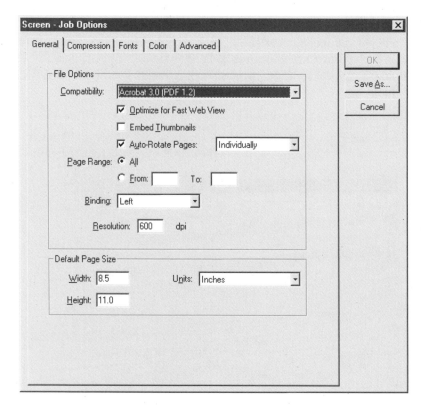

4. Save the settings and close the Job Options dialog box.

Once you have completed your Options selections, save the settings with a job name. Click the Save As Button on the Job Options dialog box. The Save Job Options As dialog box appears. Enter your job name in the File Name box and click the Save Button. The Job Options dialog box closes. You may then use that combination of settings whenever it is appropriate.

The Job Options dialog box consists of five tabs in which you can make the setting changes that you wish for a particular type of job. Each of the following sections identifies one of the Job Options tabs and the choices it contains.

# General

The settings under the General tab (refer to Figure 19-3) enable you to determine the basic settings for a job created under that job name, such as the Adobe Acrobat Reader version with which your job is compatible, the way the document is bound, and page size:

- **Compatibility**   The version you select could prevent some recipients from viewing your document. For example, if you select Acrobat 4.0, only viewers with Acrobat Reader 4.0 and 5.0 would be able to read the document. Recipients with Adobe Acrobat 3.0 would not be able to access it. Therefore, unless you know the version of Acrobat that your recipients have, it may be a good idea to select Adobe Acrobat 3.0.

   However, if it is important for colors to remain true in your document, you may want to select Acrobat 4.0 or 5.0. Acrobat 3.0 does not permit some of the color settings that maintain color across systems and output devices (see "Distiller Color Options").

   Security settings are also different for documents compatible with Acrobat version 5. See the "Security Options" section under "Setting the PDF Options" later in this chapter for more information.

- **Optimize for Fast Web View**   If your file is very large, it could take a long time for some viewers to download it from the Internet. Selecting Optimize for Fast Web View reduces the size of the file by removing unneeded backgrounds and compressing the text and art (no matter what setting you make under compression in the second tab).

- **Embed Thumbnails**   Thumbnails are small, representational images of each page in the final PDF. They are a good thing to offer in a PDF document, particularly if your document is a sales or marketing piece. Select Embed Thumbnails to create them.

- **Auto Rotate Pages**   This selection is a good one to make if your document contains some pages with an orientation that is different from the rest. For example, if your primarily portrait-oriented document has some pages with a landscape orientation to accommodate tables, charts, or graphics, with Auto Rotate Pages selected, the resulting PDF file will show each page as it should be viewed. Your viewers do not have to get a crick in their neck trying to read some material. Selecting Collectively By File turns all pages; selecting Individually turns those whose orientation requires it.

- **Page Range**   This enables you to select only certain pages to include in the PDF document. Enter the page numbers you want to include in the From and To boxes. Or enter the starting page in the From box and leave the To box empty to include pages from the start to the end of the document.

MANAGING PAGEMAKER DOCUMENTS

■ **Binding**   Your pages will not actually be bound, of course; they are displayed as an image, but this selection does affect the appearance of binding in the display of your document by displaying pages as if they were bound and laying open.

■ **Resolution**   Enter a resolution between 74 and 4000 dpi (dots per square inch) for your document in the Resolution box. Higher resolutions can slow the display of a PDF file, but low resolution can cause distortions. Unless you are certain of the resolution that you want for your document, it is a good idea to leave the default setting of 2400 dpi in place.

■ **Default Page Size**   If you want to specify a page size (8.5-by-11 inches is the default), first select the unit of measure from Points, Picas, Inches, and Centimeters. Then adjust the measurements accordingly.

## Compression

The Compression tab in the Job Options dialog box (see the following illustration) provides compression settings that enable you to reduce the size of your PDF and to control the way in which the reduction takes place.

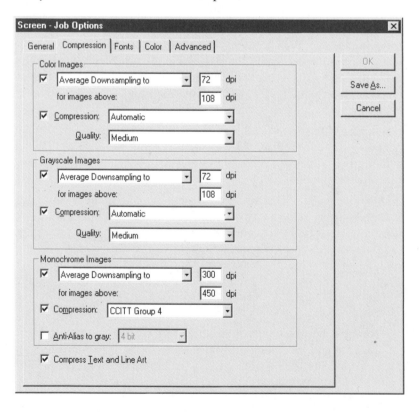

In each of three sections on this tab (Color Images, Grayscale Images, and Monochrome Images), choose the way in which Distiller reduces the particular element to produce a smaller size file:

- **Resampling**    The first box in each section enables you to choose the way in which the number of pixels that make up an object are reduced. *Downsampling* averages the color of the pixels in a certain area and replaces the area with a pixel of the average color. *Subsampling* selects a pixel in the center of a sample area and replaces the sampled pixels with the color of the selected one. Subsampling processes faster than Downsampling.

  When selecting a Resampling style from the drop-down menu, you must also set a target resolution and a threshold resolution above which the Resampling occurs.

- **Compression**    This selection determines the compression technique that is used in the reduction of the document. Select from Automatic, JPEG, and ZIP in the Color and Grayscale sections, and from CCITT Group 3, CCITT Group 4, ZIP, and Run Length in the Monochrome section:

  - **ZIP**    The best compression selection for screen shots and other images with large areas of the same color or repeating patterns. Simple graphics reduce well using ZIP, as do black and white images that contain repeating patterns.

  - **JPEG**    Works well with color or grayscale, but compresses by removing image data. Therefore, you run a risk of losing some image quality.

  - **CCIT**    A compression technique used for black and white images. Group 3 is used by fax machines. Group 4 is a good all-around compression mechanism.

  - **Run Length**    The best choice if your file contains large areas of black and white.

- **Quality**    If the quality of the graphics in the PDF document is important (such as in a product brochure), select Maximum as the choice in the Quality drop-down menu. Otherwise, select one of the other four choices. Keep in mind that the higher the quality, the larger the file.

- **Anti-alias to Gray**    This option smoothes jagged edges in black and white images by converting some areas of type to levels of gray. If you select 2-bit, you will get four levels of gray, 4-bit provides 16, and 8-bit provides 256. In small type and thin lines in graphics, some blurring may occur.

- **Compress Text and Line Art**    This choice applies the ZIP compression technique, without loss of quality, to the line art and text in the document.

## Embedding Fonts

One of the features of a PDF file is that any system can view the document. It is not necessary that the viewer have PageMaker on his or her system. However, if the fonts used in the original document are not available on the viewer's system, the viewer will see a default font (usually Courier) and the results can be chaotic. Therefore, embedding fonts into the PDF file is a good idea. In effect, this places the font file as an integral part of the PDF document, enabling the original font to display with all systems.

On the Fonts tab in the Job Options dialog box (see the following illustration), you may choose to embed all fonts contained in the original document, or you may select certain fonts to embed:

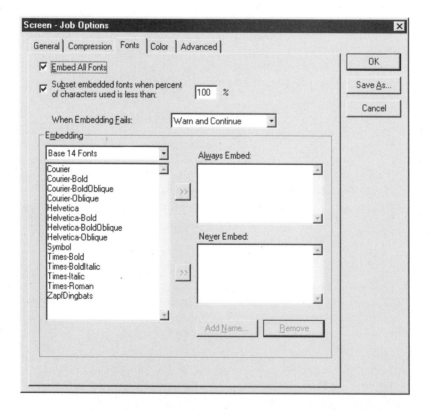

- To embed all fonts, select the Embed All Fonts box. All fonts contained in your document for which there are files on your system will be embedded in the resulting PDF document.

- If you want to select some fonts to embed, use the fonts in the Embedding section of the dialog box. Make sure that the Embed All Fonts box is *not* selected. Click on the font you wish to embed and then click the arrow to the left of the Always Embed box. The font appears in the Always Embed list.

■ If the font you want to embed is not in the list, click the Add Name Button at the bottom of the dialog box. The Add Font Name dialog box appears. Select the Always Embed selection and type the name of the font without using spaces. Click OK. The font appears in the Always Embed list.

■ If there are fonts you want never to embed, select the font in the font list and click the button next to the Never Embed list, or click the Add Name Button, select the Never Embed selection, and type the name of the font. Click OK. The font appears in the Never Embed list.

■ Indicate what you want to do if embedding fails, that is, if Distiller cannot find the font on your system. You may select for the current job to be cancelled entirely, for Distiller to warn you and continue with the job, or to ignore the request to embed fonts and proceed with the creation of the PDF file. Click the drop-down button to the right of the When Embedding Fails box and click on your choice.

# Distiller Color Options

The selections that you make in the Job Options dialog box's Color tab (see Figure 19-2) depend upon the use you are going to make of the resulting PDF. The selections available on the Color tab are discussed in the following bullet points.

■ **Settings File**   The Settings File menu, available by clicking the drop-down arrow to the right of the box, enables you to access previously saved settings that you have configured for a particular job as well as job settings that are included with PageMaker.

■ **Color Management Policies**   The choices in this menu direct Distiller to embed tags (ICC Profiles) into the document or to leave it as it is. International Color Consortium (ICC) Profiles are color management standards for use with imaging devices such as scanners, digital cameras, monitors, and printers so that color remains consistent. The Color Management Policies choices are as follows:

■ **Leave Color Unchanged**   If you are using PDF to send a file to a commercial printer *and* if the printer has counseled you on color selection based upon his or her equipment calibration, select Leave Color Unchanged.

■ **Tag Everything for Color Management**   If you elected for your PDF file to be compatible with Acrobat 4.0 or 5.0, this selection embeds ICC Profiles into the PDF as it is created. However, if you selected Adobe Acrobat 3.0 in the Compatibility section (refer to the "General" section), Distiller does *not* embed the profiles.

MANAGING PAGEMAKER DOCUMENTS

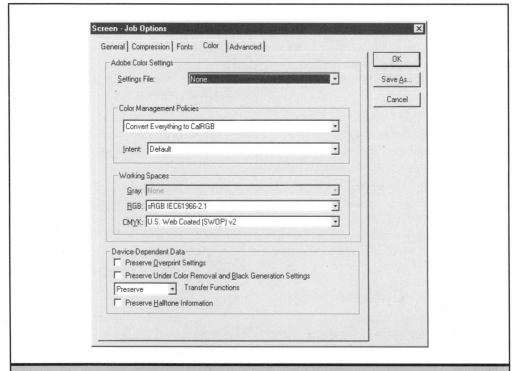

**Figure 19-2.**   *The Job Options dialog box with the Color tab displayed*

■ **Tag Only Images for Color Management**   This selection embeds the tags into images, only not into text or simple graphics. As in the Tag Everything selection discussed previously, this does not work if you have selected compatibility with Acrobat 3.0.

■ **Convert All Colors to sRGB**   This selection does not embed ICC Profiles, but calibrates the color independent of output devices.

The *Intent* menu pertains to the way colors are mapped between devices using a Color Management System. *Perception* (also called *Image*) incorporates a technique that best coordinates color for photographs. *Saturation* (also called *Graphics*) is best for simple graphics and illustrations. *Relative Colorimetric* incorporates the colors of one output device (a printer or a monitor) into the colors of another so that the colors retain their relationship. *Absolute Colorimetric* also incorporates colors from one output device into the colors of another, but maintains the integrity of signature colors such as Kodak yellow or Coca-Cola red.

Refer to Chapter 11 for more information on working with color libraries and to Chapter 21 for more information on working with PageMaker's Color Management System.

■ **Working Spaces**   Here you set the profile you wish for the management of Gray, RGB, and CMYK. The selections in this section are not available if you selected Leave Color Unchanged in the Color Management Policies menu. In addition, Gray is not available if you selected Convert All Colors to sRGB.

■ **Gray**   Select a profile to define the grayscale images in files.

■ **RGB**   Choose a profile. A good choice is sRGB IEC61966-2.1 because it is becoming an industry standard. You will find it near the top of the rather lengthy list.

■ **CMYK**   Choose a profile to define the color space of all CMYK images in the file. A good choice might be U.S. Sheetfed Uncoated v2.

■ **Device Dependent Data**   Here you select any or all of the following items:

■ **Preserve Overprint Settings**   This selection keeps the choices you made in choosing whether or not colors would overprint when designing your document.

■ **Preserve Under Color Removal and Black Generation Settings**   This box is selected by default. Remove it if you do not want device-specific settings in the file. A PDF document intended for general viewing would not require this setting to be activated.

■ **Preserve/Apply/Remove Transfer Functions**   This box enables you to choose one of the three selections. *Preserve* retains traditional functions used with commercial printing when placing an image on film. *Apply* causes the changes resulting from the transfer functions to be displayed on your computer monitor as well as on film output. *Remove*, of course, means that the transfer functions will not be used. If you are sending the PDF out to the general public, it is best to select the Remove option.

■ **Preserve Halftone Information**   Black and white photographs that are commercially printed are converted to halftones, a collection of dots that create the image with their size and frequency. Look at any black and white photo in a newspaper with a magnifying glass and you can see the dots and the way they create the image. Selecting this setting is important only if you are sending the PDF to a commercial printer for publication.

## Advanced Settings

The selections on the Advanced tab of the Job Options dialog box (see Figure 19-3) affect the fine-tuning of the structure of the resulting PDF document and govern the conversion of a PostScript document to PDF. These selections are highly technical and may not affect your document.

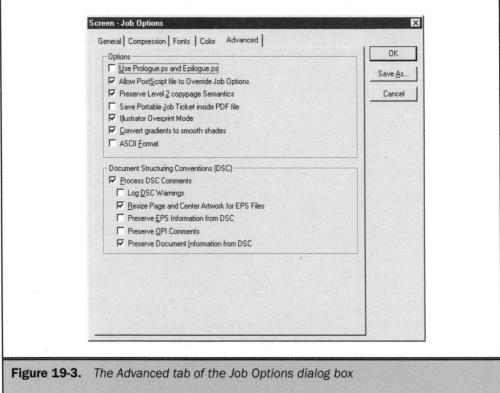

**Figure 19-3.** *The Advanced tab of the Job Options dialog box*

The issues displayed here are specific to Adobe Acrobat and require purchase of the full software (rather than that provided with PageMaker) to activate. Unless you are concerned with the issues identified in these options, I recommend that you leave the default settings in place. If you want to work with the issues reflected in these settings, refer to your Adobe Acrobat software and documentation. For more information on these questions, see the *Portable Document Format Reference Manual* on the Adobe Web site.

# Export a Document to PDF

Considering the options process, actually exporting a PageMaker file to PDF is easy. Before you start, name, save, and open the document you are exporting.

Here are the simple steps:

1.  Open the PDF Distiller.

    Select the File menu's Export command. Then choose Adobe PDF from the submenu. The PDF Distiller opens to display the PDF Options dialog box, as shown in the following illustration.

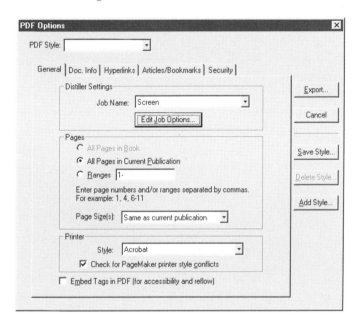

2.  Select a PDF style.

    From the drop-down menu to the right of PDF Style, select a predefined style or select a style you've created.

3.  Indicate the pages to be included.

    In the Pages section, indicate the pages you want to have included. Select from *All Pages in Book* (which will only be available if you have a book open), *All Pages in Current Publication*, or a *Range* of pages.

4.  Select the printer style.

    If there is a printer style that you have created and want to use, indicate it in the Style area of the Printer section. It is a good idea to leave the Adobe style in place. Also, select the Check for PageMaker Printer Style Conflicts box.

5.  Specify the PDF options.

    If you need to make any other settings specifically for this PDF, make those selections on the five tabs of the PDF Options dialog box. See "Setting the PDF Options" for more information on these options.

*Note that the PDF Options settings referred to here are specifically for the PDF you are currently creating. The PDF Distiller Options settings in the Job Options dialog box, described at length earlier, are general settings you may wish to establish for future use.*

6. Export the file.

Click the Export Button. The Export As dialog box opens. Specify a name and location for the file. Then click Save. The Export As dialog box closes, as well as the PDF Options dialog box. After a few moments, Adobe Acrobat Reader opens and the new PDF loads on your computer screen for you to review.

# Setting the PDF Options

Although we discussed setting job options at length earlier in this chapter, I am again discussing options you may want to consider. The difference is that these options are specifically for the PDF you are creating in the current exportation process. The earlier options are settings you may keep for use over and over again with future PDFs. It is always a good idea to consider these options as you export your PageMaker document to PDF.

## Embed Tags

This option at the bottom of the General tab is always a good selection to make. When selected, paragraph attributes of the PageMaker document are embedded in the PDF to maintain the structure of the document even in hand-held devices.

## Creating a PDF Document Summary

The second tab of the PDF Options dialog box entitled Doc. Info (see Figure 19-4) enables you to specify the author, title, subject, and keywords of your PDF. You can also create a First Page Note that will appear on the first page of your new document as a note in a note window (the Open option) or as an icon that must be clicked to open (the Closed option). Type the note in the text box and select Open or Closed.

## Setting PDF Hyperlink Options

It was mentioned earlier in this chapter that you must use PageMaker's Automatic Table of Contents and Index utilities when creating the PageMaker document if you want hyperlinks between the table of contents or index item and the topic in the PDF document. The Hyperlinks tab of the PDF Options dialog box (see Figure 19-5) lets you turn those links on and establish their appearance.

### Export Links

If you have created the table of contents and index using PageMaker's automatic utilities, select Table of Contents Links and Index Links from the Export Links section of

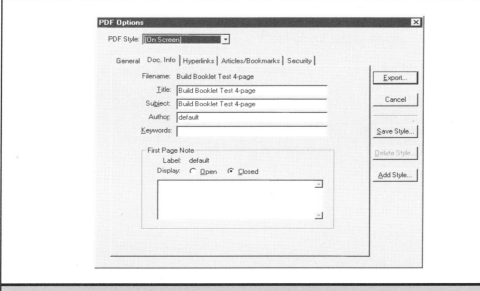

**Figure 19-4.**    *The Doc. Info (Document Information) tab of the PDF Options dialog box*

the Links tab. In this section, you may elect to have other internal hyperlinks (from one point in the document to another) or external hyperlinks (from one point in the document to a document or site on the Web) converted as well.

### Default Appearance

In the Default Appearance section, make your selections from the drop-down menus as to how you want the hyperlinks to appear in the PDF document. Then select the magnification at which you want the linked items to appear when activated.

## Creating Articles and Bookmarks

The fourth tab of the PDF Options dialog box (see Figure 19-6) provides for the creation of articles and bookmarks in the final PDF document. I suppose that these unrelated items share one tab because neither is very long or complicated.

### Creating Articles

An article in a PDF document is much the same as a story in PageMaker. An article is composed of *beads,* just as a story may consist of several text boxes. Converting long stories to articles helps maintain continuity and flow in a final PDF document.

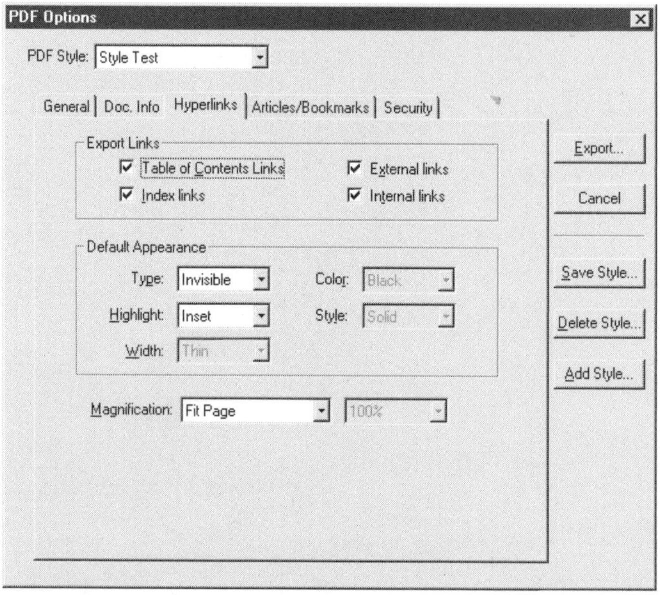

**Figure 19-5.** *The Hyperlinks tab of the PDF Options dialog box*

To allow PDF Distiller to automatically convert stories to articles, follow these steps:

1. Click Export Articles.

    Click in the Export Articles selection box in the Articles section of the PDF Options dialog box.

2. Open the Define Articles dialog box.

    Click the Define Button. The Define Articles dialog box opens.

3. Specify a threshold.

    Enter a number in the One Per Story Over ___ Text Objects box. Only stories containing more than the specified number are converted to articles.

4. Close the Define Articles dialog box.

    Click the OK button. The Define Articles dialog box closes.

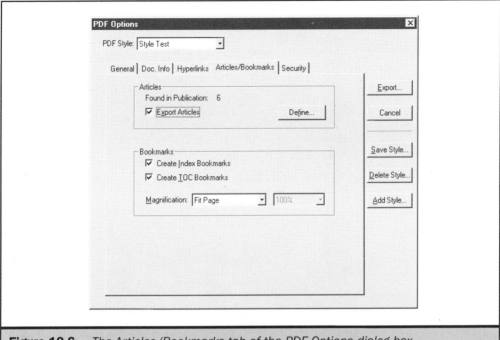

**Figure 19-6.** *The Articles/Bookmarks tab of the PDF Options dialog box*

## Create Bookmarks

Bookmarks are links built into a PDF based on the table of contents and index of a document. Although this is very similar to the hyperlinks for the index and table of contents, they are presented in a different way.

When a PDF file is viewed on a computer monitor, bookmarks, if created, appear in a pane to the left side of the body of the document (see Figure 19-7). The table of contents and index appear in the pane in a tree configuration. The reader can click on the + (plus sign) beside a topic to *expand* the topic and display the items it contains. The reader could click on the − (minus sign) to *collapse* the topic back to one line. The reader just clicks on a subtopic bookmark to move to the place in the document where that subtopic is discussed.

You can have both hyperlinks and bookmarks for the table of contents and index, or you may choose to use one or the other (or neither, of course). Merely click to select the Table of Contents or Index options. Then select an option from the Magnification drop-down menu.

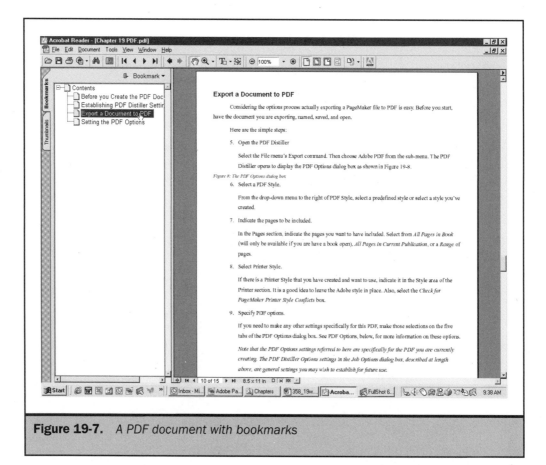

**Figure 19-7.** *A PDF document with bookmarks*

## Security Options

The Security tab of the PDF Options dialog box (see Figure 19-8) provides protection for your PDF if special security is necessary.

### Specify a Password

Select the Required to Open Document option if you want the PDF to be password-protected. Then enter the password in the box provided. You would need to communicate the password to those whom you wish to open it, of course.

If you want to set a master password, select the Required to Change Permissions and Password option and enter the master password. Only those with the master password are authorized to change the password required to open the PDF or change the Permissions settings described in the following section.

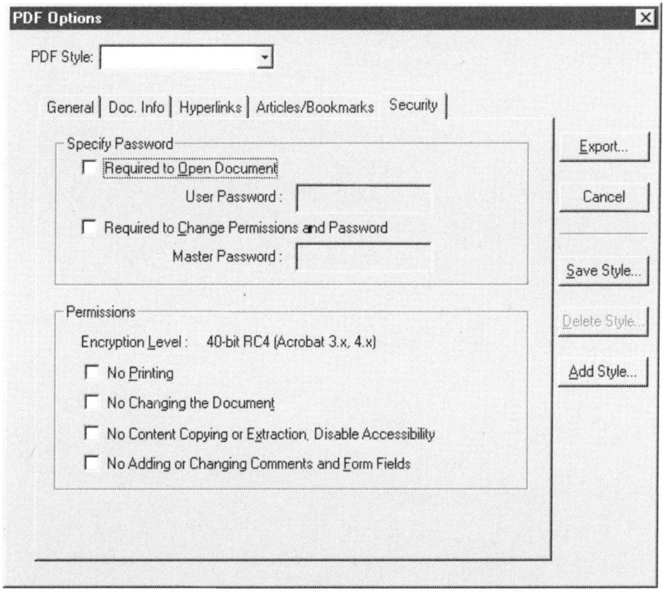

**Figure 19-8.**    *The Security tab of the PDF Options dialog box*

## Permissions

If your Job Options settings establish compatibility with Adobe Acrobat 3.0 or Adobe Acrobat 4.0, the Permissions settings are as shown in Figure 19-13. Consider allowing your readers to print your PDF, although there may be some good reasons to prohibit that. But unless you need viewers to be able to complete a portion of the PDF as a form, I recommend that you invoke the other three restrictions in order to maintain the integrity of your document.

If you have established compatibility with Adobe Acrobat 5.0, you will have a choice of encryption levels. The default is 40-bit encryption that provides the identical options described previously. If, however, you select 128-bit encryption, your choices change to those shown in Figure 19-9.

Select the options appropriate for your document. The Changes Allowed menu provides these choices:

- None
- Only Document Assembly
- Only Form Field Fill-in or Signing

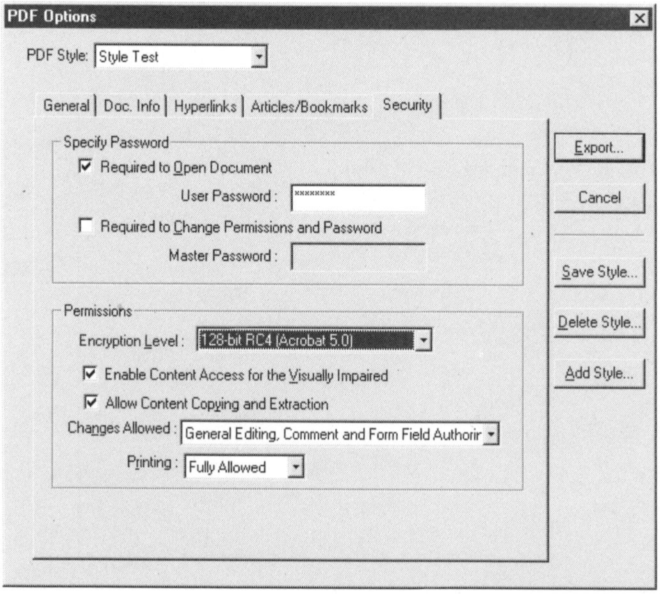

**Figure 19-9.** *Security choices for 128-bit encryption*

- Comment Authoring, Form Field Fill-in, or Signing
- General Editing, Comment, and Form Field Authoring

The Printing menu displays these selections:

- Fully Allowed
- Low Resolution
- Not Allowed

# Saving and Reusing PDF Options Settings

Although I've stated that the PDF Options settings are document specific and are made each time you export a PageMaker document to PDF, they can be saved as a PDF style if you wish to use the same settings frequently.

To save the PDF Options settings, follow these steps:

1. Establish PDF Options settings.

As described in the previous section, select the appropriate options from the five tabs of the PDF Options dialog box.

2.  Open the Save PDF Style dialog box.

    Click the Save Style Button on the PDF Options dialog box. The Save PDF Style box opens (see Figure 19-10), displaying the settings you have selected.

3.  Name the style.

    In the Save Style As box, enter a name for the style.

4.  Save the style.

    Click the Save Button. The Save PDF Style As dialog box closes, returning you to the PDF Options dialog box.

The style is added to the PDF menu for your use again.

**Note**    *The Security settings are not saved with a style. They must be reestablished with each document.*

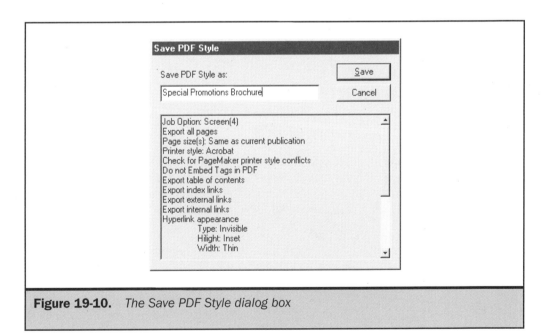

**Figure 19-10.**    *The Save PDF Style dialog box*

MANAGING PAGEMAKER
DOCUMENTS

# Summary

By exporting the PageMaker document as a Portable Document Format (PDF) document, your publication can be downloaded, viewed, and printed by just about any computer system with access to the Internet. Once you have all of the parameters established, the process is almost as easy as sending a document to print on your desktop printer.

**Before You Create the PDF Document**   Before you export the PageMaker document to PDF, you must make certain that the Adobe Acrobat components have been installed. All the software you need for most PDF conversions is available on the PageMaker 7 installation disk.

You must also prepare your PageMaker document for best PDF results. Preparation includes adjusting the PageMaker documents' page numbers to work in a PDF format, selecting colors that are compatible with Internet display, and making sure that the fonts you use are present on your system.

**Establishing PDF Distiller Settings**   PDF Distiller settings can be established at the time the PDF is created, but it is a good idea to establish in advance the settings you will most likely use. The five tabs of the Job Options dialog box provide the setting choices for you to make and save for future use.

**Export a Document to PDF**   The actual process of exporting a PageMaker file to PDF is simple. Use the PDF Options dialog to make any document-specific settings you may want and then export the document. Acrobat Reader opens and your PDF document is displayed on the screen.

**Setting the PDF Options**   Different from the Distiller Job Options settings, the PDF options are those settings that are usually document specific and are selected during the exportation process. However, if you use a lot of PDFs that are very similar, these document-specific settings can be saved and used repeatedly.

The
# Complete
# Reference

PageMaker 7

# Part IV

## Using PageMaker's Advanced Features

The
Complete
Reference

# Chapter 20

## Using Object Linking and Embedding (OLE) in PageMaker

Object Linking and Embedding (OLE) is the niftiest thing in application interaction that I have ever seen. I use it often and can think of many, many ways in which it can be a tremendous timesaver. If you are already familiar with OLE, then this may be old hat to you. But if you are new to the technique, prepare to have your socks knocked off!

OLE is a technique of connecting an object that has been placed into a document (in this case, a PageMaker publication) with its original document or the application in which it was originally created. The purpose of this process is to provide automatic updating of the imported object or ease of access to the originating application for editing the object.

PageMaker 7 is an OLE 2.0 *container*; it is *not* an OLE 2.0 *server*. That means that although PageMaker can receive objects from other OLE sources for linking or embedding, it cannot create them. For example, you can link or embed objects created in Microsoft PowerPoint into PageMaker, but objects created in PageMaker cannot be placed into PowerPoint or any other OLE application, including other PageMaker documents.

Before discussing the how-to's of OLE, it is important to understand the process.

## Understanding OLE

Let's say that at the end of the fiscal year, about a year ago, you prepared an important report in PageMaker. The report is an extensive one with a lot of data from various contributing sources. Within this report are financial projections that were originally prepared in Microsoft Excel spreadsheets. Another part of the report displays your organization's lengthy vision statement. The vision statement, officially maintained in a Microsoft Word document, is reevaluated and edited twice a year. On the first page of the report is the company's logo, originally created in Adobe Illustrator. Although the logo always stays the same, the marketing department has convinced the board to change the colors of the logo annually as a means of symbolizing a renewed pledge to excellence.

Now the current fiscal year is coming to a close, and you are faced with the prospect of updating all of the information. All of the source files are current. You just need to update the report itself. That could be a daunting job.

Because of your foresight and use of PageMaker's OLE capabilities, it is actually a simple task. When you open the PageMaker file that contains the report, the new data is automatically in place, and all you have to do is make any cosmetic changes, change the date, and double-click on the logo to change the colors. The data updates because you used OLE techniques to place files linked to their original document into the report: When the original files are updated, so are the linked objects in PageMaker. And when you double-click the logo, Adobe Illustrator opens so that you can change the logo colors in the originating application.

Now is that cool or what?

OLE is an innovation that saves time and effort, and it is far simpler than it sounds. As the name would imply, Object Linking and Embedding involves two related but separate processes: that of linking and that of embedding. Let me define the terms.

# Linking

A link is a connection that goes directly from the placed object in PageMaker back to the original *document* from which the object is copied. As long as the link is maintained (see the section "Managing Links"), whenever the original document is edited and saved, the object in PageMaker can be updated to reflect the edit. And, depending upon the settings you have established, the update can occur automatically.

# Embedding

Embedding is similar to linking. However, the connection is not back to the document, but to the *application* in which the object was created. If you wish to update an object embedded in a PageMaker document, double-click it, and the object opens *in the original application*, which provides all of the tools needed to affect the edit.

Text that is either linked or embedded into PageMaker cannot be edited in PageMaker; it must be edited using the techniques at the originating application. It is imported as an object and is treated as if it were a graphic, a picture of the original. If you want to import text that can be edited within PageMaker, use either a plain paste action or the File menu's Place command. With either of these methods, there is no connection back to the original document or application, but the text can be edited and manipulated in PageMaker.

# Importing and Updating a Linked Object in PageMaker

Naturally, the first step in utilizing the linking part of PageMaker's OLE capabilities is to import a linked object into a PageMaker document. This is pretty easy and is very similar to a regular copy and paste process but with a twist. For the linked object to update automatically, however, the correct setting must be established. The following sections lead you through these processes.

## Importing a Linked Object

There are two ways in which you may link an object you have placed in PageMaker with its original document. The first involves the Clipboard and is the technique that I recommend:

1.  Copy the object to the Clipboard.

    In the source application, save the file containing the object you wish to place in PageMaker. Then select the object and copy it to the Clipboard. In most

OLE-compatible applications, the Edit menu's Copy command does this. If necessary, refer to the documentation on the originating application.

You may leave the originating document open or closed, whichever is convenient for you.

2. Open the Paste Special dialog box.

   Open the PageMaker document in which you wish the object to be placed. Activate the Pointer tool. Then select the Edit menu's Paste Special command. The Paste Special dialog box opens, as shown next.

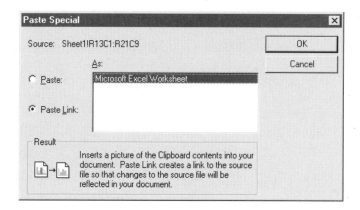

3. Select the Paste Link option.

   On the left side of the Paste Special dialog box, two radio buttons offer you the opportunity to Paste or Paste Link. Select the Paste Link option.

4. Select the object from the As list.

   In the As list in the center of the dialog box, select the appropriate object description. In most cases, once the Paste Link option has been selected, only one object remains in the As list.

   If there is more than one and you are unsure as to which one to choose, select the one that most clearly describes the object you are placing, such as Microsoft Excel Worksheet.

5. Paste the object.

   Click the OK button. The Paste Special dialog box closes, and the object is pasted into your PageMaker document.

An alternative technique is to use the Insert Object dialog box. I find that in this method I have little or no control over the objects I am pasting within an original document, so it is not good for importing a single object among many in an originating file. However, if your original document is simple, it may cut out a step or two. Follow these steps:

1. Open the Insert Object dialog box.

   Click the Edit menu's Insert Object command. The Insert Object dialog box opens, as shown next.

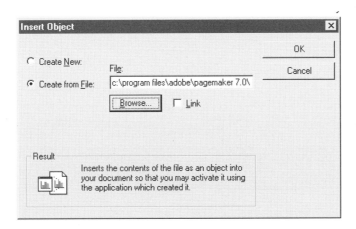

2. Select a file.

   Of the two radio buttons on the left side of the Insert Object dialog box, select Create from File. Then click on the Browse Button. The Browse dialog box opens (see Figure 20-1). Using the Browse dialog box's directory tree, locate and select the file that you want to import into PageMaker. Once the file has been selected, click on the Open Button. The Browse dialog box closes, returning you to the Insert Object dialog box.

3. Select the Link option.

   Click the Link selection box below the File menu box and to the right of the Browse Button.

4. Paste the object.

   Click the OK button. The Insert Object dialog box closes, and the object is inserted into your PageMaker document.

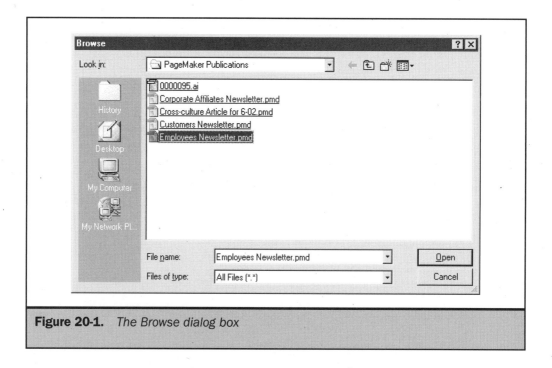

**Figure 20-1.** *The Browse dialog box*

Once a linked object is placed in your PageMaker document, you may move it or size it as you wish. The link is effective as long as the path between the PageMaker document and the original document remains intact. If the PageMaker file containing the linked object or the originating document is moved from the location it was in when the link was created, the link is broken.

## Updating a Linked Object

The most remarkable part of the OLE protocol is when an object in a PageMaker file automatically updates changes that have been made to the object's original document. If an original file has been edited, this will occur automatically only if the appropriate setting has been selected.

Here are the steps to set a linked object to update automatically:

1. Select the linked object.

   Using the Pointer tool, click on the linked object that you wish to update automatically. Sizing handles appear to indicate that it is selected.

2. Open the Link Options dialog box.

   Select the Element menu's Link Options command. The Link Options dialog box opens, as shown in the following illustration.

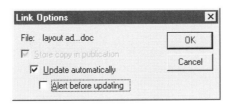

3.  Select Update Automatically.

    Click the Update Automatically check box.

    You may also select Alert Before Updating, if you wish, to require PageMaker
    to notify you with a warning box, shown below, before updating the file.

4.  Close the Link Options dialog box.

    Click the OK button to close the Link Options dialog box. When the original
    document is edited, the changes will also be made to the linked object in your
    PageMaker document.

There may be instances in which you do not want linked objects to update
automatically. You can update those objects manually by following these steps:

1.  Select the object.

    Click on the linked object to select it. Sizing handles appear to indicate that the
    object is selected.

2.  Open the Links Manager.

    Click on the File menu's Links Manager command. The Links Manager dialog
    box opens, as shown in the following illustration.

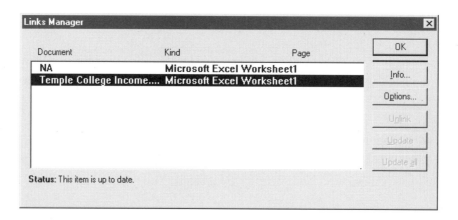

3. Update the linked object.

   The selected object is highlighted on the list. Click the Update Button. The selected Linked Object is updated immediately. The Links Manager dialog box remains open.

   You may update another link in your PageMaker document by selecting the link from the Links Manager list and clicking the Update Button.

**Note** *The Update button is only available if changes have been made to the originating document and the changes to the document have been saved.*

4. Close the Links Manager dialog box.

   Click the OK button on the Links Manager dialog box. The box closes.

## Importing and Updating an Embedded Object in PageMaker

Although the automatic updates that are a part of linking objects are pretty dramatic, embedding objects is an exceptional and remarkable task as well. An embedded object is updated by double-clicking the object in the PageMaker document. The object's originating application then opens with the object in place. You edit the object as you wish, using the originating application to do so.

An advantage of embedding over linking is that with an embedded object, the path between the embedded object and the original document does not need to remain intact. In fact, you can easily move the PageMaker document to another system on disk, but the new system *must* have the originating application installed in order to maintain the connection.

# Importing an Embedded Object

You can embed an existing object in PageMaker, or you can create a new one while working on your PageMaker document.

## Embedding an Existing Object

You will recognize the two techniques of embedding and importing as being *almost* identical to the process described in the section about linking. The difference is just enough to tell PageMaker that you want to embed the object rather than link it. Just as in the discussion on linking, I recommend the first technique over the second and for the same reason.

To embed an object using the Clipboard, follow these steps:

1.  Copy the object to the Clipboard.

    In the source application, save the file containing the object you wish to place in PageMaker. Then select the object and copy it to the Clipboard. In most OLE-compatible applications, the Edit menu's Copy command does this. If necessary, refer to the documentation on the originating application.

    You may leave the originating document open or closed, whichever is convenient for you.

2.  Open the Paste Special dialog box.

    Open the PageMaker document in which you wish the object to be placed. Activate the Pointer tool. Then select the Edit menu's Paste Special command. The Paste Special dialog box opens, as shown next.

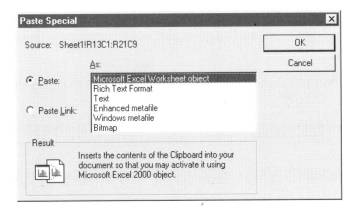

3.  Select the Paste option.

    On the left side of the Paste Special dialog box, two radio buttons offer you the opportunity to Paste or Paste Link. Select the Paste option.

4. Select the object from the As list.

   In the As list in the center of the dialog box, select the appropriate object description. As a rule of thumb, select the item that uses the term *object* as part of the description. This is usually the first item in the list.

5. Paste the object.

   Click the OK button. The Paste Special dialog box closes, and the object is pasted into your PageMaker document.

Another way to import an existing embedded object is to use the Insert Object dialog box. Just as the similar linking technique, embedding an object this way does not allow you to control how much of the object you import. If you are importing an entire file as an object, this may be a good way to do it; otherwise, I recommend that you rely on the Clipboard technique discussed previously.

The following steps lead you through the process of embedding an object in a PageMaker document using the Insert Object dialog box:

1. Open the Insert Object dialog box.

   Click the Edit menu's Insert Object command. The Insert Object dialog box opens, as shown below.

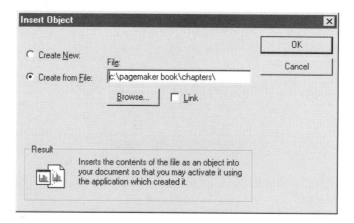

2. Select a file.

   Of the two radio buttons on the left side of the Insert Object dialog box, select Create from File. Then click on the Browse Button. The Browse dialog box opens shown in the following illustration. Using the Browse dialog box's directory tree, locate and select the file that you want to import into PageMaker. Once the file has been selected, click the Open Button. The Browse dialog box closes, returning you to the Insert Object dialog box.

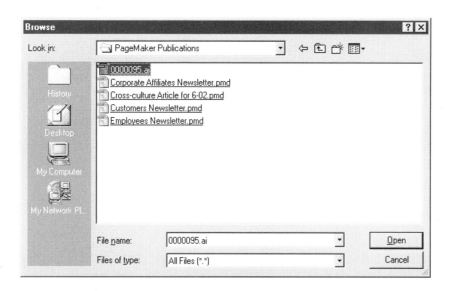

3.  Paste the object.

Click the OK button. The Insert Object dialog box closes, and the file is inserted into your PageMaker document as an object.

## Embedding a New Object

If you are working in PageMaker and realize that you need an object from an outside application that has not yet been created, it is not necessary to leave PageMaker, launch the application, and create the object. You can do it while you work in the PageMaker document. Here's how:

1.  Open the Insert Object dialog box.

Click on the Edit menu's Insert Object command. The Insert Object dialog box opens.

2.  Select Create New.

Of the two radio buttons on the left side of the Insert Object dialog box, select Create New. The Insert Object dialog box reflects the selection by displaying the Object Type list, as shown in Figure 20-2.

3.  Locate the object type.

In the Object Type list, select the application with which you want to create the embedded object.

4.  Click the OK button.

Click the OK button in the Insert Object dialog box. The Insert Object dialog box closes, and the application you selected in the Object Type list opens.

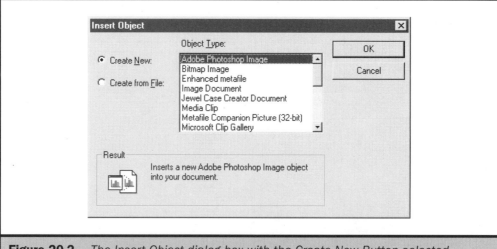

**Figure 20-2.** *The Insert Object dialog box with the Create New Button selected*

5. Create the object.

   Using the application, create the desired object.

6. Close the object.

   Once you have completed the creation of the object, save and close the application, and return to PageMaker. The new object is embedded into the PageMaker document.

## Updating an Embedded Object

Updating an embedded object is as simple as double-clicking the object in PageMaker. The originating application opens with the object in place. All you have to do is make the necessary changes using the originating application. When you return to PageMaker, the embedded object is updated. What could be simpler?

# Managing Links

In PageMaker, there are three functions for managing the connections established by OLE protocols: Links Manager, Link Options, and Link Info. Each of these plays an important part in establishing and maintaining an OLE connection, particularly links.

# Using Links Manager

The Links Manager keeps track of all OLE connections within your document, both links and embedded objects. As mentioned previously in the section, "Importing and Updating a Linked Object in PageMaker," manual updates can be made with this utility. Because the process of manually updating a linked object is an important part of the Links Manager's function, I'm repeating some information here.

The Links Manager is a great source for keeping abreast of the linked or embedded objects that you have in your document. Although embedded objects are listed in the Links Manager's list, they, by their very nature, cannot be updated from the Links Manager dialog box (refer to the section, "Updating an Embedded Object").

You can open the Link Options and the Link Info dialog boxes by clicking the appropriate buttons in the Links Manager.

## Updating Links Manually

If you do not wish your linked object to be updated automatically, do not set the option for Update Automatically in the Links Options dialog box. Then when you want the object to be updated, follow these steps:

1. Select the object.

   Click on the linked object to select it. Sizing handles appear to indicate that the object is selected.

2. Open the Links Manager.

   Click on the File menu's Links Manager command. The Links Manager dialog box opens, as shown below.

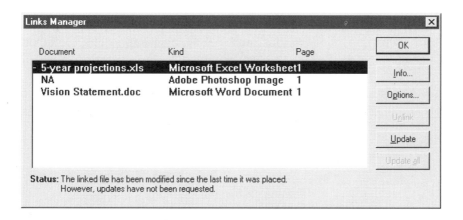

3. Update the linked object.

   The selected object is highlighted on the list. Click the Update Button. The selected linked object is updated immediately. The Links Manager dialog box remains open.

   You may update another link in your PageMaker document by selecting the link from the Links Manager list and clicking the Update Button.

   If you wish to update all links in your document, click the Update All Button.

4. Close the Links Manager dialog box.

   Click the OK button in the Links Manager dialog box. The box closes.

# Using Link Options

The Link Options dialog box concerns linked objects only and changes from one situation to another. In the Link Options dialog box, you establish whether or not you want the linked object to be updated automatically, whether you want to be alerted before an automatic update, and, in the case of linked graphics, whether or not you want the file included as part of the PageMaker document.

## Setting Options Defaults

To set the default status for linked objects, follow these steps:

1. Deselect any linked objects.

   You do not have to have a PageMaker document open to set the defaults for link options. However, if a PageMaker document is open, make sure that no linked objects are selected.

2. Open the Link Options dialog box.

   Click on the Element menu's Link Options command. The Link Options dialog box opens. The following illustration shows an example of the Link Options dialog box opened when no object is selected.

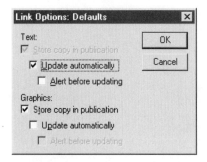

3. Select Link Options.

Make your choices from the following options for both text and graphics:

■ **Update Automatically**   As discussed previously, the selection of this option causes linked objects to be automatically updated when the original document is edited and saved.

■ **Alert Before Updating**   This selection causes a warning box to appear prior to an automatic updating of a linked object. The warning box shown below enables you to choose to update or not update any objects with original documents that have been edited. You can elect to update or not update each object individually, or you may select the Update All or Ignore All Buttons.

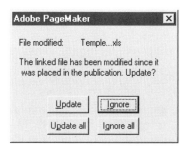

■ **Store Copy in Publication**   Available only for graphics (text is always stored in the publication so you can edit it), this selection causes a graphic file to be stored as part of the document. Select this if you are sending the file electronically for commercial printing. However, it significantly increases the file size. You may wish to deselect this option for PageMaker files that remain on your computer.

4. Close the Link Options dialog box.

Click the OK button. The Link Options dialog box closes, and the default settings are in place.

## Setting Link Options for a Selected Object

Setting link options for selected objects is identical to the setting of defaults (described previously), except that an object is selected, and the settings apply only to that object.

Although nearly identical to the previous list, I'm including the following steps for changing the settings for a selected object:

1. Select a Linked object.

With the PageMaker document open, select the linked object for which you want to set or change the options.

2. Open the Link Options dialog box.

   Click on the Element menu's Link Options command. The Link Options dialog box opens. The following illustration shows an example of the Link Options dialog box opened when an object is selected.

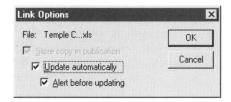

3. Select Link Options.

   Make your choices from the following options:

   ■ **Update Automatically**   As discussed previously, the selection of this option causes linked objects to be automatically updated when the original document is edited and saved.

   ■ **Alert Before Updating**   This selection causes a warning box to appear prior to an automatic updating of a linked object. The warning box shown below enables you to choose to update or not update any objects with original documents that have been edited. You can elect to update or not update each object individually, or you may select the Update All or Ignore All Buttons.

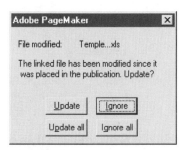

   ■ **Store Copy in Publication**   Available only for graphics (text is always stored in the publication so you can edit it), this selection causes a graphic file to be stored as part of the document. Select this if you are sending the file electronically for commercial printing. However, it significantly increases the file size. You may want to deselect this option for PageMaker files that remain on your computer.

4.  Close the Link Options dialog box.

    Click the OK button. The Link Options dialog box closes. The default settings
    are in place.

# Using Link Info

The Link Info dialog box provides information, not about the object, but about the link.
The dialog box shows you where on your system you can find the linked or embedded
object's original document. You may also use Link Info to reestablish a broken link.

## Relinking a Broken Link

In the "Importing a Linked Object" section, it was mentioned that if you moved either
the linked object or its original document, the link would be broken. I rearrange my
hard drive regularly to keep it organized and in order. Occasionally, I forget about a
document's links and break them in the organization process. Here is how you can
reestablish the link:

1.  Select the linked object.

    In the PageMaker document, select the object with the broken link.

2.  Open the Link Info dialog box.

    Click the Element menu's Link Info command. The Link Info dialog box opens,
    as shown in Figure 20-3.

3.  Select the file.

    Using the directory tree, locate the original document to which the selected
    object was linked. Double-click or click once to select and then click the Open
    button. The Link Info dialog box closes, and the link is reestablished.

**Note**

*Using the Link Info dialog box, you can change the document to which the object is
linked. If you have linked a complete file, the switch to another file should be smooth. Just
click on the file you want. However, if you have linked a portion of a file, the new link will
display a portion of the new file in about the same position on the page as the original.
This can lead to a mess. It is usually better to delete a linked object and reinsert a new
one.*

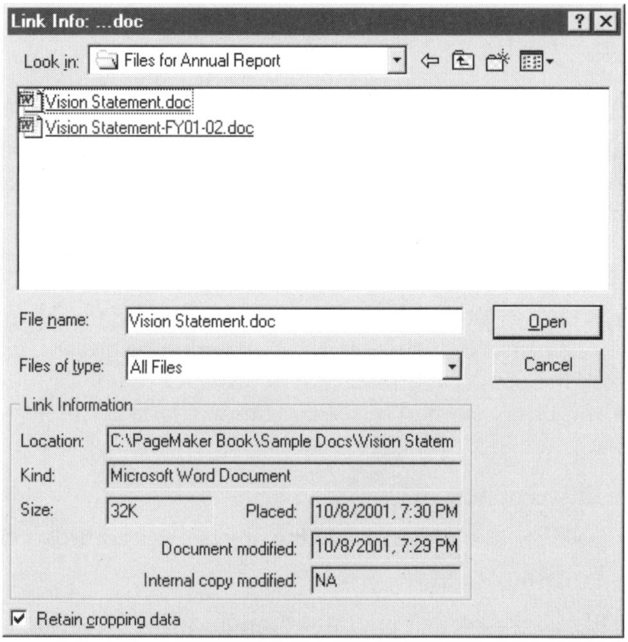

**Figure 20-3.** The Link Info dialog box

# Summary

Object Linking and Embedding (OLE) is a remarkable innovation that enables instant updates of PageMaker objects that are pasted from another application.

**Understanding OLE** If you are responsible for documents that have to be updated from time to time, OLE can save you a lot of time and energy. Placing objects that are connected to their original documents or applications makes updating your document a snap. *Linking* means that a connection exists to the object's original document. *Embedding* is a connection to the `application` in which the object was originally created.

**Importing and Updating a Linked Object in PageMaker** Placing a linked object in a PageMaker document can be as simple as the copy and paste operation of the

Clipboard. Updating can occur automatically if you set the options to do so, or you can manually update the object if you wish.

**Importing and Updating an Embedded Object in PageMaker**    It is just as easy to embed an object as it is to link one. You just make slightly different selections, and the connection is set to the originating application. When you want to update an embedded object, all you have to do is double-click it. The originating application opens, providing you with the tools to make the changes you want.

**Managing Links**    PageMaker provides you with three utilities for managing the connection between linked or embedded objects and their original document or application:

- **Links Manager**    This utility lists all of the OLE connections in a PageMaker document. If a linked object's original document has been edited, you can use the Links Manager to affect an update.

- **Link Options**    Use this to establish the settings for automatic updating and inclusion in the document.

- **Link Info**    This utility enables you to see where the originating document of a linked or embedded object is located. You can also use the Link Info dialog box to repair a broken link or change the document to which an object is linked.

# The Complete Reference

PageMaker 7

# Chapter 21

## Using a Color Management System (CMS) with PageMaker

In Chapter 11, I mentioned that when selecting the spot colors for your document, you should choose them from a color matching system swatch book, never from their appearance on your computer monitor. That, of course, is because the colors produced by your monitor are often significantly different from those produced by your printer. And the monitor colors may also differ from the matching system colors found in a swatch book.

A Color Management System (CMS) is a technology that helps you solve many of the problems associated with reproducing the same color on different devices, within different applications, and on different platforms.

# Why Use a CMS?

Today's technology provides us with powerful ways of managing and producing colors. But in spite of all the high-tech solutions, there is still the basic problem with computer color: What you see is not necessarily what you get. The color of an original image scanned into a computer is not necessarily what is shown on your computer monitor and may not be what you get when that image is output from a desktop printer or even produced by a commercial printer. The differences are caused by the color spectrum (called a *gamut*) of each device and its color profile. Some differences occur because monitors use the red, green, and blue (RGB) color model. Desktop printers may use either RGB or cyan, magenta, yellow, and black (CMYK), while high-resolution imagers and separators work with CMYK. Translating RGB into CMYK, or vice versa, results in inaccurate colors. A CMS compares the color gamut in which a color was created to the gamut of the output device or devices and essentially serves as a translator between them.

Is this important? In some cases, it is very important and in others it is just a matter of inconvenience. Consider these scenarios:

- *You are using PageMaker to create a brochure that you are producing on your desktop inkjet printer.*

  In this situation, getting the colors right is somewhat important. If you cannot judge the colors in the brochure to some extent on your computer monitor, then there is no telling what the final brochure will look like. Of course, you might like the colors that the printer produces. And when you print on a desktop printer, it is relatively easy to print a sample, adjust colors, and print again without the expenditure of much time or money. Coordination between the monitor and desktop printer would make it easier, however.

- *You are having your PageMaker flyer commercially printed using spot colors. You have picked the spot colors from a CMS swatch book at the printer.*

  Here the colors onscreen in your PageMaker document don't really matter. The final colors are mixed by the printer and applied at printing.

- *PageMaker is the layout application for a full-color catalog that you are having commercially printed. The printer uses color separations to apply CMYK inks for a four-color process job.*

In four-color process printing, like in spot colors, it is the printing press and the ink that the press operator applies to the press that create the color. Transparent inks in CMYK are printed one on top of the other to produce full color. However, before this can be done, the images in your document must be separated into CMYK so that the press applies the right amount of each color.

When process color separations come into play, it is important to have the colors accurately represented in your document because it is the colors that are recorded in the electronic document that are used for the separations.

Color management synchronizes the colors in your document with the gamut of the input devices (scanners, cameras, and so on) and the output device (separation printers) to ensure reliable color when the separations are made. What you see on the monitor is less important than how the final printed product will look. However, coordinating the color gamut of the device or devices used to input the process images with the gamut of your monitor allows you to see close approximates of the results of printing ahead of time.

- *A document is created in PageMaker for onscreen viewing. This presentation is crucial to your organization's future and it must look just right.*

For a presentation such as this, of course, accurate color is particularly important, especially if corporate colors are involved. It is important to coordinate the gamuts of the devices used to input images into the presentation with the monitor.

Now I've already said that you cannot depend on the colors on your monitor screen, and even a CMS is not going to totally change that. But it can help a lot. As I mentioned before, a CMS compares the color gamut in which a color was created to the gamut of the output device or devices and essentially serves as a translator between them. Be sure to turn on PageMaker's CMS.

A CMS comes as a part of PageMaker. The Kodak Digital Science CMS complies with guidelines established by the International Color Consortium (ICC) and is ready to use as soon as PageMaker is installed. By default, the CMS is off. All you have to do is turn it on and set the preferences.

It is possible to purchase CMSs produced by a number of software companies. I find that the Kodak Digital Science system works well for my needs.

The following steps lead you through the process of activating PageMaker's CMS:

1. Open the Preferences dialog box.

   Select the File menu's Preferences command and the General item from the submenu. The Preferences dialog box opens, as shown in the following illustration.

USING PAGEMAKER'S
ADVANCED FEATURES

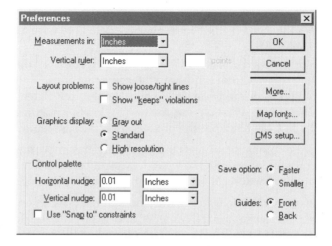

2. Open the Color Management System Preferences dialog box.

   Click on the CMS Set Up Button on the right side of the Preferences dialog box. The Color Management System Preferences dialog box opens (see Figure 21-1).

3. Turn the CMS on.

   Using the drop-down menu in the Color Management box, select On. If you have more than one CMS installed on your system, you may select the appropriate one from the icons on the left side of the dialog box. Clicking an icon turns on the CMS that it represents.

4. Close the Color Management System Preferences dialog box.

   You may close the dialog box by clicking OK. Then close the Preferences dialog box by clicking OK. The CMS is activated with defaults in place. However, you may change the default settings by selecting any or all of the options described in the following section before closing.

# Setting CMS Preferences

It is a good idea to set the preferences for the CMS. There are many ways in which a CMS can manage colors in a PageMaker document, which are all dependent upon the purpose of your document and its intended output. The following list discusses the various settings for the CMS:

■ **Monitor Simulates**   Select this from the drop-down menu.

   If you select Composite Printer, your monitor will reflect (as close as possible) the way an image will look when printed on a composite printer (a final output printer such as a desktop inkjet).

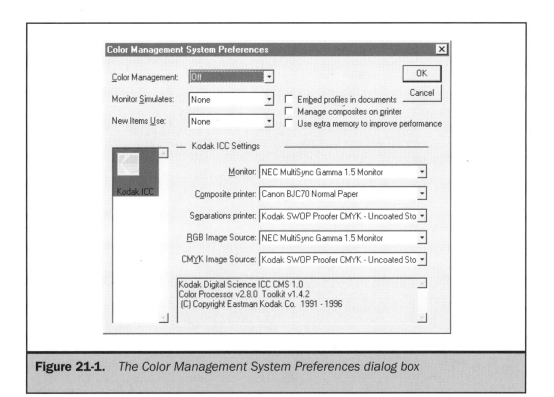

**Figure 21-1.** *The Color Management System Preferences dialog box*

If you select Separations Printer, the color gamut of the printer where the CMYK separations are produced for film or plates will be displayed on the monitor. If you are printing the separations on your desktop printer (for review, perhaps), select it. If the commercial printer is providing the separations, you may leave this at the default setting or get the information from the printer. The actual separations are not shown, however.

■ **New Items Use**   Your choices in this section are None or CMS. (If you have used the CMSs before, Kodak ICC or the names of other CMSs will appear, rather than the more generic CMS.) If you select CMS, PageMaker automatically assigns color management settings to colors as you add them to the Colors Palette's color list, documents, and imported bitmap images that do not have embedded profiles. Whether you select CMS or not depends upon how often you use CMS.

■ **Embed Profiles in Documents**   If you are saving a PageMaker document to send to another computer (perhaps the commercial printer's system), select this option. Then all of the settings you have produced are carried with the file. However, deselect this option as soon as you have created the copy of the file to send away. If you leave this option selected, it will significantly affect your computer's operations.

■ **Manage Composites on Printer** If you are printing to a PostScript device (Level 2 or 3), then you will want to select this option. This will pass the color management to the printer. Do not select this option if you are sending the file to a commercial printer that has not requested that you do so or if you are printing on your desktop.

■ **Use Extra Memory to Improve Performance** If your computer is equipped with a large amount of RAM, selecting this option can speed up the color management process. However, it can also slow down your system if it puts a strain on your memory resources.

The following options are device profiles. You may not be able to find the exact devices that you are using. In that case, choose the closest possible, leave the default setting, or contact the device manufacturer for a device profile.

■ **Monitor** Select the monitor type that most closely approximates the color characteristics of your monitor.

■ **Composite Printer** Whether you are producing the final document on a printer or just using it for proofing, locate the setting closest to the printer you are using. This, of course, is a printer that prints all page elements on one page.

■ **Separations Printer** You may need to obtain information on the printer that will produce the final separations from your commercial printer.

■ **RGB Image Source** This can be a scanner, a digital camera, or a monitor. If the majority of the RGB images in your document are produced on a camera or scanner, locate the profile that comes as close to that device as possible.

■ **CMYK Image Source** This is the same as the previous one. Just select the profile for the device you use most to produce images in CMYK.

# Adding Device Profiles

If you have obtained device profiles that are not available in the profile lists discussed previously, install those profiles by copying them in the system folder appropriate to your system:

- **Windows NT/Windows 2000**   Copy files to the folder found through the following path: Windows 2000 (or Windows NT)\System32\Color.

- **Windows 98 or ME**   Copy files to the folder found through this path: Windows (or Windows ME)\System\Color.

# Working with Color Profiles

Not only are device profiles affected by color management, but colors are also affected. Spot colors and process colors are managed differently. The CMS adjusts the values of a color to correspond as closely as possible to the color gamut of either the separations printer (process colors) or the computer monitor (RGB or hue, lightness, saturation, [HLS] color models). This attempt to match the color gamut is called a color profile.

If your CMS is activated and if you have selected CMS in the New Items Use option in the CMS preferences, any new colors created are automatically assigned a color profile by the CMS. However, if you wish to create a color profile for colors you create when the New Items Use option is not selected, you may do so.

## Managing Spot Colors

As mentioned, the only reason you need to color manage spot colors is to get a closer approximation of the colors on your monitor. Color management will not affect the final outcome in commercially printed documents because, in spot colors, it is the inks, mixed by the commercial printer, that create the final color.

If you want the colors on the monitor to more closely resemble those the printer will apply in final production, create a color profile for any colors from color matching libraries as you add them to your color list by following these steps:

1. Turn Color Management on.

   Make sure that your CMS is active. If necessary, turn the CMS on by following the steps listed previously.

2. Open the Colors Palette.

   Click the Window menu's Show Colors command. The Colors Palette opens, as shown in Figure 21-2.

3. Open the Colors Palette menu.

   Click on the right-pointing arrow to the right of the Colors Palette and below the Exit Button. The Colors Palette menu appears (see Figure 21-3).

4. Open the Color Options dialog box.

   Click the New Color command. The Color Options dialog box opens, as shown in Figure 21-4.

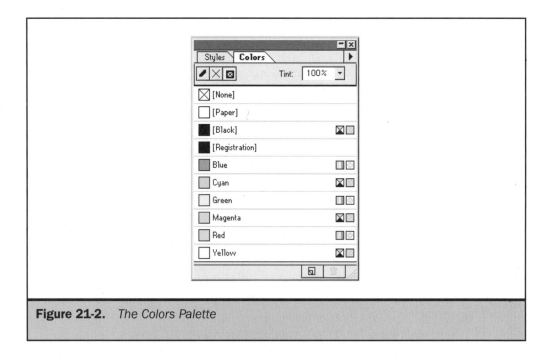

**Figure 21-2.**    *The Colors Palette*

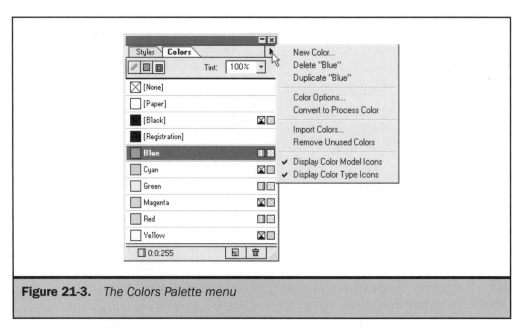

**Figure 21-3.**    *The Colors Palette menu*

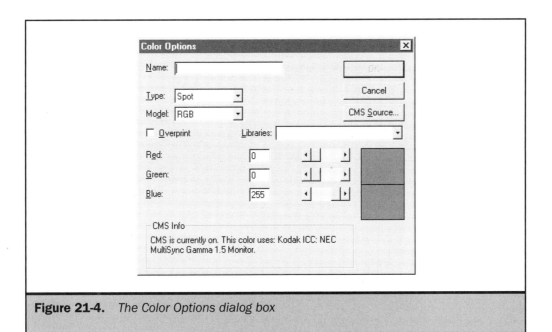

**Figure 21-4.**   *The Color Options dialog box*

5. Select a color library.

   Click on the drop-down menu beside the Libraries box to select a color library. The Color Picker dialog box opens and the library you have selected is displayed (see Figure 21-5).

6. Select a spot color.

   Using the scroll bar at the bottom of the Color Picker window, peruse the colors available until you locate the color you want to use. Double-click the color or select it and click OK. The Color Picker dialog box closes, returning you to the Color Options box.

7. Open the CMS Source Profile dialog box.

   Click the CMS Source Button on the right side of the Color Options dialog box. The CMS Source Profile dialog box opens, as shown in Figure 21-6.

8. Assign color management to the color.

   If the dialog box specifies that this color uses None, click the drop-down arrow next to the This Color Uses box and select the CMS you want to use. Unless you have installed other CMS software on your system, the only choice available to you is Kodak ICC. The CMS Source Profile dialog box then changes to reflect the source profile and rendering intent, as shown in Figure 21-7.

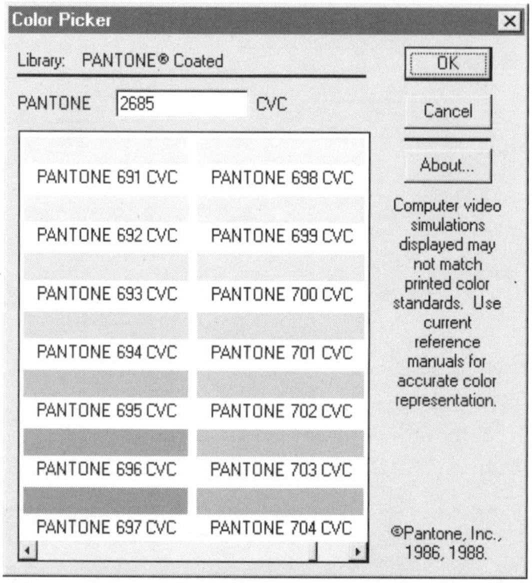

**Figure 21-5.** The Color Picker dialog box

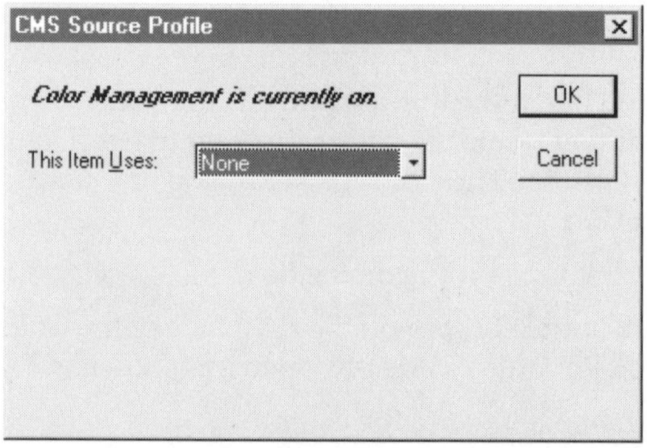

**Figure 21-6.** The CMS Source Profile dialog box

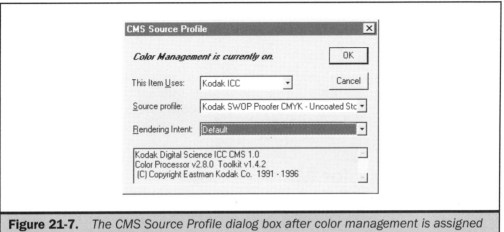

**Figure 21-7.**    *The CMS Source Profile dialog box after color management is assigned to the color*

9. Select the profile options.

   Select the profiles that are in keeping with your document and the monitor:

   ■ **Source Profile**    If the selected color is RGB, choose the same device profile you assigned to your monitor. If you are working with a CMYK spot color, choose the separation printer as the source profile. You can tell which kind of color it is by looking at the Type and Model boxes in the dialog box.

   ■ **Render Intent**    These settings determine the way in which the CMS balances two device color gamuts. *Image* incorporates a technique that best coordinates the color gamuts for photographs. *Graphics* is best for simple graphics and illustrations. *Colorimetric* is a process through which colors that are outside of the target profile's gamut are incorporated into it, causing some changes in the colors. Colors that overlap in the two gamuts are not changed.

10. Close the CMS Source Profile dialog box.

    Click OK in the CMS Source Profile dialog box. The box closes, returning you to the Color Options dialog box. The name of the selected color is placed in the Name box in the Color Options dialog box.

11. Make changes to the color.

    If you want, you may make changes to the color, selecting from the RGB, HLS, or CMYK models. If you do change the color, make sure to enter a new name so that the name will accurately reflect the color.

USING PAGEMAKER'S
ADVANCED FEATURES

12. Close the Color Options dialog box.

Click OK and the Color Options dialog box closes.

## Managing Process Colors

You can assign color management to process colors as long as you always select the profile of your separations printer as the color's source profile. The colors in CMYK images that will be separated should not be altered because their colors are predetermined to achieve the most accurate results.

# Turning Off Color Management

There may be times when you will want to use color management to improve the display of color on your screen as a publication is developed, but do not want to use it for final production. An example would be if your commercial printer or service provider is using a postprocessing application to create the process color separations. (Most printers include this in their service.)

Here's how to turn the CMS off:

1. Open the Preferences dialog box.

    Select the File menu's Preferences command and the General item from the submenu. The Preferences dialog box opens.

2. Open the Color Management System Preferences dialog box.

    Click the CMS Setup Button on the right side of the Preferences dialog box. The Color Management System Preferences dialog box opens.

3. Turn the CMS off.

    Using the drop-down menu in the Color Management box, select Off.

# Creating a Color-Managed Work Environment

There are steps you can take to ensure that the colors you see on your monitor are as close to the intended color as they can be. A lot of the distortion of colors comes from the environment in which they are viewed instead of the monitor itself. Just follow these steps:

1. View your PageMaker document in consistent light. Changes in ambient artificial lighting and sunlight can make great changes in the appearance of colors on your screen. Sunlight is always cheerful and comforting, but if you want to see colors accurately on your computer monitor, keeps the shades drawn.

Fluorescent lighting can also project a yellow cast on your monitor screen, distorting colors. If possible, replace fluorescent bulbs with lamps that do not project this cast.

2. View your publication in a neutral-colored environment. The walls and ceiling of your office contribute to the color of the elements of your document. As dull as it may be, a neutral gray is the best wall color for viewing colors on your computer.

3. Remove any busy or bright backgrounds on your desktop. Select a desktop composed of shades of gray.

4. Adjust the brightness and contrast settings on your monitor. Black should appear as true black without causing the surrounding area to appear gray.

# Summary

Color management helps you solve many of the problems associated with reproducing the same color on different devices, within different applications, and on different platforms. The Color Management System (CMS) that is a part of PageMaker 7 is the Kodak Digital Science CMS.

**What Is a CMS?**    Today's technology provides many ways of creating and applying colors to documents, but each device that you use to do so (scanners, digital cameras, printers, imagesetters, and so on) handles color in a different way. Each device has a range of color called a gamut. Color management helps to reconcile the differences between one device and another.

**Turn On PageMaker's CMS**    PageMaker's CMS, by default, is not activated when PageMaker is installed; however, turning on the CMS and setting the options is a simple operation.

**Adding Device Profiles**    The work of a CMS is based on adjusting differences in device profiles. Many device profiles are included in PageMaker's CMS; however, additional device profiles can be obtained from the manufacturer and installed into PageMaker's system.

**Working with Color Profiles**    Not only are devices affected by color management, but colors are affected as well. As each new color is added to your color list, color profiles may be added automatically or manually.

USING PAGEMAKER'S
ADVANCED FEATURES

**Turning Off Color Management**   Sometimes you just don't want a CMS to be activated. PageMaker's CMS is easily deactivated until you want to use it again.

**Creating a Color-Managed Work Environment**   If you want to make sure that the colors on your computer monitor are as accurate as possible, there are steps you can take within your office or computing environment. The type of lighting you use, the color of the walls, and the amount of sunshine available all affect the way you see colors on your monitor screen.

# The Complete Reference

PageMaker 7

# Chapter 22

## PageMaker's Color Separation Capabilities

527

In previous chapters, I have mentioned PageMaker's remarkable capability to produce color separations for both spot color and process color printing. This is, indeed, a remarkable feat and one that those of us who have used PageMaker from its earliest day applaud.

Quite honestly, however, in today's high-tech world, the capability to create separations on your desktop is becoming less and less critical. Why? Because more and more commercial printers use technology that creates separations as a part of making the plates with which the final product is printed. Instead of taking paste-up layouts to your commercial printer to photograph and turn into plates, you take an electronic file from which separations and printing plates are generated.

## Why Are Separations Necessary?

In order to understand color separations, you must first understand the commercial printing process. The printing process is discussed in part in various locations throughout this book. But I'm discussing it again here so that there is a clear understanding of the role that color separations play in the final printed product.

### Printing with a Printing Press

In order for a document to be printed, a plate is created that contains the reverse image of the document's layout. The plate is then attached to a revolving cylinder (called a press head) on a printing press, and ink is added to the cylinder's reservoir. As paper stock passes through the press, ink is added to the plate and the press head revolves, placing the ink onto the paper. If the document is a one-color piece, the job is completed. At least the printing part of a job is finished. Drying, perforating, folding, binding, and other jobs may still need to be done.

If a print job has two or more colors, a plate is created for each color. Only the items that are to be printed in a specific color appear on the plate attached to the press head for that color. When the paper stock goes through the press, first one color and then another is applied, until all the colors have been printed. If the printing press that is being used has only one press head, the first color is applied to all of the paper stock. Then the press is washed down, new ink and a new plate are added, and the stock is run through the press again. This continues, of course, until the job is complete.

Commercial printers with single-headed presses rarely print more than two colors because of the time and extra expense of washing down the press between each job. But most commercial printers have multiple-headed presses that can do a job in one pass.

The plate for each color is created from a separation, the result of a process in which the colors of a document are divided so that only the items to be printed in a single color appear together. If a document uses three spot colors, three seps (separations) are created from which plates are made for printing. In today's high-tech world, most commercial printers use technology that separates the colors and creates the plates in one step.

If you wish to produce a realistic full-color document, the process color separation is critical. In this case, the colors in the images are separated into four colors from which all the colors in the image are composed: Cyan, Magenta, Yellow, and Black (CMYK). The separation process determines how much of each of the four colors is applied as it passes through the press heads. The combination of the four colors, printed one on top of another, creates the final full-color print.

## Why Use PageMaker to Create Separations?

If the best way to get separations is to let your commercial printer do it, why bother with separations in PageMaker at all?

The primary reason for separating spot colors is for proofing purposes. Using PageMaker, you can print spot color separations and check to see if everything you want printed in black is on the black print, and the reds (or blues or greens and so on) are on the appropriate print. Even with process separations, commercial printers print copies of the separations as proofs to make sure that all items are where they should be.

If you use a commercial printer that does not automatically create the separations from your PageMaker file, you can take separation prints to the commercial printer for use in making plates. Keep in mind that each color's print will be in black, not the selected color, because it is the black on white that is photographed to make the plate. The press, of course, adds the color. For best results, if you produce the separations yourself, use the highest resolution setting possible on your printer and a high-quality coated paper, much like you would use in producing photographs. Remember to place registration marks on each color separation print (see Chapter 28).

Creating your own separations for process printing is not a good idea unless you can print to an imagesetter, a machine that produces extremely high-resolution images to film. PageMaker is perfectly capable of separating accurately; it is the resolution of most printers that may affect the quality.

If you have the option of printing to an imagesetter, creating your own separations is feasible. The quality produced by such a high-resolution imaging machine is frequently used in the production of printing plates.

## Spot Color Separations

If you want to print spot color separations for proofing, follow these steps:

1. Open the Print dialog box.

   Click the File menu's Print command. The Print dialog box opens, as shown in Figure 22-1.

2. Open the Print Color dialog box.

   Click the Color Button on the right side of the Print dialog box. The Print Color dialog box opens (see Figure 22-2).

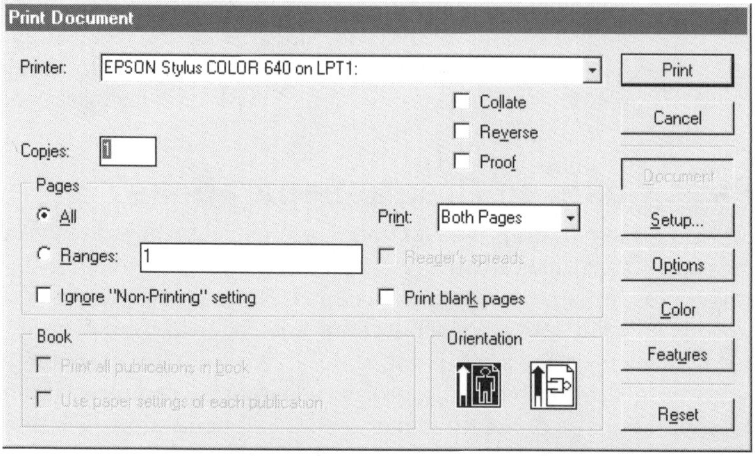

**Figure 22-1.** *The Print dialog box*

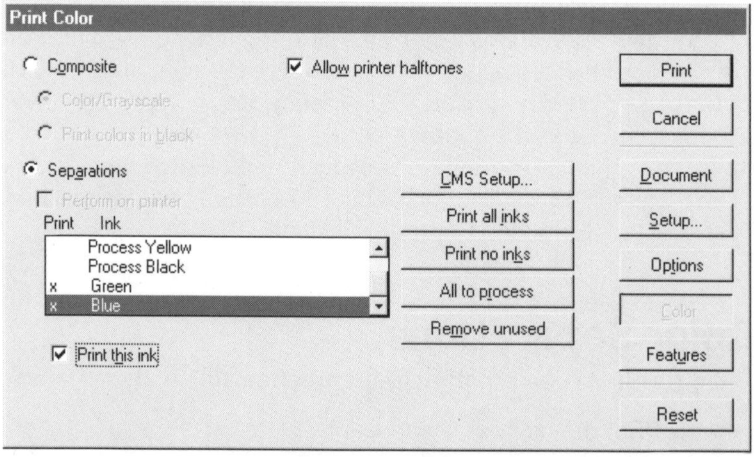

**Figure 22-2.** *The Print Color dialog box*

3. Select the Separations option.

   Click on the Separations option to select it. The colors present on your Color List in your document's Colors Palette are shown in the list below the headings Print and Ink along with the colors Process Cyan, Process Magenta, Process Yellow, and Process Black.

4. Remove unused colors.

   If your document's Color List contains colors that are not used in your publication, it is a good idea to remove them. Click the Remove Unused Button to the right of the list of colors. A confirmation message appears, asking you to confirm the removal of unused colors (see the following illustration). You may select Yes or No to confirm or decline the removal of each color, one at a time, or you may click Yes to All or No to All to confirm or decline all unused colors. Even though you are not going to use the four process colors in spot separations, they are not removed as part of this step.

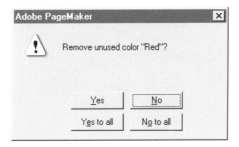

Once you have confirmed removal of the unused colors, another message box appears, informing you of the number of colors removed (see below). Click OK to close.

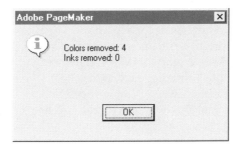

USING PAGEMAKER'S
ADVANCED FEATURES

5. Select the spot colors for separation.

Spot colors are easily identified because they are any color other than the four process colors. Click each color to select it. Then select or deselect the selection box in the Print This Ink option.

Notice that for every color that has Print This Ink selected, an X has appeared in the Print column of the list of colors.

Since this is a spot color separation, deselect Print This Ink for all four of the process colors and make sure that the X appears by each of the spot colors in your document.

6. Open the Print Options dialog box.

Click the Options Button on the right side of the Print Colors dialog box. The Print Options dialog box opens, as shown below.

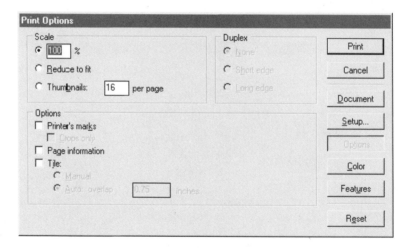

7. Select Printer's Marks.

If you are going to take the color separation prints to a commercial printer for printing or are printing with an imagesetter, place the printer's marks (registration marks and crop marks) on the documents. Registration marks enable the printer to align the separations exactly on top of one another. Also, since printed pieces are frequently produced on larger sheets of paper and trimmed to their final size, the crop marks tell the printer where to cut to produce the correct final size.

One of the problems with producing the separations yourself is this: If your final product is to be printed on letter size (8.5 × 11 inch) paper stock and if that is the size your desktop printer produces, the printer's marks will not be seen. The marks will appear outside the area of the final product.

To place the printer's marks on your document, click the Printer's Marks box. If you want crop lines only, not the registration marks, you may select the Crops Only selection box.

8.  Set the resolution of your printer.

    If you are printing color separations for proofing only, skip this step. However, if you are planning to take the separation prints to your commercial printer for printing, you need to give him or her the best possible image from which to make plates.

    Click the Setup Button in the Print Options dialog box and establish the settings particular to your printer that will give the best resolution possible. Each printer's Print Setup dialog box is different from another. The following illustration shows the Setup dialog box (labeled Epson Stylus Color 640 Properties) for my personal desktop printer. You will also want to use a high-quality coated paper for the separations, such as that used for photographs.

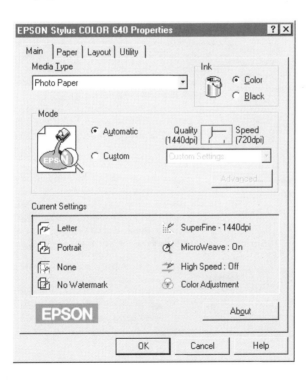

9. Print the separations.

Place the photo-quality paper in the desktop printer. Click the Print Button on the right side of the dialog box. The separations are sent to your printer.

Figure 22-3 shows the original document (you may see this document in color in the color insert section of this book).

**Figure 22-3.** *An original document and its three spot color separations*

# Process Color Separations

Although process color separations are difficult to use for proofing, you can print them out to see how the technique works. Or if you have an imagesetter, you can print the color seps to film. To do either, follow these steps:

1. Open the Print dialog box.

   Click the File menu's Print command. The Print dialog box opens, as shown below.

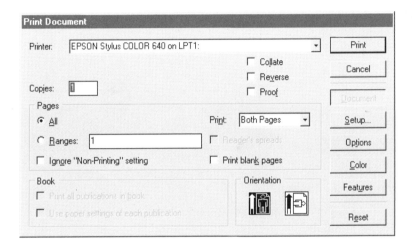

2. Open the Print Color dialog box.

   Click the Color Button on the right side of the Print dialog box. The Print Color dialog box opens (see Figure 22-4).

3. Select the Separations option.

   Click the Separations option to select it. The colors present on your Color List in your document's Colors Palette are shown in the list below the headings Print and Ink along with the colors Process Cyan, Process Magenta, Process Yellow, and Process Black.

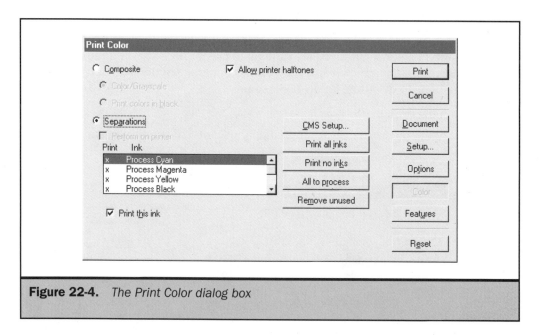

**Figure 22-4.** *The Print Color dialog box*

4. Remove unused colors.

   If you want, you may remove the colors from your Color List that are not used. Click the Remove Unused Button to the right of the list of colors. A confirmation message appears, asking you to confirm the removal of unused colors (shown below). You may select Yes or No to confirm or decline the removal of each color, one at a time, or you may click Yes to All or No to All to confirm or decline all unused colors.

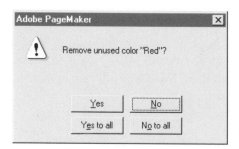

5. Select the process colors for separation.

   Click each process and then select or deselect the selection box in the Print This Ink option.

   Notice that for every color for which Print This Ink is selected, an X has appeared in the Print column of the list of colors.

   Since this is a process color separation, select Print This Ink for all four of the process colors.

6. Open the Print Options dialog box.

   Click the Options Button on the right side of the Print Colors dialog box. The Print Options dialog box opens, as shown in Figure 22-5.

7. Select Printer's Marks.

   If you are printing with an imagesetter, place the printer's marks (registration marks and crop marks) on the documents. Registration marks enable the printer to align the separations exactly on top of one another. Also, since printed pieces are frequently produced on larger sheets of paper and trimmed to their final size, the crop marks tell the printer where to cut to produce the correct final size.

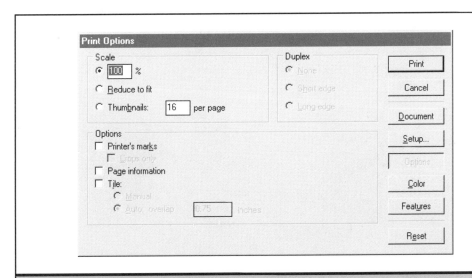

**Figure 22-5.** *The Print Options dialog box*

If you are printing for proofing purposes, you will probably not see the printer's marks. If your final product is to be produced on letter size (8.5 × 11 inch) paper stock and if that is the size your desktop printer produces, the printer's marks will not show. The marks appear outside the area of the final product.

To place the printer's marks on your document, click the Printer's Marks box. If you want crop lines only, not the registration marks, you may select the Crops Only selection box.

8. Set the resolution of your printer.

If you are printing color separations for proofing only, this step is not necessary unless you want very high-quality proofs. If you are using an imagesetter, follow the procedures for setting the resolution for that machine.

Click the Setup Button in the Print Options dialog box and establish the settings particular to your printer that will provide the best resolution possible.

9. Print the separations.

Place the photo-quality paper in the desktop printer. Click the Print Button on the right side of the dialog box. The separations are sent to your printer.

Figure 22-6 shows an original document (you may see this document in color in the color insert section of this book) and the resulting process color separations.

Cyan separation        Magenta separation

**Figure 22-6.** *An original document and its four process color separation prints*

Yellow separation

Black separation

Original

**Figure 22-6.**  *An original document and its four process color separation prints*

# Summary

Obtaining color separations, particularly for full-color documents, used to be a big—and very expensive—deal. Today PageMaker can easily do the separations for you. However, unless you are a commercial printer or have the luxury of an imagesetter, using PageMaker's color separation capabilities is not necessary. Why? Because most commercial printers do the separations for you as part of the printing process.

**Why Are Separations Necessary?**   Separations are needed because a document has to run through a press head on a printing press for each color printed. The colors must be separated out so that individual plates can be made to apply a specific color to a printed piece in just the right place and in just the right amount.

**Spot Color Separations**   You may wish to print spot color separations in order to proof your document or, if your commercial printer does not have the technology to do the separations for you, so that the commercial printer can photograph the separations to make the color plates.

**Process Color Separations**   For the untrained eye, it is difficult to proof process color separations printed on a desktop printer. But it is an interesting process and you may want to do it so that you can see the results. If you are printing to an imagesetter, use the steps in this chapter to create process separations.

The
# Complete
# Reference

PageMaker 7

# Part V

## Using PageMaker with Other Programs

# Chapter 23

## Converting Files into PageMaker 7 Documents

I f you work in an ad agency, a commercial printing company, or a graphic design shop, files will often be presented to you in a format other than PageMaker 7. Even if you just occasionally help out a friend, it is likely that you receive documents created in other page layout programs, in other operating systems, or in older versions of PageMaker.

Not all programs will open in PageMaker, of course. For example, you cannot open a Word document as a PageMaker publication. If you try to do so, PageMaker gives you a warning message (see illustration below) telling you that the document you are trying to open cannot open in PageMaker. (A Word document can be imported into PageMaker using the File menu's Place command, but it cannot be opened in PageMaker.)

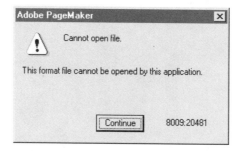

PageMaker, however, provides utilities that enable you to open the non-PageMaker 7 documents you are most likely to encounter so that you can work on them in PageMaker.

This chapter describes the process of converting documents created in older versions of PageMaker, in Microsoft Publisher, in QuarkXPress, or in PageMaker on a Macintosh operating system so that they can be managed in PageMaker 7.

## Opening Older PageMaker Documents in PageMaker 7

If you have used PageMaker for a while, as I have, you may find that you occasionally need to open older PageMaker files. In addition to PageMaker 6.5, I have a large library of PageMaker 4.0 and 5.0 documents, and occasionally, I even run across a version 3.0. PageMaker 7 will open older PageMaker documents as long as they were created in versions 4.0 through 6.5. That means, of course, that my 3.0 files are unrecoverable.

You can use two techniques to convert older documents into PageMaker 7. Each of these is simple to perform and provides similar results.

# Opening a Copy of an Older Document in PageMaker 7

The process of opening a document created by a previous version of PageMaker is almost too easy to deserve a heading of its own. Essentially, you just open it as you would any PageMaker 7 document. It takes a few seconds longer than opening a newer document, but PageMaker quickly creates an unnamed copy of the original document in the PageMaker 7 format. All you have to do is name and save the document and get to work.

The one disadvantage of this method is that in the end you have two documents, one still in the older version's format and the new one. If you open enough documents this way, you could compromise hard drive space, but the older documents are easily deleted or moved to a disk for storage.

# Using PageMaker's Publication Converter

PageMaker 7 provides a Publication Converter plug-in utility that can *convert*, rather than copy, the original file to PageMaker 6.5. In a PageMaker 6.5 format, the documents can be opened in PageMaker 7. If the Overwrite option is selected when the Converter is run, the old document no longer exists, and the document retains the name given to the original.

Another advantage of this method of file conversion is that you can convert multiple files in one operation rather than opening one file at a time.

Follow these steps to use the Publication Converter:

1. Close all open publications.

   Be sure to close all PageMaker publications before beginning the conversion process.

2. Open the Publication Converter utility.

   Click the Utilities menu's Plug-in command. Then select Publication Converter from the submenu. The Publication Converter dialog box opens, as shown in Figure 23-1.

3. Select Converter Options.

   If you want the Publication Converter utility to convert the existing documents without making a copy, select the Replace Publications option. Although overwriting the original file saves space on your hard drive (or the time and trouble of deleting or moving the original files), you may wish to leave the original in place as it serves as a backup. This selection is a matter of preference and does not affect the outcome of the conversion process at all.

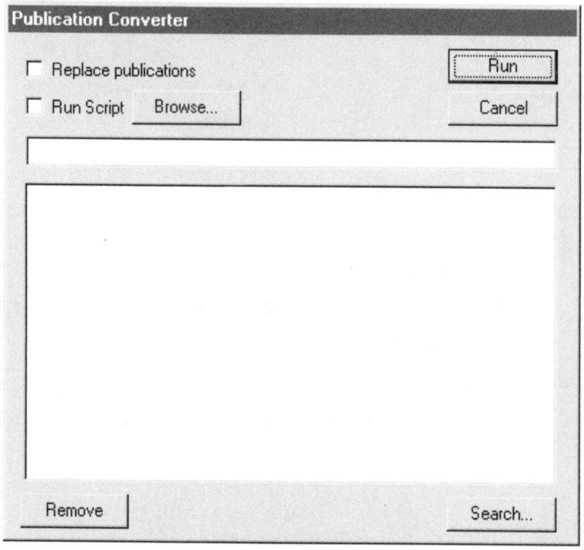

**Figure 23-1.** *The Publication Converter dialog box*

4. Open the Search for Publications dialog box.

   Click the Search Button in the lower-right corner of the Publication Converter dialog box. The Search for Publications dialog box opens (see below).

5. Enter the search criteria.

   Enter the files you wish to convert (for example, *.PM5) and the drive that you wish to search. Search for the files.

   Click the OK button in the Search for Publications dialog box. The box closes, returning the Publication Converter to your screen with a list of all the files on your system that meet the criteria you set forth in the Search for Publications dialog box. In other words, if you searched for all PageMaker 5 files in Drive C, all such files are listed in the Publication Converter list box.

6. Remove files.

   If some of the files on the list are ones you do not want to convert, they can be removed by selecting the filename and then clicking Remove.

7. Run the Converter.

   Click the Run Button in the upper-right corner of the Publication Converter dialog box. The files on the list are converted to PageMaker 6.5 files. A message box appears, telling you that the files have been converted (shown below). They can then be opened in PageMaker 7.0.

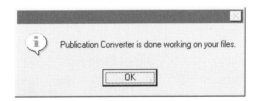

## Converting Microsoft Publisher and QuarkXPress to PageMaker 7

On occasion, you will want to open documents that have been created in other page layout programs. Not all programs will open in PageMaker, of course, but two popular page layout programs can be converted to run in PageMaker. This section discusses the process of converting QuarkXPress and Microsoft Publisher into PageMaker 7 documents.

The page layout program, QuarkXPress, usually referred to as just Quark, is a direct competitor of PageMaker and contains many of the same features. Microsoft Publisher is a similar but somewhat less powerful program. If your use of PageMaker involves receiving files from others, you may need to open Quark and Publisher documents in PageMaker.

PageMaker 7 provides the Converter for Microsoft Publisher and QuarkXPress that works with files created in Quark 3.3x to 4.1 and in Publisher 2000. For Publisher 95 to 97, a separate Converter is included. The Converter for Microsoft Publisher and QuarkXPress is located in the PageMaker 7 folder and is accompanied by a 26-page Portable Document Format (PDF) manual on its use. (The path in my computer is C:\Program Files\Adobe\PageMaker 7.0\Converter for MSP/QXP\MSPublisher Quark Converter.exe. The path in your computer should be identical or similar.) Although the essentials of using the Converter are discussed here, it is highly recommended that you refer to that manual if you use the Converter often.

**USING PAGEMAKER WITH OTHER PROGRAMS**

# Before Running the Converter

Some features in both Publisher and Quark cannot convert to PageMaker 7. These features must be adjusted before you run the Converter or the conversion may not be successful. This requires, of course, that the programs be on your system so that you can make the changes. If you are receiving files from other systems, you may not have Publisher or Quark with which to make the adjustment. If that is the case, let those who are providing the files know of the requirements.

## Before Converting a Publisher Publication

Be aware that some Publisher features do not convert. Check the following list. If the document you plan to convert contains these features, make changes or abandon the conversion.

- **Single pages larger than 42 inches by 42 inches** A 42-inch square page is the largest that the Converter will convert. If the Publisher document is larger, the page must be reduced in size before conversion.

- **Facing pages larger than 17 inches by 42 inches** Just as with a single page, a facing page that exceeds PageMaker's maximum will not convert. Make changes before a conversion is attempted.

- **Pages numbering more than 999** If the Publisher document has more than 999 pages, the pages beyond that will not convert. You may wish to divide the Publisher document into two (or more) documents before converting and then use PageMaker's Book feature to treat them as one document.

- **Banners** Banners will not convert to PageMaker.

- **Text size** Text that is larger than 650 points or smaller than 4 points will not convert accurately. Text larger than 650 will be converted as 650-point type. Likewise, text smaller than 4 points will convert to 4-point size. This may not be a big deal, but the conversion will be smoother if the text is adjusted prior to conversion.

- **Leading** Leading larger than 1300 points converts as 1300-point leading. You may adjust before conversion or after.

- **Bullets and numbering** Automatic bullets and numbering do not convert. You can manually number lines of text before conversion or use PageMaker's Bullets and Numbering feature afterwards.

## Before Converting a Quark Document

Just like Publisher, some characteristics of Quark do not convert to PageMaker. The features in the following list are ones that can be adjusted in Quark before the conversion process begins:

- **Single pages larger than 42 inches by 42 inches**   A 42-inch square page is the largest that the Converter will convert. If the Quark document is larger, the page must be reduced in size before conversion.

- **Facing pages larger than 17 inches by 42 inches**   Just as with a single page, a facing page that exceeds PageMaker's maximum will not convert. Make changes before a conversion is attempted.

- **Documents containing both single-sided and facing pages**   In PageMaker, all pages in a document must be either single or facing. Before converting, add empty facing pages to all single pages in a Quark document that contains both.

- **New column character**   The column break code in a Quark document does not convert to PageMaker. Converted text continues to flow in the text box or text frame. You may create the break in Quark using Quark techniques other than the new column character, or you may readjust the text flow after conversion.

- **Text size**   Text that is larger than 650 points or smaller than 4 points will not convert accurately. Text larger than 650 will be converted as 650-point type. Likewise, text smaller than 4 points will convert to 4 point size. This may not be a big deal, but the conversion will be smoother if the text is adjusted prior to conversion.

- **Leading**   Leading larger than 1300 points converts as 1300-point leading. You may adjust before conversion or after.

- **Horizontal scale**   Horizontal scale values greater than 250 percent convert at 250 percent. You may make the adjustment to your text in Quark before conversion or in PageMaker after conversion.

**Note**   *Many additional characteristics of Publisher and Quark do not convert accurately. Please see the "Adobe PageMaker 7.0 MSPublisher-Quark Converter" PDF document for more information. When using the features listed previously, an adjustment before a conversion is necessary or particularly helpful.*

## Running the Converter

The following steps lead you through the process of converting documents created in Publisher 2000 and in QuarkXPress versions 3.3x to 4.1. Note that PageMaker does not have to be open to run the Converter.

1. Close the documents to be converted.

   This is only possible, of course, if you have Publisher or Quark on your system. If you have been working with the files to be converted, be sure to close them prior to the conversion process.

2. Start the Converter.

   Select the Start menu's Programs command. From the Program menu, select Adobe and then PageMaker 7.0. From the PageMaker 7.0 submenu, select Converter for Microsoft Publisher/QuarkXPress. The Converter opens, as shown in Figure 23-2.

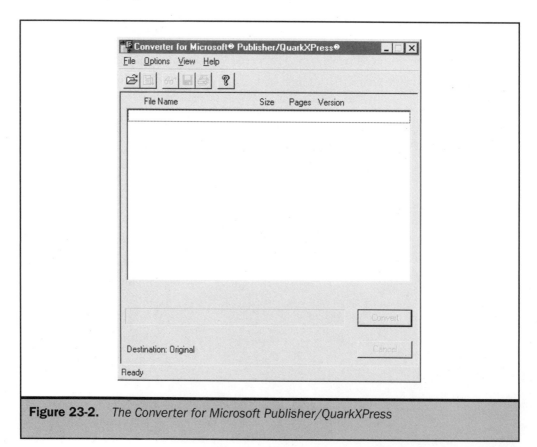

**Figure 23-2.**   *The Converter for Microsoft Publisher/QuarkXPress*

3.  Open the Select Files to Convert dialog box.

    In the Converter window, click the File menu's Select Files command. The Select Files to Convert dialog box opens, as shown below.

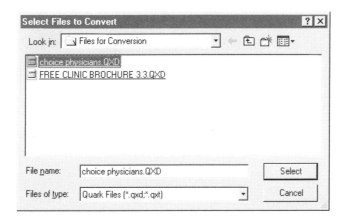

4.  Select the type of file you want to convert.

    From the Files of Type drop-down menu, select Publisher Files, Quark Files, or All Files.

5.  Locate the file or files to convert.

    Using the drop-down menu for the Look In box, open the folder in which the file you want to convert is stored. Click the filename and then click the Select Button. If you wish to select multiple files, hold the CTRL key and select each of the files before clicking the Select Button. The files appear in the list in the Converter window.

6.  Remove unwanted files.

    If you have put a file in the list that you do not want to convert, select it and click the Remove Button. The file disappears from the list.

7.  Set Conversion options.

    Open the Conversion Settings dialog box by clicking the Options menu's Conversion Settings command. The Conversion Settings dialog box opens, as shown in the following illustration. Make your selections from the following options; when through, click the OK button to return to the Converter for Microsoft Publisher/QuarkXPress dialog box.

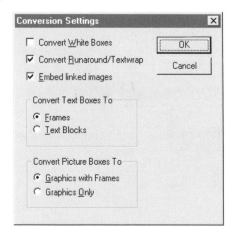

- **Convert White Boxes**   Select this option if you want Publisher/Quark boxes with a white background converted to PageMaker simple graphics with a white fill. If you want the resulting simple graphics to have a None setting (no fill), *deselect* the box.

- **Convert Runaround/Textwrap**   A runaround is a Quark setting similar to PageMaker's text wrap. Select this option if you want Quark runarounds or Publisher text wrap converted to PageMaker text wrap. All Quark runarounds and Publisher text wraps, even those customized to a shape, convert to a rectangular text wrap. This can be adjusted later in PageMaker, of course.

- **Embed Linked Images**   Selecting this option embeds images into the PageMaker file, rather than linking them. This increases the size of the file, sometimes by a great deal.

- **Convert Text Boxes To**   Text boxes created in Quark or Publisher work somewhat like PageMaker's frames. Select whether you want the Quark text boxes (or Publisher text boxes) to be converted to PageMaker text boxes or to text in PageMaker frames.

- **Convert Picture Boxes To**   Your choice in this section is to select whether Quark/Publisher graphics (not simple graphics but images and other art) convert to a regular graphic or to a graphic within a frame.

8. Specify where you want the converted files stored.

   By default, the Converter will store the converted files in the same folder as the original file. However, if you want to store them elsewhere, you must specify the folder where you want the Converter to place them once the conversion is complete.

Click the Options menu to display its commands. Click Save to Same Folder to deselect it. The Choose Destination dialog box opens, as shown in the following illustration. Use the Look In drop-down menu to locate the folder where you wish to store the file or files. Click the folder and then click the Select Button. The Choose Destination dialog box closes, returning you to the Cross-Platform PageMaker Converter dialog box.

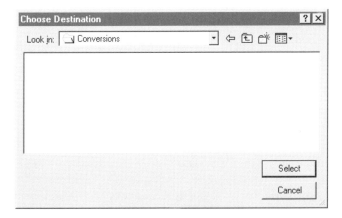

9. Convert the files.

   Click the Convert Button. The conversion status is shown in the process indicator. Once the conversion is completed, the targeted files will be shown preceded by a symbol indicating the success of the conversion. A check mark indicates a successful conversion, while an X indicates an unsuccessful conversion. If you see a yellow triangle symbol, it indicates that the conversion was successful but had some problems. You will need to check that document carefully.

## Checking the Converted Document

In addition to the several obstacles to conversion mentioned in the previous sections, numerous features of both Publisher and Quark do not accurately convert to PageMaker. All of these are adjustable to some degree once the document is converted to PageMaker. The Adobe PageMaker 7.0 MSPublisher-Quark Converter PDF file describes most of these and offers information on your options for their management. The pivotal issue here is the importance of carefully proofing the converted document.

# Converting Macintosh PageMaker Files to PageMaker 7 for Windows

PageMaker is also a popular page layout program on the Apple Macintosh platform. It is very possible, if you receive files from other systems, that you will receive a document created on a Macintosh.

If the file you want to convert is a PageMaker 6.0 or 7.0 (Macintosh) file, you can open it by using the PageMaker (Windows) File menu's Open command. The steps for doing so are described in the following section, "Opening a PageMaker 6.0/7.0 Mac Document in PageMaker 7.0."

If the file or files are PageMaker 5.0 or 6.0 (Macintosh), you must use the Cross-Platform Converter. See the section "Using the Cross-Platform PageMaker Converter."

## Opening a PageMaker 6.0/7.0 Macintosh Document in PageMaker 7.0 for Windows

As previously mentioned, if the PageMaker for Macintosh document was created in version 6.0 or 7.0, you can open it using PageMaker 7's (Windows) Open command. And, if you wish, you can return the document to the Macintosh platform using the same process. There are some selections that you need to make in the process. Here are the steps:

1. Transfer the Mac file to the hard drive of the Windows computer.

   If the file is on disk, place the disk in the appropriate drive on the Windows computer where PageMaker 7 (Windows) is installed. If the file has been received electronically, download it and save it to the hard drive.

2. Start PageMaker 7 (Windows).

   Launch PageMaker as usual.

3. Open the Open dialog box.

   Click the File menu's Open command. The Open Publication dialog box appears (see Figure 23-3).

4. Select the file.

   Use the Look In drop-down menu to locate the folder where the document you want to convert is stored. Select the file.

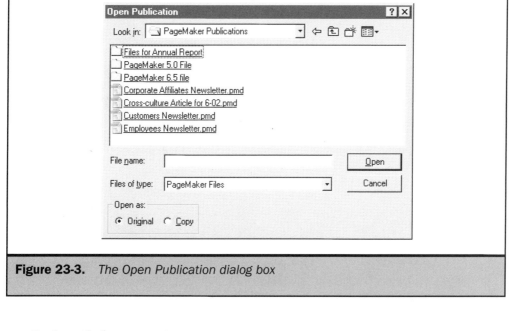

**Figure 23-3.**    *The Open Publication dialog box*

5.  Launch the conversion.

    Click the Open Button in the Open dialog box. A Conversion dialog box appears, as shown below.

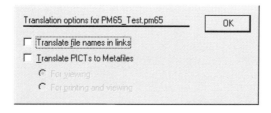

6.  Specify the settings.

    Select the appropriate settings for the conversion as described in the following list:

    ■ **Translate Filenames in Links**   Select this option if you are moving the document to the Windows environment permanently. This enables PageMaker to link to externally stored files.

- **Translate PICT to Metafile (Windows)**   Only if you need to view graphics or print the final output (the conversion is temporary) should you select this option. Leaving the option unselected enables it to be reopened in PageMaker for the Mac if it is sent back to that platform.

- **For Viewing**   If the conversion is temporary but you do need to see the graphics, select the For Viewing option. PageMaker will convert Metafiles screen representations so they can be viewed. However, printing will not print at high resolution.

- **For Printing and Viewing**   Use this selection if you are moving the document to PageMaker 7 permanently or for final output. PageMaker will convert the graphics so that they print accurately.

*Metafiles and PICTs must be embedded in the document before conversion to allow accurate printing at high resolution.*

## Using the Cross-Platform PageMaker Converter

If you want to convert PageMaker5.x and 6.x documents created on the Apple Macintosh platform, you must use the Cross-Platform PageMaker Converter. This utility is placed on your hard drive at the time you install PageMaker 7.

Easy to use, the Cross-Platform Converter works essentially like the Converter used to convert Publisher and Quark documents discussed earlier. Here are the steps:

1. Transfer the Mac file to the hard drive of the Windows computer.

   If the file is on disk, place the disk in the appropriate drive on the Windows computer where PageMaker 7 (Windows) is installed. If the file has been received electronically, download it and save it to the hard drive.

2. Start the Converter.

   Using either My Computer or Windows Explorer, follow this path to locate the Cross-Platform Converter:

   C:\Program Files\Adobe\PageMaker 7.0\Extras\XplatConv\XPMConv.exe

   Then double-click XPMConv.exe to launch the Converter (see Figure 23-4).

3. Open the Select Files to Convert dialog box.

   In the Converter window, click the File menu's Select Files command. The Select Files to Convert dialog box opens, as shown in Figure 23-5.

4. Select the type of file you want to convert.

   From the Files of Type drop-down menu, select the version in which your target file was created or All Files.

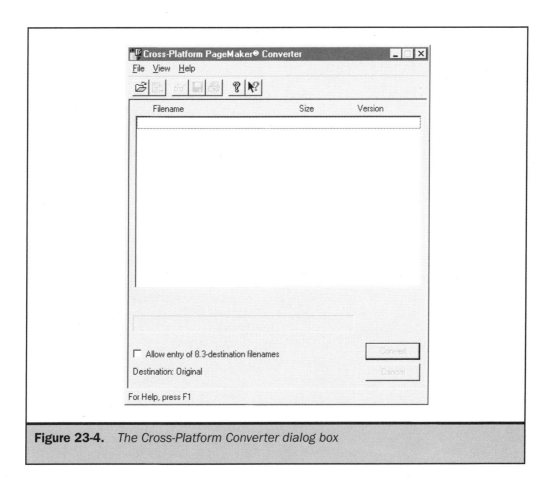

**Figure 23-4.**   *The Cross-Platform Converter dialog box*

5. Locate the file or files to convert.

   Using the Look In box drop-down menu, open the folder in which the file you want to convert is stored. Click the filename and then click the Select Button. If you wish to select multiple files, hold the CTRL key and select each of the files before clicking the Select Button. The files appear in the Converter window's list.

6. Remove unwanted files.

   If you have put a file in the list that you do not want to convert, select it and click the Remove Button. The file disappears from the list.

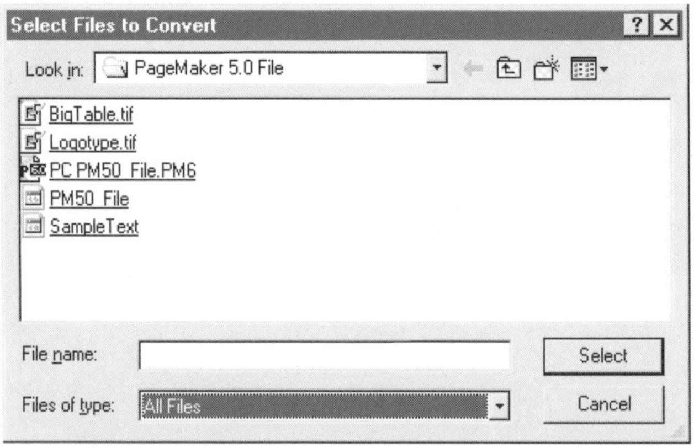

**Figure 23-5.** *The Select Files to Convert dialog box*

7. Specify where you want the converted files stored.

   By default, the Converter will store the converted files in the same folder as the original file. However, if you want to store them elsewhere, you must specify the folder in which you want the Converter to place them once the conversion is complete.

   Click the File menu to display its commands. Click Save to Original to deselect it. The Choose Destination dialog box opens, as shown in Figure 23-6. Use the Destination drop-down menu to locate the folder where you wish to store the file or files. Click the folder and then click the Select Button. The Choose Destination dialog box closes, returning you to the Cross-Platform PageMaker Converter dialog box.

8. Determine the naming convention.

   PageMaker 7 (and its Windows environment) enables filenames to contain as many as 256 characters. However, some older networking software requires the former convention of a limit of eight characters followed by a three-digit extension. If you are working within such a system, select the Allow Entry of 8.3 Destination Filenames box.

9. Convert the files.

   Click the Convert Button. The conversion status is shown in the process indicator. Once the conversion is completed, the targeted files will be shown

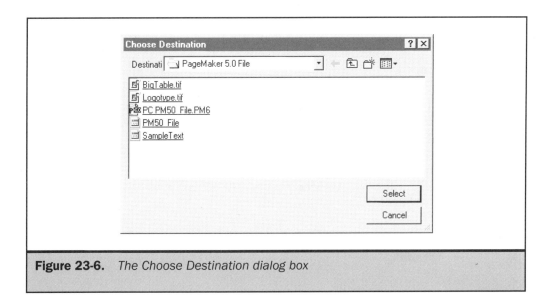

**Figure 23-6.**    *The Choose Destination dialog box*

preceded by a symbol indicating the success of the conversion. A check mark indicates a successful conversion. An X indicates an unsuccessful conversion. If you see a yellow triangle symbol, it indicates that the conversion was successful but had some problems. You will need to check that document carefully.

When the conversion is complete, close the Converter by clicking the Exit Button or click the File menu's Exit command.

# Summary

If you work with PageMaker in situations where you receive files from other people and, perhaps, other systems, then you may need to convert those files in order to work with them in PageMaker 7. PageMaker provides the conversion utilities you need for the most likely situations when files must be converted.

**Opening Older PageMaker Documents**    I've worked with PageMaker through many versions. As a result, I have disks containing documents that go way back, even as far as PageMaker 3.0. For PageMaker 3.0 documents, I'm out of luck; they cannot be opened in PageMaker 7, but for the newer versions, PageMaker 4.0 through 6.5, they can be opened in PageMaker 7 or converted to a form in which they can be opened.

**Converting Documents Created in Microsoft Publisher and QuarkXPress to PageMaker 7**    Not all documents can be opened in PageMaker, of course. However, documents created in two of the most popular programs, Microsoft Publisher and QuarkXPress, can be. PageMaker provides two utilities that convert Publisher and Quark files.

**Converting Macintosh PageMaker Files to PageMaker 7 for Windows**    If you receive files from others, there is a very good chance that at some point you will receive PageMaker files that were created in PageMaker on the Macintosh operating system. Depending upon the version of PageMaker (Mac) in which they were created, you may merely open the file using the PageMaker (Windows) Open command, or you may use the Cross-Platform PageMaker Converter to do so.

# Chapter 24

## Interfacing with the World Wide Web

The Internet, and most particularly, the World Wide Web, have become an integral part of our culture and our lives. The World Wide Web, which has only been around for about ten years, has revolutionized the way products and services are marketed. And e-mail is an important personal and business communication tool. Just as it is hard to imagine life without cars and telephones, life without the Internet would be far different.

With all the colorful and dramatic graphics available on the Web, it is predictable that a PageMaker designer would want to incorporate some of them into a layout. And, quite obviously, PageMaker's capability to create striking and attention-getting layouts makes it a prime candidate as a web design tool. This chapter explains the ins and outs of importing from and exporting to the Web.

# Importing Graphics and Text from the Web

To those of us who work with layouts every day, as well as to the part-time designer, the World Wide Web seems a cornucopia of images and information for use in our designs. I remember when clip art had to be purchased on disk and installed on the hard drive. I got a lot of really good material that way, and still use some of it today. But it is so much easier to just download it from the Web. In this section, I talk about the process of obtaining material from the Web and some considerations you must take before doing so.

## Copyright Considerations

If you have Web access, you have easy access to a world of images and text. However, one of the burgeoning Web industries is tracking and settling copyright violations. I won't attempt to give a tutorial on copyright, but the fines are very stiff, and tracking usage is not as hard as you might think.

Before you use graphics or files from the Web in a PageMaker document, make sure you have a right to do so. Most sites that provide graphics clearly outline the requirements for use. When you use these graphics, you do not own the graphic, of course, but are given a "license" to use it. Some sites will allow you to use their graphics on a personal site, but not a commercial one. If you wish to use graphics or text with requirements that are not clearly defined, you must obtain permission before you use it. If you cannot obtain permission, *do not use it*. Find another graphic or text to take its place. Unless there is explicit notice that material is in the public domain, anything that is created is copyrighted in the name of the creator or his or her employer.

Please do not treat copyright considerations lightly. Because of the large number of infractions that occur every day, copyright owners are very aggressive about locating and prosecuting violators.

## Setting Online Preferences

Make sure you have your online settings in place. Click the File menu's Preferences command and select the Online command. Then set your proxy settings appropriately.

Put the address of your default browser in the web browser text box at the bottom of the Online Preferences dialog box.

# Importing Text or Graphics with the Place Command

We use the Place command to import graphics and text from our files. We can use it to import graphics and text as well:

1. Copy the URL of the image or text you want to import.

   Use your web browser to access the page containing the image. Right-click the image and select Copy Image Location if you are using Netscape. If you are using Internet Explorer, select Properties and drag through the path shown to the right of Address (URL) in the Properties dialog box. Press CTRL-C to copy.

2. Open the Place dialog box.

   Return to the PageMaker window. Select the File menu's Place command. The Place dialog box opens, as shown in Figure 24-1.

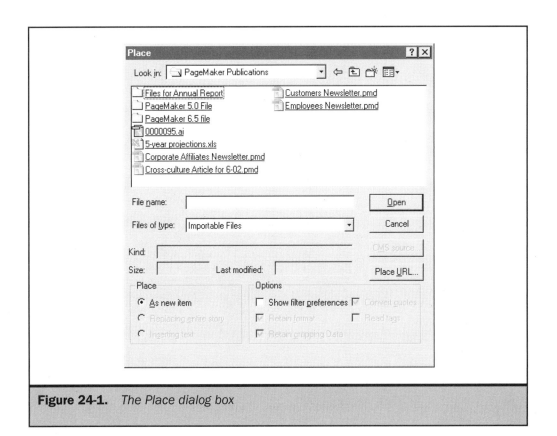

**Figure 24-1.** *The Place dialog box*

3. Open the Place URL dialog box.

   In the Place dialog box, click the Place URL Button. The Place URL dialog box appears, as shown in the following illustration.

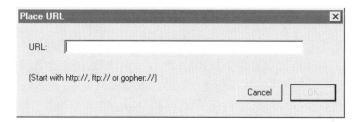

4. Paste the address into the URL box.

   In the Place URL dialog box, click in the text box and press CTRL-V to place the address of the file into the text box.

5. Click OK.

   When you click the OK button, a warning dialog box appears, as shown below, reminding you to be cognizant of copyrights and copyright infringement laws. It is a good idea to check the Don't Show This Again Next Time box, or you will see the warning box each time you place a file from the Web. Click the OK button.

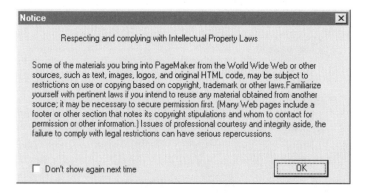

6. Place the graphic or text in your PageMaker document.

   Once you have closed the warning box, the mouse pointer will change to a square with an X. (If your computer is a slower one, you may first see a progress gauge indicating how much of the image has been downloaded.) Click your PageMaker page approximately where you want the text or graphic to be located. The image appears.

If the object is not exactly where you want it to be located, just move it by clicking and dragging it to a new location. If you have imported a graphic, it can be sized as well. However, enlarging the graphic may decrease its resolution and distort the image.

## Importing Text or Graphics with Drag and Drop

Another way to place an object from the Internet is to merely drag and drop it from the browser into your PageMaker document. Here's how:

1. Display the PageMaker page on which you want to place the object.

   If necessary, open the PageMaker document. Then display the page where you want the graphic or text to appear.

2. Position the PageMaker window and the browser window side by side.

   Restore both the PageMaker window and the web browser that you have located the target object with, and place them side by side on your computer screen, as shown in Figure 24-2.

3. Drag the object from the browser to the PageMaker page.

   If you want to import a graphic, just click and drag the object from the browser to the PageMaker page. If you want to import text, the text must first be selected in the browser window. (Just click and drag through the text you want to import.) Then it can be dragged just as a graphic.

*I have found that many graphics would not import this way but that all selected text appears to do so.*

How simple!

## Importing Graphics with a Right-Click

Of course, the most common way to import a graphic is by right-clicking it and selecting the Shortcut menu's Save Picture As command. Just name and save the graphic to the appropriate location on your hard drive. Then use the Place command to place the picture.

## Exporting PageMaker Layouts to HTML

In PageMaker, you can export layouts to HyperText Markup Language (HTML) so that they can be loaded onto the Web. This is a fairly simple operation, but due to the nature of the Web, many elements of a PageMaker document may not appear correctly or may not export at all. Therefore, the first thing to look at in this section are the limitations of the export process.

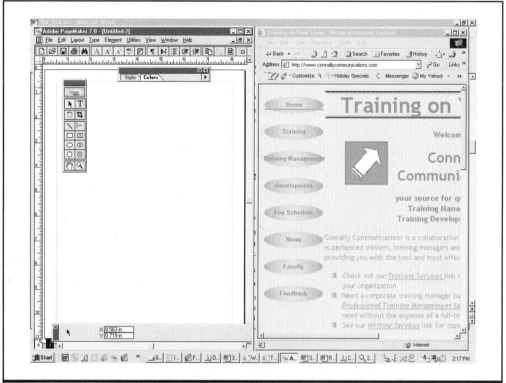

**Figure 24-2.**    The PageMaker window and the Internet Explorer window displayed side by side

## Limitations and Considerations

HTML was created as a means of displaying text and images on the Web in a manner that allows all types of computers to view them. The same document files cannot be read in Windows, Mac, or Unix machines without conversion, but all of these systems can read HTML files. However, in the development of this remarkable language, certain limitations were created. In addition, Web browsers display some elements of a design differently. Before you export your PageMaker file to HTML, you should be aware of these limitations and address them in your PageMaker document.

### Type Limitations

Many of the typographical features that fine-tune our text in PageMaker do not translate to HTML. Specifically, the following are lost when a PageMaker file is exported:

- Font, type size, and leading
- Horizontal scale
- Tracking and kerning
- Outline- and shadow-type styles
- Paragraph alignment (unless Preserve Approximate Page Layout is selected)
- Indent and tab positions

Web browsers display only specific fonts, so the text in your web page may look one way in Internet Explorer and another in Netscape Navigator. Trial and error is the best way to see the differences.

## Graphic Limitations

HTML supports only the GIF and JPEG formats. The good news is that PageMaker automatically converts imported graphics to that format as part of the export process. The not-so-good news is that simple graphics, those drawn with PageMaker simple graphic tools, are lost when exported. The one exception is the horizontal line, which is converted to a HTML horizontal rule.

## Page Layout Limitations

The following are unsupported features in HTML. You should make page layout changes to adjust your PageMaker layout to produce an acceptable layout in HTML:

- **Transformations**  Transformations, such as rotation, skewing, or flipping, are lost in the exportation process. You can, however, transform the object in a graphics program, resave the image in its transformed state, and replace the object in your PageMaker document. Then the image will appear correctly in HTML.

- **Overlapping**  Any objects that are overlapping in the PageMaker document are separated in HTML. Revise your design before exporting so that you have control over placement.

- **Text wrap**  Text wrap shapes, other than rectangular, are also lost. Revise any other text wrap styles to display the rectangular shape.

- **Frames**  The content of a frame is exported, but not the surrounding frame itself. If you select the Preserve Approximate Page Layout option, discussed later in this chapter, images that extend beyond the frame border are cropped to approximate the effect of the frame. If that option is not selected, the cropping does not take place.

■ **Masking**   Masked objects are unmasked. You can re-create an approximate version of a masked graphic by cropping it with PageMaker's Cropping tool. If you masked text, re-create it in an illustration program and place it back into PageMaker as an object before exporting to HTML.

## Color Limitations

Only certain colors are available for display on the Web. Before exporting your PageMaker document, open the Online Colors library, as explained in Chapter 11 and use the colors from it. That way the colors you select will be the colors used in the HTML document.

# Setting HTML Export Preferences

It is a good idea to set the Export options before beginning the exportation process. Access the Export options page (see the following illustration) by selecting the File menu's Export command and choose HTML from the submenu. Then click the Options Button on the Export HTML dialog box. The Options page appears. The various settings are explained in Table 24-1.

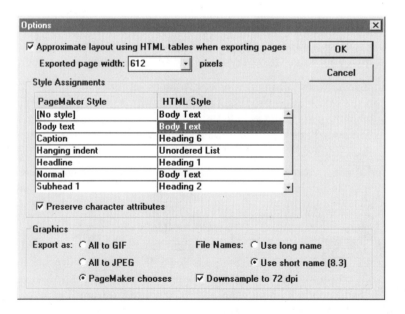

| Settings | Explanation |
|---|---|
| Approximate Layout Using HTML Tables When Exporting Pages | When this is checked, PageMaker will use tables to make the layout of the HTML page look as much like the PageMaker page as possible. Columns will be retained as well as possible. If this is not checked, columnar text appears in one column that fills the page between the margins. |
| Exported Page Width | This is important. Virtually all PCs can display windows wider than 640 pixels (the basic VGA horizontal resolution), but you may want to restrict your pages to this width so that no one will have trouble seeing your web page or have to scroll over to see it all. Adjusting this size will result in the proportional scaling of the images and column widths in your pages. Try the default of 612 pixels. It is a good average size. |
| Style Assignments | This section of the Options dialog box enables you to determine which HTML style is substituted for a specific PageMaker style. Suggested substitutions are listed with the PageMaker style on the left and the corresponding HTML style on the right. If you want to change the HTML style, click the HTML style you want to change. A list of HTML styles appears. Select the HTML style you want to substitute for the PageMaker style. |
| Preserve Character Attributes | This selection retains color and typestyle in the exported text as much as possible. |

*continues*

**Table 24-1.**   *The Export HTML Options*

| Settings | Explanation |
|---|---|
| Export As: | **All to GIF** This works well for most images, but may result in some loss of resolution and color depth in a very complex image. |
| | **All to JPEG** Converting all the graphics to JPEG may result in slower downloads of your page. JPEG images are larger than GIFs. |
| | **PageMaker Chooses** This is a good choice because during the exportation process PageMaker assesses the images and makes a decision as to which format is better. |
| File Names: | Check the radio button next to Use Long Name or Use Short name (8.3). Since most operating systems can now function with long, complex filenames, it is recommended that you stick with the long ones. |
| Downsample to 72 dpi | This selection reduces the resolution from the print resolution (probably 300 dpi or more) to the computer monitor resolution of 72 dpi. Failing to downsample does not affect the appearance of your web page, but it multiplies the download time required to access each image. |

**Table 24-1.** *The Export HTML Options (continued)*

# Exporting to HTML

With all limitations considered and with the options set, you are ready to export your PageMaker document to HTML. Just follow these steps:

1. Open the PageMaker document you want to export.

   If necessary, open the PageMaker document you want to export and display the appropriate page.

2. Open the Export HTML dialog box.

   Choose the File menu's Export command. Then select HTML from the submenu. The Export HTML dialog box appears, as shown in Figure 24-3.

3. Open the Export HTML: New Document dialog box.

   Click the New Button. The Export HTML: New Document dialog box appears (see Figure 24-4). Type a document title in the Document Title text box. In a web browser, this title will appear at the top of the browser window.

4. Assign PageMaker pages or stories.

   If Assign PageMaker Pages is selected, click the document's pages on the left, and click Add for each page you want to export to HTML. To export all pages, of course, click the Add All Button.

   If Assign PageMaker Stories is selected, click the PageMaker story or stories, shown on the left, that you want to export and then click Add or Add All. If this option is selected, you will not be able to export the layout of the stories.

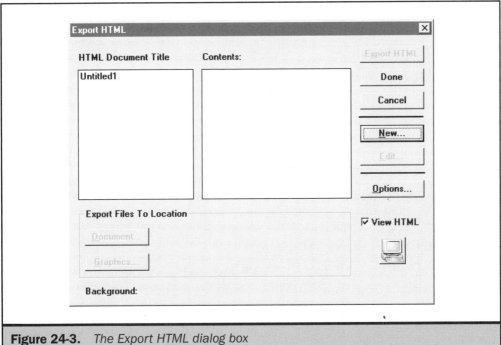

**Figure 24-3.**   *The Export HTML dialog box*

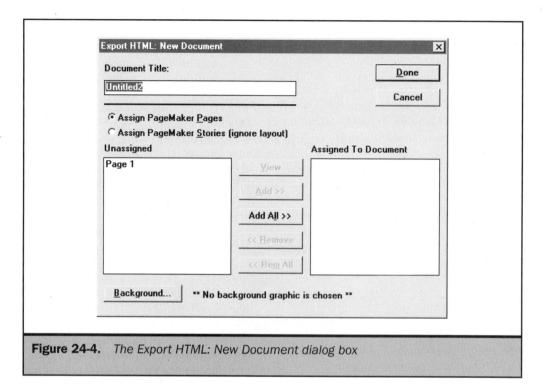

**Figure 24-4.** The Export HTML: New Document dialog box

*The order in which you add pages or stories is the order in which they will be exported to HTML.*

5. Select a background.

   If you wish to apply a tiled background image for the document, click the Background Button, and the Choose a Background Image dialog box appears. Then locate and double-click the image you want to have tiled as a background.

   Return to the Export HTML dialog box.

   Click Done to save the selections you have made so far. The Export HTML: New Document dialog box closes, revealing the Export HTML dialog box again.

6. Select a storage location for the HTML document.

   Click the Document Button at the lower part of the dialog box. The Document Save As dialog box appears. Enter a name in the File Name text box and use the Save In menu (accessed by clicking the drop-down arrow to the right of the

Save In box) to locate the folder where you wish to save the completed HTML file.

7.  Click OK.

At this point, you are not actually saving the document but are defining its storage location.

8.  Specify the web browser to be used for the document preview.

Click the Application icon in the lower-right corner of the dialog box, and the Choose a web Browser dialog box opens. Use the Look In menu to locate the web browser you wish to use. Click the Open Button and an icon representing your selection appears.

9.  Generate the HTML document.

Click the Export HTML Button, and the new HTML document is created in the location you have selected. If you want to leave the process and come back later to complete the export, click the Done Button.

The first time you export a publication as HTML, PageMaker checks it for compatibility. If incompatibilities are found, PageMaker displays a dialog box identifying the parts of the PageMaker document that do not export correctly. You may correct the problems and export again.

Once the export process is completed, you can open the HTML document in a web browser by selecting the File menu's Open command and then locating and opening the file. The publication is not yet posted on the Web, of course. In order to do that, you must interface with a web server. Many web servers are available for small amounts of money or as a complimentary service by an Internet service provider.

# Summary

In today's world, the Internet and the World Wide Web are integral parts of the way we communicate and do business. We can easily import graphics and text from the Web, and PageMaker 7 provides a means to use the layout of a PageMaker document as the basis for a web page.

**Importing Graphics and Text from the Web**    The most important consideration in importing graphics and text from the Web is the honoring of intellectual property laws. Make sure you have permission of the web site's creator before using any graphic or text found on a site. Many sites state the permissions right up front.

You will want to set your online preferences before importing an object. Once that is all set, importing is an easy process with any one of several techniques.

**Exporting PageMaker Layouts to HTML**   PageMaker provides an easily used feature for converting a PageMaker document to a format that can be posted on the Web. The Export HTML feature converts the document to HTML, a language that is used on the Web and that virtually all computer systems can read. All elements of a PageMaker layout may not be able to convert to HTML, however, so some adjustments may need to be made in the original PageMaker publication.

Once the export limitations are acknowledged and dealt with, you can set the HTML export preferences and export the document.

The
# Complete
# Reference

PageMaker 7

# Chapter 25

## Preparing for Output

Whether you are having your PageMaker publication produced by a commercial printer, are printing it on your desktop printer, or are exporting it to the Web, final checks or preparations need to be performed. This chapter identifies those actions that must be made in order for you to get the best results.

# Printing Proofs

Before you send a document to a commercial printer, the Web, or your desktop printer for final output, you should print proofs of the document and any color separations (refer to Chapter 21). Carefully check to see that the colors are separated appropriately and that all items appear on the correct separation. As mentioned in Chapter 21, if you are not accustomed to looking at full-color separations, it may be difficult to envision the way the Cyan, Magenta, Yellow, and Black (CMYK) seps work together because each separation prints in black only, but you can check to see that things such as type and simple graphics appear where they should.

# Proofing Your Work

In a previous chapter, I took the opportunity to wax philosophical about the importance of saving your work and keeping your hard drive organized. I'm going to do that again, but this time my topic is the importance of proofing your work.

Just as there is more that is practical about saving and organizing than there is philosophical, proofing your work is truly crucial to a quality document. If there is any lesson that I have learned over the years, it is the importance of careful, considerate proofing. Even if time is at a premium, verifying the accuracy of your work is not where time should be cut.

We all understand how important it is to catch and correct any errors in a document, but catching the error after it has gone to the commercial printer could cost you dearly. Commercial printers will stand by any work that they do, but if you send a PageMaker document that contains an error to a printer, you will have to pay for redoing the output to the point where the error is discovered, even if you find the error before the final printing.

In a recent conversation with the typesetting manager of a local print shop, I asked her what preparation she would want her clients to make before sending a PageMaker document to her for printing. With a sigh, she said that there are three things that a client could do to make her job easier and the final document better: proof his or her work carefully, provide her with a printout of the piece, and use the Save for Service Provider utility included with PageMaker (see "Using the Save for Service Provider Feature" later in this chapter).

In this section, I admit, I'm primarily focusing on documents that will be produced by a commercial printer. But the principle here is just as valid if you are exporting to the Web or producing the document on your desktop. The effectiveness of the best document is reduced by at least half if it contains a typo. If I see a typo or a grammatical error in a Web site, the site's credibility is automatically reduced considerably in my mind. If you are trying to sell something (even yourself) in a printed document, a Web page, or a document that you publish on your desktop, you cannot afford to overlook an error.

One of the biggest mistakes made by a designer is for him or her to be the only proofreader of his or her work. No matter how carefully you read and consider your work, you are less likely to find your own mistakes than someone who brings a fresh eye to the document. I remember, painfully, an important catalog that I worked hard to produce when I managed the marketing materials department of a national manufacturing company. The piece was beautiful and well done, but I failed to place some important symbols in a certain section. As many times as I read and looked over the catalog, I never saw the absence of those symbols. It went to press and we later had to take a rubber stamp to provide the symbols to thousands of pieces. A person who was not so intimately involved with the catalog would have spotted it right away. Actually, someone did just that. It was the big boss and it was after the piece had been printed.

The following steps are the very minimum of proofing necessary:

1. Proof it yourself carefully.

   This is obvious. Read through the piece. Try to put yourself outside of the connection that you have with it as the creator.

2. Have someone else proof it carefully.

   This is the most important step of all. Take the piece to someone you can trust and ask him or her to read and consider the document carefully. If you absolutely do not have anyone who can do that for you, editing services exist on the Web that will provide the service for a fee. Actually, these professional organizations do the very best job of proofing your work, and they are totally objective. Keep in mind, however, that editing services may find typos and obvious omissions, but are not necessarily going to be able to provide content analysis.

   If you absolutely cannot have another individual proof your work, then step away from it for a period of time, at least overnight, if possible, but as long as you can. Then come back to it and read it with a fresh eye.

3. Have your client proof it carefully.

   This, too, is obvious. If you are working for a client, make sure that the client has the opportunity to peruse the piece before it is sent to print. Also make sure that the client understands that it is his or her responsibility to find any inaccuracies at that point. Most design professionals require the client to sign off on the proofs presented right before final output.

4. Proof it again.

I don't want to appear obsessive. I'm really an off-the-wall kind of person, but one with very high standards. I've just learned from experience that I would rather put a lot of effort into finding errors before press than apologize to the client afterwards.

So give the piece one last look.

**Note** *In reviewing your document over and over, I'm not suggesting that you keep on making essential changes. It is really easy to keep on making changes every time you review your piece just because you can. Continuing to change the document usually results in a poor-quality piece. Once the document is done, let it be done. But do look for errors.*

# Using the Save for Service Provider Feature

When I first started working in graphic design, I produced mechanical layouts. That means that I pasted every element of my design onto a paste-up board using T-squares to make sure the lines were straight and applied hot wax to make them stick. I then took the paste-up board to the commercial printer for him or her to photograph for plates. Today, through the wonders of computers and other high-tech advances, of course, we take the printer a disk. Or better yet, we send the file to the printer electronically.

With mechanical layouts, everything that the printer needed was pasted to the layout board. Today, however, it is important to see that nothing gets left behind. You see, just as the printer of the "olden days" needed every little scrap of paper that was pasted to the layout board, the printer of today needs every font, graphic, and photograph to make the entire project work.

The purpose of the Save for Service Provider plug-in utility is twofold. First, it makes sure that everything the printer needs to output the document is included with it. When you run your PageMaker document through the Save for Service Provider utility, PageMaker checks to see if all the linked objects are with the document and all the fonts are included. If you use this utility, you know that everything your printer needs is with the file. The Save for Service Provider utility's second purpose is to package the document and its peripherals so that you can just put it on disk and take or send it to the printer.

Here's how it works:

1. Open the PageMaker publication to be saved for the printer.

The document you are preparing to send to the commercial printer must be open, of course, before you can check or package it. If you have recently made changes, save the document.

2. Open the Save for Service Provider dialog box.

   Click the Utilities menu's Plug-in command. Then select Save for Service Provider from the submenu. The Save for Service Provider dialog box opens, as shown in Figure 25-1.

3. Preflight the document.

   Depending upon whether you are sending your document to a commercial printer as a publication file or as a PostScript file, click either the Preflight Pub or Preflight PS Button. (For information on which form to use, see the section "Sending a Publication or a PostScript File.") The utility checks the document, linked files, and fonts, and it displays information on whether they are available to be packaged for printing. Figure 25-2 shows a preflighted document in which all the information needed to accurately print the document is available. If there had been problems, the font or link items

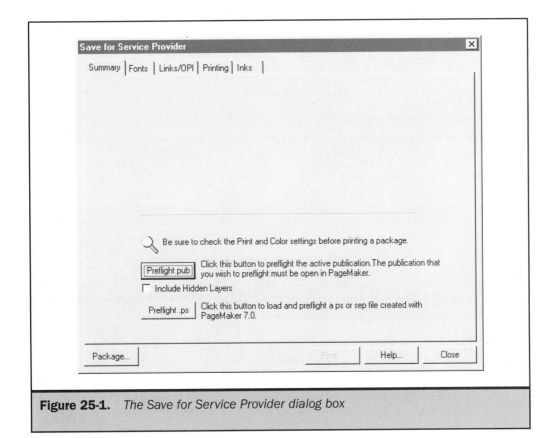

**Figure 25-1.** The Save for Service Provider dialog box

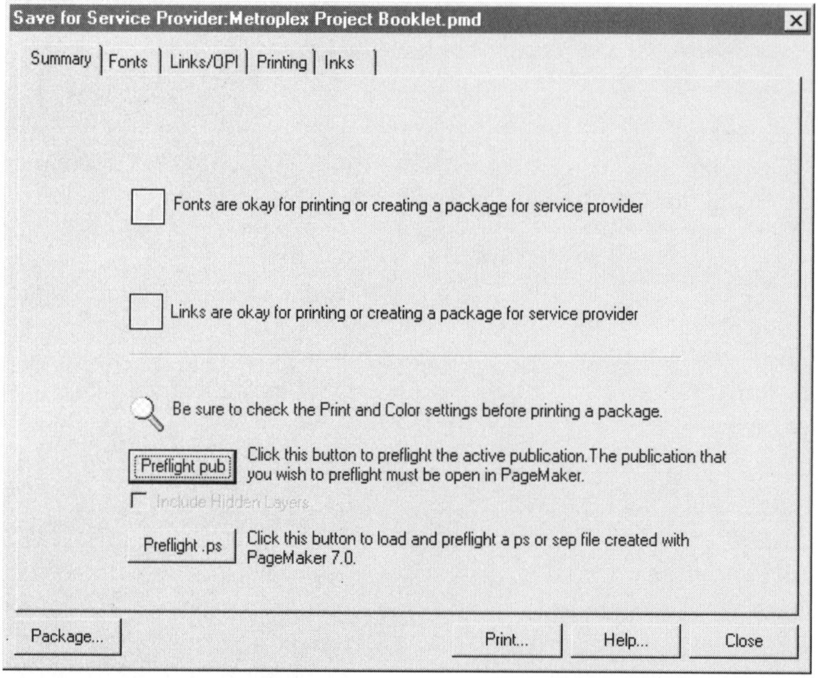

**Figure 25-2.**   *The Save for Service Provider dialog box after preflight*

would have a red X instead of a green check mark. In that case, click the appropriate tab and the Help Button to obtain more information on the problem so you can correct it.

4. Save the publication as a package.

   Click the Package Button. A Save As dialog box opens, as shown in Figure 25-3.

5. Select the packaging Save As options.

   Choose from the following options:

   - **Report Type**   Select Formatted from the drop-down menu.
   - **Auto Open Package Report**   The utility provides a report containing information that your commercial printer needs for fonts, linked graphics, print settings, and so on. If you want the report to appear in a separate window on your desktop, click this selection.

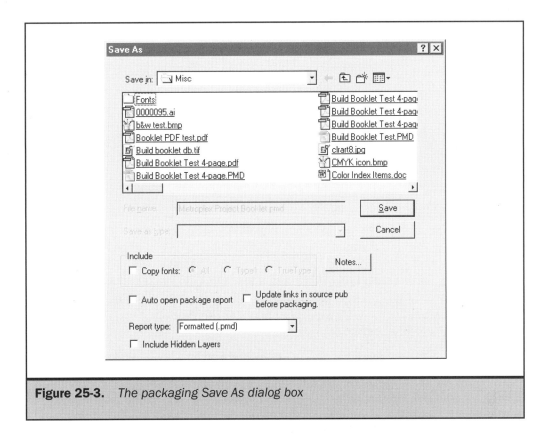

**Figure 25-3.**   *The packaging Save As dialog box*

- **Update Links in Source Pub Before Packaging**   This selection causes PageMaker to automatically update all links before packaging the publication.

- **Include**   Select the Copy Fonts option to make sure the commercial printer has the fonts you have used in your document. Then choose the type of fonts. Select from All, Type 1 (PostScript), or TrueType. (If you do not have a PostScript printer and are not using a type management system, chances are good that all of your fonts are TrueType fonts.) The All option would be used when you want to use both PostScript and TrueType fonts.

- **Notes**   You can use the Notes section to enter any information you need to communicate to the commercial printer. For example, you probably want to include your contact information so that you know it is always with the file. Just click the Notes Button and enter the information in the Notes box.

6. Select a location.

Using the drop-down menu from the Save In box at the top of the Save As dialog box, locate the folder in which you want the packaged file to be stored.

7. Save the packaged files.

Click the Save Button. The necessary files are copied to the destination folder and the Save As dialog box closes. Although you can save directly to your floppy or CD drive, it is always a good idea to keep a copy of the packaged file on your hard drive, just in case. If you are short on hard drive storage space, save a backup copy of the packaged file.

The packaged file can then be sent to your commercial printer by copying it to disk or by sending it electronically.

# Sending a Publication or a PostScript File

You have a choice of two ways to prepare and send your document to the commercial printer. You can send the file as a regular PageMaker publication or you can convert the document into a PostScript file.

## Sending Your Document as a PageMaker Publication

Sending the file as a PageMaker document skips the step (discussed in the following section) of converting it into a PostScript file. This method enables the commercial printer to make changes to your document, verify print settings, or perform prepress tasks. If you are new to the process of creating documents to be commercially printed, this could be a good way to do it. The printer could help you with any concerns you may have and could advise you in the best way to configure some of the settings to suit his or her technology. If you choose to use this method, you may package the document just as it is in PageMaker and take it to the commercial printer.

## Sending Your Document as a PostScript File

Converting your document into a PostScript file before you package it for the printer has some advantages over sending the PageMaker document. Principally, you maintain absolute control over the document and all its settings. If you are an experienced designer with confidence in your work, this may be the right method for you to use. You need to be familiar with the technology used by your commercial printer to make sure that the print settings you use in the document, before it is converted to PostScript, are appropriate. Another advantage is that you do not have to have the same version of PageMaker or even the same platform that your printer uses.

Make sure to consult your commercial printer before using this method. Use the following steps to create a PostScript file:

1. Open the Print dialog box.

   Click the File menu's Print command. The Print Document dialog box opens, as shown in Figure 25-4.

2. Choose a PostScript Printer Description (PPD).

   You must select a PPD in order to save the file as PostScript. If you are having your document printed by a commercial printer, the PPD must match the imagesetter on which he or she will image your file. For the correct PPD to be available to you, the imagesetter must be installed on your system as one of the printers, even if you never use it personally. Check with your service provider to see what imagesetter is used and to obtain the appropriate drivers.

   **Note** *If you have a non-PostScript printer selected as your default printer, the PPD menu is not available on the Print dialog box. When you select a PostScript printer from the Printer list, the PPD menu appears. You do not have to have a PostScript printer to install its driver.*

   Click the drop-down arrow to the right of the PPD box to display the PPD menu. Select the appropriate PPD from that list.

3. Set the print options.

   Using the Document, Paper, and Color Buttons to display the various pages of the Print Document dialog box, select the print options that you want to use for your document. See Chapter 27 for a description of these pages.

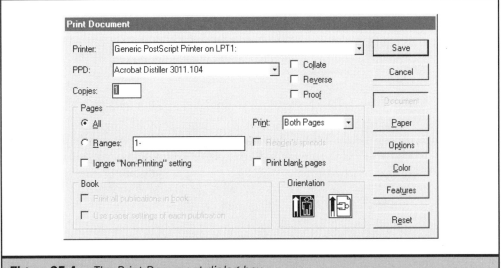

**Figure 25-4.** *The Print Document dialog box*

4. Establish the PostScript options.

Click the Options Button in the Print dialog box. The Print Options box is displayed in the following illustration.

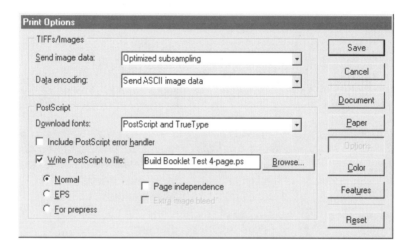

 *Although the Print Options box of the Print dialog box contains options for TIFFs/images as well as PostScript options, it is only the PostScript section that we are concerned with here.*

Choose from the following items on the Print Options box of the Print dialog box:

- **Download Fonts**   Select from the drop-down menu. If you select None, no fonts will be included with the file. If you know for sure that your commercial printer has your fonts, leaving the fonts out makes the PostScript file smaller, which is good. However, if you need to send the fonts with the file, choose one of the other two choices. PostScript and TrueType is a good choice.

- **Include PostScript Error Handler**   This selection enables you or your commercial printer to troubleshoot printing problems by using the information provided by the PostScript error handler. When this feature is included and printing problems occur, the error handler prints a page describing the error, common causes for the error, and remedies for the problem.

■ **Write PostScript to File**   When this box is selected, additional PostScript options are displayed. First, verify that the default file name in the Write PostScript to File box is the one you want to process as PostScript. If it is not, type the name of the correct file in the box or use the Browse Button to locate the file.

Then choose the type of PostScript file you want to create:

■ **Normal**   This selection creates a file that contains information on every element of your publication. Link files are included as well as instructions specific to the output device that you have selected on the document page of the Print dialog box.

■ **EPS**   This choice is not one to use when you are preparing a file for a commercial printer. When this radio button is selected, PageMaker creates a separate Encapsulated PostScript (EPS) file for each page of the active document. This is useful when you want to import a page from your document into another document using a program that imports EPS images.

■ **For Prepress**   Although it would seem that this would be the selection to make when sending your publication to a commercial printer, it is not. The file created when this selection is made is optimized for functions such as trapping and imposition. All the printer-specific instructions are removed.

■ **Page Independence**   When this box is selected, PageMaker downloads font information separately for each page in your publication. This is useful if the pages need to be reordered, but it seriously adds to the size of your file. When you select EPS or Prepress as the type of file, this box selects automatically. If you choose Normal, then it is a good idea to make sure that this box is not selected.

■ **Extra Image Bleed**   If you have chosen Normal as the type of file, this selection is not available to you. A bleed is the printing of an image beyond the page size so that when the final document is trimmed, the image goes all the way to the edge. The selection of this box with EPS and Prepress selections permits the bleed to extend one inch beyond the image's original boundaries.

5. Create the PostScript file.

Click the Save Button. The PostScript file is created.

# Summary

Once your document is completed, there are still several steps to take before handing it over to a commercial printer.

**Printing Proofs**   Before you send your document out to be printed commercially, print proofing copies of your document along with color separations. Even if you are not accustomed to viewing full-color separations, you will still be able to determine if certain items, such as text, are present in the appropriate color.

**Proofing Your Work**   No step in the process of creating and publishing your work is more important than proofing. It is important that you have someone else go over the document as well as proof it carefully yourself. It is just a fact of human psychology that we do not readily find our own mistakes. If you are working for a client, have the client review the piece and sign off on it before going to press.

**Use the Save for Service Provider Feature**   PageMaker's Save for Service Provider feature packages your document with all the fonts, images, and linked items needed to produce your document correctly. If you use this feature, you can be sure that you will not forget to give the printer some font, graphic, or document that he or she needs.

**Sending a Publication or a PostScript File**   Whether or not you are packaging your document using the Save for Service Provider feature, you have two ways to prepare and send it to the commercial printer. You can send it as a PageMaker document or as a PostScript file. If you are new to the process of creating documents to be commercially printed, this is a good choice. It enables the commercial printer to take responsibility for print settings and prepress tasks such as trapping. However, if you are experienced and confident about your work, you can send the file to the commercial printer as a PostScript file. This prevents any changes being made to your work.

# The Complete Reference

PageMaker 7

# Part VI

## PageMaker Printing

# The Complete Reference

PageMaker 7

# Chapter 26

## Printing

hen I first started using PageMaker in the late 1980s, you had to use a
PostScript printer if you wanted to print a PageMaker document. Today,
PageMaker prints on any Windows-compatible printer, and PageMaker offers
a wide selection of printing options that enables you to select the settings you need to
achieve the results you want.

In this chapter, I discuss the process of sending your document to print and go over
the many options from which you may choose.

# The Print Process

Sending a publication to print from PageMaker is similar to sending a document to
print from any other Windows-compatible application; however, PageMaker provides
more than just the reproduction on paper of the document's pages. The five pages that
make up PageMaker's Print dialog box provide choices such as printing thumbnails,
creating a PostScript document and printing it to file, printing color separations, and
printing large documents in tiles, just to name a few.

In this section, I first describe the essential steps to sending a publication to print on
your desktop printer; then I discuss each of the pages of the Print dialog box and the
options that they present.

Take the following steps to print a PageMaker document:

1. Open the Print dialog box.

   With the document open, select the File menu's Print command. The Print
   dialog box opens with the Print Document page displayed as shown in the
   following illustration.

2. Select a printer.

When the Print dialog box opens, the default printer is automatically selected as the target printer. It may well be that your default printer is the one you want to use and, if so, you may skip this step. However, if the printer displayed in the Printer box is not the printer you wish to print to, use the drop-down arrow to the right of the box to reveal the Printer menu. Select the printer of your choice.

3. Select a PostScript Printer Description (PPD).

This step is only necessary if you select a PostScript printer. When a PostScript printer is selected, a second box opens beneath the Printer box for selection of a PPD, as shown below. Using the drop-down box to the right of the PPD box, select the PPD that is appropriate for your printer.

4. Select Document options.

Select the Document options that you want to use. The Document options are discussed in the following subsection.

5. Establish other Print settings.

Use the Paper, Options, Color, and Features pages (accessible by clicking the appropriate button) to configure your print job as you wish. These pages are discussed individually in the following subsections.

6. Send the document to your printer.

Click the Print Button. Your document is sent to the selected printer.

# The Document Page

The Document options are the most frequently selected Print options. Look at the document settings and make the appropriate changes each time you print. Choose from the following options:

- **Printer** As described in the previous section, the printer that you have selected as your default printer will appear in the Printer box when the Print dialog box is opened. You may, however, change to another printer if you wish by clicking the drop-down arrow to the right of the box.

- **PPD** As mentioned previously, this selection is only available if you select a PostScript printer. Select the PPD that matches your PostScript printer.

- **Copies** This selection determines the number of copies of your document you wish to receive. Change the setting by selecting the current number and typing in another.

- **Collate** When the Collate box is selected, PageMaker will print one complete copy of your document before printing another. (When this is deselected, each page will print the required number of copies before going on to the next page.) Using the Collate option causes the print job to progress slightly slower than it would otherwise.

- **Reverse** This option changes the order in which your document's pages are printed. If your printer normally prints page one first, selecting this option will cause page one to be printed last. The method of printing differs from one printer to another; however, if you have to reorder your printed pages each time you print, this option would print them in the correct order for convenience.

- **Proof** This option is used when you want to print your document rapidly but do not require high resolution or for the graphics to be displayed. For more information, see the section "Printing Proofs" later in this chapter.

- **Pages** This group of options governs what pages print. Choose from the following:

  - **All** This option prints all pages in the document.

  - **Ranges** If you wish to print only specific pages of your document, you may use this selection to tell PageMaker which pages to print. Click the Ranges selection box, and then enter the page number of the page or pages in the box to the right of Ranges. Indicate a group of pages by listing the first and last pages separated by a hyphen—for example, 23-27. To add additional page groups or individual pages, separate them by a comma— for example, 23-27,31,35-38. Note that no spaces are placed in the Ranges box. The Ranges box accepts up to 64 characters.

- **Ignore "Non-Printing" Setting**   If you have created nonprinting objects but wish to print them in this instance, select this box.

- **Print**   This option allows you to print all pages, only the odd pages, or only the even pages.

- **Print Blank Pages**   Use this option to print blank pages. When this option is deselected, blank pages in your document will not print.

- **Book**   If you are printing a book, you have two additional options:

  - **Print All Publications in Book**   With this option selected, the entire book list prints. If it is deselected, only the active document prints.

  - **Use Paper Setting of Each Publication**   If you chose a PostScript printer, select this option. This causes PageMaker to use the paper size and source information saved in each publication. This selection is not appropriate if you are using a non-PostScript printer because the settings are saved in the printer driver.

- **Orientation**   Click the appropriate preview to select a tall (portrait) or wide (landscape) orientation for your document.

## The Setup Page

The Setup page is available with non-PostScript printers and is used frequently in establishing printing parameters. The Setup page differs from one printer to another. Figure 26-1 shows the Setup page for my Epson Stylus Color 640 desktop printer. The Setup page is where you make selections such as printer resolution, paper size and quality, color or black ink, and other selections unique to your printer. For more information regarding this page, refer to your printer's documentation.

## The Paper Page

This page is available only when a PostScript printer is chosen (see Figure 26-2). This page enables you to see how your document fits on the selected paper and to select the following print options:

- **Paper**   These options select the size and source of the paper on which you are printing and other options that pertain to or affect the paper or paper size. Choose from the following options:

  - **Size**   As you would expect, this option enables the selection of the paper size on which you will print. The options that are available to you depend upon the information stored in the PPD regarding what sheet sizes your printer accepts. Use the drop-down arrow to the right of the Size box to select the paper size appropriate for your print job.

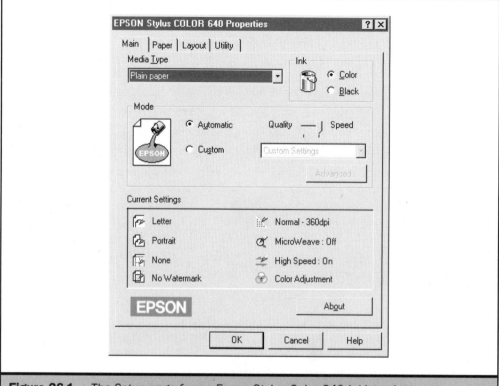

**Figure 26-1.**   *The Setup page for an Epson Stylus Color 640 inkjet printer*

- **Source**   Select the paper tray or trays from which the paper stock for your print job will be selected.

- **Printer's Marks**   Selecting Printer's Marks places marks on your document to indicate crop lines so the commercial printer will know where to crop the document, registration marks to assist the printer in correctly aligning separations, and density-control and color-control bars to assist the printer in determining print quality. These marks require .75 inches in addition to the document size so they may be trimmed away.

- **Crops and Bleeds Only**   This selection limits the type of printer's marks that are placed on your document.

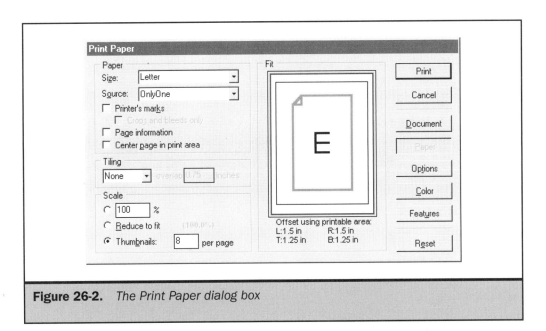

**Figure 26-2.** *The Print Paper dialog box*

- **Page Information** The document's filename, page number, current date, and spot- or process-color separation's names are printed in the printer's marks area of the document when this option is selected. Page information is printed in 8-point Arial type.

- **Center Page in Print Area** Some printers have a printable area that is not symmetrically centered on the selected paper. Since PageMaker automatically centers the document on the selected paper, you must check this option to center the document in the print area rather than in the paper.

- **Tiling** For a document that is greater than your desktop printer can produce, you can choose to print the document in tiles. Choose *None*, *Auto*, or *Manual* from the drop-down menu. None, of course, turns tiling off. The Auto setting sends the document to print in blocks overlapping according to the setting in the Overlap ___ Inches box. Selecting the Manual option sends to the printer only the page-size section of your document that is identified by the Zero indicator as the upper-left corner of the page. You would move the Zero indicator to print various segments of your document.

- **Scale** This section of options enables you to select the size of your document for printing. If the document page is smaller or larger than you wish on the paper, you may use the percentage box to set a scale larger or smaller than 100 percent; or you may select *Reduce to Fit*. The *Thumbnails* selection prints miniature versions of your document pages, several to a sheet. The size of the miniature pages depends upon the number that you enter in the *Per Page* box.

■ **Fit** The Fit section of the Print Paper dialog box previews the fit of your document on the selected paper size. Double-click the preview image to view the numerical fit information.

# The Options Page

The Print Options dialog box displays a completely different set of options if you are using a PostScript printer from those of a non-PostScript printer. The following subsections describe these two dialog boxes.

## Non-PostScript Printer

The Print Options page for a non-PostScript printer (shown in the following illustration) contains some of the same information as that which is contained in the PostScript printer's Paper page:

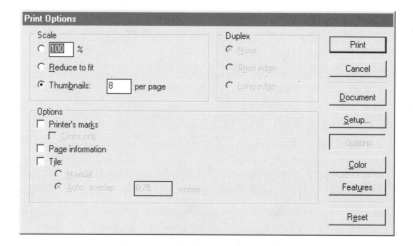

■ **Scale** This section of options enables you to select the size of your document for printing. If the document page is smaller or larger than you wish on the paper, you may use the percentage box to set a scale larger or smaller than 100 percent, or you may select *Reduce to Fit*. The *Thumbnails* selection prints miniature versions of your document pages, several to a sheet. The number of miniature pages and, consequently, the size of the thumbnails depend upon the number that you enter in the *Per Page* box.

■ **Options** The Options section contains selections pertaining to Printer's Marks, Page Information, and Tiling. Choose from the following:

- **Printer's Marks**   Selecting Printer's Marks places marks on your document to indicate crop lines so the commercial printer will know where to crop the document, registration marks to assist the printer in correctly aligning separations, and density-control and color-control bars to assist the printer in determining print quality. These marks require .75 inches in addition to the document size so they may be trimmed away. The *Crops Only* selection limits the type of printer's marks that are placed on your document to crop lines.

- **Page Information**   The document's filename, page number, current date, and spot- or process-color separation's names are printed in the printer's marks area of the document when this option is selected. Page information is printed in 8-point Arial type.

- **Tiling**   For a document that is greater than your desktop printer can produce, you can choose to print the document in tiles. Selecting the *Tiling* option enables the Tiling feature. Selecting the *Manual* option sends to the printer only the page-size section of your document that is identified by the Zero indicator as the upper-left corner of the page. You would move the Zero indicator to print various segments of your document. The *Auto* setting sends the document to print in blocks that overlap according to the setting in the Overlap ___ Inches box.

- **Duplex**   If you have a duplexing printer—one that prints on two sides of a sheet of paper—the options in the Duplex section determine how the pages print:

  - Select *None* to deselect the duplexing feature.

  - The *Short Edge* option prints duplex pages so that the top of the back side of the page is printed opposite the bottom of the front page—in other words, upside down. This makes the pages readable when they are bound at the short edge.

  - If you want to duplex so that pages can be bound at the long edge and read like a book, select the *Long Edge* option.

## PostScript Printer

If you are using a PostScript printer, the Print Options page, shown in Figure 26-3, controls the way bitmap images are sent to print, as well as PostScript settings.

The *TIFF/Images* section of the Print Options page (PostScript Printers) governs how high-resolution bitmap images such as TIFF, PCX, and GIF graphics are sent to the printer:

- **Send Image Data**   With the options in this section, you select how the images in your document are sent to the printer. Some of these options are particularly useful when printing proofs (see the section "Printing Proofs" later in this chapter); you can select a method of printing that takes less time (and less printer toner) to produce proof-quality results. Choose from the following options:

■ **Normal**   This setting sends all of the graphic's data to the printer. This would be the preferred setting for most normal printing operations and for proofs that are black and white.

■ **Optimized Subsampling**   If your document contains high-resolution images and you are proofing on a low-resolution desktop printer, this selection is the best to use. The Optimized Subsampling selection sends only the amount of data to your printer that it can use. This saves significant time in printing the proof.

■ **Low-Resolution**   The Low-Resolution option sends all graphics to the printer at 72 dots per inch (dpi), significantly reducing printing time.

■ **Omit**   This selection, of course, eliminates the graphics from the printing entirely. This is also handy if you are printing to file (packaging the document for your commercial printer) and the printer is inserting high-resolution images during prepress operations.

■ **Data Encoding**   If you are saving your document as a PostScript file, consider one of the two Data Encoding choices in this section. A binary image file is half the size of an ASCII image file and takes half the time to transmit when sending

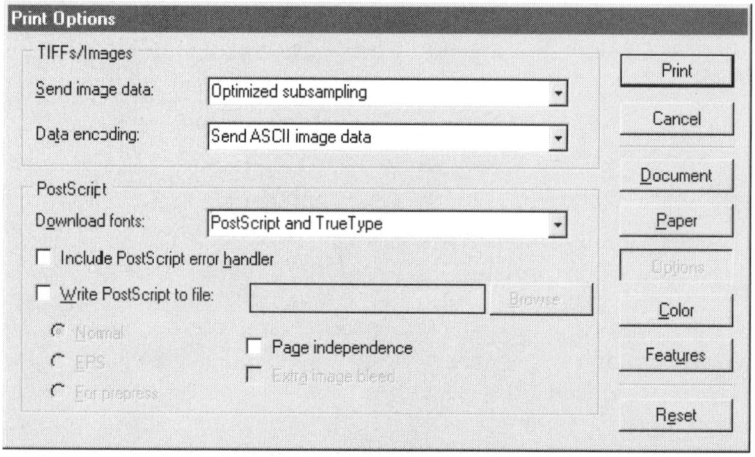

**Figure 26-3.**    *The Print Options display for a PostScript printer*

the file electronically. However, not all systems support the transmission of binary data. Select *Send Binary Image Data* if you know your system and the system of the commercial printer support this format. Otherwise, select *Send ASCII Image Data*.

The *PostScript* section of the Print Options dialog box is for establishing PostScript settings. These options are important in creating a PostScript file from your document so that it may be packaged to take to a commercial printer (see Chapter 25):

- **Download Fonts**    Select from the drop-down menu. If you select None, no fonts will be included with the file. If you know for sure that your commercial printer has your fonts, leaving the fonts out makes the PostScript file smaller, which is good. However, if you need to send the fonts with the file, choose one of the other two choices. PostScript and TrueType are good choices.

- **Include PostScript Error Handler**    This selection enables you or your commercial printer to troubleshoot printing problems by using the information provided by the PostScript error handler. When this feature is included and printing problems occur, the error handler prints a page describing the error, common causes for the error, and remedies for the problem.

- **Write PostScript to File**    When this box is selected, additional PostScript options display. First, verify that the default filename in the box to the right of Write PostScript to File is the one you want to process as PostScript. If it is not, type the name of the correct file in the box or use the Browse Button to locate the file. Then choose the type of PostScript file you wish to create from the following options:

  - **Normal**    This selection creates a file that contains information on every element of your publication. Link files are included as well as instructions specific to the output device that you have selected on the Document page of the Print dialog box.

  - **EPS**    This choice is not one to use when you are preparing a file for a commercial printer. When this radio button is selected, PageMaker creates a separate Encapsulated PostScript (EPS) file for each page of the active document. This is useful when you wish to import a page from your document into another document using a program that imports EPS images.

  - **For Prepress**    As much as it would seem that this would be the selection to make when sending your publication to a commercial printer, it is not. The file created when this selection is made is optimized for functions such as trapping and imposition. All of the printer-specific instructions are removed.

- **Page Independence**   When this box is selected, PageMaker downloads font information separately for each page in your publication. This is useful if the pages need to be reordered, but it seriously adds to the size of your file. When you select EPS or Prepress as the type of file, this box selects automatically. If you choose Normal, then it is a good idea to make sure that this box is not selected.

- **Extra Image Bleed**   If you have chosen Normal as the type of file, this selection is not available to you. A *bleed* is the printing of an image beyond the page size so that when the final document is trimmed, the image goes all the way to the edge. Selection of this box with EPS and Prepress selections permits the bleed to extend 1 inch beyond the image's original boundaries.

# The Colors Page

The Print Colors dialog box displays options that determine the color production of your document. If your document contains colors but you wish to print it in black and white on your color printer, this box provides the setting that does that. If you want to print color separations, this is the place to do it. Choose from the following options:

- **Composite**   Select Composite if you want all colors printed together as they are in the final product. A composite setting produces the final product if you are printing proofs, or if you are producing your document on your desktop printer. The settings in this section determine how a composite is printed:

  - **Color/Grayscale**   Prints colors on a color printer or grayscale color equivalents on a black and white printer. Grayscale equivalents show colors as visually representative shades of black. For example, a 20 percent tint of yellow is shown as lighter than a 20 percent tint of black because visually yellow appears lighter than black. Keep in mind that the colors produced by a desktop printer only approximate the actual colors that are achieved by commercial printing. (See Chapters 11, 21, and 22 for more information about using and printing in color.)

  - **Print Colors in Black**   This sends the document to your desktop printer in tones of black, rather than in color.

  - **Allow Printer Halftones**   A halftone is a printing technique that produces images such as photographs. Selection of this option enables your printer driver to create the halftones rather than PageMaker's Image Control settings.

- **Separations**   If you want to print separations, select the Separations box. The selection of this option activates other Separation settings.

  - **Perform on This Printer**   This option is only available if you are using a PostScript level 2 or PostScript 3 device. This selection speeds the printing process by enabling the printer to perform the separations rather than the computer.

- **Print This Ink**   The ink list displays the colors present on your Color List in your document's Colors Palette. When an ink color is selected, you can click the *Print This Ink* option to identify the ink as one selected for separation printing. An X beside the color indicates its selection.

- **CMS Setup**   Clicking this button displays the Color Management System Preferences dialog box so that you can activate CMS and establish your preferences. See Chapter 21 for more information on PageMaker's CMS.

- **Print All Inks**   This button causes all ink colors to be selected for printing. It is a good idea to use the Remove Unused Button to remove any unused colors before using this shortcut.

- **Print No Inks**   This button, of course, deselects all ink colors so that none are sent to print.

- **All To Process**   If you click the All To Process Button, all colors are converted to process colors and are separated as such. When this button has been used to convert spot colors to process, the button changes to *Revert to Spot* so that you can reverse the process.

- **Remove Unused**   If your document's Color List contains colors that are not used in your publication, it is a good idea to remove them. Click the Remove Unused Button; a confirmation message appears asking you to confirm the removal of unused colors. You may select *Yes* or *No* to confirm or decline the removal of each color, one at a time, or you may click *Yes to All* or *No to All* to confirm or decline removal of all unused colors.

## The Features Page

The Features dialog box is provided to display any special features provided by your printer. Although it is conceivable that a non-PostScript printer may have special features, I have never seen the Print Features dialog box contain any information unless I was using a PostScript printer. Figures 26-4 and 26-5 shows the Features page for a generic PostScript printer.

# Printing Proofs

It is a good idea to print out proof copies of your document periodically to make sure that things look the way you want them to look from their appearance on your monitor. Colors may not print accurately, but printing color proofs does give you an approximation of their final appearance. Any printing of your document can be used for proofing purposes, of course, but you can save printing time and printer toner by using proofing options available in PageMaker. The following sections describe how to use these options.

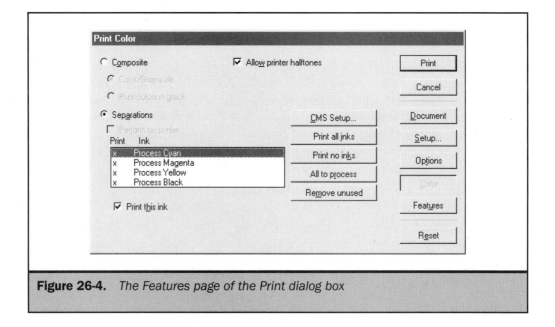

**Figure 26-4.** *The Features page of the Print dialog box*

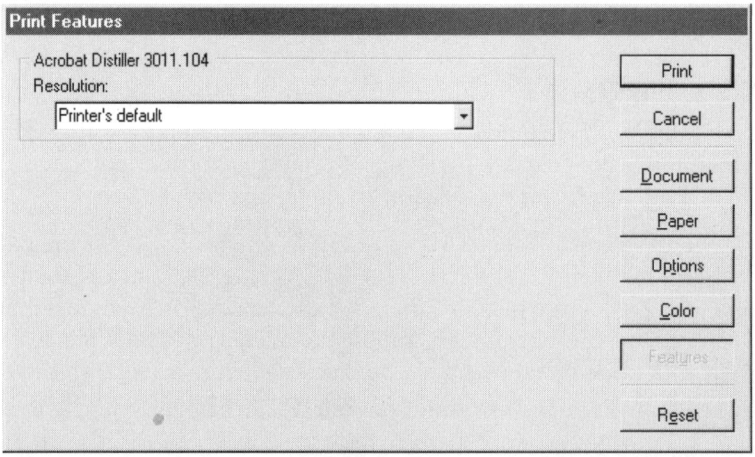

**Figure 26-5.** *The Features page of the Print dialog box*

## Printing Proofs Without Graphics

You can print your document without printing the graphics. Placeholders in the form of rectangles with large Xs in them take the place of the images. To do this, select the Proof option on the Print Document dialog box. Then select any other Print options you require and send the document to print.

## Printing Thumbnails

Thumbnails are miniature versions of your pages. You can print out a page (or pages) with thumbnails so that you can review your document, its design, and its flow. If you are using a PostScript printer, select the Thumbnails option on the Print Paper dialog box. If your printer is not PostScript, make this selection on the Print Options dialog box. Whichever way you make the selection, be sure to state the number of thumbnails you want printed on each piece of paper.

## Printing Reader's Spreads

This proofing option is only available for documents with facing pages. The Reader's Spreads option prints two facing pages together as if they were bound. This is useful when two pages flow together with one image. It lets you see the document as it will look when completed. To print this kind of proof, select the Reader's Spreads option on the Print Document dialog box. Make sure to deselect the option before packaging the document to send to your printer.

# Printing Oversized Documents

PageMaker can create documents up to 42 inches square. Chances are, however, that you do not have a desktop printer that can produce a print that large, so PageMaker provides a handy technique called Tiling to produce your oversized document, without an oversized printer, for proofing or for final production. With Tiling selected, PageMaker prints page-sized portions of your document until the entire page (or pages) is produced. Then you can fit them back together to create the total effect. I know that producing a large page in small pieces and pasting them together sounds less than high quality, but I have seen composite images produced this way and put together with a lot of care that could not be discerned from a single sheet without close inspection. To print an oversized document, follow these steps:

1. Activate the Tiling option.

   If you are using a PostScript printer, the Tiling option is located on the Paper page of the Print dialog box where you will select either Auto or Manual from the Tiling menu. The None selection, of course, turns the Tiling option off.

   For non-PostScript printers, locate the option on the Options page. Click the Tiling radio button to activate the Tiling options.

2. Select Automatic or Manual.

This selection is made as part of the activation step if you are working with PostScript printer options. However, for non-PostScript printers you must click the radio button for Automatic or Manual:

■ **Automatic**   This selection sends the entire document to print in page-size tiles with an overlap that you enter into the Overlap ____ Inches box.

■ **Manual**   Selecting the Manual option sends to the printer only the page-size section of your document that is identified by the Zero indicator as the upper left corner of the page. You specify the section of the document page that you want to print by moving the Zero indicator.

3. Send the document to print.

Click the OK button on the Print dialog box. The document is sent to your printer and will print in tiles according to your selection.

# Summary

PageMaker documents print on PostScript printers or non-PostScript printers. The process is largely the same with a few variations in the Print options.

**The Print Process**   Printing in PageMaker is similar to printing in any other Windows-compatible application. But PageMaker offers a wide range of options that provides for many variations on the usual printing process. The Print dialog box is divided into five pages, accessible by clicking buttons that appear on every page, which are dialog boxes in their own right. Some of these pages change when using a PostScript printer, but, with a few exceptions, you can produce the same effect with whatever printer you are using.

**Printing Proofs**   It is always a good idea to print proofs periodically during the development of your document. PageMaker provides options for printing proofs that save on time and printer toner. You can print proofs without printing the graphics, you can print miniature versions of your document's pages, called thumbnails, or your can print reader's spreads that show how two-page spreads will look when published and bound.

**Printing Oversized Documents**   If you create a document page in PageMaker that is larger than your printer can produce, the Tiling option can print the oversized piece in sections, or tiles, that you can put together to construct the full-size page. Select Auto (or Automatic for non-PostScript printers) for PageMaker to send the entire page to print in tiles, or Manual to specify the segments yourself.

# Index

## M

# INTERNATIONAL CONTACT INFORMATION

**AUSTRALIA**
McGraw-Hill Book Company Australia Pty. Ltd.
TEL +61-2-9417-9899
FAX +61-2-9417-5687
http://www.mcgraw-hill.com.au
books-it_sydney@mcgraw-hill.com

**CANADA**
McGraw-Hill Ryerson Ltd.
TEL +905-430-5000
FAX +905-430-5020
http://www.mcgrawhill.ca

**GREECE, MIDDLE EAST,
NORTHERN AFRICA**
McGraw-Hill Hellas
TEL +30-1-656-0990-3-4
FAX +30-1-654-5525

**MEXICO (Also serving Latin America)**
McGraw-Hill Interamericana Editores S.A. de C.V.
TEL +525-117-1583
FAX +525-117-1589
http://www.mcgraw-hill.com.mx
fernando_castellanos@mcgraw-hill.com

**SINGAPORE (Serving Asia)**
McGraw-Hill Book Company
TEL +65-863-1580
FAX +65-862-3354
http://www.mcgraw-hill.com.sg
mghasia@mcgraw-hill.com

**SOUTH AFRICA**
McGraw-Hill South Africa
TEL +27-11-622-7512
FAX +27-11-622-9045
robyn_swanepoel@mcgraw-hill.com

**UNITED KINGDOM & EUROPE
(Excluding Southern Europe)**
McGraw-Hill Education Europe
TEL +44-1-628-502500
FAX +44-1-628-770224
http://www.mcgraw-hill.co.uk
computing_neurope@mcgraw-hill.com

**ALL OTHER INQUIRIES Contact:**
Osborne/McGraw-Hill
TEL +1-510-549-6600
FAX +1-510-883-7600
http://www.osborne.com
omg_international@mcgraw-hill.com

# From Windows to Linux, check out all of Osborne's Hacking books!

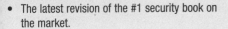

# New Offerings from Osborne's
# How to Do Everything Series

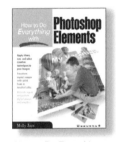